The Directors

Edited by
Alain Silver & James Ursini

This anthology is dedicated
to our late colleague
Carl Macek.

Published in 2012 by Limelight Editions
An Imprint of Hal Leonard Corporation
7777 West Bluemound Road
Milwaukee, WI 53213

Trade Book Division, Editorial Offices
33 Plymouth St., Montclair, NJ 07042

Permissions can be found in the Acknowledgments on page 7

Book and cover design by Alain Silver

Printed in the United States of America

Library of Congress Cataloging-in-Publication Data is available upon request.

ISBN No. 978-0-87910-394-1

www.limelighteditions.com

Front Cover: Alfred Hitchcock with cast and crew on the set of *Shadow of a Doubt* in 1943.

Back Cover: Robert Siodmak positions Yvonne de Carlo and Burt Lancaster in *The Killers*; Rita Hayworth with Orson Welles on the set of *The Lady from Shanghai*; during the shooting of *Hard, Fast and Beautiful,* pioneer woman director Ida Lupino with producer Carleton Young and actor Claire Trevor.

Frontispiece: Robert Aldrich displays a copy of *Film Noir* by Raymond Borde and Étienne Chaumeton on the set of *Attack!* in 1956.

Contents page: Fritz Lang shows Joan Bennett how to hold the phone for a scene in *Scarlet Street*.

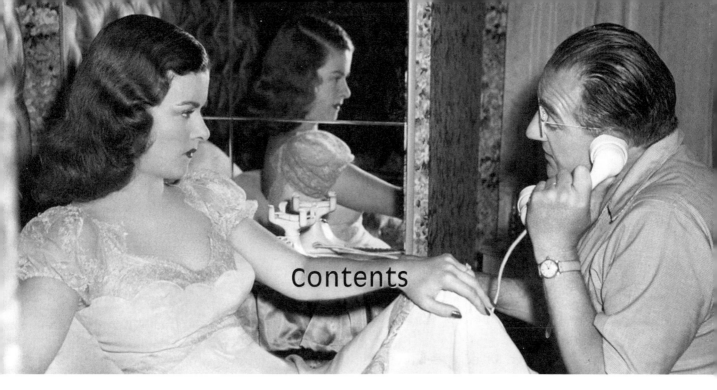

Contents

Acknowledgments

Thanks first of all to our various contributors and to our frequent collaborators Robert Porfirio, Elizabeth Ward, and Linda Brookover for their suggestions about this volume. Besides our present publisher John Cerullo at Limelight, we would like to acknowledge the long-term support we received from his predecessor, the late Mel Zerman, on the entire Film Noir Reader series, of which this volume is an informal continuation. An earlier version of our essay on John Farrow appeared in the first *Film Noir Reader;* and since that time, it has been our hope to produce a volume about directors of the classic period. A few of the directors discussed in this book were still alive when the *Film Noir Reader* series began (including André de Toth and Robert Wise who graciously participated in *Film Noir Reader 3*). Sadly all these directors and all but a few contributors to the classic period movement are now gone. Among the actors still living, five are pictured below

Most of the illustrations in this volume are from our personal collection, but for many others we are grateful to Lee Sanders, Timothy Otto, Adell Aldrich, and visual archivists, too numerous to cite individually, who share their material online. Chris D. and Todd Erickson provided extensive image files with their essays.

An abridged version of "John Farrow: Anonymous Noir," which originallly appeared in *Film Noir Reader* (copyright © 1996) is reprinted herein. All previously unpublished essays are also copyright © 2012 by the individual authors and are printed here by permission. Stills are courtesy of Allied Artists, American International, Columbia, MGM/UA, Paramount, PRC, Republic, Universal, Warner Bros. and many other production companies and distributors.

Clockwise from below: Constance Towers gives Sam Fuller a naked kiss; Peggy Cummins in *Gun Crazy*; Audrey Totter telephones in *The High Wall*; Dolores Dorn in *Underworld U.S.A.*; and Valentina Cortese with Robert Wise on the set of *House on Telegraph Hill.*

Introduction

Alain Silver

"More for Less" says the sign on the wall of Jerry's Market. "More for Less" could be a motto for film noir. Those cops around director Billy Wilder and stars Barbara Stanwyck and Fred MacMurray on location for *Double Indemnity* were not uniformed extras but real "flat feet" hired by Paramount to protect valuable food props from wartime pilfering. Even on studio pictures loss and damage had to be minimized, although budgets there were a bit more generous than on poverty row productions. That's where Edgar G. Ulmer and, for a while, Anthony Mann labored. Nonetheless on their pictures or the under-funded independents of Joseph H. Lewis and Ida Lupino, the style and sensibility of film noir crossed all the lines from performance to payroll, from major to minor studio, and always gave the viewer more for less.

The first audiences of classic period noir were born in the era of hard-boiled fiction that filled the pages of *Black Mask*, where gamblers dodged lead from blazing gats and dames in trouble looked for help wherever they could. Such an audience seldom expected high-key lighting and A-class actors, just action, suspense, with maybe some obsessive love or ironic mischance thrown in. They listened attentively in *Double Indemnity* as MacMurray portraying Walter Neff confessed to a dictaphone that "I killed him for money—and a woman—and I didn't get the money and I didn't get the woman. Pretty, isn't it?"

Film noir was not pretty, nor elegant, nor particularly uplifting unless one could find some edifying aspect to the classic period's collection of mostly sordid stories. As Paul Schrader observed in his seminal essay, "*Double Indemnity* was the first film which played film noir for what it essentially was: small-time, unredeemed, unheroic." ["Notes on Film Noir" (1972), reprinted in the first *Film Noir Reader*]

This volume is partly inspired by another of Schrader's observations: "Some directors did their best work in film noir (Stuart Heisler, Robert Siodmak, Gordon Douglas, Edward Dmytryk, John Brahm, John Cromwell, Raoul Walsh, Henry Hathaway); other directors began in film noir and, it seems to me, never regained their original heights (Otto Preminger, Rudolph Maté, Nicholas Ray, Robert Wise, Jules Dassin, Richard Fleischer, John Huston, Andre de Toth, and Robert Aldrich); and other directors who made great films in other molds also made great film noir (Orson Welles, Max Ophuls, Fritz Lang, Elia Kazan, Howard Hawks, Robert Rossen, Anthony Mann, Joseph Losey, Alfred Hitchcock, and Stanley Kubrick). Whether or not one agrees with this particular schema, its message is irrefutable: film noir was good for practically every director's career."

Some will wonder what happened to many names from Schrader's list, to Budd Boetticher or Jean Negulesco, to Karlson, Kazan or Kubrick, to Rudolph Maté or Robert Rossen, to Hawks, Heisler, Douglas, Cromwell, Fleischer, and the rest, most of whom were certainly worthy of inclusion but did not make the cut over Gerd Oswald or Felix Feist or John Brahm. The only answer is that, in the spirit of Schrader's notes, the best directors are not necessarily the best examples.

Kiss Me Deadly: on a soundstage set at Enterprise Studios, Robert Aldrich instructs Gaby Rodgers as Lily Carver/Gabrielle on how to open the prop box which other characters call "the great what's-it."

Robert Aldrich

Tony Williams

Although Robert Aldrich will always be associated with the baroque climax of classical film noir in *Kiss Me Deadly* (1955), a trait he shares with another climactic film in this first phase–Orson Welles' *Touch of Evil* (1958)–his creative appropriation of this quintessential American film style is much more diverse than it may initially appear. He was certainly familiar with the style both creatively and professionally as that well known still showing him with Borde and Chaumeton's *Panorama du Film Noir* attests. However, Aldrich's work in this stylistic category is not merely confined to the familiar dangerous urban jungle but also encompasses diverse realms of war movies, stage adaptations, neo-noir and melodrama (especially *What Ever Happened to Baby Jane?* and *Hush...Hush, Sweet Charlotte* that anticipate the family horror films of the 1970s). In fact, a case may be made for extending the noir category to other Aldrich films that do not represent territory familiar to classical definitions of this very challenging film style. If Robin Wood once argued that it is a mistake to regard Hollywood genres as self-contained when they really provide different avenues to understanding ideological problems affecting American society, today we have many theoretical approaches in cultural studies and materialism that emphasize the hybrid concerns affecting representations that appear to be easily definable on first analysis. As several critics have shown, color films such *as Leave Her to Heaven* (1945) and *Slightly Scarlet* (1956) also appeared in the classical film noir period as did Westerns such *as Pursued* (1947) and *Ramrod* (1947) that have many recognizable noir features. Similarly those 1940s RKO horror films produced by the Val Lewton unit such as *The Cat People, I Walked with a Zombie, The Leopard Man* (derived from a Cornell Woolrich novel), *The Ghost Ship*, and *Bedlam* contain several noir elements. This is not surprising since many talents working on these films participated in Orson Welles' *Citizen Kane* (1941). Whether we define this as a key example of film noir as Thomas Schatz does in *Hollywood Genres* or not, the fact remains that *Citizen Kane* was a key influence on RKO noirs as Robert Porfirio earlier pointed out in his excellent doctoral dissertation on film noir. Despite the fact that extending the parameters of Aldrich's involvement with film noir may frustrate any critic seeking a convenient categorization, the fact remains that the style is fluid in nature. Recognizing this helps us appreciate Aldrich and his work even more as a cultural explorer of the "dark side of the screen," something that exists in other genres as well.

Like his contemporary Samuel Fuller, Aldrich recognized that "film is like a battleground" but also saw such features within both the war film and the melodrama. *Attack!* has a definite stylistic and thematic connection to the family melodrama of *Autumn Leaves*, a film that is much more than its supposed basic plot of a dysfunctional marital relationship between older woman and younger man. The noir works of Robert Aldrich always display much more than may meet the eye especially in his perception of the social aspects of that visual style, something he may have learned from his early association with Abraham Polonsky while he worked as assistant director in Enterprise Studios during the filming of *Body and Soul* (1947) and *Force of Evil* (1949). His association with Joseph Losey during the 1951 filming of *The Prowler*, *M*, and *The Big Night* should also not be neglected. Many of the Los Angeles locations used in those productions reappeared in *Kiss Me Deadly*. The death of Nick the mechanic in that movie is foreshadowed in *Red Light*, where a truck-yard stalking ends with a character crushed by a freight trailer. Like Soberin in *Kiss Me Deadly* only the killer's lower legs and feet are visible until a final low angle, visual devices that Aldrich freely borrowed. As with his early television work during the 1950s on Four Star Playhouse, these were all important learning experiences that he would use to great effect in his later collaborations with accomplished noir cinematographers such as Joseph Biroc, Ernest Haller, and Ernest Laszlo.

Aldrich's first noir as director was *World for Ransom* (1953). Based on the *China Smith* TV series starring Dan Duryea (some episodes of which Aldrich directed), scripted by blacklisted screenwriter Hugo Butler and photographed by Biroc, the film begins with its hero alone on the foggy noirish streets of Singapore before he finds himself trapped in an abstract setting of a staircase, his exit blocked by two men. Stylistically, the visual area of entrapment complements the theme of a romantic knightly hero also trapped by his own solipsistic forms of desire and his inability to read objectively the real nature of his "lady fair." The film ends as it begins leaving its hero more psychologically isolated than he was in the beginning.

Below, foggy, noirish street in *World for Ransom* Opposite, *The Big Knife*..

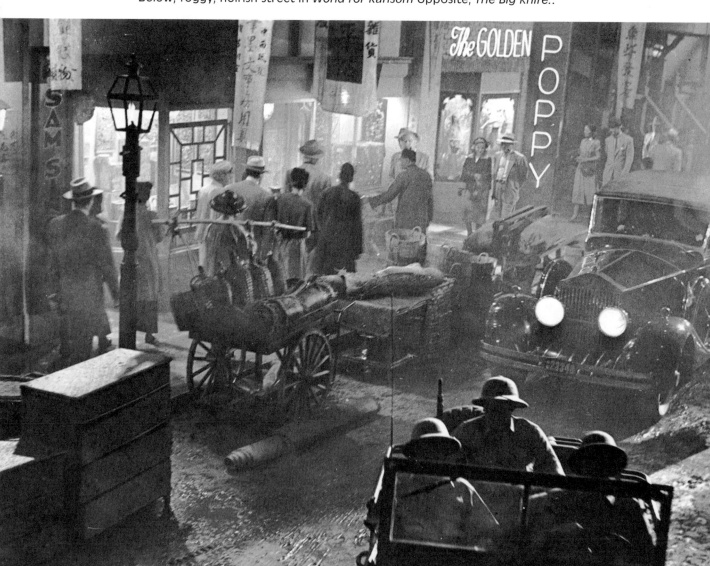

The Big Knife also transcends its origins as a Clifford Odets stage play originally starring John Garfield with whom Aldrich hoped to work with before that actor's tragic victimization by HUAC. Rather than belonging to the "Hollywood on Hollywood" genre exemplified by Vincente Minnelli's *The Bad and the Beautiful* (1953) and other works, *The Big Knife* is a psychological study of personal and social entrapment aided by Ernest Laszlo's cinematography that depicts the lush interior of Charlie Castle's Bel Air mansion as an affluent, but claustrophobic, psychological cage stifling both the creativity and vitality of its main protagonist. Its opening credit sequence by Saul Bass represents Charlie as a film noir version of that tormented character in Norwegian artist Edvard Munch's famous Expressionist painting *The Scream* and it is by no means accidental that the screen fragments like a broken mirror at the end, abstractly illustrating its hero's psychological crisis.

Then an uncredited voice-over commentary by Richard Boone introduces us to successive shots of Charlie's Bel Air environment before the audience remains confined to his "playroom" as Odets described it in his original play. These shots utilize canted angles (mercifully brief in contrast to those dominating Carol Reed's *The Third Man*) to suggest the instability lurking beneath this affluent material façade. Once inside Charlie's mansion Aldrich and Laszlo employ relevant camera angles, cutting, deep focus photography, and the presence of ceiling shots evoking those in *Citizen Kane* to suggest an environment of emotional entrapment tending to limit human agency.

The final overhead crane shot at the end of *The Big Knife* depicting the torment of Marian Castle reveals also the dangerous environment of a studio that has destroyed a character who has retreated into self-indulgent masochism and chooses a defeatist solution after making his one heroic stand against the system. Although Charlie may believe that it is his only possible act of rebellion, he leaves a psychologically devastated widow behind and a young son who will certainly be traumatized by this event as much as the aged heroines later played by Bette Davis and Joan Crawford who suffer from family dysfunction. Like *Autumn Leaves*, noir is the only possible style that can appropriately represent such dilemmas.

Below, Ida Lupino and Jack Palance as the dysfunctional Castles in *The Big Knife*. Opposite, the pillar of salt becomes one of fire: Lily Carver about to die in *Kiss Me Deadly*.

Kiss Me Deadly has also received detailed treatment especially in a definitive essay by Alain Silver (originally published in a 1970s issue of *Film Comment* and afterwards available in *Film Noir Reader*) that any further comment may seem superfluous. However, like *World for Ransom* and *The Big Knife*, noir is the only possible stylistic treatment for a world heading towards destruction. It is a film that deliberately employs visual instability as the opening credits rolling up the screen in reverse show. The same feature of instability applies to certain aspects of sound. As Silver and Ursini point out in *What Ever Happened to Robert Aldrich?*, sound is used creatively in this film and deserves study in its own right. When Christina dies, we still hear the

sounds of her screaming on the soundtrack although her legs do not move in the background. It is a technique going against the grain of normal Hollywood practices and another example of how Aldrich was very aware of the acoustic aspects of cinematic modernism and his work here bears comparison with Hitchcock's techniques in *Blackmail* (1929). A.I. Bezzerides' screenplay depicts key characters with few redeeming features whose material greed leads to nuclear destruction. Described by critics as diverse as C.G.Infante and Francois Truffaut as the first real film of the Atomic Age, *Kiss Me Deadly* also displays those largely vanished Los Angeles environments seen in Joseph Losey's *M* as well as the funicular railway doomed to obsolescence in a world dominated by freeways, recording machines, and a deadly modernist environment creating new and "fabulous" treasures that will also result in the extinction of humanity itself.

Like all Aldrich noir films, *Kiss Me Deadly* is capable of so many alternative and rich readings in which its baroque visual style stands out as an appropriate representation for a dark era in American history often buried beneath the banal world of Eisenhower conformity. However, there were also other directors such as Samuel Fuller, Anthony Mann, and Douglas Sirk who would visually contradict the ideological and material certainties of the 1950s in their films. Like *Citizen Kane*, *Kiss Me Deadly* is a key work of cinematic modernism belonging to a tradition that influenced both Aldrich and Welles. Its use of deep focus, wide angle lens, and discordant shot syntax places it not only within this context but also within contemporary modernism as Mike Grost has shown in his very informative essay on his *Classic Film and Television Web Page* that also analyzes *World for Ransom* within this context.

Attack! is another film from a stage play that interested John Garfield. As well as being a war film attacking the authoritarian military system, it also analyzes the personal factors that make the system rotten to the core. Captain Cooney anticipates Burt Hanson of *Autumn*

Leaves in being an "adult child" traumatically destroyed by an abusive father and lacking a maturity that leaves him not only dangerous to himself but also to the men under his command. Placed in control by the calculating manipulative father figure of Colonel Bartlett who sees Cooney as the key to his future post-war political ambitions, the cowardly and irrational character of the Captain is significantly depicted by the noir lighting of Joseph Biroc. Our second view of Cooney is ominous. Accompanied by the discordant and fragmented score of Frank De Vol, chiaroscuro lighting and mail room pigeon holes obscure the face of a commanding officer first seen in a distant long shot. De Vol's musical accompaniment ideally complements a masterly use of noir technique making the film easily recognizable according to Richard Combs in his 1978 monograph as the work of "a director whose worlds are always in turmoil, his characters *in extremis*, and his intense, battering style productive of more *angst* than the narratives can comfortably contain."

Like other characters in Aldrich's universe, Lt. Costa finds himself "too late the hero" and Aldrich himself casts doubt on the obligatory happy ending by framing Lt. Woodruff in isolation as he begins to inform the high command as to what has really happened. He will end up as another victim in a court-martial dominated by a prosecuting counsel "bucking for a majority." Aldrich anticipates this "unhappy ending" by displaying a diagonal shadow bar across Woodruff's chest after he shoots Cooney. No matter how well motivated his act is, the officer finally becomes trapped within the unstable world of film noir no matter how much he has attempted to distance himself from facing its implications throughout most of the film. In an earlier scene, Aldrich ironically employed a sarcastic use of sound montage to express his understanding of Woodruff's plan to Costa concerning the removal of Cooney from the command by using a goat bleating in the background.

Scripted anonymously by blacklisted writer Jean Rouverol Butler, *Autumn Leaves* is much more than the asocial melodrama that may have initially attracted Joan Crawford. Although Aldrich lacked his usual cinematographers on this film, Charles Lang's camerawork contains the director's distinctive noir touches. He had also previously shot Joan Crawford in *Queen Bee* (1955) but was also adaptable to noir cinematography. However, what makes *Autumn Leaves* most notable is not its category as a melodrama but the manner in which Aldrich significantly inserts elements of noir into the narrative to emphasize the psychosis existing in all the main characters. This film anticipates not only his later collaboration with Bette Davis but also the 1970s family horror film where the threat exists internally within the family. As Richard Combs notes in his 1978 British Film Institute monograph on the director, the introduction to Millie's apartment not only evokes the opening scenes of *The Big Knife* but also foreshadows the opening scenes of Alfred Hitchcock's *Psycho*. Millicent has masochistically turned down her chances for marriage to devote herself to her ailing father who ironically rejects her attentions. Now a spinster she sees in Burt a second chance to recover what she lost but it is one where she re-enacts that past role of maternal nurturer that had trapped her initially.

Burt is an adult child, the victim of an incestuous father and cheating wife who has chosen to retreat into a world of fantasy rather than confront the conditions that cause his schizophrenia. In one scene, Aldrich also employs a reverse form of that mirror imagery he used in *Kiss Me Deadly* where Mike appears to see Velda as he enters her apartment but in reality sees a false double imagery. The shot begins in the earlier film with Mike watching Velda perform her ballet exercise. It is only when the camera moves right that the audience learns that what we understood as a real image was actually a reflected mirror image. In *Autumn Leaves*, after Millicent visits a pre-*Bonanza* Lorne Greene, the camera moves left in a different direction to that of the scene in *Kiss Me Deadly* revealing a mirror showing the entrance of Burt's cheating wife. The scene not only symbolically depicts the secret incestuous relationship existing

Opposite, Lt. Costa (Jack Palance) and a prisoner in *Attack!*

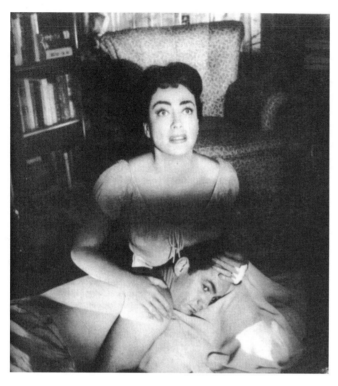

between father-in-law and his former daughter-in-law but also subtly suggests the dark nature of the attraction between Burt and Millicent. Age difference links all these characters. When Burt weeps in Millicent's lap in a manner evoking the "Pieta" a horizontal shadow bar (similar to those used in *Attack!*) appears before her body revealing both her recognition of an unhealthy relationship that she has entered into as well as her realization that it has to cease despite the fact that she may lose Burt.

This imagery reveals Aldrich's sophisticated understanding of the noir style and its transgeneric nature. Similar uses of shadow bars occur in *Attack!* emphasizing the very different natures of Bartlett and Costa, one a devious manipulative father figure and the other a sacrificial victim trapped within the claustrophobic world of an authoritarian military institution as well as being a pawn of his own self-destructive tendencies. In *Autumn Leaves*, diagonal shadow bars cast ominous patterns intimating the very problematic and symbiotic relationship existing between two characters who pathologically need each other but also must engage on a difficult road towards personal maturity before any possibility of positive psychological change can develop.

Due to the fact that it is now impossible to ascertain what sections of *The Garment Jungle* Aldrich actually directed, it is best to pass on to his two family horror melodramas starring Bette Davis. Both *What Ever Happened to Baby Jane?* and *Hush...Hush, Sweet Charlotte* benefit from the black and white cinematography by Ernest Haller and Joseph Biroc respectively as well as the director's association with a scenarist who also echoed his radical undermining of Hollywood genres–Lukas Heller. Heller had also collaborated with Anthony Mann on *Man of the West* (1958) and *God's Little Acre* (1959) creating appropriate dark overtones for these anti-establishment films. *Baby Jane* and *Charlotte* present their respective heroines as victims of a dysfunctional family whose mental instability results from the role of a malevolent sibling figure in the past. Like Millicent and Burt in *Autumn Leaves* they have never gained sufficient maturity to cope with advancing years and changing times. Both are fragile victims of a past that has left indelible traumatic traces on their personalities. Aldrich's choice of the noir style is again creatively motivated recognizing the plight of an aging woman in a changing society, leaving her at the end with either the choice of regressive insanity that will spare her from further pain or theatrically performing the role her contemporary Southern society has forced on her despite the fact that she discovers the truth and takes justified vengeance on her persecutors. Often relegated to the realm of camp melodrama, these films are really poignant studies of fragile individuals whose personalities have been ruined by personal and social factors over which they have no control. The dark overtones and tragic aspects of both these

What Ever Happened to Baby Jane and *Hush...Hush, Sweet Charlotte* where Bette Davis alternates between tormentor, with Joan Crawford above, and tormentee, with Olivia de Havilland

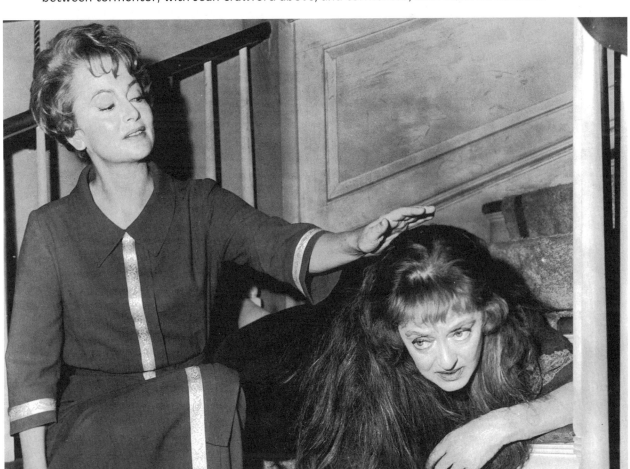

Above, Robert Lansing as an "old school" private eye in *The Grissom Gang.*

films receive appropriate visual representation by a very different noir style.

No longer confined to the familiar urban jungle, the noir element now depicts a different, but also very familiar type of *American Tragedy,* earlier explored by Theodore Dreiser in his novel of the same name as well as in *Sister Carrie,* that also has undeniable associations with literary naturalism as Foster Hirsch has noted in his 2008 study *The Dark Side of the Screen: Film Noir.* Like Samuel Fuller's battleground, in Aldrich's universe the family can also be a dark representative of cinematic emotion. Once viewers ignore the misleading camp reputation of both these films, they can then appreciate Aldrich's own form of visual style merging film noir, the deep focus cinematography associated with the Welles-Toland collaboration of *Citizen Kane*, and the influence of Alfred Hitchcock's *Psycho* that would be a key influence on the 1970s family horror film movement. Aldrich sympathized with the tragic victims portrayed by Bette Davis in both these films and it was no accident that Baby Jane's "I'm Writing a Letter to Daddy" and the theme to *Hush...Hush, Sweet Charlotte* were played at the director's memorial service.

Aldrich and Biroc also collaborated on *The Grissom Gang* (1971). As one of the first neo-noirs in American cinema, it was more than appropriate that these two key talents would contribute further refinements beyond the classical film style that new developments in lighting, high-speed film stock, and cameras made possible at this time. As a remake of the novel by James Hadley Chase, *No Orchids for Miss Blandish*, *The Grissom Gang* owed nothing to the 1948 British film noir set in America starring Jack La Rue embodying the pulp fiction threat of the American gangster tradition that affronted the sensibilities of critics such as George Orwell and the British cultural establishment. Instead, it presented a very grim view of the 1930s American Depression era often glamorized in contemporary Warner Brothers productions and disavowed in later films. Biroc's harsh color cinematography and Aldrich's unglamorized direction of his leading actors, that provided no easy type of audience identification, presented a dangerous Social Darwinist world where humans operated as predators towards each other very much in the manner of volumes in Emile Zola's Rougon-Macquart series that also influenced American fiction. The director's characters sweat in a non-air conditioned world of the 1930s, prey on each other, and often change according to whatever personal and social circumstances occur as the tender, but doomed, romance between Slim Grissom and Barbara Blandish reveals.

By the time *Hustle* (1975) appears cinematic technology has developed to such a state that Biroc can reproduce the visual contrasts of classical noir cinematography within the world of color. *Hustle* is thus a more advanced cinematic neo-noir than *The Grissom Gang*, allowing Aldrich to return again to a visual style he contributed to and bring out its bleak dimensions in an appropriately bleak world of color. The neo-noir color style influencing *Hustle* is clearly recognizable. It is an advance on the cinematography employed in *The Grissom Gang* due to its sophisticated variation of lighting techniques. While the earlier film resembles the Technicolor cinematography employed in *Leave Her to Heaven* and *Slightly Scarlet*, *Hustle* is one of the first recognizable examples of neo-noir that influenced the future development of film noir.

Basically, the film may be categorized as an American "film policier" but to do so would mistakenly misrepresent Aldrich's particular type of authorship that is displayed throughout most of his films, one that interrogates the different ways characters may survive or not in a different historical era from the one of their formative years. Lt. Phil Gaines is nostalgic for old movies featuring Humphrey Bogart and John Garfield and his musical tastes reflect those of the 1930s. By contrast, Nicole is a sophisticated European woman who prefers the more critically reflective compositions of Charles Aznavour, one of which questions past nostalgia–"When I was Young." Furthermore, like Blanche and Charlotte, both are adult victims of past family trauma. Phil is a "red diaper" baby whose father died in the Spanish Civil War. Nicole's military father engaged in terrorism during the Algerian war for independence. The lavish apartment that Phil and Nicole share appears positively lit up by the California sunshine outside as we see in the opening scene. But inside, it is a world of darkness whose interior is lit up in a similar manner to Phil's office in the police station.

Furthermore, Korean war veteran Marty Hollister (a brilliant, non-characteristic performance by Ben Johnson) appears as Phil's "secret sharer," a man out of touch with both a changing world and his growing daughter, somebody who "wants his day in court" like a Warner Brothers character from the studio social-conscience movies of the 1930s but who is more likely to end up as "Juliet to some faggot's Romeo" in prison. *Hustle* is another of Aldrich's key films where everything is interconnected through a glass darkly and the most appropriate form of visual representation for its subject matter is the stylistically pessimistic mirror of "neo-noir," a new style used by Aldrich and Biroc in an interrogative manner before it became more superficial in later representations such as the misbegotten remake of *D.O.A.*

Robert Aldrich had a very diverse career and worked in several different cinematic genres. But most of his films evoked indelible traces of film noir, even works that appeared to bear very little relationship to that visual style. In *The Killing of Sister George*, the camera tracks upwards above Beryl Reid's tragic figure showing her alone in a dark and deserted television studio in the same way that it does at the end of *The Big Knife* and *Attack!* Like those Aldrich heroes in both these films, George ends up not only betrayed by others but also the victim of her own self-destructive tendencies. In *Too Late the Hero*, Lt. Lawson is shot in noir lighting in compositions that denote his deadly refusal to help Captain Hornsby in a mission that might have worked as well as another that clearly reveal his guilt as the dead eyes of his superior officer gaze at him in condemnation. Even the problematic *The Choirboys* (1977), photographed by Joseph Biroc, also contains examples of dark neo-noir cinematography that reveal the deep anguish in the minds of its L.A.P.D. characters in a revealing expressionistic manner. As Raffaele Caputo points out in his stimulating 1992 *Continuum* essay, "*Film Noir*: You Sure Don't See What you hear" Aldrich's *Twilight's Last Gleaming* contains a strong gallery of actors well known for their roles in film noirs such as Burt Lancaster, Richard Widmark, Joseph Cotten, Charles McGraw, Leif Erickson, and Richard Jaeckel, as well as William Marshall who played the District Attorney in Richard Fleischer's neo-noir *The Boston Strangler* (1968) that also used split screen techniques similar to Aldrich's film. This is also appropriate for a film complementing the apocalyptic nature of *Kiss Me Deadly* where Nick's "Va, Va, Voom! Pretty Pow" nearly occurs as a result of the instability of a hero audiences may think they are supposed to identify with. Also, Joseph Biroc's cinematically bleak depiction of an American industrial wasteland in Aldrich's last film *...All the Marbles* (1981) also contains very relevant neo-noir features of a culture and society beginning its decline in the Reagan era. Robert Aldrich thus left a very important legacy for cinema both in terms of his creative authorship as well as his artistic reworking of the classical film noir legacy into new directions in terms of his collaboration with other creative personalities of the movement.

Biography

Robert Aldrich was born in Cranston, Rhode Island on 9 August 1918. His father was newspaper publisher Edward B. Aldrich. He was a grandson of U.S. Senator Nelson W. Aldrich and cousin to Nelson Rockefeller. Studying economics at the University of Virginia, he left to take a minor job at R.K.O Studios and, despite his privileged background, gained experience by working his way up from the bottom to eventually work as assistant director for Jean Renoir, Joseph Losey, Lewis Milestone, Charles Chaplin, and Abraham Polonsky. His formative period was his time at Enterprise Studios where he began a lifelong friendship with the soon-to-be-blacklisted Polonsky. Wanting to be a fully-fledged director, he worked in that capacity on East and West Coast television productions, especially on Dick Powell's *Four Star Playhouse*. This led to his first feature *The Big Leaguer* (1953) starring Edward

Above, assistant director Aldrich's cameo as a fight fan with a bottle in Joseph Losey's *The Big Night*.

Opposite, unexpected encounter with an armed robber at the conclusion of *Hustle*.

Bottom, Aldrich directs Jack Palance and Ida Lupino in *The Big Knife*.

G. Robinson (who had recently emerged from blacklisting problems) and his two initial noir films *World for Ransom* and *Kiss Me Deadly*. Aldrich also directed two westerns starring Burt Lancaster (*Apache, Vera Cruz*) that may also be regarded as blacklist allegories before working on a diverse number of genres such as the war film (*Attack!*), stage adaptation (*The Big Knife*), melodrama (*Autumn Leaves*), syndicate drama (*The Garment Jungle*–from which he was replaced by Vincent Sherman), Rubble Movie (*Ten Seconds to Hell*) before relocating to Europe and directing *The Last Days of Sodom and Gomorrah*. Aldrich returned to Hollywood directing two films with Bette Davis and achieved box-office success with *The Dirty Dozen* allowing him to purchase his own studio. Following its collapse, he directed *Ulzana's Raid* starring Burt Lancaster and the neo-noir *Hustle* (1975). After his last film *...All The Marbles* (1981) Aldrich died on 5 December 1983 following complications from surgery.

Noir Films

World for Ransom (1954)

The Big Knife (1955)

Kiss Me Deadly (1955)

Autumn Leaves (1956)

Attack! (1956)

The Garment Jungle (1957)

What Ever Happened to Baby Jane? (1962)

Hush...Hush, Sweet Charlotte (1964)

The Grissom Gang (1971)

Hustle (1975)

John Brahm

James Ursini

Over a career as a movie director that stretched from 1936 to 1967, John Brahm consistently explored the archetype of the femme fatale in film noir. Although his movies have largely been ignored by film historians until recently, Brahm has nevertheless left a body of work which demonstrates a consistency of style as well as an obsessive fixation on the image of the powerful if conflicted female archetype in film noir. Like many of his contemporary noir directors, whether consciously or unconsciously, Brahm also investigated the issue of female power and the ways in which the patriarchy attempts to limit or even destroy that power.

Actor Laird Cregar in collaboration with Brahm and writer Barré Lyndon forged with *The Lodger* (1944) and its companion piece *Hangover Square* (1945) two classics of the period noir with special emphasis on the image of the femme fatale. *The Lodger*'s opening scenes set the mood appropriate for a tale of Jack the Ripper (the source is the same novel used by Hitchcock to tell the story in a very different manner seventeen years earlier) as well as a film noir. The camera ranges through the foggy streets of Whitechapel (the area where most of the

Brahm's period femme fatales: a saucy Linda Darnell (left) in *The Lodger* and a more demure Merle Oberon (right) in *Hangover Square*.

Ripper murders occurred in the late 19th Century). We are introduced to the denizens of the city: entertainers, prostitutes, beggars, and working class stiffs as they go about seeking money and entertainment. Bobbies patrol on horse and foot searching out an elusive serial killer who brutally murders and then disembowels women.

After this moody opening, Laird Cregar as the killer (the audience infers this by his furtive actions and disturbing demeanor), who has once again escaped the police patrols, emerges from the fog and dark. He looms over the camera, both his height and bulk adding to his sense of menace. But when the camera finally moves into a close-up, the audience sees in his soulful eyes a gentleness and melancholy which helps give dimension to this "monster." Cregar, as he did in most of the performances of his sadly abbreviated career, conveyed the alienation and despair of a noir protagonist with a style reminiscent of the great expressionistic actors of the 1920s like Emil Jannings and Lon Chaney. The camera most often shoots him from below, exaggerating his already larger dimensions, in scenes such as the one in which he

Below, in *The Lodger* Cregar's size facilitates his physical dominance in a frame, plus Brahm positions him at the center, flanked by Sir Cedric Hardwicke (Bonting), Queenie Leonard (Daisy), Merle Oberon (Kitty) and Sara Allgood (Mrs. Bonting). Opposite: same visual effect in *Hangover Square*.

clutches the Bible of the family he has taken up lodgings with, the key light focused on his large eyes, as he tells the lady of the house in his soft voice, "Mine too are the problems of life and death."

Brahm spends a great deal of his capital in the film drawing the audience into the mind of the killer: his obsession with his dead brother (he blames women for his brother's early death), which verges on incestuous homoeroticism; his attraction to the flirtatious yet sympathetic cabaret performer Kitty, the femme fatale of the piece (Brahm himself had two marriages to actresses which ended with divorce and long periods of depression, clearly influencing his approach to the femme fatale icon), who simultaneously stimulates and repulses him—intensifying his desire, as he says, to "cut the evil" out of her beauty.

One of the most remarkable scenes of the movie and a tribute to Brahm's talent as well as Cregar's acting abilities is the final chase through the galleries of the theater. The killer is shot several times and finally cornered by the police in the top tier of the theater. As the killer cringes in a corner like a wounded animal, Brahm drops out everything on the soundtrack except Cregar's labored breathing. And then as the camera moves in, the killer suddenly turns and leaps to his death through a window into the Thames River below, the waters which he had earlier described as "full of peace." Kitty pronounces his eulogy over the river, expressing her sympathy for this man who had not only murdered a string of innocent women but threatened her. In closing the film with her utterance, the filmmakers suggest that their mission has been to humanize the seemingly "inhuman."

In *Hangover Square* (1945) as Netta (the name invokes the unfaithful wife in the Leoncavallo opera *Pagliacci*) actress Linda Darnell debuts on the stage of a seedy Edwardian music hall, where she displays her long legs as she sings a provocative ditty to an audience of drunken men. As she moves off stage to meet her lover/composer, she expresses her disdain for the men as well as the mediocre music she is forced to sing. She, like any self-respecting femme fatale, has ambition. And that ambition finds its tool in the person of the emotionally crippled classical composer George Bone (played in his last performance with typical sympathy and depth by Laird Cregar). Like a siren, she keeps him in line with promises and brief kisses. And when he begins to stray back to the world of his beloved piano concerto (which he is working on throughout the movie), she pulls him back with her prodigious sex appeal, sitting on his piano to obstruct his composing and convincing him to use part of his concerto as the theme for one of her music hall ditties.

Below, prototypical noir lighting for a period street scene in *Hangover Square*.

The twist, of course, in the plot is that Bone is a murderer who commits his crimes in a trance, about which he remembers nothing. When Netta betrays him by keeping up an affair with her former lover as well as a new lover, in the person of a theatrical director who can offer her more than George, he becomes enraged. In one of his trances, he strangles her and feeds her to the bonfire set to celebrate Guy Fawkes Day.

With *Guest in the House* (1944), taken over by Brahm after Lewis Milestone fell ill, the director began a series of movies (including *The Locket, The Brasher Doubloon*, and *Singapore*) which delved more specifically into the psyche of the conflicted femme fatale. The protagonist/antagonist of the piece, Evelyn Heath (Anne Baxter), is a brilliant creation, a manipulative mass of fixations, phobias, and delusions. Her entry into the bright and sunny seaside house of the Proctors (the relatives of her fiancée Dan) produces a bit of frisson in both the audience and the unsuspecting family. As they wait for Dan and his patient/fiancée to enter by one door, suddenly a voice and a jarring cut draw us in an opposite direction. There, as if appearing out of thin air, stands Evelyn, dressed in black in contrast to their lighter colored clothes. She proceeds to dominate the "stage" (the movie was based on a stage play), circling her "audience" and winning them over with her sweet voice and treacly compliments ("I saw Bernhardt make an entrance like that once").

Above, the Proctors (Ruth Warrick and Ralph Bellamy) encounter Evelyn Heath (Anne Baxter) in *Guest in the House.*

From that point on, Evelyn works her magic on the family. Within a few days they are designing negligees and a robe for her, serving her breakfast in bed, and tiptoeing around her room as she plays over and over again her favorite recording, "Liebestraum" ("love dream"). Soon the delusional and highly romantic Evelyn has constructed her own "love dream," fixating on the artist husband of the house, Douglas Proctor (Ralph Bellamy). Using her influence to rid herself of her fiancé—she first teases and denies him sexually, then taunts him with talk of infidelity, she then begins her campaign to win Douglas. She infects the young daughter Lee (Connie Laird) with the suspicion that her father is having an affair with his curvaceous model Miriam (Marie McDonald). The infection then spreads to Ann Proctor (Ruth Warrick), Douglas' wife. In this manner Evelyn rids herself of her first rival, Miriam.

Evelyn then begins work on rupturing the once erotic and joyful relationship between Ann and Douglas (in early scenes we see them "roughhousing" playfully and sensually in the bedroom). Using her porcelain face, Evelyn leads Douglas to believe that she would be the perfect model for the church mural of Saint Cecilia. As Evelyn and Douglas grow closer, ensconced in the darkened chapel to work, the once-happy Proctor house descends deeper into disorder and misery. Lee begins to imitate Evelyn, refusing to leave her own room and playing

"Liebestraum" on her record player continuously. Douglas drinks heavily and sleeps on the couch while Ann keeps herself busy with work, letting her appearance and dress deteriorate. Even the lighting changes radically (prestigious cinematographer Lee Garmes photographed the film). The now chiaroscuro lighting externalizes the darkness descending on the family.

Like a psychic vampire Evelyn thrives as her "victims" weaken. During a night storm in which the lights go out, Evelyn parades her new found strength in front of a depressed Douglas who has now lost his daughter and wife. Declaring her unabashed love for him, she advances on the besotted artist. Shocked back to his senses, Douglas runs off in the night to find his wife and child and bring them back.

The final scene of the movie is an impressive tour de force. Evelyn has turned the tables once more and called back her "love-slave" Dan, who tells his family they have offended Evelyn and that they are to be married. As the "vampire" stands victorious, the family, except for the wise Aunt Martha (Aline MacMahon), exits the scene in defeat. Intent on protecting her brood no matter the cost, Martha convinces Evelyn that Lee's bird is loose in the house (Evelyn has an hysterical fear of birds, significant as they represent to her a loss of control). Brahm uses the sound of flapping wings and "flying" camera shots to subjectify Evelyn's inner state as she runs about the house madly. Leading her outside, Martha stands at the door, her arms covered in a shawl stretched out like two huge wings, and tells Evelyn that even more birds are threatening her outside. The audience hears her scream and the sound of the waves below the cliff. As the music rises, Martha bows her head, victorious in saving her family but marked psychologically by her deed.

The protagonist/antagonist of *The Locket* (1946), Nancy, is a somnambulist (a la Cesare in the German Expressionist classic *The Cabinet of Dr. Caligari*) femme fatale. As portrayed by Laraine Day in the movie, Nancy is a schizophrenic who leaves a trail of destruction (narrated within a complex structure of flashbacks within flashbacks) in her wake, including a suicide and a possible murder. However, she commits all her crimes with a child-like innocence, unaware of the reality of her actions. Our first introduction to the character says it all. Described as "perfect" several times, she appears to the crowd at her wedding celebration like a vision of joy and light. The only note of darkness is from an amateur astrologist who, after reading all the positive qualities of a Scorpio (Nancy's astrological sign), begins to list the negative characteristics of the sign.

Like many noirs of that period (including, most notably, Brahm's own *Guest in the House*), Freudian psychology informs the discourse of the movie. And so it is fitting that Nancy's psychologist husband Dr. Blair (Brian Aherne), who invades the happy celebration to warn Willis (Gene Raymond) about his wife-to-be, relates part of the complex story of this complex woman.

As with most Freudian analysis, the tale begins in childhood trauma—in this case the accusation of stealing a locket and the consequent bullying by the lady of the house, leading to young Nancy's feelings of guilt and humiliation. As Nancy grows up she becomes a kleptomaniac drawn always, in a simplistic Freudian construct, to jewelry. So much so that one act of theft leads to the murder—accidental?—of her employer, Bonner (Ricardo Cortez). Her theft of these trinkets seems largely unconscious. When confronted with the items by her lover, the artist Clyde (Robert Mitchum in an unusually sensitive performance), and later by her husband Dr. Blair, she seems genuinely shocked and confused—telegraphing to the audience her split from reality.

What saves Nancy from exposure are the messianic older men who are drawn to this child-woman. All of them refuse to accept that this bright and lovely woman can be corrupt and so reject the information given to them by former lovers. Even Clyde, who pursues Nancy in order to save a man condemned for her crime, gives up and commits suicide, jumping dramatically from the window of Dr. Blair's high rise office.

Again invoking the Freudian paradigm, Nancy can only find release if she revisits, literally or figuratively, the scene of her trauma. And Nancy chooses, unconsciously that is, the literal method by marrying Willis, whose mother is the same woman who accused and bullied her as a child. Even though Willis is warned by Dr. Blair regarding Nancy's background, he refuses to believe it, much like Blair before him. In the final scene, Mrs Willis (Katherine Emery), unaware of Nancy's identity, gives her the very same locket she had accused her of stealing. The sight of the locket on her breast and the action, repeated from her childhood, of knocking over the music box and setting off its haunting tune sends Nancy into a hypnotic state. As she walks down the aisle she starts to faint, her eyes focused on the design of the rug which turns into images from her past. Collapsing she finds no simplistic cure but instead retreats into the safety of her mind as she is led away to the hospital.

Singapore (1947) draws inspiration from both *Casablanca* and *Double Indemnity* in its tale of amnesia, smuggling, and obsessive love. Noir regulars Fred MacMurray and Ava Gardner are at their best. MacMurray, as the cynical pearl smuggler Gordon, again projects the image (as he would in a number of noirs into the 1950s) which Wilder created for him in *Double Indemnity*—the oversized, flabby "chump" with a weak moral center. Gardner as Linda Grahame is as radiant as usual in her role as a sultry femme fatale of circumstance (she only betrays her lover Gordon and marries the wealthy Van Leyden because she suffers from amnesia).

Below, Nancy (Laraine Day), the clearly troubled protagonist of *The Locket*, flanked by Norman (Robert Mitchum) and Dr. Harry Blair (Brian Aherne).

The situations in the movie are also affectingly noir. Gordon's flashback to the lovers' whirlwind affair and his despair over Linda's supposed death during a Japanese bombing hits the right noir tone. Brahm's fetishization of Gardner also nicely enhances her role as a femme fatale: whether dressed in black silk in an overheated tropical hotel room, appearing on the dance floor of a nightclub as if out of Gordon's wet dream, or lying comatose in her veiled bed as both her lover and her husband hover about

Above Ava Gardner and Roland Culver in *Singapore.*

Opposite, Nancy Guild and George Montgomery in *The Brasher Doubloon.*

the object of their own particular obsessions. Even the "happy" ending works as a transgressive affirmation of love beyond the bounds of society's rules as the cuckolded husband delivers his wife to the arms of her lover at the airport (a witty reversal of the ending of *Casablanca*).

By *The Brasher Doubloon* (1947) Brahm had become an expert in mentally disturbed movie femme fatales. The movie was an adaptation of Raymond Chandler's *The High Window* and featured Chandler's cynical knight-errant Marlowe (here played by George Montgomery with a lighter, more suave tone than other movie Chandlers). Merle Davis (Nancy Guild) is a victim femme fatale, a victim not only of her own psychology (like Linda in *Singapore* and Nancy in *The Locket*) but of yet a second femme fatale, Nancy's employer and the matriarch of the Murdoch clan—Mrs. Murdoch (Florence Bates).

Mrs. Murdoch hires Marlowe to find an invaluable gold doubloon but in the process he discovers the true murderer of Mr. Murdoch who had plunged to his death from his Pasadena mansion during the Rose Parade. Mrs. Murdoch blames her servant/secretary Merle, who it is implied was having an affair with the much older Murdoch. Merle herself alternates between helpless victim, firing up Marlowe's savior complex, and seductive siren. In the early scenes Marlowe finds himself drawn to her physical beauty as well as her gentleness. When he makes a move on her and she responds by telling him she has an aversion to being touched by men, Marlowe is even further intrigued, suggesting night school with him to overcome her phobia. But later, when Merle turns up, gun in hand, dressed like a traditional femme fatale (Mrs. Murdoch has told her she should use her "assets" to retrieve the doubloon she believes Marlowe has discovered), she seems to have lost her aversion to close contact.

Marlowe, of course, uncovers the truth within the labyrinth of deception and misdirection common to all noir. He finds a missing reel of film shot by a photographer who was blackmailing Mrs. Murdoch. By blowing up the frame of the film, he reveals to his audience of

Above, Guild, Montgomery, and Florence Bates in *The Brasher Doubloon.*

suspects and police that in fact Murdoch was pushed from the window by Mrs. Murdoch. In the final scene, Merle has obviously lost all her inhibitions as she aggressively suggest they spend the night together and hangs up on a potential client to drive her point home.

In the film Brahm uses to great effect the Santa Ana winds of Southern California (a favorite motif of Chandler) to create an eerie and tense mood through many of the scenes, amplifying the sounds of the wind as the moving trees and bushes create shifting patches of light in the Murdoch mansion. Like the home by the sea in *Guest in the House* or the boarding house in *The Lodger*, the upper class Pasadena manor traces its roots to the Gothic mansions and castles of 19th Century Romantic literature. It is at the center of the mystery and as much a character as any of the humans in the story.

Queen Antinea (played by statuesque and regal cult star Maria Montez) of *Siren of Atlantis* (1949) makes the manipulative femme fatale of *Guest in the House* seem like an amateur. Co-directed with Arthur Ripley (although the editor's name often appears on the credits as director because of a legal dispute), the idiosyncratic director of artsy noir films like *The Chase* and *Voice in the Wind, Siren* is based on the oft-filmed fantasy novel *L'Atlantide* by Pierre Benoit about the lost city of Atlantis and its queen, Antinea.

In the production design for Atlantis Brahm and Ripley create a dream/nightmarescape which reflects the personality of its ruler, the imperious Antinea. Like her, it is at times languid and sensual. Antinea and her lover of the moment watch sensual dances while they make love. Incense floats through the air as Middle Eastern-style music wafts down the chiaroscuro caverns and chambers of the city. Obsessed captive males languish, while waiting for Antinea to send her bodyguard with a token, a necklace, which symbolizes that they are chosen to be her consort for the night.

At other times, this erotic dream can turn frightening. Captives who try to escape or defy Antinea are killed and then encased in gold by a scientist whose tongue has been ripped out by Antinea so that he will be a more compliant chess partner and servant. One drunken and obsessed drone slits his wrists with a broken cocktail glass, given to him by the effete, impotent Blades (Henry Daniell), who taunts the virile men, clearly jealous of their physical attributes. As one of the captives tells the others, the air is almost stifling at times, oppressing the idle men as they await their turn with the beauteous queen.

The film itself centers primarily on one of the captives, St. Avit (played by Jean-Pierre Aumont, Maria Montez's husband at the time) who is the most romantic of the group of consorts. He argues with the uptight and puritanical would-be monk Morhange (Dennis O'Keefe), who resists Antinea's will, that love is the most important ideal. And it is his love for Antinea, particularly after she estranges herself from him, which drives the jealous St. Avit to stab Morhange whom he believes has becomes Antinea's newest lover.

Distraught with his act, however, St. Avit flees Atlantis but cannot forget his queen. Antinea— partially out of pride, partially out of love—sends her servant to fetch her straying lover. He finds St. Avit and presents him with the symbolic necklace. Without losing a beat, St. Avit mounts his camel and heads into a dust storm to find Antinea and Atlantis. In a powerful bit of crosscutting, we see Antinea looking out into the desert from her rooms, her face expectant and even a little sad; and then more cuts: the storm in the desert and finally St. Avit's body half-buried in a dune, his hand clutching the token of his obsession.

Like many noir directors (Ida Lupino, Gerd Oswald, etc.), used to working in the limited budgets of B-films, Brahm moved in the 1950s to the new medium of television. Soon he was directing some of the most innovative shows on the networks: *Alfred Hitchcock Presents*, *Johnny Staccato*, *Naked City*, *Twilight Zone*, *Thriller*, and *The Outer Limits*. Brahm brought his noir ethic to these shows, at times even invoking themes, archetypes (including of course the femme fatale) and even scenes right out of his classic period noirs.

In 1962 Brahm directed a memorable episode from the *Thriller* series called "A Wig for Miss Devore." The episode opens on the gallows in 18th-century England. A beautiful witch, Meg Peyton, stands defiantly before the rope and her two hangmen. After dismissing the bishop disdainfully and insulting the king, she steadies the hand of the one of her executioners, asking not to have her fiery red wig removed before her death. He agrees. But as she falls through the trap door, her wig flies off, revealing the aged body and face of a crone.

Cut to modern Hollywood and the home of aging star Sheila Devore (Patricia Barry). The platinum blonde Sheila, with her baby-doll voice and mincing ways, is a caricature of the 1950s blonde bombshell who often replaced the powerful femme fatale of the 1940s as America returned to its puritanical and conformist roots. Waited on by her lovestruck servant Herbert (John Fiedler), Sheila has finally chosen a script for her comeback, the story of Meg Peyton. Sending Herbert off to the studio head Max (Herbert Rudley) to prepare for her return to the screen, she rehearses the execution scene the audience has just witnessed in the prologue. However, Max is not interested in bringing back this aging "sex kitten." And so Herbert uses blackmail (the studio head has stolen profits from Sheila's movies) to convince Max to agree.

On Sheila's request, Herbert buys from a London museum the wig Meg Peyton wore so that Sheila can transform herself into the legendary witch. And it is quite a transformation. When she enters the soundstage, the cast and crew applaud as her director and former lover, Machik (John Baragrey), stands in awe. Not only does Sheila seem younger but more impor-

The sultrily-posed Maria Montez in *Siren of Atlantis*.

tantly she has become a full-fledged femme fatale, like her legendary model. As the production of the film goes swimmingly, everyone around Sheila comments on how more "exciting" she has become, even her baby-doll voice has become smokier and her intelligence much keener.

Like Meg, Sheila now is intent on claiming what she considers her own and punishing males who stand in her way. Learning of the duplicity of Max, she seduces him and then drowns him. She then forces Machik, who was also involved in the scheme to cheat Sheila, over his balcony (a favorite form of death in Brahm films since *Guest in the House*). However, Sheila's undoing is, appropriately, another woman—the Hedda Hopperish Arabella (Linda Watkins). Discovering the legend behind the wig, she confronts Sheila and "unwigs" her. Sheila runs out into the studio street and falls to the ground. As her pursuers turn lights on to identify her, they see her aged and decaying face.

Brahm revisited the terrain of *Guest in the House* in an episode of *The Outer Limits* called, onomatopoeically, "ZZZZZ" (1964). This isolated cottage is not by the sea but in the country. And the transgressive feminine force which disrupts the life and bourgeois marriage of its owners is an exotic mutant, a queen bee who has transformed herself into a human in order to mate with the scientist who studies the life of her "people." The entomologist, Professor Fields (Philip Abbott), finds Regina (played sensuously by Joanna Frank) lying on the grass of his yard. Regina is Isis or Astarte fallen to earth. Her voluptuous body is encased in a form-fitting tunic; her strong Middle Eastern features peek out beneath tufts of black hair which cross her face; her voice is honey-sweet yet commanding.

Regina, like any queen such as Antinea in Brahm's earlier *Siren of Atlantis*, wastes no time in pursuing her "human drone" as she calls him. Realizing that because he is human he must love her in order to mate, she sets about alienating him from his conventional and aging wife Francesca (Marsha Hunt). Playing upon her own child-woman qualities, she invokes the memory of his dead daughter as he stares dreamily at her over the dinner table while his wife fumes. During one of her barefoot romps in the moonlight, Regina purposely kneels beneath Francesca's window and as the wife looks down sticks her tongue in the center of a flower to collect pollen and transforms herself into her original form—a bee.

When Francesca tells her husband what she saw, he dismisses it as a symptom of her jealousy. Doubting her own sanity, she takes to her bed for rest while Field and Regina become closer in the intimacy of his laboratory. As the shadows deepen over the house, much as they did in *Guest in House*, Regina gains complete dominance when Francesca dies and Fields is left vulnerable. Wearing a wedding veil (intimations of the "mad" wedding in *The Locket*) to taunt Fields about their future union (she had spoken before of the beauty of the sacrifice of drones who mate with the queen and then die), Fields seems defeated. But when he listens to the tapes of her conversations with her drones, translated by the analyzer, and remembers his love for Francesca, he gains the courage to defeat her. Attacking her with platitudes about love and marriage, he pushes her back against the second story window and she falls to the ground (much like Evelyn in *Guest*). However, this is 1964, not 1944, and the U.S. is on the edge of a cultural and feminist revolution. So, unlike Evelyn, Regina does not die but survives in her queen bee form, flying off to rendezvous with her drones.

Biography

John Brahm (born Hans in Hamburg, Germany on August 17, 1893) was the son of German actor Ludwig Brahm. Brahm himself was both an actor and director for such acting troupes as Deutsches Kunstler Theatre and the Lessing Theatre. He was also married to famed stage and screen actress Dolly Haas, whom he would direct in his first feature film, a moody remake of D.W.Griffith's *Broken Blossoms* (1936). The film was made shortly after Brahm fled the continent for England in response to the rise of Hitler. Brahm then came to America in 1937 to work for both Columbia and 20th Century-Fox. Fox head Darryl Zanuck was so impressed with Brahm's ability to make low-budget movies like the proto-noir *Let Us Live* (1939) and the horror film *The Undying Monster* (1942) look stylish, he "wedded" him with actor Laird Cregar to make two classic period noirs—*The Lodger* (1944) and *Hangover Square* (1945). After the success of these films, Brahm made a series of noirs redolent with the Expressionist style he learned in Germany, e.g. *Guest in the House* (1944), *The Locket* (1946), *The Brasher Doubloon* (1947), etc. Brahm also travelled to Europe to make films with the cult siren Maria Montez, including *Siren of Atlantis* (1949) and *The Thief of Venice* (1950), Montez's last movie. After the collapse of the studio system, Brahm made a smooth transition to television where he became one of the most sought after directors for fantasy/horror/sci-fi shows like *The Outer Limits*, *Alfred Hitchcock Presents*, and *Thriller*, to name but a few. Brahm died in Malibu, California on October 13, 1982.

Noir Films

The Lodger (1944)
Guest in the House (1944)
Hangover Square (1945)
The Locket (1946)
The Brasher Doubloon (1947)
Singapore (1947)
Siren of Atlantis (1949)

Brahm with Jean Parker.

Jules Dassin

Tom Ryall

Introduction

Jules Dassin directed four titles often referred to in discussion of the American film noir: *Brute Force* (1947), *The Naked City* (1948), *Thieves' Highway* (1949), and *Night and the City* (1950). *Night and the City*, though featuring prominent Hollywood stars, was shot in London by Twentieth Century-Fox as a "runaway" production and exists in two different versions. The most familiar version is the American release print endorsed by Dassin himself but a British version was also released with a different musical score, additional scenes, and a different ending. The film acquired an emblematic status for the film noir cycle when a still featuring the star, Richard Widmark, was used for the cover of Borde and Chaumeton's classic *Panorama du film noir americaine* 1941-1953 published in 1955. In addition Dassin directed *Du rififi chez les hommes* (1955) in France, a film often located within the history of the French film noir and praised by François Truffaut as "the best crime film I have ever seen."[1] The five titles constitute a some-what diverse and oblique contribution to the film noir cycle; none feature the hapless males enveloped in the webs spun by the femmes fatales of James M. Cain, or the world weary private eye heroes of Chandler and Hammett, the familiar constituents of emblematic noirs such as *Double Indemnity* (1944) and *The Big Sleep* (1946). All five titles though had the cycle's crime subject matter, its violence, murder, and robbery. Some had the cycle's characteristic urban settings, the seedy rooming houses, and the night clubs; some had iconic noir stars such as Richard Widmark, Gene Tierney and Burt Lancaster; and, some had the stylistic qualities, the distinctive lighting and camera angles, and, in thematic terms, the bleakness, the fatalism, associated with the cycle in the immediate postwar period.

James Naremore has suggested that the Dassin films belong to a distinctive branch of the film noir associated with a group of film makers on the political left. Along with Robert Rossen, Abraham Polonsky, Joseph Losey, Nicholas Ray and others, Dassin's films are marked by "humanism and political engagement" in contrast to the "cynicism and misanthropy" of film makers such as Alfred Hitchcock and Billy Wilder. They belong to one of the "two major branch-es in the 'family tree' of film noir."[2] The other branch, which includes *Double Indemnity* (1944), *The Killers* (1946), and *Out of the Past* (1947), embodies the cynical and misanthropic dimen-sions of the cycle often considered to be at the center of noir. The grouping with which Dassin is associated occupies a more marginal position, overlapping in some respects both in terms of theme and style with the titles conventionally regarded as central, but providing a "social-realist spin to familiar noirish plots."[3] Unsurprisingly, it was actors, directors, and writers from this grouping that were centrally involved in the investigations of communist influence on Hollywood in the late 1940s and early 1950s. Dassin himself had been a member of the Communist Party USA in the 1930s and he was blacklisted in 1950.

Dassin's films before the noir titles included war films, comedies and an adaptation of an Oscar Wilde story, *The Canterville Ghost* (1944). *Two Smart People* (1946), a comedy about con-artists, was the nearest indication of the crime themes that were to feature in the noir films but there is very little indication in his early work of the bleak and desperate world constructed in films such as *Brute Force* and *Night and the City*. How do the Dassin films relate to the noir cycle? The following will identify aspects of the Dassin films which relate to the cycle.

Brute Force

The Hollywood prison film was well established by the 1940s when Dassin embarked upon *Brute Force*, the first of two films he was to direct for producer Mark Hellinger who had made a considerable impact on the noir cycle with his production of *The Killers* (1946). Films such as *The Big House* (1930), *The Criminal Code* (1931), and *Each Dawn I Die* (1939), mixtures of the gangster and the social problem film, had generated a set of conventions deriving from the realities of prison life—physical and mental confinement, escape planning, the visits from loved ones and from lawyers, the informers, liberal administrators and authoritarian guards, the prison riot—many of which are present in Dassin's film. Prison films were often marked by a liberal antipathy to the hardship and suffering endured by convicts and a political and social commitment to reform often communicated in exhortatory title cards and in lengthy scenes where dignitaries and officials discuss the treatment of prisoners. In *Brute Force* the harsh disciplinary position is embodied in a senior official remonstrating with the prison governor,

Below, the cell mates in *Brute Force.*

while the compassionate approach is outlined by the prison doctor, an amiable liberal drunk. Such a scene anchors the film in Hollywood's prison melodrama strand though the perspective developed in the film is one of "humanism and political engagement" locating *Brute Force* within the left-leaning strand of the noir cycle, in what Brian Neve has termed the "social *film noir*"[4] Other dimensions of the noir cycle are discernable in the film. *Brute Force* is marked by a brutality, a degree of violence, prompting Borde and Chaumeton to include the killing of the "stoolie" involving blow torches and a compression machine in their litany of the "unprecedented panoply of cruelties and sufferings" which the noir cycle brought to the screen.[5]

This sequence, together with the notorious episode in which the chilling authoritarian Captain Munsey (Hume Cronyn), stripped to his vest, beats Louie (Sam Levene) with a rubber truncheon to the strains of Wagner on the sound track, certainly present striking images of brutality. In particular, the depiction of Munsey with its fascist overtones hints at a post-Auschwitz view of human capabilities and indicates the "humanism and political engagement" noted by many as a feature of Dassin's work in the late 1940s.

The film incorporates a number of short sequences outside of the prison in which the central characters—the inmates of Cell R17—reminisce about their lives and misfortunes. Spencer (John Hoyt) tells his fellow prisoners about the woman who robbed him of his gun and money; Lister (Whit Bissell) ponders his crime—embezzlement from his firm in order to buy his wife a fur coat; Becker (Howard Duff) recalls the incident in wartime Italy when his wife shot her father and he took the blame; and Joe (Burt Lancaster) thinks of his last meeting with his wheelchair-bound wife. If the prison film elements of the film noir are on the margins of the cycle, these brief sequences embody a key narrative feature of the film noir—the flashback—and they also present some of the key themes of the cycle. Spencer's story is a condensed classic film noir complete with a femme fatale who lures the hapless male to his fate; Lister is a white collar criminal desperate to please his beautiful wife; Joe's visit to his wife is while he is on his way to his "last job" with the promise of a future ahead of them. Becker's story is slightly different with the wartime Italian setting and the theme of interaction between the GI and indigenous population evoking Rossellini's *Paisa* (1946) and the Neo-realist cinema just beginning to make itself known to American audiences and film makers, and acknowledged by Dassin as an influence on his work.

The Naked City

The Naked City, Dassin's second film for producer Mark Hellinger, is best known for its documentary-influenced style. The film belongs with semi-documentaries such as *The House on 92nd Street* (1945), *Boomerang!* (1947), and *Call Northside 777* (1948), films which blended criminal and espionage investigative dramas often based on real life cases with the techniques of documentary cinema such as extensive location shooting and "voice of God" commentary. It is a significant and interesting contribution to the broad noir cycle which draws together influences from newsreels such as Louis de Rochemont's *The March of Time*, wartime documentaries, Italian Neo-realist film, and crime photojournalism. The film's title is taken from *Naked City* (1945), a book of images of New York by the famous crime photojournalist, Arthur Fellig (Weegee). Mark Hellinger had acquired the rights to the book's title and, according to some accounts, hired Weegee as a consultant for the film. Weegee's brutally realist work is often cited as an influence on the film noir and, indeed, some of the images in Dassin's film have a similarity to some of the photographs in *Naked City*. However, Dassin's own well-documented dismissal of the film was mainly on grounds of the cutting of Weegee-like images of the seamier side of New York City—shots of the Bowery, of a rough sleeping derelict—which compromised the realism to which the director was committed.

The semi-documentary police drama amalgamates several elements including violent

Above, *Naked City* : an early police procedural where young and old homicide detectives compare notes with a white-coated version of a forensics officer while standing by the victim's corpse.

crime and murder, in particular, often drawn from actual cases, mystery and investigation, and a detailed focus on the procedures of detection and arrest. Its dominant defining feature, however, is location shooting, often in live situations involving crowds of bystanders at resonant urban landmarks such as public buildings, train stations, and major bridges. The realism and authenticity derived from the location shooting had to be matched with the melodramatics of Hollywood narration as the films were offered as part of the entertainment mainstream and aimed at the conventional cinema-going audience. *The Naked City* embodies much of the semi-documentary repertoire. Its documentary credentials are emphasized in the film's opening sequence when the voiceover spoken by producer Mark Hellinger proclaims that the film "was not photographed in the studio." "Quite the contrary," the producer/narrator continues, the actors "played out their roles on the streets, in the apartment houses, in the skyscrapers of New York itself. And along with them a great many thousand New Yorkers played out their roles also." It is also a police procedural with an emphasis on the mechanics of crime detection. Indeed, screenwriter Malvin Wald, who wrote the story treatment on which the script was based, prepared for the project with a one month stint observing the work of the New York Police Department from the inside. But, it begins firmly in the world of noir with two murders. The first, in an apartment, is presented obliquely in the rhetoric of noir with the female victim and the two male perpetrators hidden in shadows; the other, on the riverside, is in the cold light of dawn. Yet both are set in the context of a "city profile" montage, "a social, economic, and geographic cross-section of a day in the life of New York" familiar from the city documentary genre and films such as *Berlin: Symphony of a Great City* (1927).[6] The violent crimes along with other aspects of New York life are presented as routine occurrences in the pulsating diversity of city life.

Hellinger envisaged the film as a portrait of New York and while the thrust of the film following the opening sequence is that of the intricate murder mystery requiring unravelling by the dogged police team, the frequent location sequences embed the drama in the familiar streets and buildings of the city, and in the life of its people on the subway, its children playing in the streets, giving the film a hybrid quality in its merger of documentary and drama, and positioning it on the margins of the noir cycle.

Thieves' Highway

Dassin's next film is another "marginal" case. In Thom Andersen's words, *Thieves' Highway* is one of a group of "noir films in which a social critique carries more weight than a psychological diagnosis."[7] Andersen termed this grouping *film gris* to distinguish films such as *Force of Evil* (1948), *They Live by Night* (1948), and *Thieves' Highway* from more emblematic noirs such as *The Killers* and *Out of the Past* while also signalling their affinities as films of the same broad cycle or genre. The grouping, which he also termed "Hollywood neorealism" overlaps with Naremore's identification of the major noir strand defined by "humanism and political engagement" mentioned above. The social realism of *Thieves' Highway* lies in the subject matter. The film is an adaption of his own proletarian novel, *Thieves' Market*, by A. I. Bezzerides, and focuses upon truckers working in the corrupt and violent world of the San Francisco fruit market. It is a distinctively working class film concerned with the harsh competitive and dangerous lives of the ordinary truckers and their exploitation by the wholesale buyers. The social realist dimensions of *The Naked City* lay in the extensive location shooting grounding the film in the detailed reality of New York, and the careful presentation of procedural detail. Its delineation of the principal characters was somewhat restrained and perhaps distant, and subordinated to the film's documentary impulse. In contrast, *Thieves' Highway* presents its working class characters in a more engaging fashion, placing them in tense and dramatic situations with less of a stress on illustrating the social and class dynamics of the situation, and more of a conventional Hollywood focus on audience involvement.

Thieves' Highway incorporates noir elements to a greater extent than its predecessor, *Brute Force*. As in films such as *The Blue Dahlia* (1946), *Dead Reckoning* (1947), and *Crossfire* (1947), the central character, Nick (Richard Conte), is a veteran of the Second World War returning from abroad. He has a settled relationship with Polly (Barbara Lawrence) and becomes engaged to her on his return. In the course of the film, however, he meets Rica (Valentina Cortese), in some respects a classic femme fatale, who lures Nick to her room to keep him occupied while Mike Figlia (Lee J Cobb), the corrupt fruit wholesaler, disposes of the lorry load of apples which Nick has brought to market. Polly is conventional, representing the path of marriage and respectability for Nick; in contrast Rica is immoral though vibrant and exciting. It is a pairing of female characters familiar in the noir cycle. For example, in *Out of the Past*, Jeff (Robert Mitchum) has a similar set of alternatives with a conventional marriage partner in Ann (Virginia Huston) and a seductive alternative in Kathy (Jane Greer). Jeff's reluctant involvement with the latter, however, leads to his death while *Thieves' Highway* ends atypically for a film noir with Nick rejecting Polly and convention, and heading for a new life with Rica.

The Naked City has been described by Thomas Schatz as "a crime film with virtually no trace of *noir* stylistics";[7] in contrast *Thieves' Highway* has a number of sequences which utilize noir lighting to great dramatic effect. Indeed, the film is shaped in terms of a descent into

Below and oppsite *Thieves' Highway* where Nick Garcos (Richard Conte) flashes the same smirk for a cop and, opposite, for a working girl (Valentina Cortese)

darkness typical of noir. The opening sequences of Nick's homecoming and the scenes in the orchard are filmed documentary-style in bright sunlight; in contrast, the long drive to the wholesale market, and the scenes in the market itself, are largely at night in the shadowy darkness of a noir underworld including the bars and rooming houses, and the dark alleys, the essential backdrop to the harsh and violent world of the cycle. Two sequences in particular stand out. The drive to market is through the night and Nick's truck has a tire blowout. He attempts a repair but the jack slips and the truck pins him to the ground but his partner, Ed (Millard Mitchell), following in another truck, comes to his rescue. The sequence is filmed in near-darkness with the flickering lights of passing traffic on the highway occasionally illuminating the agonized Nick as he struggles with the breakdown. The second is when Nick and Rica are walking back to her room after he has done the deal with Figlia. They stroll through noirish surroundings—the railroad, the boxcars, the rain-washed streets, the neon sign of the hotel—a typical and appropriate setting for the outbreak of violence when Figlia's henchmen attack and rob Nick of the money which their boss has just given him.

Night and the City

Dassin's previous titles converged with noir in some respects though they also contained social realist elements which suggested a different temper and sensibility to that of the cycle. *Night and the City*, however, despite being made in England, is regarded by many as a quintessential film noir. The film "may well be the definitive *film noir*,"[9] suggested Foster Hirsch while

Glenn Erickson regarded the film as "a graphic showcase of the style at its most extreme" with a title "that best exemplifies the textbook definitions of the *noir* sensibility."[10] Yet, *Night and the City* has also been claimed as a substantial contribution to British cinema, as a major instance of the British "spiv cycle" of the late 1940s, a companion piece to films such as *Brighton Rock* (1947), and *The Third Man* (1949), and one of the "six great spiv films" according to Peter Wollen.[11] In fact, the film is an adaptation of a late 1930s British crime novel written by Gerald Kersh, and its central character, Harry Fabian (Richard Widmark), is called a "cheap spiv" in a scene included in the British version but cut from the American release print of the film.

Though the film was British-based, the regulations governing runaways enabled American personnel to take the principal creative roles of direction, writing, and acting. Dassin, of course, had made three noirs in America but other members of the production

team also had experience in the cycle. The screenplay was written by Jo Eisinger who previously had worked on *Gilda* (1946) as well as adapting his crime novel, *The Walls Came Tumbling Down*, for the screen. Star Richard Widmark had sprung to prominence a few years earlier playing a neurotic killer with a trademark high-pitched laugh in *Kiss of Death* (1947). Harry Fabian, though, the central character of *Night and the City* played by Widmark, was more of a petty criminal, a hapless figure striving for the easy life, without the psychopathic dimensions of

Richard Widmark as the desperate Harry Fabian in *Night and the City* (with Francis L. Sullivan, opposite, and Gene Tierney, below)

Widmark's earlier role. Gene Tierney, his female co-star, had established a high profile with her role as the enigmatic heroine of *Laura* (1944) though her role as Mary, Fabian's girl-friend, is a relatively minor one. However, the exemplary noir stylistics of the film, its bold expressionist visual style—low key lighting, the use of shadows, night for night shooting—is the work of a British-based German, cinematographer Max Greene. Greene, whose real name was Mutz Greenbaum, had been working in Britain since the early 1930s. Yet even this was in keeping with the situation in Hollywood where a number of contributors to the American film noir (Fritz Lang, Robert Siodmak, Karl Freund, etc.) had worked in the German cinema of the 1920s, bringing its distinctive cinematographic style to the cycle. Many of the interiors, shot at Shepperton Studios, are shot in a highly charged expressive style, especially the sequences in the night club office with Phil Nosseross "in a glass-paned cage whose bars throw broad web-like patterns across ceilings and walls" creating an archetypal noir mise-en-scène.[12]

The "British" qualities of the film derive from two sources, firstly, the supporting actors and, secondly, the distinctive London location. Francis L. Sullivan as Nosseross, a sinister night club owner resembling Sidney Greenstreet, and, especially Googie Withers as his wife, a variant of the femme fatale figure, provided strong support to the American stars. Herbert Lom, though a Czech refugee from the Nazis, had established a strong profile in British crime films of the postwar period, and played a ruthless criminal boss pitted against the doomed Harry Fabian. Lom, along with a number of British character actors in smaller roles, gave the picture of London's underworld a strength in depth and more than an echo of the petty criminal gangs, the pickpockets, traceable in literary terms back to Dickens and Victorian London. Indeed, according to Googie Withers, many of the bit-parts were played by real gangsters, "ponces, racketeers, very dangerous men"[13] endowing the film with a minor dose of neo-real-

Du rififi chez les hommes.

ism. Indeed, for Charlotte Brunsdon, the depiction of the London underworld with its array of small-time operators, provides the film with a strong "contrast of an unscrupulous American hustler with a mundane and local British criminality."[14]

The film's setting, the distinctively British cityscape incorporated potent London landmark icons such as Big Ben, St Paul's Cathedral with its wartime resonance, Soho, Piccadilly Circus, Trafalgar Square, and the River Thames with its dramatic bridges and looming power stations. The studio publicity material lists 54 separate filming locations ranging from the familiar—Trafalgar Square, Piccadilly Circus—to the myriad anonymous back alleys of central London through which Harry Fabian is chased, and in which he conducts his shady business. The film's publicity made much of the London backdrop suggesting that "a bigger slice of London has been put on the screen than in any previous picture taking the city as its subject." The stress on location shooting links the film with the Hollywood semi-documentary trend, and much of the film exploits the streets of London to great effect as in the opening with St Paul's Cathedral looming over Harry Fabian as he runs through streets, fields, and alleyways, the Shot Tower on the South Bank into which Harry runs to evade capture towards the end of the film, and the chilling finale with Kristo (Herbert Lom) the wrestling racketeer looking on from Hammersmith Bridge as Fabian is killed and his body thrown into the river. Though not as striking as the Williamsburg Bridge finale in *The Naked City*, the sequence is chillingly effective, sealing the bleak trajectory on which Fabian is set from the opening images of the film. The bleak ending is somewhat softened in the British release print which ends with Mary walking across the bridge with her long-time admirer Adam (Hugh Marlowe), to a new romantic future without Harry.

Du rififi chez les hommes

Night and the City was Dassin's final American film for some time. It marks his fugitive status and his vulnerability to the HUAC investigations. Indeed, according to many accounts, producer Darryl Zanuck deliberately sent Dassin to London for the film fearing his imminent summons to appear before the committee. His American career ground to a halt and like many American film makers of the era, he tried to reconstruct his career in Europe after his inclusion on the Hollywood blacklist. There were a number of projects in France including a Fernandel vehicle which "was envisioned as a send-up of American film noir and mobilized all the clichés of the genre."[15] However, it was not until *Rififi* (as it is usually known in Britain and the USA) that Dassin's film career resumed.

Rififi relates to the American noir cycle; its Hollywood predecessors as "heist films" include *Criss-Cross* (1946) and *The Asphalt Jungle* (1951) but is also part of "the French school of noir,"[16] the cycle of *policier* and crime films of the 1950s which includes *Touchez pas au grisbi* (1954), *Razzia sur la chnouf* (1955), *Bob le flambeur* (1955), and the Lemmy Caution films starring American actor Eddie Constantine. Like *Night and the City*, the film is an adaptation of an indigenous crime novel, a *serie noire* written by Auguste Le Breton, and, like *Night and the City*, the city—Paris in this case—is a constant backdrop . The film is best-known for a cinematic *tour de force*, the lengthy robbery sequence shot without dialogue or music. Other aspects of the film, however, may be more relevant to its relationship to the film noir than the "crime procedural" dimension, suspenseful and accomplished though that is.

Central to *Rififi* is the melancholic figure of Tony (Jean Servais), a seasoned criminal recently released from prison, who masterminds the audacious burglary at the jewelery store. Servais' doleful features embody the noirish gloomy trajectory of the character which begins early in the film when Tony emerges as a loser after an all-night poker session and continues with a vengeful meeting with his ex-lover who has taken up with a rival gangster. The robbery itself, both the planning and the execution, are a kind of interlude when things go well and

Tony displays his consummate though criminal professionalism. The fatalistic odyssey, however, resumes after the robbery when things unravel. Tony rescues his kidnapped godson but is shot by his rival and dies after returning the child to his mother. Tony, in many respects, is a noir hero, and like Harry Fabian in *Night and the City*, is caught up in the relentless and fatalistic world of crime, betrayal, violence, and the inevitable climax of death. Though much of the film is set indoors—the L'Age d'Or nightclub, various apartments, cafés, the jewelry store—the location shooting in Paris is both extensive and distinctive; like Dassin's London in *Night and the City*, it is in some respects rendered as a noir city, "a mist-shrouded and hostile big city"[17] appropriate for the dark thematics of a film in which all of the protagonists end up dead.

Dassin noir?

Dassin's contribution to the film noir is, in some senses, on the margins of the cycle. Also, given that two of his five noirs were made outside America, the contribution has to be seen in the context of a broad inclusive definition of the cycle, elastic enough to accommodate a range of films which overlap in some respects despite spanning different national cinemas. The five titles are mentioned in Raymond Durgnat's wide-ranging noir survey but all have a peripheral relationship to James Damico's narrower definition based on headline noir titles such as *Double Indemnity* and *The Killers*.[18]

Brute Force, a prison film, is closer to the gangster genre though its truncated noir flashbacks provide a link with the cycle; *The Naked City* is a striking example of the documentary-style *policier* with limited noir dimensions; *Thieves' Highway*, though based on a work of proletarian literature, incorporates aspects of noir especially in its treatment of Rica, a sympathetic femme fatale, saved from the usual fate of such a figure and united happily with the hero of the film in a decisively non-noir ending; *Night and the City* has strong affiliations to noir especially in its leading characters yet also can be incorporated into the British postwar "spiv cycle"; *Rififi* is a "heist" film with a strong resemblance to *The Asphalt Jungle* both in terms of the robbery subject matter but also with its doomed hero. Like *Night and the City*, however, the film also reflects its domestic origins as a key contribution to the 1950s French crime film. Across the five films Dassin emerges as a strong and distinctive director working within the conventions of the crime film but with a strong socially committed impulse which surfaces intermittently. There is also another dimension to Dassin's work identified by Colin McArthur as a tendency towards "dream, hysteria and ritual," towards spectacle and excess.[19] McArthur suggests that these were disciplined and controlled by the generic framework of the film noir, producing the tense, exciting, uneven, contradictory, experiences provided by "Dassin noir."

Notes

1. Francois Truffaut, *The Films in My Life*, 1978, p. 209.

2. James Naremore, *More Than Night*, 1998, p. 125.

3. Ibid.

4. Brian Neve, *Film and Politics in America*, 1992, p. 119.

5. Raymond Borde and Etienne Chaumeton, *A Panorama of American Film Noir 1941-1953*, Trans, Paul Hammond, 2002, p. 10.

6. Edward Dimendberg, *Film Noir and the Spaces of Modernity*, 2004, p. 59.

7. Thom Andersen, "Afterword," in Frank Krutnik *et al* (eds), *Un-American Hollywood*, 2007, p. 267.

8. Thomas Schatz, *Boom and Bust*, 1997, p. 392.

9. Foster Hirsch, *The Dark Side of the Screen*, 1981, p. 128.

10. Glenn Erickson, "Expressionist Doom in *Night and the City*," in Alain Silver and James Ursini (eds), *Film Noir Reader*, 1996, p. 203.

11. Peter Wollen, *Paris Hollywood: Writings on Film*, 2002, p. 194.

12. Erickson, "Expressionist Doom", p. 206.

13. Brian McFarlane, *An Autobiography of British Cinema*, 1997, p. 612)

14. Charlotte Brunsdon, "Space in the British Crime Film," in Steve Chibnall and Robert Murphy (eds), *British Crime Cinema*, 1999, p. 155.

15. Rebecca Prime, "'The Old Bogey': The Hollywood Blacklist in Europe," *Film History*, Vol. 20, No. 4, 2008, p. 479.

16. Borde and Chaumeton, *A Panorama*, p. 130.

17. Ibid., p. 136.

18. Raymond Durgnat, "Paint it Black," and James Damico, "*Film Noir*: a Modest Proposal." Both in Alain Silver and James Ursini eds, *Film Noir Reader*, 1996.

19. Colin McArthur, *Underworld USA*, 1972, p. 95.

Biography

Jules Dassin was born in Middletown, Connecticut, in 1911 to parents of Russian origin. The family moved to New York and the young Jules was raised in Harlem and went to High School in the Bronx. He studied drama in Europe during the 1930s and, on his return to America, became actively involved in various New York theatre groups and also wrote for the radio. He moved to Hollywood in the early 1940s and, after a brief stint at RKO, made a number of routine films at MGM. He then moved to Universal teaming up with producer Mark Hellinger and with *Brute Force* and *The Naked City* began the cycle of noir films which remain central to his reputation as a director. He moved to Twentieth Century-Fox and made two noirs (*Thieves' Highway*, *Night and the City*) for another strong though supportive producer, Darryl Zanuck. It was during this time that Dassin, who had been in the Communist Party during the 1930s, was named at a hearing of the House Un-American Activities Committee and subsequently blacklisted. He went into exile but re-established his career in France with *Du rififi chez les hommes*, a critical and commercial success and a strong influence on subsequent American "heist" pictures. His career thereafter includes a number of films with his second wife, Greek actress Melina Mercouri, including the highly successful *Never on Sunday* (1960), *Topkapi* (1964), another "heist" picture, and *Up Tight!* (1968), an improbable remake of John Ford's *The Informer*, but set in 1960s African-American urban America. Dassin's last film *Circle of Two* was made in 1981 and he died in Athens in 2008.

Noir Films

Brute Force (1947)
The Naked City (1948)
Thieves' Highway (1949)
Night and the City (1950)
Du rififi chez les hommes (France, 1955)

Dark Waters: Merle Oberon listens to Andre de Toth.

Andre de Toth

R. Barton Palmer

Andre de Toth became involved in the noir project that was to become *Dark Waters* through his association with Alexander Korda, who was romancing star Merle Oberon and wanted de Toth to save her from what he considered a disastrous script that might ruin her career, as well as a relationship with cinematographer Lucien Ballard. In a development where art seemed to imitate reality, Oberon was to play a young woman whom impostor relatives try to lure into an "accidental" death after establishing she is insane in order to obtain the considerable property she has inherited after her parents' deaths. Screenwriter Joan Harrison's doctoring of the original script delivered a tight, suspenseful plot to producer and director. De Toth was to deliver the film's Gothic atmosphere: a feeling of imminent threat, of destructive forces lurking beneath a seemingly benign surface, with all of these corresponding interestingly to obvious aspects of the protagonist's psychologically damaged and increasingly bewildered character. In this he was very successful, providing the talented Oberon with an ideal platform for her portrayal of a woman whose urge to live (and love) proves stronger than the "dark waters" of the past and present that urge her toward destruction. Plans to shoot on location were quickly abandoned when de Toth decided that an actual Louisiana setting (he visited several) might prove an aesthetic mistake. As he maintained later in an interview, his aim was to "fuse" the characters and location into "one integral unit," considering it a mistake to let locations "override the story." *Dark Waters* is set in a backwoods Louisiana of the mind in which a stately manor house, reminder of a bygone gentility that has mysteriously vanished, dominates an otherwise primitive culture of poor if hospitable Cajuns and the trackless bayous that threaten strangers with unseen dangers.

Traveling from her plantation home in Batavia ahead of the Japanese advance with her wealthy parents, Leslie Calvin (Oberon) finds herself shipwrecked off the Louisiana coast, one of only four survivors of a German submarine attack. Taken to a hospital to recover, she is haunted by memories of the attack and guilt at having survived when her parents did not. With the advice of a psychiatrist, Leslie makes contact by letter with her only other relative, an aunt, Emily Lamont, she has never met who lives in New York City. After some delay, she receives an answer from Lamont, who informs her niece that she and her uncle Norbert have moved to a family estate in nearby Belleville; they invite Leslie to convalesce with them once she's able to travel, which she does directly, sending a telegram to advise her aunt and uncle of her arrival. Nothing, however, seems quite right when she is dropped off from the train at the sleepy town's station. Neither Norbert nor Emily is there to meet her, and the pair seems unknown in town, and Leslie is bewildered about what to do next and seemingly at the point of relapse. Fortunately, the town physician, George Grover (Franchot Tone), answers the call for help and drives her to the estate, which is some distance from town and where she is greeted first by another man who identifies himself as Mr. Sydney (Thomas Mitchell). Explaining that no telegram in fact arrived, Sydney, despite his effusive affability, however, seems immediately suspect, especially because of his unexplained presence on the estate. That something is amiss is quickly confirmed when Sydney takes Leslie's telegraph from his pocket and throws it into the trash. Leslie is introduced in short order to both Norbert (John Qualen) and Emily (Fay Bainter), and she soon meets up as well with Cleeve (Elisha Cook, Jr.), who seems to be something of a hired hand though he is not from the local area. Grover warns Sydney, who seems in charge (Norbert has little to say to any of the guests), that Leslie's mental health is precarious.

No one, Grover warns, should bring up the subject of the shipwreck or the sequence of frightening events that made her family flee their home in Indonesia. But when the family sit down to dinner soon after Grover's departure, Sydney does just that, reducing Leslie to tears and forcing her to take to her room. The next day Sydney and the Lamonts take Leslie to the local movie theater, where the program's newsreel details a submarine attack on a merchant ship; once again, Leslie is reduced to tears and, fearing that she might have a relapse, the group take her home to bed. The next day, as she walks around in the garden, Leslie is approached by Pearson Jackson (Rex Ingram), the native-born caretaker of the estate who was

Below, *Dark Waters:* Lamont (John Qualen) looms ominously in the foreground while his wife Emily (Fay Bainter) and her niece Leslie (Merle Oberon) talk. Opposite, there is some "stylistic exuberance" in the posed shot of Merle Oberon, hand on an off-kilter banister with wedges of light behind.

dismissed. Jackson tells her that something is not right with the new arrivals. Grover has taken a romantic interest in her, and Leslie reciprocates his affection, but rejects any further commitment, fearing that her unstable mental condition would make a permanent relationship impossible. Talking to Emily soon after, Leslie realizes to her horror that the woman is an impostor who knows nothing about her ostensible sister; that same day Leslie discovers Jackson's dead body and attempts to flee the estate, but is prevented by her "aunt."

The Lamonts, it turns out, are indeed impostors whose real names are May and Pinky, and they were hired by Sydney and Cleeve, who have conspired to murder the real Lamonts. Since Leslie arrived, revealing the existence of a relative who might have a claim against a considerable estate, Sydney has plotted to drive her insane, hoping that she would either kill herself or make it possible for her to be eliminated by an "accident." Grover tries to rescue Leslie, but is himself taken captive by the crafty Sydney. Grover turns the tables, however, when Sydney and Cleeve try to take the pair into the swamp. Tipping over the boat, he helps Leslie hide in the water lilies as Sydney's motorboat passes dangerously overhead. She bursts energetically to the surface after that frightening immersion, and Cleeve soon sinks into a pool of quicksand. Lost in a wilderness and now lacking his more knowledgeable partner, Sydney surrenders, and the film ends with Grover joined to a Leslie who, having survived yet another hazardous trial with dark waters, seems cured of her fear and guilt.

Dark Waters is neither a stylistically exuberant nor thematically rich production The film is quite competently made, certainly a notch or two above the average studio release. De Toth's carefully restrained use of mise-en-scène lends the rather simple script just the right touch of decadent Southern-ness, authenticated by an occasional dose of realism, most notably when Grover and Leslie pay a visit to a family of nearby Cajuns and have dinner with their huge brood of frolicsome children. A more complex investment in psychologism might have been achieved through a deeper exploration of the connection between Leslie's recurring waterish nightmares, but de Toth does make the connection, establishing the final escape as therapeutic in the way that such adventures are in similar films by Alfred Hitchcock or Fritz Lang. *Dark Waters*, to be sure, also avoids engaging with the moral issues raised by the plot designed and carried out by Sydney and Cleeve, a backstory to which only scant reference is made, but this seems more a fault of the script with its generally two-dimensional handling of character and less a failing on the part of the director. That de Toth was fascinated by the various questions posed by psychopathology is clear from the subtlety with which he handles a similar character arc: the decline into unfeeling cruelty of the German protagonist in the noirish *None Shall Escape*, who is at first a somewhat sympathetic character made to feel a stranger in his own land, to which he returns hoping to make a new life after the debacle of the Great War.

Pitfall, above: injured insurance investigator John Forbes (Dick Powell) is comforted by his family (Jane Wyatt and Jimmy Hunt) in a drab bedroom. Opposite, there is more "expressionistic richness" when Powell poses with Lizabeth Scott in front of a menacing Raymond Burr.

Pitfall, like *Dark Waters*, lacks the expressionistic richness that lends a distinctive look to so many noir melodramas of the 1940s. Based on a grimly realistic novel by Hollywood old hand Jay Dratler (whose other credits include such classic noir films as *Laura* and *Call Northside 777*), *Pitfall* deals with the ennui that a respectable citizen and father of a certain age might feel at the constraints that a steady, responsible job and unwavering marital monogamy have imposed upon him. It is perfectly understandable that a bored and self-despising insurance agent like John Forbes (Dick Powell) would find himself liable to the temptation of a revitalizing adventure that, inevitably, brings upon him a kind of moral ruin even if the film's conclusion holds out some possibility of a limited kind of moral self-reclamation. The middle-class family man, unable to resist the charms of an available, helpless woman who lacks the bourgeois stability he enjoys, descends into a noir underworld that is both geographical and moral, the liminal space of petty criminals who steal to impress a woman, seedy private detectives with dangerous erotic obsessions, and nightclub singers who are the unwitting recipients of stolen property.

With exteriors filmed at a number of Los Angeles locations, *Pitfall* suggests the proximity of morally divergent neighborhoods as a sprawling city, traversable only by the automobile, indifferently includes all types, making it possible for that thin line separating the law-abiding from the lawless to be easily breached. The worst kind of criminality comes in the end to threaten the assumed safety of a bourgeois home, tucked neatly away from the dangerous downtown in a suburb of well-maintained, single family dwellings.

The "pitfall" in the film's title perhaps means principally the beautiful blonde, Mona Stevens (Lizabeth Scott), who, if by no means a femme fatale in the classic noir sense, is the lure that draws Forbes away from the straight and narrow. Yet de Toth's handling of the film's complex dramatic interactions, including his firm refusal to deal in limiting stereotypes, suggests that "pitfall" should also be understood in a larger sense, as referring to that dangerously appealing other side of respectability, with its ultimately false promises of escape from stultifying routine, from the conformity to those unvarying patterns that settled life demands. De Toth's version of the dark underside of the everyday goes beyond the formulas of self-destructive aggrandizement and character weakness regularly found in other noir films where crossing the line into the attractively illicit structures of the narrative separates protagonists from success or redemption; de Toth's characters are truly three-dimensional, unglamorized people trapped into an entangling morass of their own creation.

Like *Double Indemnity*'s Walter Neff, John Forbes works for an insurance company, a legitimate enterprise that, of necessity, must deal continually and profitably with criminality, offering continuing opportunity for malfeasance of one kind or another. On a day when a domestic scene at the family home, with his worried wife Sue (Jane Wyatt) in attendance, has demonstrated his aggressive dissatisfaction with all that he has (and all that seems too much), Forbes learns from a private detective the firm uses as an investigator, J.B. MacDonald (Raymond Burr), that Mona Stevens, the girlfriend of now-jailed embezzler Bill Smiley (Byron Barr), now has some of the property bought with the funds Smiley converted to his own use. Mona, MacDonald tells Forbes, is very attractive, and he has hopes of a romantic attachment. Forbes calls on Mona, and she is not at all the moll he has been expecting, but a respectable young woman caught up unwittingly in Smiley's plans to impress her with expensive presents, including a speedboat. These Forbes cannot help returning to the insurance company. But like MacDonald, Forbes finds Mona attractive, and a second encounter leads to their beginning an affair.

Figuring out what has happened, MacDonald is furiously jealous and waylays Forbes in his own driveway, beating him severely. Forbes had left his attaché case in Mona's apartment, and when she drives to his home to return it discovers that he has a wife and young son. Heartbroken, Mona ends the affair, and Forbes, having experienced the dangerous thrills of a different way of life, seems contented with Sue and his son. But the precarious balance of desire and intention that makes normal life possible has been disturbed. Forbes has revealed to MacDonald that Mona is "available," and the detective begins stalking her. Helpless under this assault on her privacy Mona rings up her erstwhile lover to ask for help. Forbes obliges by giving MacDonald a thorough beating.

But the detective has another trick up his sleeve. Smiley is now to be released from jail since the bulk of the funds he has taken have been retrieved by Forbes, and MacDonald tells him of Mona's relationship with Forbes, even furnishing him with a pistol to exact vengeance on her seducer. In the film's most suspenseful sequence, Smiley makes his way to Forbes's home, where the threatened homeowner shoots the "prowler" and claims self-defense. Informed of what MacDonald has done, Mona shoots the detective. The police call Forbes in for questioning about the possible connections between the two shootings, and he tells them the truth, eliciting a severe condemnation from the district attorney for his role in the death of Smiley even though he was within his rights to defend himself. At film's end, Forbes has returned to his wife, who cannot decide yet whether they can begin again, while Mona waits in custody to see if MacDonald will die of his wounds.

Pitfall is certainly a cautionary tale, a frightening warning against any weakening of moral self-regulation, of any thoughtless surrender to passing interests or dissatisfactions. Yet the film avoids simplifying moralization. None of the principal characters—Forbes, MacDonald, Mona, and Smiley—is evil as such, even though each is responsible for serious breaches of the law and conventional morality. MacDonald is as much the prisoner of desire as the other two men—all of them want Mona. Yet she is no siren, flirtatious and scheming, but rather a young woman lacking the stability of marriage who finds herself connected to men who lead her to act against her self-interest. She is no victimizer but a victim of forces she has not put into motion and cannot control. The illusion of free will, of a desire that can put limits on the damage it has caused, is dispelled after the break-up of the erstwhile lovers by MacDonald's continued pursuit of a woman whom, perhaps understandably, he wants even more now. He has seen her wanted by another man whose good looks and more secure place in the social order MacDonald obviously resents from the beginning, so the love triangle is motored by considerable energy.

This dramatic complexity is well served by the film's carefully unostentatious deployment of real Los Angeles locations and Marty Wild's restrained cinematography. Pitfall was a film that challenged the Production Code's strictures with its ambiguous ending; both Mona and Forbes, it was argued, avoid proper punishment for their transgressions and there is no satisfying compensating moral value in the restoration, if that is what it is, of the family or the social order. De Toth said that in making Pitfall, he "wanted to pose a question so many people don't dare face or talk about," and the finished film shows that the director provides no easy answers to the connections, if any, between fall and redemption or between injury and forgiveness.

If the secret to the dramatic success of Dark Waters is, as mentioned earlier, de Toth's fusing of character and mise-en-scène "into one integral unit," that mark of directorial intelligence is also on display on Pitfall, in which careful casting, well-coached acting, and proper attention to the rhetoric of imagery produces one of the noir's most effective, character-driven dramas. As de Toth put it, somewhat poetically, referring to his interest in the characters, "their image is imbedded in their milieu," a comment that can be applied justly to all his films and, most especially perhaps, to his taut thriller Crime Wave. In its carefully calculated realism (once again resulting from the use of real locations) and collective narrative that eschews that most sacred of Hollywood conventions, the main character, Crime Wave recalls John Huston's masterful caper film, The Asphalt Jungle, released some four years earlier. As in The Asphalt Jungle, narrative focus is divided between the criminals and the police pursuing them, but de Toth adds a third element: an ex-con determined to go straight, Steve Lacey (Gene Nelson), who finds himself, along with wife Ellen (Phyllis Kirk), unwillingly in the dangerous middle. Crime Wave is arguably more melodramatic than Pitfall in the sense that the Laceys find themselves safe and free at film's end, a testimony to their essential innocence, achieved only through the running of great risks and Steve's forced resumption for a time of the criminal

Above, Doc Penny (Ted de Corsia, center) with his minions portrayed by Charles Bronson (left) and Timothy Carey (on the floor grinning) pitches a caper to Steve Lacey (Gene Nelson).

identity he had forsworn. Unlike John Forbes, Lacey exits morally unsullied from entangle-ments that promise several times to destroy him, even as the real criminals (who are not pre-sented sympathetically, in the way that Smiley and MacDonald are in *Pitfall*) are apprehended in the end by Detective Sergeant Sims (Sterling Hayden), whose apparent unconcern about Lacey's innocence is revealed in the end as part of a test: Sims had been hard on Lacey only because of his righteous interest in separating absolutely the good from the bad. This is once again a thematic movement not anticipated in *Pitfall*, whose hallmark is a persistent moral ambiguity.

Crime Wave opens with one of the most effectively staged action sequences in any film noir: the robbery of an L.A. filling station by escaped convicts, Doc Penny (Ted de Corsia), Ben Hastings (Charles Buchinsky, aka Charles Bronson), and Gat Morgan (Matt Young). In the struggle that follows the robbery, which is initially achieved with a minimum of violence, a policeman is killed, but not before shooting Gat. Left behind by his erstwhile comrades, Gat drives to the home of Steve Lacey, whom he knew in prison, and enters the apartment at gun-point and then dies. Gat had asked a crooked doctor, Otto Hessler (Jay Novello), to meet him at the Laceys, and when he arrives, Hessler takes the money Gat had intended to pay him and leaves the Laceys with the problem of what to do with Gat's body. Steve is rightly afraid to call the police, thinking that they will assume he was harboring Gat, but Ellen persuades him to call his parole officer and tell the man the truth. Or at least part of the truth, because Steve does convince his wife that they should not mention Hessler's visit, on the theory that it would make them seem too guilty.

Meanwhile Sims has figured out the identity of the robbers from the gas station atten-dant's description, and he assumes they will make their way to their former prison mate Lacey. Sims arrives in time to listen to Lacey's story, which he does not believe, deciding to arrest the

Crime Wave: stylized pose and lighting as the obsessive Det. Sims (Sterling Hayden) draws down on Lacey.

man and keep him in jail for three days. He only releases Lacey after asking him to help in capturing the two remaining escapees. Lacey refuses, but Sims releases him anyway, in the belief that he will lead them to Penny and Hastings. And the criminals do make their way to and into the Laceys' apartment, where they intend to stay despite Steve's admonition that the police are watching him. Sims, meanwhile, confronts Hessler, thinking that he might have been engaged to help Gat, and the doctor confesses, agreeing then to return to the Laceys to see if the convicts are there, establishes that they are, but, overheard by Hastings, returns to his office where the gangster kills him. Steven and Ellen are then forced to help Doc on his next caper—robbing a bank—and Steve finds himself driving the getaway car after a shootout in which Doc and Hastings are shot by police posing as bank personnel. Desperate to return home where a new member of the gang, the psychopathic Haslett (Timothy Carey), is holding Ellen hostage in order to insure Steve's cooperation, a fight between the two men is eventually broken up by the police, who take Haslett into custody. After reproving Steve for not calling the police when Gat had first appeared at his apartment, Sims decides to release him. If not as memorable as *Pitfall*, *Crime Wave* is a competently made thriller, its byzantine plot developments expressed clearly by its careful imaging and excellent ensemble acting.

Biography

Andre de Toth was born Sâsvári Farkasfalvi Tóthfalusi Tóth Endre Antal Mihály in the city of Mako, which was then part of the Austro-Hungarian empire in 1913. After obtaining a law degree in Budapest, he decided to focus on his considerable and varied artistic talents, taking up both playwriting (and working with the internationally acclaimed Ferenc Molnar) and also sculpture. Molnar introduced the young man to the leading lights of the Hungarian artistic scene, and this enabled him to work on several projects as a camera operator. But de Toth (as he soon styled himself) was not satisfied working only in Eastern Europe and soon traveled to the UK, the U.S., and other European countries, looking for work. He later claimed to have worked for the Korda brothers and to have done some uncredited script doctoring for William Dieterle's noteworthy biopic *The Life of Émile Zola* (1937). De Toth liked to amuse others with outrageous stories of these years of wandering during which he turned himself into a citizen of the international cinema, but it is hard to establish the truth of tales such as his claim that one morning, after participating in a student riot in Vienna, he awoke in the city morgue. In later years, he would claim to be a "Hungarian-born, one-eyed American cowboy from Texas," and this fanciful self-description nicely captures something of his larger-than-life personality.

Returning to Hungary after working on the Dieterle project, de Toth (now spelling his first name as Endre) made something of a sensation in the national industry, directing five films in one year; several of these enjoyed a U.S. release. When war broke out, he immediately left Central Europe and returned to the UK to work for the Kordas, receiving onscreen credit for the very successful *The Jungle Book* (1942). Moving to the United States, he was hired by Harry Cohn at Columbia Pictures to direct *Passsport to Suez*, the tenth entry in the "Lone Wolf" B picture series starring Warren William. Though blatantly propagandistic, the film is an effective actioner, and this prompted Cohn to let de Toth make a more personal film, *None Shall Escape* (1944), which uses the fiction of an Allied war crimes trial to trace the political career of an East Prussian ethnic German who, disgruntled that his homeland has been turned over to a revived Poland, joins the Nazi movement and, after German victory in 1939, returns as their military overlord to oppress and destroy the people he had grown up among. With its flashback narrative and frequent use of expressionist effects, including chiaroscuro lighting and entrapping framings, *None* is interestingly noirish, as are a number of his other productions: *The Other Love* (1947), which traces the self-destructive indulgence of a tubercular concert pianist; *Slattery's Hurricane*, in which a pilot working as a drug smuggler examines his moral failings in a complex flashback as he undertakes a desperate mission to salvage his reputation; *Monkey on My Back* (1957), a biopic that features the descent of Barney Ross, champion boxer and World War II hero, into a whirl of self-destructive heroin addiction. De Toth also directed three international thrillers that make use of occasional noir stylings: *Hidden Fear* (1957), essentially a hard-boiled detective story focusing on counterfeiting and set in Denmark; *The Two-Headed Spy* (1958), based on the true account of a British double agent's activities during World War II; and, most successful of the trio, *Man on a String* (1959), in which an all-star cast (including Ernest Borgnine, Alexander Scourby, and Colleen Dewhurst) dramatize the true story of a Russian double agent, with famed producer Louis de Rochemont and de Toth pushing for and receiving permission to do location and background shooting in both East Berlin and Moscow.

De Toth, however, made three films that are fully noir and for which he is justly celebrated. These include: *Dark Waters* (1944), a southern gothic about recovered memory; *Pitfall* (1948), a melodrama of mischance that drags down a solid citizen into an erotic tangle; and *Crime Wave* (1954), a taut thriller done in the noir realist style. De Toth also is reported to have engaged in an uncredited collaboration with John Brahm on *Guest in the House* (1944), which centers on the near-destruction of a happy family by a neurotic young woman. Like many studio directors of the postwar era, de Toth also turned his hand to making a number of Westerns, including some—most notably the noirish *Ramrod* (1947), *The Stranger Wore a Gun* (1953) and *Day of the Outlaw* (1959)—that are among the finest of the genre in a period when it arguably enjoyed its most substantial success.

Noir Films

Dark Waters (1944)

Pitfall (1948)

Crime Wave (1954)

Edward Dmytryk on the set of *Mirage* with Gregory Peck and Diane Baker.

Edward Dmytryk

Geoff Fordham

Any consideration of Edward Dmytryk is inevitably overshadowed by one incident that irrevocably shaped his career: his summons in 1947 to appear before the House Committee on Un-American Activities (HUAC), to answer questions about Communist influence in Hollywood. He refused to testify, a decision that was eventually to lead (in 1951) to a 12-month prison sentence. He became one of the "Hollywood Ten," a designation by which, as he said in his autobiography, he "...would be known from here to eternity." Yet either side of the HUAC episode, his career spanned more than seven decades, during which he served as messenger, editor, prolific director, writer and teacher. His filmography as director includes more than 50 movies, although no more than four or five can be considered "noir".

Despite the pivotal significance of the HUAC hearings in Dmytryk's career trajectory, he was a reluctant, ill-disciplined and above all temporary member of the Communist Party. In his autobiography, Dmytryk says he was approached in late 1944 or early 1945, he "...was ready to be had," and he remained in the party for little more than a year. His broadly left-wing sympathies had of course been apparent before this, but he did not succumb willingly to party discipline. Throughout his association with the CPUSA, whether as fellow-traveler or member, he resented their attempt to interfere with his artistic freedom. In particular, the party's attempts to restore overtly Communist themes at the post-production stage of *Cornered* (1945) led him to say "If this is the way things are going to go, I think I want out." Adrian Scott, his producer in *Cornered* and *Murder, My Sweet* (1944), a fellow member both of the CPUSA and the Hollywood Ten, apparently agreed.

B. F. Dick, in his 1989 book *Radical innocence – a critical study of the Hollywood Ten*, divides Dmytryk's career as director into four phases:

1939-42 – directing melodramas at Paramount and Columbia

1942-47 – the RKO years, during which his best-known noir films were made

1948-51 – the blacklist years

1951-75 – the recant years

By the time he made his first film noir Dmytryk had already cut his teeth on a series of low budget B movie melodramas, many of which displayed, embryonically, the combination of stylistic characteristics and working practices that would eventually define the noir approach, certainly as it was pursued at RKO. These early films often used the dark lighting and high contrast photography that were to characterize the noir style; and just as importantly, Dmytryk developed a reputation for meeting tight schedules and delivering within – and even below – budget, a particular attraction for one of the smaller studios like RKO, for whom he made his principal noir films.

There is rarely consensus on which movies in any director's filmography should be

Above, Dick Powell and Claire Trevor in *Murder, My Sweet*. Opposite, Powell with Walter Slezak in *Cornered*.

described as film noir. However, in the case of Dmytryk, most critics recognize four of his movies as unambiguously noir – *Murder, My Sweet* (1944), *Cornered* (1945), *Crossfire* (1947) and *The Sniper* (1952). However, a much later offering – *Mirage* (1964) – has sufficient noir ingredients to warrant consideration alongside the other four.

His first and probably best known film noir, *Murder, My Sweet,* was made in 1944 as an adaptation of Raymond Chandler's *Farewell My Lovely*. The movie was initially released with the same title as the book, but poor previews led the studio to conclude that the previous screen persona of its male lead, Dick Powell, had confused movie-goers into thinking it was a romantic comedy.

Dmytryk claimed much later that *Murder, My Sweet* had helped to establish the stylistic conventions of film noir: deep shadows, unsettling camera angles, and a narrative driven by flashback and voice-over – much of it drawn directly from Chandler's use of the first-person in the original novel. The opening sequence for example displays precisely the characteristics that are now seen as defining the noir visual style.

In the opening shot, from above, a bright light illuminates a table. Over the credits, the camera tilts down, the music builds, and as the dialogue begins, unseen voices accuse a man of murder. We see three figures in shadow, all in matching trilby hats, and, just in shot, a man – Marlowe – whose head is swathed in bandages. With the shadow of one of the be-hatted figures cast against a white wall, we hear Marlowe's voice-over account of what happened, leading into flashback, as the camera pans out of the window, taking us down mean streets in a city at night time, lit up by glaring neon.

Dmytryk's use of chiaroscuro no doubt reflects the influence of German Expressionism, not to mention, rather closer to home, Welles' *Citizen Kane,* made for RKO in 1941; but ever the pragmatist, his techniques and visual style were also appropriate for, if not driven by, the constrained budgets demanded by the studio's finances. A significant reason why RKO proceeded with Scott's recommendation to make *Murder, My Sweet* at all was the fact that the studio already owned the film rights, having purchased them for an earlier (and unmemorable) attempt to film Chandler's book, *The Falcon Takes Over* (1942), one of a series based on the adventures of the eponymous gentleman troubleshooter.

Another of his early noir films, *Crossfire* (1947), also demonstrated Dmytryk's economy as well as his artistic ability. Like *Murder, My Sweet,* the movie made substantial use of exaggerated shadows and harsh lighting, in its attempt to tackle racial discrimination, one of the first Hollywood movies to do so. Because of its controversial subject matter, the studio was reluctant to risk large sums on what was regarded as an experimental venture, and Dmytryk was asked to work within a $500,000 budget, a higher proportion of which than usual was invested in star names – Robert Young, Robert Mitchum and Robert Ryan (as the chillingly racist killer). Compensating for the stars' salaries necessitated a brief shooting schedule (22 days according to Dmytryk), and savings in below-the-line production costs. According to Dmytryk simple high-contrast lighting was quick and cheap to set up: "It was a lot faster to light the people and then throw a couple of big shadows on the wall."

Film noir of course is defined not just by design, cinematography and presentation: the noir "style" encompasses themes, issues, characterization. One common ingredient focuses on individual paranoia and psychological disturbance, reflecting among other things a growing awareness in the 1940s of psychoanalysis and the work of Freud. Much of Dmytryk's noir offering explores the behavior and motivation of psychopathic or mentally disturbed characters.

The most notable perhaps is Robert Ryan's Monty Montgomery in *Crossfire,* a chillingly psychotic anti-Semite, a performance for which Ryan won an Oscar nomination for Best Supporting Actor, (one of the film's five nominations, including Best Film and Best Director). Montgomery murders a Jewish man who has invited him, together with his comrades, back to his apartment for drinks, and then tries to pin the blame on another soldier. His simmering resentments – of which anti-Semitism is only one – come to a head with the sadistic on-screen murder of a potential witness.

Above, Robert Ryan as the menacing anti-Semite in *Crossfire*, Opposite, Adolphe Menjou (an actor of decidedly different political persuasions than Dmytrk) as the Inspector in *The Sniper*.

In different ways the central protagonists of *Cornered* and *The Sniper* also display obsessive or psychopathic behavior. In the former, Laurence Gerard (Dick Powell) plays a world weary war veteran seeking revenge on the French collaborator who fatally betrayed his fiancée to the Nazis. His pursuit is relentless, and the violence his search generates is starkly brutal. In *The Sniper* Eddie Miller (played by Arthur Franz) is a young mentally disturbed World War II veteran who stalks the streets of San Francisco, shooting young women in an early version of what was to become the serial killer formula. The police employ a psychologist both to explain his condition and help track him down.

While all three films explore the psychological conditions of these troubled characters, there is an important underlying theme which overshadows their individual motivations. In each, the post-war malaise is exposed as we see the weariness and disillusion of returning GIs, unsupported in their transition back into civilian life, and uncertain whether the world to which they have returned justifies the sacrifice they have made. To varying degrees in the three, Dmytryk balances the horror of their individual brutality with a liberal's sympathy for the circumstances which led to it: for example society's failure to deal effectively with the consequences of mental disturbance.

There is little doubt that his politics influenced his film-making as well as his career, before and after the HUAC incident. Apparently it was principally the anti-Semitism of

Crossfire that attracted HUAC's attention in the first place; and his disenchantment with the Communist Party arose in part because of their attempts to interfere with his work. But the political dimensions of his movies predated both his party membership and his work on noir films.

In 1943, for example, Dmytryk directed *Tender Comrade,* (written by a fellow member of the Hollywood Ten, Dalton Trumbo). Ginger Rogers plays a young defense plant worker whose husband is in the military during World War II, and shares a house with three other similarly placed women. They live along co-operative lines, designed to show how collaborative action helps the war effort. But during the McCarthy era such sentiments could appear dangerously radical. Rogers' mother testified to HUAC that her daughter had been asked to say "Share and share alike, that's democracy, "as evidence of Dmytryk's subversive quality. Reflecting Roosevelt's encouragement of Hollywood to support the war effort, the film may have condoned collectivism and egalitarianism, but the demands of the war – and perhaps the memories of the Depression – made these concepts acceptable in a way which, by the 1950s they had ceased to be.

Dmytryk had also been involved in more explicitly propagandist and anti-fascist wartime films (*Hitler's Children, Behind the Rising Sun* [1943,] *Back to Bataan* [1945,]) and his early noir films continued with these anti-fascist and anti-racist themes. And while *Murder, My Sweet* embarked on a different tack, its appeal for him was nevertheless at least in part, a reflection of his political views.

According to Jon Tuska (*Dark Cinema: American Film Noir in Cultural Perspective*, 1984) what most appealed to Dmytryk about filming a Chandler novel was that the "...story permitted the camera to venture among the lower levels of society where crime was far more commonplace, even a product of the milieu itself." Thus, it was possible to portray social evil as a consequence of an unjust society, rather than the result of individual failings. The film presents a deeply cynical view of a society which is corrupt and dysfunctional.

Dmytryk's last film that could be described as noir, *Mirage,* describes an individual's attempt to rediscover himself as he gradually recovers from amnesia. Gregory Peck's scientist, David Stilwell, learns, in the process of regaining his memory, that a discovery he had made and which he thought was to be used to help promote world peace has in fact been sold to the head of a large corporation at the heart of the military-defense establishment. Within a complex noirish narrative, Dmytryk presents a critique of corporate America as corrupt and self-serving. As Dmytryk says in his autobiography, the movie describes "...a conflict between those working for the greater good of society and extremely cynical and selfish private interests." The film script was based on a novel by Howard Stone, writing with an alias as he like Dmytryk was a former member of the CPUSA who had been blacklisted.

Although the camera work in *Murder, My Sweet* may have incorporated some *homage* to Welles and *Citizen Kane, Mirage* makes a subtle reference to *The Third Man* (1949). Charles Calvin (Walter Abel), the head of the not-for-profit and Stilwell's mentor, looks down at the street from a window in his office high up in a New York skyscraper (and from which he is about to fall to his death). In justification of his sell-out, he says to Peck's scientist: "Do they look like human beings or ants?" The shot of tiny specks moving in the street below reminds us of the fair ground scene in *The Third Man* when Welles' Harry Lime says: "Would you feel any pity if one of those dots stopped moving forever?" Lime is a black marketeer selling scarce medicines for personal profit; the reference emphasizes that for

Above, *Murder, My Sweet.* Below, Gregory Peck in *Mirage.*

Dmytryk, Calvin, for all his corporate respectability, embraces the amorality of the black marketeer.

Dmytryk's politics may suffuse his films but the demands of the studio system and the Production Code meant they often had to be diluted. A variety of critics have complained that Chandler's forensic treatment of police corruption – and not just in *Farewell My Lovely* – are lost in Hollywood treatments like *Murder, My Sweet* or Hawks' *The Big Sleep* (1946). In Chandler's novel, Florian's, the bar where Moose Malloy fell for Claire Trevor's Velma (an archetypal film noir femme fatale,) is a run-down, Black bar. But in 1944, race remains largely untouchable in Hollywood and Florian's clientele become white. *Crossfire* also had to undergo a similar dilution: in the novel on which the film was based, the Robert Ryan character is homophobic rather than anti-Semitic, his victim gay not Jewish. However, a critique of anti-Semitism was deemed to be safer than a critique of homophobia.

His politics may have surfaced in the themes he tackled: anti-fascism, anti-racism, opposition to corporate greed and corruption. But finally, they did not fundamentally affect the style and tone of his movies, noir or otherwise. As B. F. Dick concludes, "Dmytryk would have been a director of melodrama and film noir in any era, whether he had joined the John Birch Society or the Communist Party."

Biography

Edward Dmytryk was born in 1908 in Canada, to Ukrainian immigrants. When he was six his mother died and his father moved to San Francisco. His was an unhappy childhood, and after he ran away from home, juvenile authorities placed him with a family in Hollywood. At the age of 15, he started as messenger boy at Paramount, working in various departments at the studio until in 1930. The director Cyril Gardner hired him as editor, a role he occupied throughout the 1930s, his credits including the Marx Brothers' *Duck Soup*. He directed his first film, *The Hawk*, a low-budget Western, in 1935, but his career took off when Paramount gave him a contract in 1939 to direct a series of B movies. After a brief spell at Columbia, he moved to RKO in 1941, for whom he made a number of brutal propaganda films, including *Hitler's Children* and *Behind the Rising Sun* (both 1943). Over the next three years, his best-known films noir were made for RKO, until in 1947, he was summoned to appear before HUAC. His refusal to testify (as one of the "Hollywood Ten") led to a trial for contempt, and after a period of exile in England he was sentenced to a year in prison in 1951. Once he had served his time, he recanted, the only one of the Ten to do so, and gradually restored his career, making mostly non-noir films such as *The Caine Mutiny* (with Bogart),*The Young Lions* (with Brando) and *The Carpetbaggers*. He directed his last film in 1975, thereafter focusing on writing, and from 1981, teaching as a professor of film-making at the University of Southern California. He died in California in 1999.

Noir Films

Murder, My Sweet (1944)

Cornered (1945)

Crossfire (1947)

The Sniper (1952)

Mirage (1964)

Dmytryk directs Young with Mitchum off-camera in *Crossfire*.

Maureen O'Sullivan and John Farrow (far right) on the set of *The Big Clock*.

John Farrow

Alain Silver and James Ursini

Like many filmmakers who worked through the noir cycle, John Farrow's motion pictures melded seamlessly into the fabric of the classic period. In fact, his films were such an anonymous part of the total output of Hollywood in the 1940s and 50s that most film encyclopedias do not even list him. In some circles, Farrow is better-known as a Roman Catholic apologist, who wrote books on Thomas More and Father Damien's efforts with the lepers of Molokai.

Farrow directed nearly fifty features but only five standard noir films—six with the inclusion of the hard-boiled, supernatural melodrama *Alias Nick Beal*. This was a couple more than Joseph Losey or Max Ophuls, around the same number as Nicholas Ray and Otto Preminger, and considerably less than Fritz Lang or Anthony Mann. Like most of these men, Farrow's noir films were made within the studio system, first at Paramount and then at RKO. Farrow's cinematographers, John F. Seitz at Paramount, Nick Musuraca and Harry Wild at RKO, worked on other, better-known noir films, such as *Double Indemnity*, *Out of the Past*, and *Murder, My Sweet* respectively, and with better-known directors from Billy Wilder to Joseph von Sternberg. Most of Farrow's other collaborators, from screenwriters and composers to stars, worked on as many or more noir films, particularly actor Robert Mitchum.

I. The Paramount Films

As a contract director who theoretically worked on assignment, Farrow typifies how fully engaged in the noir cycle America's film industry, as represented by the major studios, was. Farrow's other pictures range from Westerns and war films to screwball comedies and costume dramas. His pre-noir work included the series detective feature *The Saint Strikes Back* (1939) and the downbeat war adventure *China* (1943) starring Alan Ladd. Ladd also starred in Farrow's first film noir, *Calcutta* (1947), playing a Paramount equivalent of Bogart's Sam Spade in a plot heavily derived from *The Maltese Falcon*: a cynical protagonist, the death of a partner, a duplicitous woman, smuggled jewels. After he beats a confession out of his dead partner's widow, Ladd's character, Neale Gordon, turns her in with the sardonic admonishment: "You counted on your beauty with guys. Even ones you were going to kill." As our late colleague Bill MacVicar put it, Gordon "drifts from hotel to casino to airfield encountering a rogues' gallery of grotesques [including] Edith King, as a stogie-puffing prototype of Baby Jane Hudson."

From the first Farrow stylistically favored occasional foreground clutter and wide-angle close-ups as visual counterpoint. He was second to none of his contemporaries, not even Ophuls, in his passion for the long take and often staged entire sequences without a cut. Farrow's films in the 1950s ranged from the bizarrely plotted Western, *Ride, Vaquero*; the World War II drama starring John Wayne as a German freighter captain, *The Sea Chase*; and a final semi-noir melodrama of sexual paranoia and betrayal, *The Unholy Wife*. Farrow also used

71.

Alan Ladd strikes an
action pose in *Calcutta*.

the actors he was assigned to manipulate audience expectation. As he would later with Faith Domergue, Farrow uses the wide-eyed, ingenue-like appearance of Gail Russell in *Calcutta* to undercut audience anticipation of her true nature: a conniving femme fatale. The smooth and charming Ray Milland would soon provide the same counter-effect in *Alias Nick Beale* (1949).

After *Calcutta*, Farrow's fully noir pictures of the classic period at Paramount, *The Big Clock* and *Night Has a Thousand Eyes* (both 1948) were produced back-to-back. Although the producers were different, Farrow worked with essentially the same scenarist, cinematographer, costumer, sound recordists, art department, and composer on both pictures. While *Night Has a Thousand Eyes* does have some location exteriors, both movies were mostly shot on sound stages. Both feature flashbacks from the point of view of a troubled protagonist.

The Big Clock uses a miniature, process photography, and optical effects to open with a low angle panning shot across a night skyline then to move into a building. A matte optical takes the camera past the letters that identify "Janoth Publications" and inside to a dark corridor, where a figure comes out of an elevator. As he does, he begins a tortured narration, wondering how he has ended up here, hunted, hiding in the darkness, how everything was different only "thirty-six hours ago," a phrase he repeats like a litany. An unbroken shot, typical of Farrow, follows him into the mechanism of a giant clock, around an interior catwalk then

moves out of the clock to its exterior display of the date and time. A dissolve begins a flashback to a day-lit lobby, thirty-six hours before. The narration and long take are combined to enhance suspense. The viewer knows that the figure (who names himself when he says, "Think fast, George!") is portrayed by Ray Milland, the star of the film and thus the character with whom to identify. But the other items of noir style, the dark cityscape, the camera moves, the low-key sets, all these confuse and disorient the viewer. Point of view is established and expressed both in narrative terms as the character prepares to tell his story and in figurative terms as the audience co-experiences his tension and uncertainty.

As the character's flashback tale begins, Farrow uses another long take as George enters the *Crimeways* magazine bureau. Turning from a blackboard that reads "Crimeways Clue Chart" to the full-lit reception area and moving back with George into his private office, the camera

The titled "Big Clock" inside and out with Ray Milland, above, as the trapped George Stroud.

dollies and pans as he passes and speaks to co-workers, tightening slightly with each movement until it frames him in medium close-up when he calls his home. The cut, which breaks the high-key elasticity of the image, is to his wife. Georgette Stroud (Maureen O'Sullivan) mirrors George, in name and in framing. She does not believe that Janoth (Charles Laughton) will permit him to leave for an extended vacation. On this first note of discord, there is a dissolve to a staff meeting that George must attend. Rather than a typical establishing shot,

Laughton (at center) as Janoth: "It's a mechanical thing. It can go wrong!"

Farrow opens the scene with a tight close shot of Steve Hagen (George Macready), Janoth's executive assistant. Hagen's severe mien and harsh voice are an immediate contrast to the pleasant banter at the *Crimeways* office. The camera pulls back all the way to the other end of the table, reducing Hagen to a distant figure, as the clock sounds signaling the hour and all stand in anticipation. From this Farrow cuts to a high angle, as Janoth enters via a private elevator at the back of the conference room. In just two shots, the tone has shifted again. Acting and staging create an edgier atmosphere and a different stylistic undercurrent with the framing and angles. The camera follows Janoth all around the table as he makes a speech and asserts his control. In the foyer a door opens and Stroud comes in. He disrupts the careful order of Janoth's world by coming late, and Farrow underscores that by timing the end of the long take to Stroud's entrance.

While it may predate the use of the term, Janoth himself is a classic "control freak"; and the clocks are the obvious symbols of that. His obsessive scheduling of his time down to the minute, his fastidious grooming, his inflected speech with syllables modulated like the swinging of a pendulum–these are all exaggerated traits, suggestive of a parody, even of a cartoon. There is an element of parody also in the way that representational reality is subtly questioned. Many aspects of the Janoth Building, the "big clock" itself being just one such item, are extremely stylized; streamline- moderne decor creates an atypical almost antiseptic atmosphere. Stroud's entire career has been spent under Janoth's control. He is trapped now, literally first inside Janoth's building and later within the confines of his clock; but figuratively Stroud is also trapped inside Janoth's head. This condition creates the twists most typical of noir. Stroud the narrator never realizes completely, as he tells his own story, either the real dimensions of his dilemma or how he himself has caused it. After being fired, Stroud goes to a bar and encounters an acquaintance named Rita Johnson, who he does not know is Janoth's mistress. Rita ends up dead, and Stroud realizes he might be the prime suspect. When Janoth rehires George to find himself, it is the ultimate existential irony.

Farrow's visual scheme complements the circular movement of the narrative. The figurative circle is closed the second time Stroud enters the clock in a repetition of the first scene. This time the camera follows Stroud out of the elevator in a tighter, medium close shot. Again he evades the guard, and without a cut another unbroken but different shot follows him inside the clock and up the short spiral staircase. The flashback never really ends as much as it merges back into the narrative and, since we have already heard what George is thinking, into itself through this overlapping action.

When George, having taken refuge in the big clock, inadvertently turns it off, Janoth and his associates in the building above notice that the office clocks have also stopped. "It's a mechanical thing!" Janoth exclaims after frenziedly shaking a desk clock; "It can go wrong." In Janoth's universe, where time, where all things are tied together in mechanized harmony, dissonance is anathema. Stroud now knows that Janoth killed Johnson and when he elbows the clock switch shortly after this discovery, it metaphorically underscores the turning point in the plot, the transfer of control from Janoth to Stroud. In the end, it is the loss of control that sends Janoth to his doom and spares George.

The concept of control is also a significant factor in *Night Has a Thousand Eyes*, which is based on a novel of the same name by Cornell Woolrich whose fiction inspired a dozen noir films. Like most of Woolrich's work the story revolves around images of darkness and time, images that threaten to swallow up the main characters fighting desperately for their lives against these two inexorable forces. In this case it is a young woman, Jean Courtland (Gail Russell), and a haunted seer named Triton (Edward G. Robinson), who predicts her doom and ultimately his own. The audience's identification with Triton is established early in the film and sustained through flashback. Unlike Stroud, Triton tells his story to other characters: the camera tracks around him, hunched over the table of the dimly lit, dingy bar, as he tells his

Below, Edward G. Robinson as Triton works in the audience in *Night has a Thousand Eyes.*

Above, Triton's hard-scrabble life hiding from his gift.

Opposite, the prophecy fulfilled in *Night Has a Thousand Eyes.*

story to the distraught Jean and her skeptical beau. Then it holds on a close-up of Triton as he confesses that "I had a crazy feeling I was making the things come true."

Convinced that he can no longer control his fate, Triton retreats into a world of run-down hotel rooms and isolation. The camera pans across Bunker Hill and Angel's Flight, iconic settings in many noir films, to one of the area's seedier apartments where Triton has taken up residence. The use of practical locations in *Night Has a Thousand Eyes* is limited to the sequences at Bunker Hill and the train yard. The effect is to add a graphic reality to Triton's self-imposed exile in a neighborhood that mirrors his voice-over: "I was living in a world, already dead." Triton only ends that exile to save Jean, the daughter of his former fiancée and partner. The vision he has of her fate is delivered to him in bits and pieces: a flower crushed under a shoe, a sudden gust of wind, the talons of a lion, a broken vase, a voice saying "there's no danger now." But the most disturbing part of his vision is the one he sees in the mirror. In a three-quarter medium shot of Triton in double image, the audience witnesses his face turn to shock as he feels his side, looking for blood on his shirt. The scene is not subjectified. The audience does not see what he "sees" in his mind but is left to infer it from his face and actions.

Eventually each of the images from Triton's vision becomes "real" in that they are visually reified for the audience. Finally Triton himself is shot trying to save Jean. As the camera pans around the baffled faces and down to the prone figure of Triton, the viewer realizes as do the characters that the parts of his vision were correct but not the whole, that it was not Jean's doom he saw but his own. As in *The Big Clock* literal and figurative time are again crucial elements but with a twist typical of Woolrich. The flashback structure freezes and distorts time but cannot reveal the real truth because the narrator does not yet know it.

Like Janoth's $600,000 timepiece in *The Big Clock*, the grandfather clock in the Courtland house also is a key symbol. As 11:00 p.m., the time Triton had predicted for Jean's "doom," draws closer, a series of close shots of the assembled characters are cut to the sound of the chimes. When nothing untoward occurs, the characters are relieved. The audience,

however, has been put in a superior position and is aware of the irony of the scene: it is not really 11:00 p.m. The time setting has been altered by an unidentified hand, which moved the clock forward. As in *The Big Clock*, the control of time is tied to survival. Unlike Stroud, Triton is a tormented figure unable to stop the "big clock" or reset the fabric of predetermined events, which override everything else.

The supernatural aspects of *Night Has a Thousand Eyes* pale in comparison to *Alias Nick Beal*, Farrow's penultimate assignment at Paramount. Adapting a screen story rather than a novel as *The Big Clock*, Jonathan Latimer's script is a pastiche of Faustian elements that Farrow overlays with a noir style. Nick Beal (Raymond Milland) is a third-person narrator who introduces the saga of Joseph Foster (Thomas Mitchell). Farrow opens with a signature long take: one assistant exits an elevator and brings a casebook into an office, hands it off to a second assistant who opens another pebbled-glass door to reveal District Attorney Foster in conference. As a hard-bitten D.A., Foster is more intent on prosecution than prestidigitation and has little of the lust for knowledge or acclaim that plague the Doctors Faustus of Marlowe, Goethe, and Mann. He flatly rejects a sleazy mouthpiece's offer to back him as a candidate for governor. Foster's offhanded remark that he'd "give his soul to nail" a particular criminal coincides

with Beal's appearance, or should one say manifestation. Farrow uses a long tracking shot down a wharf to reveal a silhouette in the fog then follows this figure back to a waterfront version of the Auerbach's Cellar, the wine bar in Goethe's *Faust*. While he never turns the middle-aged Foster back into a young man, Beal does serve up Gretchen/Marguerite in the form of a floozy named Donna Allen (Audrey Totter). Foster is irrevocably caught on the road to perdition, until Rev. Garfield (a less sinister turn by George Macready) drops a Bible (literally) on Foster's contract, Beal smugly remarks, "You've jockeyed me into some sort morality play haven't you? We've a pier instead of the nave of a cathedral, but props are the same: it's always been bell and candle or that worn-out book of yours." In the end no amount of fog can cover the seams.

Above, the Mephistofelian Mr. Beal and his middle-aged victim. Below, Audrey Totter as a troubled femme fatale in *Alias Nick Beal*.

II. The RKO Films

Farrow moved to RKO because Howard Hughes promised him bigger budgets and more control. Farrow quickly realized the trade-off was Hughes' interference particularly where the leading women were concerned. The visual depiction of both Faith Domergue in *Where Danger Lives* (1950) and Jane Russell in *His Kind of Woman* (1951) had to live up to Hughes' expectations: highly eroticized and glamorous.

Farrow reacted to these constraints in the first of his RKO noirs by creating a femme fatale unusual even for noir. Many of the cycle's "spider women" are heartless schemers empowered by a deadly eroticism, sometimes deadlier for themselves than for their male victims. Margo, the deadly woman of *Where Danger* Lives, is an out-of-control schizophrenic, who seems truly to believe in the fantasies she has concocted to ensnare her hapless lover, Dr. Jeff Cameron. In this she is unlike such classic femme fatales as the cold and cunning Phyllis Dietrichson of *Double Indemnity* but anticipates a later, more conflicted heroine such as Diane Tremayne of Otto Preminger's 1953 *Angel Face*. The viewer's first close-up glimpse of Margo is from Cameron's point of view as he bends over her supine body and questions her regarding her attempted suicide. Her naked shoulders peek out seductively from beneath the hospital sheets. Her black hair frames her softly focused face like a demonic halo. His attraction is immediate as he sees in her both sexual object and damsel in distress. By the time she asks rhetorically, "Why should I live?" Cameron has already supplied an answer.

Margo is driven by an hysterical intensity that propels all the persons around her, including the submissive protagonist, into violence. Cameron's confrontation with Margo's husband (who she originally tells him is her father) is particularly illustrative. The

Physical dominance cannot save Jeff Chambers from the disturbed Margo and her heartless husband in the twisted dynamics of *Where Danger Lives*.

scene is staged largely in three-shots which reify the triangular conflict of Margo, her husband Lannington, and Cameron. When the fatal fight between Cameron and Lannington finally breaks out, it is instigated by another of Margo's hysterical fits. Cameron responds violently to her claim that her husband has ripped an earring from her ear and is consequently beaten over the head by Lannington. When he regains consciousness he discovers the husband dead and himself a fugitive. The fight between Cameron and Margo's husband is only the beginning of Margo's control over Cameron. His association with Margo erodes his will as it sucks him into the back draft created by her frenetic energy. Only in a sleazy border-town hotel, where the concussion from his fight with her husband has left him drained and delirious, does he begin to sense the truth.

In terms of Farrow's work, Cameron resembles George Stroud much more than Triton. The other link with *The Big Clock* is Maureen O'Sullivan as Cameron's girlfriend, Julie. As Georgette Stroud in *The Big Clock*, O'Sullivan's jealousy was never focused. When she came upon George with Rita Johnson, she momentarily suspected an affair. In fact, if there is a triangle in *The Big Clock*, it involves the Strouds and Janoth, whose desire to control has a defi-

Once she has him by the lapels, the only time the needy and grasping Margo will take her hands off Jeff is to hold on to the steering wheel.

nite sexual component. Julie is a more passive character than Georgette Stroud.

Even though it violates his medical oath, his code of morality, and common sense, Margo's sexual magnetism and control drag Cameron into becoming half of a fugitive couple on the run to Mexico. He does this with a woman any trained doctor could plainly see is suffering from serious mental illness. The appeal this neurotic woman holds for him is two-fold: she is a dangerous and exciting object of desire, who stimulates him from the first shots of her bare shoulders and sultry expressions. More importantly, especially considering his profession, he sees her as a fulfillment of his messiah complex. Or as Lannington says when they first meet, "...a clinging vine brings out your protective side." Lannington's words are visually complemented by a two-shot a few minutes later in which Margo clutches him desperately and whispers in his ear, "How much I need you now." Margo needs saving and Cameron wants to be a savior no matter what he has to sacrifice.

As Margo alternates between loving partner and ruthless exploiter, Cameron grows weaker and weaker, bodily and mentally. His physical decline is an externalization of his psychic/spiritual wound. While his strength diminishes, hers grows. Like a dominatrix or an emotional vampire the femme fatale feeds off the weakness of her victim. Margo hectors him constantly to keep moving towards "freedom" and the Mexican border by saying, "If you love me, you'll make it," even though she realizes his paralysis and possible death is imminent. In a seedy motel on the border Cameron and Margo await a

"coyote," who will conduct them across the international line. A neon sign flashes into the dimly lit room. In a stunning sequence shot, an unbroken seven-minute take locks onto Margo at her most frenetic, pacing the room as Cameron writhes in pain in the foreground. Gradually she reveals the truth about herself, that she was under psychiatric care, that she actually murdered her husband. An anguished Cameron expresses his disgust for her behavior but is too weak to run away. When he collapses, Margo attempts to smother him with a pillow. To the end she is consistent in her emotional inconsistency. [For a more detailed discussion of Farrow's use of three sequence shots at the climax of *Where Danger Lives* see the entry in *Film Noir the Encyclopedia*.]

As a limping Cameron pursues her, Margo sees him from her hiding place, and Farrow's staging again underscores the twisted relationship between the two. The injured Cameron staggers along a line of porch posts, clinging to them as he pursues the source of his pain. An extreme low-angle frames Margo as she slips from the truck and holds her in a medium close shot as she pulls out a pistol. Even after she shoots him, the masochistic Cameron keeps coming. Margo flees but is brought down by a police bullet. In a final reversal, she clears Cameron of the murder of her husband. While clinging to the chain-link fence, she defiantly delivers her own epitaph: "Nobody pities me." The practical night exteriors in *Where Danger Lives*, such as the scene at the border, are a departure from the studio work of the Paramount films. As with Bunker Hill in *Night Has a Thousand Eyes*, the border town where Jeff and Margo take temporary refuge provides a graphic context for Cameron's fall: from manors to shacks, from doctor to transient on the lam.

Like many writer/producer/directors before him including Max Ophuls, Howard Hawks and Preston Sturges, Farrow soon discovered that Howard Hughes was the ultimate authority at his studio. After Farrow shot *His Kind of Woman* back-to-back with *Where Danger Lives* in late spring of 1950, Hughes brought in a long-line of writers to re-imagine the script and restructure the movie. The part of mobster Ferraro was recast with Raymond Burr, and director Richard Fleisher was brought in to reshoot scenes and fashion a "bigger" action ending. Except for that Farrow shot most of what became the final cut.

Because it is set almost entirely at night, on a literal level this film by diverse hands is among the most oppressively dark of film noir. Narratively it balances comedy that verges on

Whether on the dark streets or a shadowy interior, Mitchum's Milner plays it casual.

slapstick (as vacationing actor Mark Cardigan played by Vincent Price leads his unlikely band of rescuers against Ferraro's ship) with the graphic violence of Milner's prolonged beating and torture. The effect of such abrupt shifts in narrative tone and content is both grisly and chaotic. Mitchum, Burr, and even Price, reprising his effete role of *Laura,* were already familiar icons of film noir who are isolated and exaggerated almost to the point of parody here. Ultimately Ferraro and his minions become less and less real, not so much characters than the embodiment of the vague, impersonal peril that has threatened Milner throughout the film. Each cutaway to inept Cardigan reemphasizes the illogical chaos of Milner's situation and prolongs his ordeal in a manner suggestive of the hazards and incongruities of the noir universe.

In this sense, *His Kind Of Woman* deals almost self-consciously and exclusively in archetypes of the noir world. As portrayed by Mitchum, Milner is both archetype and stereotype: weary, sardonic, unexcited but critically unaware that the components of a fateful narrative, which will ensnare him and compel him into action, are already in motion. The mise-en-scène combines long takes with compositions in which wedges of light and bizarre shadows clutter the frame and distract the viewer. The plot is a pastiche of ambiguous characters and events such as the songstress Liz Brady (Jane Russell) "playing" the role of the heiress Lenore Brent and the insecure Mark Cardigan unable to escape his film star persona. Casting Vincent Price in the role of the would-be classical actor trapped in a career as a movie star overtly plays with the audience's genre expectations for comic effect. Using Jane Russell as Liz/Lenore subtly does the same thing. Many other characters are drawn with touches of parody. Some are visual: Krafft wears dark glasses while he plays chess with himself. Others are verbal, as when the dispassionate Thompson proclaims himself "ignorant and happy to be that way." In this mix,

When the locale shifts to
Mexico, shadows on ceiling
pieces and tangled land-
scapes help sustain suspense.

Milner is the only predictable element, the only emblem of stability, however uncertain.

Milner's introduction in the late night diner is fully stylized as he explains to an acquaintance behind the counter that he is out of money and has just spent thirty days on a county road gang for an implicit vagrancy. The counterman gives Milner a free meal but his stance with his back to the gambler betray his working stiff's inability to understand a gambler's lifestyle. The suggestion that Milner inhabits the noir underworld is reinforced in the next sequence. First, a long shot isolates Milner on a dark street, where he climbs a set of wooden steps to a cheap second-floor apartment. Inside Milner finds three men waiting. In the course of a long take, Milner shrugs off their accusations of reneging on a bet and finally, after telling them it would "be nice if you guys cleaned up this mess before you got out of here," snubs out a cigarette in the palm of one of the men. The sustained shot is broken as Milner falls out of frame under the fists of the other two.

Milner's self-destructive defiance is symptomatic of his existential ennui. After this first of many beatings that he will endure during the course of the film, Ferraro's man calls with his proposition and Milner offhandedly tells him, "I was just getting ready to take my tie off...wondering whether I should hang myself with it." For all his postures of fatigue and weariness, Milner is most at home in the noir underworld. Clearly the white-walled, expensively furnished home he visits to hear Ferraro's offer makes him uncomfortable, As he discusses the proposition in a sustained three shot, Milner paces back and forth, finally slumping against a Greek-styled column and remarking on the offer, "I'm not knocking it, man, I'm just trying to understand it."

Milner, who understands the complexities of odds, finds the offer of something for nothing a puzzle. He moves through Mexico almost like a somnambulist in search of a waking reality. In typically noir values, some degree of that reality are to be found, but only in money and in sexuality as represented by Lenore. At that, Milner's relationship with sex and money is somewhat eccentric. Although he is clearly drawn to Lenore, her claim to being wealthy is not enticing to him. It is her off-screen voice that draws him around the bar at the cantina where the choker close-ups of both of them, suddenly inserted as he watches her sing, suggest an immediate fascination with her. There is also an indication of an underlying sexual tension between them in their initial conversation after Milner buys her champagne; but their awkward movements when they find themselves together in the plane to the resort reinforce the sense of a mutual reluctance toward a precipitous intimacy. Nonetheless, Lenore is more real for Milner than any of the film's other characters. The only day scene, which occurs midway through the narrative, features Milner with her at the resort's private beach. Ultimately her presence provides a serio-comic counterpoint to the darker elements. "What do you press when you're broke?" she asks Milner: "When I'm broke, I press my pants." This kind of banter permits sequences of relative verisimilitude that contrast with Milner's other encounters. In terms of film noir conventions, because Lenore is his kind of woman, Milner's relationship with her, despite its sexual tension, is crucial to his survival. He survives; and the tension is finally dissipated in the film's last shot, the comic sexual metaphor of an iron burning Milner's pants while he and Lenore embrace.

III. Afterthoughts

After his disheartening sojourn with Hughes, Farrow returned to Paramount but never fully ventured back into film noir. Reunited with John F. Seitz, there were noirish stylistic touches in the period prison drama set in Farrow's native Australia, *Botany Bay* (1953). Farrow then hop-scotched around the studios replacing John Ford on *Hondo* (1953) for Warner Bros.

then to Columbia for *A Bullet is Waiting* (1954). As much or more Western than noir, *A Bullet is Waiting* does have some Farrow touches beginning with the moving shot that introduces the downed plane. The limited cast and isolated setting are like those of contemporary noirs *Bait* (1954) and *Storm Fear* (1955) but Farrow does not underscore the sense of a deterministic noir underworld. Farrow then returned to a Hughes-less RKO and made a crash-survivor movie: *Back to Eternity* (1956) was a remake of his own 1939 *Five Came Back*.

Farrow had come narratively close to noir at MGM with the fatalistic Western *Ride Vaquero!* (1953). Then as the classic period neared its end Farrow returned to the subject he explored so well in *Where Danger Lives*—the noir femme fatale—with *The Unholy Wife* (1957). The British "blonde bombshell" Diana Dors effectively conveys the various moods and complexities of the archetype, here named Phyllis Hochen. Not even the commanding presence of actor Rod Steiger as Phyllis' husband and patriarchal California vineyard owner Paul Hochen can overshadow the scenes with Phyllis (Dors).

Farrow uses the Technicolor process to fetishize garishly the image of Phyllis. Her torturously teased and coiffed blonde hair and her dozen or more costume changes (all in vibrant colors) set her apart from the chiaroscuro lighting of the movie. Farrow makes Phyllis the emotional and psychological center of this often overly moralistic tale. The priest brother of Paul fulfills the function of judge and jury, awkwardly conveying Farrow's own Catholic ideology. Moralizing aside, Farrow does give Phyllis her due, as he did with Margo in *Where Danger Lives*. Phyllis narrates the story of murder and deception from her death row jail cell to her clerically garbed brother-in-law. With her face scrubbed of make-up and in her drab prison garb, the glamorous Phyllis is gone. From a B-girl pick-up, with whom Paul spends a weekend, to a restless, pouting wife searching for the excitement her older husband cannot give her, Farrow makes Paul as complicit in the relationship's dysfunction as Phyllis. He even admits marrying Phyllis in order to gain an heir. His domineering manner and lack of true affection rival those of Smith Ohlrig in Ophuls' *Caught*, and Farrow uses framing and movement to suggest the noir web that underlies the narrative.

While his commitment to the noir style was unsurpassed, Farrow may never get the recognition of Ophuls, Fritz Lang, or Anthony Mann. His movies, however, reveal as profound an understanding of the movement as any director of film noir.

Biography

John Villiers Farrow was born in Sydney, Australia on February 10, 1904 and left an apprenticeship as an accountant to sail the South Seas. After a brief stint on the crew of Robert Flaherty's *Moana*, in 1926, Farrow came to Los Angeles and found employment as a marine technical advisor then as a writer at DeMille Studios, Paramount and RKO during the transition from silent to sound eras. After assisting G.W Pabst on the multi-lingual *Don Quixote* (1933), on his return to the U.S. Farrow was arrested and given a five-year probation for having an expired visa. Despite this Farrow found work as a director in the specialty, second and B-units at MGM (where he met his second wife actress Maureen O'Sullivan) and Warner Bros. In two years at RKO he made eight features and graduated to A-budgets then left for Canada to join the Royal Navy. After a medical discharge Farrow returned to Paramount as a director and enjoyed considerable success with his first assignment, *Wake Island.* At Paramount he worked in comedy and drama, Westerns and war movies, and his first noir films. Howard Hughes lured Farrow to RKO with the promise of greater autonomy, but Farrow quickly discovered that working for Hughes was anything but liberating. Farrow left after just three projects. Most of Farrow's last movies were made under the banner of John Farrow Productions and financed through individual studio deals. Farrow won an Academy Award for co-writing *Around the World in 80 Days* but never recaptured the critical success as a filmmaker that he had enjoyed at Paramount. He also wrote novels and biographies, most notably *Damien the Leper* (1937), and proselytized heavily for Roman Catholic causes. Nonetheless he was one of 27 directors who signed an open letter opposing Cecil B. DeMille's attempt to take over the Screen Directors Guild in 1951. Farrow was beginning to work in episodic television when he died of a heart attack on January 27, 1963.

Noir Films

Calcutta (1947)
The Big Clock (1948)
Night Has a Thousand Eyes (1948)
Alias Nick Beal (1949)
Where Danger Lives (1950)
His Kind of Woman (1951)
The Unholy Wife (1957)

Opposite, Diana Dors as Farrrow's last femme fatale in *Unholy Wife*. Right, on a beach location with Dors and Rod Steiger.

Felix Feist caught without his toupee outside a Los Angeles courtroom in 1957.

Felix E. Feist

Jake Hinkson

Over the course of directing twenty-one feature films, Felix E. Feist never developed an impressive reputation among critics, a situation which has continued to this day. Despite contributing four notable noirs during the classic period—*The Devil Thumbs a Ride, The Threat, The Man Who Cheated Himself*, and *Tomorrow Is Another Day*—he remains a virtually unknown figure even within the rather insular world of noir studies.

A closer look at his work, however, reveals a shrewd craftsman well-attuned to the noir style sweeping through the Hollywood system in the late 1940s and early 1950s. His films demonstrate a particularly deft usage of a difficult narrative mode—the alternating POV. Abjuring the first-person (he doesn't use voiceovers), Feist divides his audience's point of identification between two characters, often with one character having a dominant POV while the second character has a POV that is uneasily subordinate to the first. Further complicating the audience's entry into his crime stories, Feist often flips the conventional POV, with the antagonist or villain dominating the narrative as well as shaping the perceptions of the conventional protagonist or hero. These competing POVs create a dissonance in the narrative mode of the film, intensifying the volatility of the protagonist's world as he attempts to achieve, or regain, stability. Feist played different variations on this narrative dissonance while working within the structure of four of noir's sturdiest plotlines: the lethal hitchhiker, the prison break, the femme fatale, and the lovers on the lam.

The Lethal Hitchhiker: *The Devil Thumbs a Ride*

After directing musical comedies for most of the 1940s, Feist made his noir debut with RKO's *The Devil Thumbs a Ride* (1947). He wrote the screenplay, adapted from a novel by Robert C. Du Soe, about a psychopath named Steve Morgan (Lawrence Tierney) who, after robbing and killing a theater manager making a night deposit, hitches a ride with Jimmy Ferguson (Ted North), the affable regional manager for a ladies hosiery business. When Ferguson stops for gas, Morgan picks up two women looking for a lift. Spotting a roadblock, Morgan commandeers the car and takes his hapless good Samaritan and the unsuspecting women for a ride the long way around. After nearly killing a police officer, he convinces his fellow travelers to stop at a beach house in Newport where most of the last act unfolds.

The Devil Thumbs a Ride inverts the usual point of identification in a hitchhiker narrative by focusing on the dangerous hitchhiker rather than the innocent motorist. The first shot of the film begins on a street clock in the middle of the night, floats down to the window of the Bank of San Diego, and finds an old man at the night deposit box who is suddenly surprised by Morgan. After a short tussle, Morgan shoots the man, and the camera cranes up quickly to show Morgan taking the money and running away. In an unbroken shot of thirty-four seconds, Feist establishes the time and location of the story, initiates the plot, and sets up this brutal

Above, "Sometimes," as Al Roberts laments in *Detour,* "Fate puts the finger on you." Other times it's a kid in a drab uniform that does it to Morgan's mug-shot in *The Devil Tumbs a Ride.*

killer as our main character. Moreover, since the shot doesn't reveal Morgan's face until the moment he shoots the man, the revelation has immediate impact. Compared to this dramatic opening, the casual introduction of Ferguson in a standard two-shot denotes relative indifference.

As scenarist for the film, Feist diverges from Du Soe's source novel mostly to differentiate the competing POVs of Morgan and Ferguson.[1] First, he changes Ferguson from a boorish drunk driver into an affable, happily married man, thus pushing him into sharper contrast and quicker conflict with Morgan as things fall apart; however, since Steve Morgan supplies the film's dominant POV—which is to say that in nearly every scene he's the only one onscreen who knows what's going on—this change has the curious effect of turning the film's mandatory representative of decent society into an ineffectual dupe. Our ostensible protagonist, genial Jimmy Ferguson, finds himself reduced in a matter of minutes to the level of pure victim. Likewise, Detective Owens (Harry Shannon), the cop investigating the robbery/homicide, is transformed by Feist into little more than comic relief.

Feist's most important addition to the plot is Morgan's theft of Ferguson's identity.

Upon first exchanging names, Morgan dubs Ferguson "Fergie"—taking casual ownership of the other man's name. This rechristening sticks once the hitchhiking women pick up on it, and Ferguson begins his process of transmogrification into Fergie. Whereas "Ferguson" was a respectable married man and the regional sales manager of a clothing company, "Fergie" is a weakling who is manipulated and bullied at every turn by Morgan. At the end of the film, Morgan takes this transference to the limit when he steals the other man's wallet, forges his signature, successfully passes himself off to the police as Ferguson, and frames Fergie for his own crimes. Only the sudden *deus ex machina* of Mrs. Ferguson's unexpected appearance saves the real Jimmy Ferguson and reinstates his identity.

While Morgan is the devil of the title, he presides over a hell of various demons, each of whom helps him to diminish Fergie and reinforce his position as the dominant POV. One of the women is Agnes Smith (Betty Lawford) a callous wisecracker who spills booze on Fergie and then tries to blackmail him for free samples of women's stockings. When he doesn't come across with the hosiery, she interrupts his frantic phone call to his wife by cooing,

Above, in *The Devil Thumbs a Ride* Lawrence Tierney's chiseled features recall Hammett's description of Sam Spade: "his chin a jutting v under the more flexible v of his mouth.... He looked rather pleasantly like a blond Satan."

"Fergie darling..."—thus jeopardizing Ferguson's relationship with his wife by reasserting "Fergie's" new identity. Later, when Morgan attempts to pass himself off as Ferguson, Agnes pretends to be Mrs. Ferguson to help him. Likewise, Fergie's life is complicated by the appearance of Joe Brayden (Andrew Tombes), the drunken night watchman who is easily intoxicated and manipulated by Morgan. Once the police arrive, it's Brayden, drunk and confused, who lends official credence to Morgan's claim to be the real Jimmy Ferguson.

The Devil Thumbs A Ride deserves its place among other notable hitch-hiker noirs such as *Detour* (1945), *The Hitch-Hiker* (1953), and *The Night Holds Terror* (1955)—though of the four, it is the least despairing and the least focused on sadism.[2] In part, this is due to the lightness of the director's touch and his infusion of good-natured comic asides, but it is also because the studio demanded a cheery resolution. After Morgan is gunned down by the cops, we return to Ferguson in his car, this time joined by his wife who giddily announces she's pregnant—a cue for celebratory music and the fade out. While Feist hated the upbeat ending and argued against it [3], it functions here as it did in so many noirs from the classic period—as an ironic counterpoint to the insanity which has preceded it. Ferguson's plunge into chaos, his glimpse of the void personified by Morgan and his demonic henchmen, is only reinforced by the ending's nervous reassertion of familial, middle-class security.

The Prison Break: *The Threat*

Feist's second RKO noir was *The Threat* (1949). It stars Charles McGraw as a convict named Kluger who escapes from Folsom and kidnaps the men who put him behind bars, Detective Ray Williams (Michael O'Shea) and District Attorney Baker MacDonald (Frank Conroy). As the police search for them, Kluger and his gang escape to the California desert with their hostages in the back of a moving van. The cop and the DA attempt an escape but only succeed when an old girlfriend of Kluger's named Carol (Virginia Grey) shoots down the criminal. The films ends with the cop rejoined with his pregnant wife (Julie Bishop) as she announces she is going to have twins.

Below and opposite, dynamic staging and framing in *The Threat*.

As with *The Devil Thumbs a Ride*, once again the focus is on the villain of the piece. Tellingly, the staging of the domestic sphere in *The Threat*—Detective Williams and his wife decorating the baby room—is prosaic, a few mid-level shots lacking visual interest. The married couple exchange trite (and conventionally gendered) dialog in which she worries about his safety while scolding him for taking too many chances at work.

Only when the story addresses its villain does it spark to life. Once he shows up in the DA's office, Kluger dominates the rest of the film. Part of this has to do with the forcefulness of McGraw's performance (he is by far the most dynamic performer in the piece), but his dominance also owes something to the construction of the film's narrative. Once again, the ostensible hero of a Feist film, Michael O'Shea's Detective Williams, is wholly ill-prepared to cope with the anarchy represented by the villain. O'Shea spends the majority of the film literally bound and gagged. In the final confrontation between hero and villain, Kluger wrestles the policeman to the ground and smashes a chair over his head. If not for the intervention of Carol, we have no reason to doubt that Kluger would have emerged as the victor of this struggle between good and evil.

Every aspect of Feist's direction, in fact, serves to highlight the villain and diminish the hero. Contrasted with the banality of the hero's first scenes, Kluger is introduced with great fanfare. Before we see his face, he is mentioned by name *seventeen times* in the film's opening eight minutes. When he first appears, Feist frames McGraw from the shoulders down, only revealing his face in a flourish once he bursts into the DA's office. This framing sets up a motif throughout the film in which shots begin on feet or bodies rather than on faces. Feist's visual scheme, introduced by the villain, thus splinters the stolid world established by the opening scenes in the police offices and the Williams home.

The most intense sequence in the film, set at a flop house before the gang takes to the road, involves the torture of DA MacDonald. When Detective Williams refuses to make a phone call to throw off the dragnet, Kluger orders one of his henchmen to "give the treatment" to the DA with a pair of pliers until Williams finally capitulates. Not incidentally, this is the scene in which the noir style becomes most fully evident. The director, preferring to shoot from furniture-level, often with a couch or table at the bottom of a shot, is characteristically judicious in his use of close-ups.[4] The scene is shot almost entirely in tilted angles, with cinematographer Harry J. Wild's shadows slashing across walls in the background

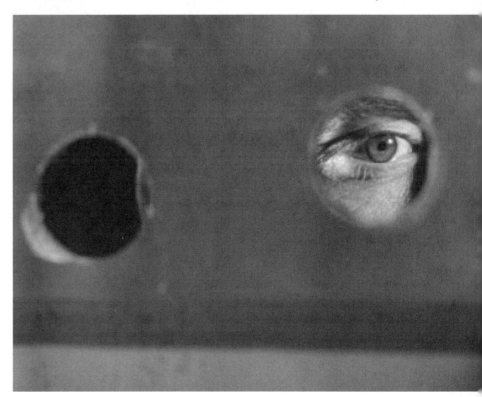

Above, Lee J. Cobb and Jane Wyatt in *The Man Who Cheated Himself*.

and the actors moving in diagonal relationship to each other within the frame. The break from the steady world of the Williams home is complete.

Interestingly, it is Carol, whose motives remain a mystery throughout the film, who returns Williams to his world of normality. At the climax, Kluger turns to find Carol pointing a gun at him. In a POV-shot through Kluger's eyes, the camera rises from the gun up to her face, devoid of all emotion except the slightest hint of a smile. This is the third time she is framed in a shot that begins at her feet. The first occurs when she tries to slip away from Kluger in an early scene, the second as she slides off a cot to seduce Kluger at the hideout. Only here, however, does Kluger understand that she's the one person capable of killing him.

With Kluger dead, the film returns to a mid-level static two-shot for a final scene of Detective Williams reunited with his wife, but this happy ending is even less reassuring than the one in *The Devil Thumbs a Ride*. Feist once again creates a world in which a feckless hero is unbalanced, and nearly destroyed, by his exposure to a darker side of the world. Dominated by a stronger man, he is saved once again by the intervention of a stronger woman.

The Femme Fatale: *The Man Who Cheated Himself*

The Man Who Cheated Himself, the only film produced by Jack M. Warner Productions, tells the story of Ed Cullen (Lee J. Cobb), a San Francisco police lieutenant who's having an affair with a married socialite named Lois Frazer (Jane Wyatt). When he witnesses Lois kill her husband, Ed covers up her involvement by moving the body. Once he is assigned to the murder case, he attempts to stop his brother Andy (John Dall), a newly minted police detective, from indentifying Lois as the killer. Andy, however, cracks the case, and Ed and Lois flee, pursued by Andy, and are arrested after hiding out for a day at Fort Point, a deserted army outpost beneath the Golden Gate Bridge.

Most critics of the film have correctly identified its main weakness: the performance of Jane Wyatt in the role of the femme fatale. Since the narrative is constructed around Ed's dominant POV, a great deal of weight is placed on the audience's identification with his desire for Lois. The film is hampered by Wyatt's sexless turn as Lois Frazer, but Feist's failure to eroticize the interactions between his leads is actually the larger problem. Because the film lacks a scene that vividly defines their relationship in terms of either sex or power, it's difficult to know why this man is so infatuated with this woman—a serious flaw for what is, after all, a conventional femme fatale story.

The absence of a strong female lead in *The Man Who Cheated Himself* reflects a characteristic lack of interest in eroticism on the part of the director, but it also points to the real focus of the film, the two brothers. Feist again splits his film's POV between the ostensible antagonist (Ed) and the ostensible hero (Andy). The differences between this film and Feist's earlier work are that Ed is less a villain than an antihero, and Andy is more resourceful than any other Feist protagonist. Since we are privy both to Ed's criminal acts and Andy's investigations, the audience's point of identification is bifurcated between two evenly matched opponents, creating a narrative tension that carries throughout the film. At the end, when Ed seeks refuge in the abandoned spaces of Fort Point, he does so because he and Andy played there as children. As Andy searches the fort for his brother, Feist accentuates the vast emptiness of the space, the whistling of the wind, the echo of Andy's footsteps. Ed, waiting to escape to his freedom, is trapped by his brother in an empty remnant of their childhood.

Feist's visual scheme for the film includes longer takes and more complicated shot compositions than his previous noir work. The murder, for example, is followed by a long shot of Ed and Lois going into a room, walking back through the hall, into another room, to the body, to the phone, and then back to the body. Though broken at the end by two quick inserts of the man on the other end of the phone, the shot sweeps us along with Ed as he decides to cover up the murder. Later, Feist stages an interrogation scene in which Ed and Andy question a thief named Nito Capa (Alan Wells). The shot, beginning with Nito's nervously tapping foot, moves up into a tilted angle that places Nito's sweaty face in the foreground, with Ed looming over him at the top of the frame, and Andy sitting in the lower left of the frame. The men move subtly as the dynamic of the scene changes: Nito nearer to the camera, Ed hovering over him, Andy watching them both. As Nito gets closer to breaking, Ed tries to frame him for the Frazer killing, which in turn causes Andy to become suspicious of his brother. The scene is three minutes without a cut, and by the end of it the split between the brothers has been established. From this scene forward, Andy is torn between his policeman's instinct and his devotion to his brother.

Feist uses the apartment shared by Andy and his new wife, Janet, to further dramatize his protagonist's discombobulated POV. Designed under the direction of ex-RKO art director Van Nest Polglase, the apartment is made up entirely of diagonals—sharply rising staircases, slanted ceilings and windows—and only appears in the film once Andy can no longer deny his suspicions that his brother is involved in the Frazer murder. Feist frames this scene from a low position to emphasize the angles of the architecture and then places Andy and Janet at angles to each other as they discuss the case. Andy's moral confusion—should he confront his brother with what he knows to be true—is alleviated only when he runs out of the apartment to find Ed.

Though flawed, *The Man Who Cheated Himself* is an important addition to Feist's noir work. Significantly, it is the only one of his noir films without a perfunctory happy ending. In the final scene, we see Ed being escorted into court by his brother. Lois passes by with her lawyer, with whom she is now clearly romantically involved. She and Ed exchange looks, he lights her cigarette, and she walks away.

"Why?" Andy asks his brother. "Why?"

"You said it once," Ed replies. "'Under the skin.'"

With that the film ends, on an ambiguous note to be sure, and one that leaves the fractured point of view in place. Ed is satisfied by the futility of his explanation, but Andy clearly is not.

Lovers On The Lam: *Tomorrow Is Another Day*

The last noir Feist made was the 1951 romance *Tomorrow Is Another Day*. It stars Steve Cochran as Bill Clark, a recently released ex-con who meets a jaded dime-a-dance girl named Cay Higgins (Ruth Roman). Things are going good until Cay's cop/pimp boyfriend Conover (Hugh Sanders) shows up, starts a fight with Bill, and is shot in self-defense by Cay. The fugitives flee New York and settle down among lettuce pickers in California, but their past follows them in the form of a pulp magazine article about the shooting. When Bill, convinced that a suspicious neighbor has betrayed them, attempts to kill a police officer at their door, Ruth shoots him in the shoulder. The film ends with the sudden revelation that the lovers have been cleared of all charges.

Although *Tomorrow Is Another Day* pulls itself into contortions in its final moments in order to arrive at a happy ending, it is deeply noir. With an excellent script by Art Cohn and Guy Endore, from a story by Endore, it is Feist's fullest work. It follows his previous films in the way Feist dramatizes its narrative through competing points-of-view, but this time the viewpoints form a complex nexus of guilt between a femme fatale and an antihero.

The film begins with Bill Clark being released from prison. His release is observed by a newspaperman eager to get an interview. The reporter approaches Bill at a diner without revealing his profession or motives, befriends him, and offers him a lift to a prospective job site. Only when Bill gets the evening paper does he realize that the newsman has betrayed him. This opening sets up a pattern in the film wherein Bill Clark, our protagonist, will almost always be in a position of being watched. He is an object that other characters observe, often with condescension, malice, or scorn. Feist's use of the focalizing gaze subtly establishes the narrative tension. When the reporter follows Bill, for instance, Feist positions the camera inside the car over the shoulder of the reporter, objectifying the convict (whom the reporter regards as little more than a good story). Likewise, when Bill meets Cay in the Dream Land Dancing club, we first see her as she stands with her back to us, observing Bill as he fumbles through an interaction with another dancer.

The major turning point comes during the fight with the crooked cop Conover. When Bill is knocked unconscious, the film stays with Cay. From this point on, in fact, we are prima-

Opposite, Steve Cochran and Ruth Roman as the fugitive couple in *Tomorrow Is Another Day*.

rily positioned in Cay's point of view. The audience sees her grab the gun and shoot Conover. When Bill regains consciousness, Cay lets him believe that he shot the cop. Bill is prepared to believe this because he is a former killer, having served eighteen years in prison for the murder of his father.

For the rest of the film, until the climax, Cay will allow him to believe that he is a murderer. Because she harbors this secret, a secret the audience shares, Cay's conflicted perspective effectively becomes the dominant POV of the film. Even within the context of a romantic narrative, Bill Clark is positioned as the observed, not simply as an object of romantic or erotic interest (as in a conventional romance) but as a pitiable figure tormented by guilt and anxiety. As the film progresses, Bill is isolated even further by other characters. When his new neighbors, the Dawsons (Lurene Tuttle and Ray Neal), see his mug shot in a pulp magazine, they discuss turning him in for a reward. After Mr. Dawson is injured in a traffic accident, Mrs. Dawson, desperate for money, alerts the police to Bill's presence. Feist frames Bill more and more inside the small shack he shares with Cay, pacing like an animal, left in a single shot to heighten his confinement.

Alain Silver and Linda Brookover have pointed out that the noir sensibility of *Tomorrow Is Another Day* is established through *amour fou*—with the obsessive love between Bill and Cay becoming a consuming passion.[5] Their reliance on one another will preclude everything else, a dependency that is dramatized in a skillfully realized set piece in which the fugitives attempt to hide away in a car atop an auto-transport truck. The sequence is suspenseful—with Bill and Cay silently scrambling to avoid detection as they break into the car— but it also marks the moment the two begin to rely on each other to the exclusion of literally everyone else. The bonding that results from this dangerous experience makes plausible the subsequent scene in which Bill proposes marriage and Cay accepts.

What is important to note, however, is that the romance's noir sensibility is given shape by the split POV that separates these characters, before and even after this bonding, from one another. Though Cay loves Bill, she lets him believe he is a murderer. Although joined by passion, they are unable to function happily together because of the dishonesty at the core of their circumstances. Her lie about the shooting creates a new kind of prison for the ex-con, a prison from which she is then expelled. The way in which Cay's lie turns back on her summons the femme fatale's essential contradiction as first articulated by Borde and Chaumeton: "[She] is also fatal unto herself. Frustrated and guilty, half man-eater, half man-eaten, blasé and cornered, she falls victim to her own wiles."[6] Feist's keen handling of this pivotal disarticulation is what gives the romance its noir hue.

Tellingly, Felix Feist did not regard himself as an artist, nor even a craftsman, but rather as a storyteller.[7] His films are notable for their speed and a certain

Below, the virginal ex-con courts the blonde "taxi dancer" in *Tomorrow Is Another Day.*

unfussiness of style, and while he was not a stylist as distinctive as Welles or Siodmak, his films do have consistent qualities: breakneck momentum, strong-willed female characters, weak-willed male protagonists, and the dominance of evil. Above all, giving them tension and depth, his films have competing POVs that layer and complicate his narratives and suffuse them with the noir ethos.

Notes

1. Robert C. Du Soe. *The Devil Thumbs A Ride.* (Robert M. McBride and Company, 1938.)

2. See also: Mark Osteen. "Noir's Cars: Automobility and Amoral Space in American Film Noir." *Journal of Popular Film & Television* 35.4 (2008): 183-192.

3. From an interview I conducted with the director's son, Raymond E. Feist on February 21, 2010. On *The Devil Thumbs a Ride:* "Pop was mostly happy with it...but he disliked the suddenly upbeat ending. But that was a studio call and he did was he was told to do."

4. Ibid. Mr. Feist quoted his father as saying, "If you're not doing action, you're doing talking heads. If you're doing talking heads, they better be saying something important."

5. Alain Silver and Linda Brookover. "What Is This Thing Called Noir?" *Film Noir Reader*. Eighth printing. Limelight Editions, 2006. p. 266

6. Raymond Borde and Etienne Chaumeton. *A Panorama of American Film Noir: 1941-1953*. City Lights Books, 2002. p. 9.

7. From my interview with Raymond E. Feist: "You asked earlier if Pop considered himself an artist or a craftsman. I don't think he thought of it that way. I think he saw himself as a narrator, a story teller, and his job was to do the best he could with whatever he was given."

Biography

Felix Ellison Feist was born in 1910 in New York City, the son of Felix F. Feist, MGM's general sales manager. When he was nineteen, Feist moved to Hollywood and took a job at the studio loading film for cameramen. By the early 1930s, he was placed in charge of directing screen tests for future stars such as Maureen O'Sullivan, Deanna Durbin, and Judy Garland. Following his apprenticeship in the MGM shorts department (as well as a fluke feature film assignment with the 1933 disaster movie *Deluge*), Feist moved to Universal to make features in the early 1940s, specializing in comedies and musicals. After directing one last musical comedy, *George White's Scandals* (1945) for RKO, he drifted around various studios and start-up production companies directing more serious fare. In addition to his work in noir, he made melodrama (*This Woman is Dangerous*), Westerns (*The Big Trees, The Man Behind the Gun*) and science fiction (*Donovan's Brain*). By the mid-1950s, he switched to television, directing multiple episodes for shows such as *The Californians* and *Voyage to the Bottom of the Sea*. He was working as a line producer on *Peyton Place* when he died of cancer, at age 55, in 1965.

Noir Films

The Devil Thumbs a Ride
The Threat
The Man Who Cheated Himself
Tomorrow Is Another Day

Left, Feist close to the beginning of his career

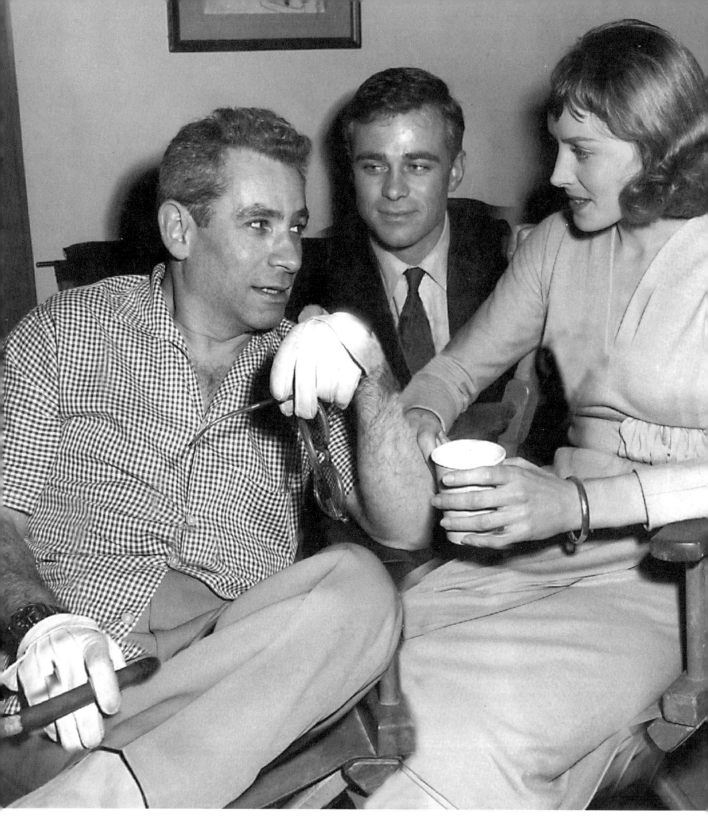

Above, with white-gloved hands holding a cigar and sunglasses, Sam Fuller talks with Glenn Corbett and Victoria Shaw on the set of *The Crimson Kimono*.

Samuel Fuller

Grant Tracey

Samuel Fuller is one of the most arresting noir directors of the 1950s and '60s. His style is raw, explosive, an in-your-face aesthetic full of an irrational chaos that somehow all makes sense. In Jean-Luc Godard's *Pierrot le Fou* (1965), Fuller makes a cameo appearance and describes his cinematic philosophy: "A film is like a battleground. There's love. Hate. Action. Violence. In one word, emotions." Later, in an interview with Lee Server, Fuller acknowledged his indebtedness to the American tabloids (he worked as a crime reporter for the *Evening Graphic*) and said that he plotted his hard-hitting melodramas on a blackboard with different colored chalk to balance out the story's three-levels of composition: red (action), white (exposition), and blue (love or romance).[1]

So what exactly is Fuller's tabloid aesthetic? He relies on the long-take or master shot for love scenes, creating rich subtexts through internal blocking, and opts for rapid cutting for action sequences.[2] He once commented that a close-up is like a newspaper headline, but his visual style is all about narrative rhythm. Similar to the dynamics of competing stories on a newspaper page ("Co-ed Murder Suspect to Tell All; "Saw Parade of Beauties Unclad in Worker's Room"; "Furriers Fail to Quit in Needle Strike"[3]), Fuller often shifts narrative modes, mixing action, exposition, and romance (red, white and blue) in wondrous, offbeat ways. Fuller will have collisions within scenes: lovemaking will turn violent (blue to red). Or he'll position collisions across scenes (an expository conversation followed by violence [white to red]) to create moods of noir-like disequilibrium.[4]

Moreover, like a journalist questioning social ills, Fuller will use expository moments to foreground larger issues, such as racism. Although many noir critics, including Raymond Durgnat, Robert Porfirio, and Paul Schrader, respond to the existential absurdity and cruelty in American noir, Fuller's vision is less bleak and more modernist. Like a reporter giving us the story in a seemingly objective, yet caring tone, Fuller is a moral filmmaker, fighting for social change.

Fuller's first two noirs, *Pickup on South Street* (1953) and *House of Bamboo* (1955), were made for Twentieth Century Fox and weren't as outlandish as his later work. Fuller didn't have complete control on these projects (*Bamboo* was a re-make of *Street with No Name*), and thus the "weirder" Fuller moments are absent. Both films are tightly written (all of the narrative's causal links fit), but they do showcase Fuller's tabloid aesthetics.

Pickup on South Street has an anti-hero at its center. "You waving the flag at me," asks Skip McCoy (Richard Widmark) with a noticeable "kink" in his mouth. He doesn't care about jingoistic patriotism and if he accidentally grifted communist secrets so what, or as he says, "who cares," with a kind of laidback Frank Sinatra cool. Widmark's McCoy is a self-centered sadist.

But Fuller balances McCoy with two female characters (Mo and Candy), the film's moral centers, who together nudge him toward redemption. "What's the matter with you? Playing footsie with the commies . . . I never figured you for a louse," Mo chastises Skip at a diner. Later she sacrifices her life for him, by refusing to give Joey (Richard Kiley) the street address he covets. Her death scene is a great Fullerian set piece, a meditation on ageing and dying. She discusses how she's run down, living in a state of near despair, but she won't give in to Joey's demands and as the camera swish pans to a needle stuck in the final grooves of a record, Joey shoots her. Her death reforms Skip. Upon hearing of Mo's murder, he recovers her body from a tugboat headed to a potter's field and gives her a proper burial.

Candy (Susan Peters) begins the film lacking knowledge. In the gripping opening sequence on a subway train, pickpocket Skip grifts her purse, and Fuller has her looking away, unaware of Skip's machinations or why two federal agents are tracking her. Later, her absent stare is converted into a series of seven penetrating eye-line matches. When she meets with Joey and his two associates, Candy rails against Skip for "calling us commies." As Fuller cuts in to Candy's perspective, a man smokes a cigar, another talks about "security" in portentous tones, and she slowly discovers the painful truth: they *are* communists. In Fuller's worldview communists are evil, the equivalent of totalitarianism.

Fuller makes his final moral case regarding the rightness of Candy's actions of defying the "commies" late in the film. As Skip visits Candy in the hospital, Fuller uses a highly subjective shot/reverse shot sequence in which Skip's close-ups are framed through the bars of Candy's hospital bed. This cheat shot indicates his lack-of-faith in her devotion. But as the intercutting continues, his blindness dissolves. The bars no longer frame Skip as he asks, "Did Joey kick your face in?" He's now committed to loving and avenging her.

The film has several additional memorable Fullerian set pieces: three love scenes that shift quickly to violence (blue to red), including Candy whacking Skip over the head with a beer

Below, Fuller's early underworld couples: Jean Peters and Richard Widmark in *Pick-up on South Street.* Opposite, Robert Stack and Shirley Yamiguchi in *House of Bamboo.*

bottle, and Joey's brutal beating of Candy. This scene begins as exposition as he wonders how she got the film (white), and then once he discovers a frame missing shifts to violence (red)— as he batters her about the room and lamps and end tables shatter.

House of Bamboo (1955) doesn't have as strong a Fullerian presence as his other noir films, in part because the movie was a big-budget actioner (shot on location in Japan and not Fuller's typical "in-betweener," a project between an A and B picture made to fit on a double-bill).[5] The script also wasn't Fuller's. He did punch up Harry Kleiner's original story, adding grit to the dialog and an interesting wrinkle in which the gangsters run their organization like a military outfit (including a stunning raid by their "five-star general" Sandy on a Tokyo munitions factory). This sequence involves variable framing, fast-paced intercutting, and smoke bombs clouding the screen with a mood of swirling chaos.

The center of the story involves Army sergeant Eddie Kenner (Robert Stack) who poses as wannabe tough guy Eddie Spanier and infiltrates a heist mob run by Sandy (Robert Ryan). The film is essentially about betrayal, as Sandy forms a homoerotic bond with Eddie and brings about his own demise through a series of misjudgments. Sandy is also crazy.

A second story revolves around interracial love as Kenner and his "kimono," Mariko (Shirley Yamaguchi), fall in love. She helps him solve the murder of her husband, and their relationship allows Fuller to make some biting social commentary. Most of the Japanese community assumes that Mariko is sleeping with Kenner and at the market several women shun her. On her way home, Mariko greets a young neighbor kid, and the mother pulls him away from her and closes their apartment door. "Living with you here like this brings dishonor on them," she eventually explains to Eddie. It's not clear if the dishonor stems from a relationship outside of marriage or if the community rejection is a result of Eddie being White.

In terms of Fuller's tabloid aesthetics, there are moments of collisions in and across scenes. The most memorable involve Mariko. Sandy invites her to his pagoda for tea. The pleasant conversation slowly shifts from casual conversation (exposition) into menace as rationality breaks down: "What's a matter, do I make you nervous? (beat) You're what's bothering him." He shoves her around, calls Mariko a two-timing "tramp," and the scene moves from white to red.

A collision also occurs across an earlier scene. After being asked where he's been, Eddie lies: "To see a kimono." In truth, he was being briefed by military intelligence. A shock edit follows as

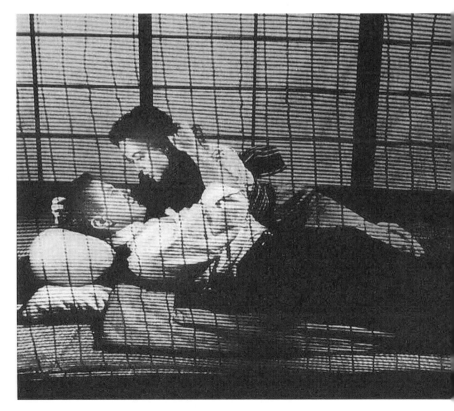

Sandy's hoods smack around an uncle of Mariko's (white to red). When Mariko denies spending time with Spanier, the violence escalates as Spanier himself steps in and hits her: "Was I here today?" he barks. She acquiesces with her own lie, swearing "yes." Prior to this beating, Spanier, during his military briefing, hinted at falling for Mariko and his bosses tell him, "Forget her." Thus these two scenes shift from blue to red, creating noir-like disequilibrium.

From 1956-61, Fuller became an independent producer/writer/director, creating films for his own Globe Enterprises and distributing them with the major studios such as Columbia.[6] Fuller was upset over having projects turned down by Fox, including an early draft of what would become *Forty Guns* (1957), so he opted for greater autonomy.

Crimson Kimono is one of Fuller's most personal films. Fuller was a fervent anti-racist and here sought to tell a hard-hitting story of love and loss. Like a reporter, he takes us on a multi-cultural journey, showing us parts of Los Angeles that other filmmakers hadn't. We travel into the Japanese-American community of Little Tokyo. We visit a Buddhist temple, see Japanese-American nuns, learn about the rituals of karate and kendo, and visit Evergreen Cemetery. There Fuller pays tribute to the 442nd Nisei Memorial, a monument to the Japanese-American unit who fought with valor in WWII and experienced 9,486 wounded and 600 killed. This cinematic moment is unmotivated narratively and is pure exposition. Fuller shows us a figure of a soldier at the top of the column, tilts down, and highlights quotes by Generals Dwight D. Eisenhower and Mark W. Clark, praising "the loyalty and courage of Nisei troops in Italy" and how America is in their "debt." Fuller, wearing his reporter's hat, shows how Japanese-Americans are part of the national fabric.

In terms of the story, it's a love triangle involving two cops, Charlie Bancroft and Joe Kojaku (Glenn Corbett and James Shigeta) as roommates and former soldiers in Korea, in love with the same woman, Chris Downs (Victoria Shaw), and trying to find the killer of a stripper. When Chris, a White woman, opts for the man of Asian ancestry, the film takes an interesting twist and explores questions of identity.

As in many Fuller films, love in *Crimson Kimono* is dangerous and threatening. As Charlie kisses Chris, the phone suddenly rings. Charlie tells Joe not to "do anything foolish" and then Fuller cuts to a disorienting shock edit of an arm chopping down, followed by an extreme close up of Shigeta's face, and a brawl in a pool hall with Shuto. The sequence quickly moves from blue to red.

But *Crimson Kimono*'s real collision course lies in the clash between Fuller's world view

Below and opposite dangerous love in *Crimson Kimono*.

(all are equal) and Joe's self-loathing (his feeling of inferiority to Whites). At first it appears that Joe is worried about hurting Charlie and ruining their friendship, but when he visits a Sensei, Joe asks "how do I rate her?" which suggests that he has a low opinion of himself. The Sensei is confused by Joe's comments. When Chris asks about kendo dress, Joe describes it as a "monk in a catcher's outfit." Interesting word choice: during W.W.II, the Japanese were portrayed in editorial cartoons as monkeys, and "monk" certainly has that trace sound, and could subtly hint at Joe's own self-loathing. And during the kendo match, Joe crosses the line, beating Charlie into submission, knocking him out. He projects his self-hatred onto a White man who seems full of entitlement and privilege.

In the end Joe "solves his own case." After capturing the stripper's killer, Joe cradles the wounded killer, a jealous woman, in his arms and hears a double-voiced confession, words that apply to him as well as her: "I died when I saw her figure. That's why I killed her. . . . It was all in my mind." As she confesses, Fuller cuts away to eight shots of Asian faces gathered around the wounded woman. The cutaways aren't motivated through Joe's eye-line matches. Instead these cutaways function as descriptive commentary by Fuller that highlight his theme: Joe Kojaku's fear of his own skin, his own people, and their collective gaze at his guilt.

Underworld USA (1961) revisits *Pickup on South Street* stylistically. Street urchin turned small-time hood Tolly Devlin (Cliff Robertson) wants to avenge the murder of his father and punish the four men responsible. In a prison hospital he tracks down the dying Vic Farrar and extorts a confession. Farrar wants to go out "with a clean slate," names names, and asks forgiveness. Here Fuller repeats the cheat shot from *Pickup*: high/low, shot/reverse shots centering around Farrar on a bed. The shots of Farrar are uncluttered; those of Robertson are shrouded in the bars of the bed, suggesting what he's doing is criminal. He refuses to forgive Farrar and calls him a "fink" just as the gangster dies. In *Pickup*, the bars of the bed slowly disappear, no longer framing Skip McCoy once he acknowledges Candy's love. Devlin, by contrast, is a darker figure, full of demons—he's a borderline sociopath, a classic noir anti-hero.

Moreover, like *Pickup*, there's a love interest (Cuddles played by Dolores Dorn) who becomes the moral center of the film and seeks to help Tolly become a better person. But it's rough going. Tolly does eventually do the right thing: risking his own life to protect her; however prior to these actions he has an incredibly irredeemable moment of cruelty. Cuddles confesses she loves him, says she wants his child, and Fuller shifts the tone of the scene from blue to red. Robertson pulls slightly away from her, says, "Marry you. Marry you?" And then brutally laughs at her. Here the violence or action isn't physical but emotional and palpable.

In terms of tabloid poetics, the film relies on the newspaper reporter's need to get the facts to the public. Forty minutes into the film, the narrative stops for a descriptive essay on organized crime by D. A. Driscoll (Larry Gates). Shot in consecutive long takes, Driscoll informs us of how the syndicate traffics drugs and recruits girls into prostitution by targeting coffee houses and soda shops. He also comments on how their organization is run like the military: "Lording it over the generals in the field is Earl Connors, their Chief of Staff. Shrewd. Warm. Charitable. An animal." His pulpy dialogue reads like newspaper headlines.

Three times Fuller freezes the narrative with tableaux effects, opening his story up to larger social issues: First, when corrupt Chief Fowler, who's on the take, commits suicide, Fuller moves to a shock cut-in, Fowler saying, "God forgive me," and then cuts to a bullet lodged in a photograph of uniformed police officers, suggesting how Fowler's corruption has besmirched cops everywhere; Second, after hit-man Gus (Richard Rust) runs overs Mencken's daughter with his car, Fuller recreates a Weegee–like crime scene photograph, framing the moment with a mangled bicycle, two discarded shoes, and a dead girl lying on her side. And finally after Tolly murders Connors, he stumbles out of the gangster's headquarters and dies

Above, another Weegee-like tableau: a dead mobster and his pool chair float around a headline.

in the same back alley that claimed his father. The camera tracks in on his fist and freeze frames into a final, grainy image.

All three moments circumscribe the action and invite us to write a caption, to ponder these images separate from story: the dead girl isn't just a girl, but a victim—nobody is innocent or safe; the lodged bullet is a synecdoche for Fowler's death but also suggests corruption within police departments across the country; Tolly's clenched fist doesn't represent only his pain and obsessions, but the drive and failure many experience trying to fight their way out of the gutter.

This is one of Fuller's darkest noirs and most satisfying. Here his style is more abstract, "weird," less locked into narrative causal links, and he's taking greater risks. *Underworld*'s undercover theme, of a man infiltrating an organization to find truths, gets revisited in Fuller's next film, the outlandish and somewhat crass and insensitive, in its treatment of mental illness, *Shock Corridor*.

Fuller often uses his mise-en-scène to comment on the fallibility of his lead characters, their inability to truly see and feel (recall the bed-framed sequences from *Pickup on South Street* and *Underworld USA*), but what complicates that fallibility in *Shock Corridor* is that perspectives get blurred between authenticity and performance, sanity and insanity, rationality and irrationality.[7] For example, Stuart (James Best), an inmate who thinks he's a Civil War general, discusses battle plans for Antietam, and suddenly through his eye-line matches Fuller gives us discordant 16 mm images of Japan (a Buddha statue; trains, Mount Fuji; and an amusement park in Tokyo). Objective and subjective images collide, creating a mood of disequilibrium. Similarly, late in the film, Johnny (Peter Breck), hears a thunderclap. He looks up. The sound appears to be diegetic, but when spots of water hit his open palm we realize he's having an expressionistic moment, the line between reality and illusion blurring.

Collisions within scenes are also affected by questions of sanity. Trent (Hari Rhodes), another inmate, is an African-American student who attempted to integrate into an all-white university. The trauma of that experience has converted him into the very thing he hates: a bigot, a KKK follower who carries a placard that reads: "Integration and Democracy Don't Mix. Go Home, Nigger!" The sentiments are obviously absurd: democracy is about the freedom of all. Moreover, two of his scenes quickly shift from white (exposition) to red (violence). In one, he's discussing the catatonic symptoms of a patient next to Johnny when suddenly Trent chases a fellow African-American down the long corridor, shouting "America for Americans" and thus begins a "race riot." Later, in sickbay, Trent's rationally recounts for Johnny his experiences as a student and the failed integration experiment. In the middle of his descriptive essay

Below, another underworld couple: Tolly (Cliff Robertson) and Cuddles (Dolores Dorn).

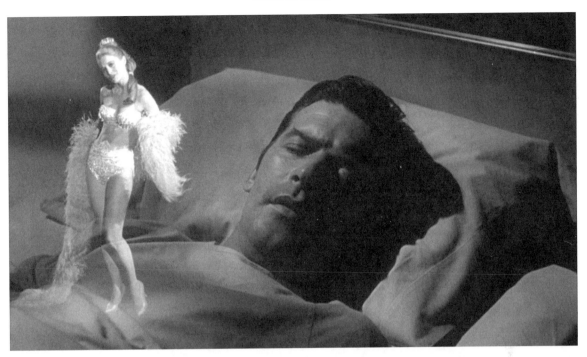

Above and below, the dreams and nightmares of *Shock Corridor.*

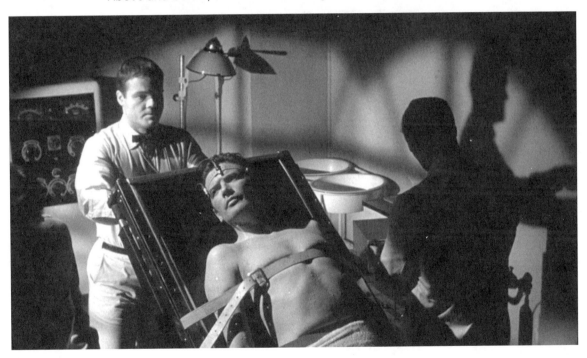

(exposition), he suddenly shifts into madness, snapping up in bed, his lip curling back, as he shouts "Get That Nigger!"

Johnny too slowly shifts from rational order to catatonic chaos. He goes undercover, pretending to have incestuous desire for Cathy (his alleged sister who is really his lover), so that he can find out who killed Sloan, a mental patient at the hospital, and thereby win the

Above, the violent attack that opens *The Naked Kiss*.

Pulitzer. Cathy (Constance Towers), like so many Fuller women the moral center of the film, disapproves, arguing that what he's about to do is disgusting and dangerous: "You're in a hopped-up, show off stage. Get off it." Johnny's convinced that he can play-act at being mad without the performance having any ill effects. But, of course, he's wrong. He infiltrates the hospital, solves the case, but along the way slowly disintegrates, at times losing his ability to speak, and has restless dreams in which Cathy, in her stripper clothes and a boa, tells him she can't wait, she has the right to find someone else. Very late in the film, Johnny has a meeting with Cathy to pass on information. The moment collides blue (love) with red (violence). Cathy kisses Johnny, and he pushes her away, slipping into an authentic fit (not a play-acted one). "Don't ever do that. Don't you ever kiss me like that again." He's actually starting to think she *is* his sister.

Fuller's final noir masterpiece is *The Naked Kiss* (1964). This time he makes the moral center of the film (Constance Towers as Kelly) his lead character. A former prostitute, Kelly arrives in Grantville, and local cop Griff (Anthony Eisley) tries to shoo her away, saying he likes a "clean" town, and suggests she become a "bon-bon" across the river. But Kelly refuses to be defined by him, takes up residency, reforms, and works as a nurse for handicapped children at a local hospital, dedicating her life for the betterment of others. She eventually gains Griff's begrudging approval and falls in love with J. L. Grant (Michael Dante), the town philanthropist. Grantville seems like a nice picturesque town, a bright lit energetic locale out of a *Leave It to Beaver* backlot, but a noir-like darkness envelopes the apparent contented sheen. Kelly later discovers J. L. Grant to be a child molester.

Kelly and Grant's relationship is founded on artifice and contains one of the most bizarre scenes in Fuller's catalog, a moment that blurs the lines between reality and fantasy, and sadly suggests that Kelly's dream is unattainable.[8] She and Grant sit on a couch and watch home movies of a gondola floating in Venice as leaves fall. Grant says if you listen carefully you can hear the song of the gondolier, a wacky moment in which the objective moment is made subjective. And as she hears the

Left, a variant of fated figures posed on a bed in *The Naked Kiss*.

gondolier's song, Fuller cuts from the home movies, to a theatrically staged moment: Kelly on a makeshift couch/gondola, "imagined" leaves fluttering intermittently on her dress, everything resembling an ironic moment out of a Douglas Sirk melodrama or an expressionistic scene from an Ingmar Bergman chamber film. And when he kisses her, she hesitates, pulls back, and senses, although she can't articulate it yet, the naked kiss, the "kiss of a pervert."

Moreover Fuller has his usual memorable collisions within scenes. The opening, pre-credit sequence is a stunner. Farlunde (Monte Mansfield) had the camera attached to his chest, so that when Kelly attacks him we can feel it. As he bounces about the room, he pushes off Kelly's wig to reveal that she's bald. He falls, she sprays seltzer in his face, and takes seventy-five dollars from his wallet. "I'm taking only what's coming to me," she explains. Her pimp was holding out on her. And thus a sequence that begins in red (violence) winds up with brief exposition (white) and a quick explanation for the explosive energy we've just witnessed.

Perhaps the most famous collision occurs when Kelly kills Grant. Kelly arrives unexpectedly at Grant's estate with her wedding dress. Fuller cuts from long shot to a close up of her face as her joy gives way to disgust. A little girl skips out of the shadows and exits. Grant, unapologetic about being caught molesting a child, lurches slowly forward and in a tight choker close-up confesses, "Now you know why I never could marry a normal woman. That's why I love you. You understand my sickness." He drops to his knees and promises that their "marriage will be a paradise because we're both abnormal." A shock edit follows as Kelly clubs him to death with a telephone: white (exposition) to red (violence). The moment resonates with us because what she most desires—acceptance and normalcy—is shown to be a mirage. She wanders the mean streets of film noir disillusionment, and in the end leaves town, exonerated of her crime, but still feeling like an outcast.

Fuller's tabloid aesthetics can also be witnessed in his non-noir films, especially *The Steel Helmet* (1950) with its expository pauses on African Americans being forced to ride at the back of the bus and Niseis being sent to stateside interment camps. In *Verboten* (1959), Fuller transcends story through grainy images of the horrors of the holocaust, working to ensure that it never happens again. But the six noirs discussed here show an auteur working at the top of his craft to paint various shades of tabloid poetics into the noir canon.

Notes

1. Lee Server, *Sam Fuller: Film Is a Battleground* (North Carolina: McFarland and Company, 1994), pp. 4-5, 12-17.

2. Lisa Dombrowski, *The Films of Samuel Fuller: If You Die, I'll Kill You!* (Wesleyan University Press, 2008), pp. 18-19.

3. *The Evening Graphic* (20 June, 1929), p. 5.

Fuller's ironic vision of the tabloid world: Broderick Crawford and John Derek in *Scandal Sheet*.

4. Many of the ideas in this essay I explored in an earlier piece: Grant Tracey, *"Film Noir* and Samuel Fuller's Tabloid Cinema: Red (Action), White (Exposition), and Blue (Romance)" in *Film Noir Reader 2*, eds. Alain Silver and James Ursini (New York: Limelight Editions, 1999), pp. 158-75.

5. Dombrowski, pp. 81-83.

6. Dombrowski, pp. 93-95.

7. Dombrowksi, pp. 148-49.

8. Dombrowski, pp. 163-64.

Biography

Samuel Fuller was born in Worcester, Massachusetts to Jewish immigrant parents on August 12, 1912. At twelve he became a newspaper copyboy and at seventeen was working as a crime reporter on the *New York Evening Graphic*. There he covered Jeanne Eagels's death. From the mid-1930s on he became a pulp writer and his novel *The Dark Page* later became the source material for a Phil Karlson noir, *Scandal Sheet*. During World War II, Fuller served with the Big Red One and saw heavy fighting in North Africa, Czechoslovakia, and Italy. He was present at D-Day and the liberation of a German concentration camp at Sokolov. Fuller reached the rank of corporal and was awarded a bronze star, a silver star, and a Purple Heart. Fuller's wartime experiences combined with his work on a tabloid, helped inform his visual style: a combination of shifting moods that counterpointed long-take master shots with sequences full of rapid inter-cutting. Fuller's third film for Robert Lippert, *The Steel Helmet*, launched his career. There he portrayed the ordinariness of the life of a grunt, and showcased several of his cinematic touches, including collisions among narrative modes (exposition, violence, and romance) and his use of narrative essays, pausing the story to educate an audience on issues such as racism. From 1953-64, through a variety of companies (20th Century Fox, his own Globe Enterprises, and Allied Artists), Fuller made six outstanding noir films that featured ambiguous heroes, tough-talking dames, and lovable mother figures. Most of his noirs were low-budget genre pictures made to fit on a double bill and packed with action and lurid sensationalism. Between 1967-80, Fuller directed only two films. After *Naked Kiss* and *Shock Corridor* lost money for Allied Artists, Fuller found it hard to make movies for a teen exploitation market. His efforts in this era were among his weakest: *Dead Pigeon on Beethoven Street*, a neo-noir, winds up being a pale pastiche of his better films (especially *Pickup on South Street*). Moreover, *Shark* was a mess and a film Fuller disassociated himself from. In 1980 he completed his final masterpiece, the autobiographical *The Big Red One*, which has been recently "re-constructed" by Richard Shickel to its full epic grandeur. Fuller died on October 30, 1997.

Noir Films

Shockproof (1949) (screenplay only)

Scandal Sheet (1952) (novel source only)

Pickup on South Street (1953)

House of Bamboo (1955)

Crimson Kimono (1959)

Underworld USA (1961)

Shock Corridor (1963)

The Naked Kiss (1964)

Henry Hathaway (left of camera) directs Richard Widmark and Victor Mature in *Kiss of Death*.

Henry Hathaway

R. Barton Palmer

By 1945 Henry Hathaway had established himself as one of Hollywood's most reliable directors, a minimal stylist with a flair (nurtured by his work as an assistant for Victor Fleming) for well-designed, object-rich mise-en-scène. It seemed unlikely at the time that he would shortly become noted for his work in a dark version of the classic Western, as well as in various forms of the crime melodrama, what French journalists would soon identify as an American version of the film noir, already a feature of French filmmaking in the 1930s. Aside from his quite noteworthy work in suspense thrillers such as *Diplomatic Courier* and *Fourteen Hours*, Hathaway's six fully noir projects (which will be the focus of discussion here) constitute one of the most consistently fine bodies of work in the series, rivaled only by such more widely acknowledged masters as Fritz Lang, Billy Wilder, and Alfred Hitchcock.

Below, *The House on 92nd Street.*

Early in his career Hathaway had fancied himself as something of a documentarian, traveling in India and collecting material for a film on pilgrimage, so it was perhaps appropriate that he was chosen to direct when documentary producer Louis de Rochemont determined to make a film that married fiction and documentary approaches to the recreation of a historical event from the recent past, whose hitherto secret nature could now be revealed. The producer intended the film to fit into the then current fashion for crime melodrama, what later critics identified as the film noir, and to appeal to audiences whose tastes for cinematized current events had been whetted by a flood of wartime documentaries. Released in September 1945, a little more than a month after final victory in the Pacific, *The House on 92nd Street* moved noir in a substantially different direction than it had assumed in earlier entries such as *Double Indemnity* (1944), a dark romance that meditates on the destructiveness of the relentless pursuit of self-interest. Hathaway's wartime thriller is fictional only in the sense that it expands its spare story with some imagined scenes and dialogue, combining the visual style and formal conventions of documentary filmmaking with the exaggerated naturalism of the film noir, especially the genre's probing of hitherto off-limits themes and its Zolaesque preoccupation with the seedier side of contemporary American life, which are here effectively evoked in expressionist visuals of the espionage netherworld.

The House on 92nd Street is "true," or at least so its authoritative narrator declares; the film re-enacts a real case of German espionage foiled during the early stages of World War II by timely and expert police work, the so-called Duquesne Spy Ring case. FBI files from that case were made available to the screenwriters. Many sequences were shot in locations around the New York City area, where the plot to steal nuclear secrets was discovered and foiled, and in Washington, D.C. at the FBI complex, where the investigative work was done. Much of this footage is straightforwardly documentary in its apparently unstaged recording of police activities and its dispassionate account of law enforcement procedure. Non-professional actors were used in minor parts (with some of the roles being played by actual police personnel), and the FBI cooperated by furnishing a technical advisor, one of its distinguished agents, Howard R. Hawkins. Sequences shot silent are explained by the self-assured and omniscient narrator (Reed Hadley, in a role that he would repeat many times in subsequent films for Hathaway and other directors, as well as on early television).

And yet *The House on 92nd Street* is more than a re-creation of a "true case." The film's narrative focus is uneasily split between the Nazi agents (memorably incarnated by Leo G. Carroll and Signe Hasso), those fascinating perpetrators of an unfathomable and perverse evil, and their pursuers, led by FBI agents Bill Dietrich (William Eythe) and George Briggs (Lloyd Nolan), whose unalloyed and rather flat virtue proves much less interesting and appealing, even though they naturally emerge victorious in a finale that celebrates the invincibility of American institutions. A largely neutral, unglamorized visual style attests to the film's accurate re-enactment of the official response to the discovered threat, but the sequences detailing the machinations of the reptilian villains strain to evoke a different atmosphere. These sequences are, as it were, overly theatrical, barely contained by Hathaway's otherwise subdued and objective approach to his material. Hathaway exerted significant influence on subsequent entrants in the noir semi-documentary, most of which manifest the same unstable melding of two opposed story worlds: the well-organized modern state, knowable as well as knowing, its irregularities surveilled and corrected by government agencies of enormous power that are always put in service of the public good; and an underworld of the maladjusted and dissatisfied, whose transgressions, moral and legal, are not only self-defeating, but otherwise easily disposed of by an unchallengeable authority. As in many films of the noir documentary cycle, what stitches the plot together is the leading role played by Dietrich as a double agent, who, recruited because he is an ethnic German, is sent to Germany, with the connivance of the FBI, to receive training by the Abwehr secret service and then return to the USA, where, it is hoped, he will help roll up the network of spies that the Germans have planted in key American cities. Their target is information about American atomic bomb research, and, as the narrator informs the film's viewers, that the FBI was able to protect these secrets proved vital to American final victory, an event in the very recent past when the film was released in late the fall of 1945, just weeks after the Japanese surrender. In the manner of the studio thriller, the narrative climaxes with a violent confrontation that generates suspense about Dietrich's escape from his erstwhile comrades, now aware that he is an FBI agent, and the successful capture or killing of the enemy agents. An epilogue features documentary

A posed shot of James Cagney for *13 Rue Madeleine*: exaggerated noir lighting of a stylized setting is superimposed over the documentary-style of the narrative.

footage of the capture of the actual German agents and their trial, with Hadley drawing the appropriate moral about the haplessness of America's enemies.

Hathaway and de Rochemont were eager to capitalize on their initial success. Though not always considered noir because of its focus on foreign espionage, *13 Rue Madeleine* is a virtual sequel to *The House on 92nd Street*, with the Gestapo headquarters in Le Havre taking the place of the spies' New York City headquarters that furnishes the initial project of Hathaway and de Rochemont with its title. Here the focus is not on successful American counterespionage efforts, but on the founding of the OSS, the antecedent to the CIA, and its operations in occupied Europe. Hathaway and de Rochemont once again made excellent use of a distinguished technical advisor from the OSS, Colonel Peter Julien Ortiz. The original plan was to model the main character on the OSS's spymaster "Wild Bill" Donovan, but the famous man objected and the script was rewritten to obscure the resemblance, but many viewers might not have been fooled. As was the case in *House*, the film begins with documentary footage of official Washington, accompanied by a stirring musical score, and a brief history of the origins and functioning of the fledgling counterespionage agency, with Reed Hadley reprising his role as narrator. Mixing re-enactments with documentary sequences, Hathaway and de Rochemont follow the rigorous training of a new class of American agents, effecting a seamless transition to the narrative proper and a focus on a case of particular importance: a mission to gather the precise locations and architectural details of a series of V-1 missile sites trained on the port of Southampton and intended to be fired in a destructive volley as the D-Day invasion fleet gathers to cross the channel. Bomber command needs that information in order to decide what type of explosive to use in a mission to destroy these facilities as a prelude to D-Day.

Once again, the plot features a double agent, but in this case his loyalty is to the German side (Wilhelm Kuncel, played by Richard Conte, has for a long time been in deep cover as Bill O'Connell). The senior agent in charge of the mission, Bob Sharkey (James Cagney), knows that O'Connell is a German agent and deliberately sends him to France along with two OSS operatives after having provided the group with persuasive misinformation about the date and site of the invasion. Sharkey reveals O'Connell's real identity to one of the operatives, Lassiter (Frank Lattimore). Lassiter acts nervous around the wily O'Connell, who concludes that his cover has been blown and cuts Lassiter's parachute cord before the team jumps from their air transport. Landing, he seeks out the German authorities and assumes his real identity as a Gestapo officer. Meanwhile, the one surviving team member, Suzanne de Beaumont (Annabella), makes contact with the Resistance, but cannot complete the mission until Sharkey comes to her aid.

At this point, Sharkey becomes the main character, and the narrative follows him until he and Suzanne obtain the necessary intelligence. She is killed by the Germans just after sending the coded message to London, and Sharkey is taken prisoner and moved to intelligence headquarters at 13 Rue Madeleine in Le Havre. Tortured by the Gestapo and his erstwhile comrade Kuncel/O'Connell, Sharkey refuses to reveal what he knows. Improbably, he has been informed about the plans for Operation Overlord, but does not tell the Germans when D-Day will come and, more important, exactly where the allies are to land. The film ends abruptly with its most unforgettable image: Sharkey, bound to a chair where he has been whipped for hours, hearing Allied planes overhead and thus knowing that Suzanne got the message through to London. He breaks out in hysterical laughter as bombs destroy the building and all within. In this project, Hathaway decided against a closing documentary epilogue, probably because the "true case" on which the film is based is more fiction than fact, however accurate a portrayal of OSS operations in general Hathaway and de Rochemont purport to offer. The duo made a substantial effort to give this film authenticity; though many of its "French" sequences were obviously shot on a Hollywood back lot, there are a number of shots that open out into the "real" (most notably, several exterior sequences that present a flat country-side of small farms divided by hedgerows, filmed not in Normandy, the ostensible location, but in rural Quebec, where a similar countryside could be found). As in *The House on 92nd Street*, the noirness of *13 Rue Madeleine* consists largely in its evocation of an atmosphere of constant threat where characters who are pretending to be other than what they really are must struggle to prevent the exposure of the truth, creating the same suspense as the dark tale of the conspiring murderous lovers in *Double Indemnity* and many other noir romances.

As in these two productions, in *The Dark Corner* the balance between story (also "real" of course in the case of the two films discussed thus far) and recorded reality tips more deci-sively toward the fictional and away from history per se. *The Dark Corner* is based on no true story, nor does it reference the workings of a government institution like the OSS or the FBI. Based on a screenplay by Hollywood professional Jay Dratler, the film is a hard-boiled detec-tive yarn in the tradition of Dashiell Hammett and Raymond Chandler. Despite the fact that many of its exteriors, like those in *House,* were filmed by a second production unit on the

A posed shot of Richard Conte and James Stewart for *Call Northside 777*: again exaggerated noir light-ing and a stylized setting contrast with documentary-style narrative.

streets of New York City, *The Dark Corner*'s visuals are in general more characteristically noir, with many framed or "entrapping" compositions and, overall, a darker photographic style. This is due in part to the excellent cinematography of Joseph MacDonald, who would go on to work on several other projects with Hathaway, providing an excellent atmospheric look to other noir films, notably *The Street with No Name* (1948). If *House* and *Madeleine* are noir largely in the sense that they locate their main characters in a dangerous underworld (the lair of a spy ring or an enemy-occupied country), with its focus on a private detective, jailed for a crime he did not commit and only recently released, *The Dark Corner* has more in common with similar films in the early noir cycle. Detective Brad Galt (Mark Stevens), just released from prison and now relocated in New York City, discovers that he is being followed by a man known as White Suit (William Bendix), who it turns out is working for a lawyer, Anthony Jardine (Kurt Kreuger), whom Galt knew in California. Galt discovered that Jardine was an embezzler, framing the detective for a vehicular homicide that landed him in prison. The villain of the piece, however, is really art gallery owner Hardy Cathcart (Clifton Webb), who hates Jardine for having seduced his young wife Mari (Cathy Downs) and intends to get rid of his rival, using White Suit against his former employer. Acting for Cathcart, White Suit kills Jardine with a fireplace poker that he then puts in the hand of Galt, whom he had previously knocked out by a dose of ether. With the help of his secretary Kathleen (Lucille Ball), Galt manages to escape the frame-up this time despite passing through a moment of despairing helplessness. Cathcart, meanwhile, gets rid of the now-inconvenient White Suit, pushing him out an open window in the skyscraper where they meet in one of film noir's most unusual and startling murder sequences.

Eventually, again helped by Kathleen, Galt manages to track down Cathcart, who attempts to get rid of him but is foiled by Mari who, aware that he murdered her lover, shoots him dead. Kathleen and Galt immediately thereafter set out in a taxi for city hall, where she has determined they are to be married that very day, in a finale that reflects the hurriedly improbable happy ends of many films noirs, as exemplified by *Murder, My Sweet* (1944), a highly popular release (and now thought a noir classic) that Hathaway's film otherwise interestingly resembles. Noted reviewer Bosley Crowther found much to admire in Hathaway's hard-boiled, well-paced narrative, praising *The Dark Corner* as "tough-fibered, exciting entertainment" (*The New York Times*, 9 May 1946). With its byzantine plot, straining credibility at almost every turn, *The Dark Corner* moved decisively away from the realism, however forced it may be at times, that dominates Hathaway's first two noir entries.

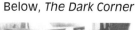

Below, *The Dark Corner*

Interestingly, however, Hathaway at this point in his career abandoned this thoroughly fictional approach to what he would have called the crime melodrama, returning for a time to the semi-documentary formula he had so successfully inaugurated with de Rochemont in the *The House on 92nd Street*. Both *Call Northside*

777 (based on a "true story") and *Kiss of Death* (whose fictionality Hathaway strives mightily to disguise) aim to create and foster an atmosphere of realism. The opening credits of *Call Northside 777* proclaim that "this is a true story" that was filmed insofar as possible at the actual locations in the state of Illinois where the "case" it deals with took places. An elaborately staged process shot introduces the city of Chicago, burning up in its famous fire, as the film's setting, with once again the stentorian Reed Hadley introducing important institutions, this time the various newspapers whose function it is to surveil and help correct, as possible, errors that are made by the state, thus providing the rationale for "freedom of the press." These real locations most interestingly include not only the building fronts of the various Chicago dailies, but also the Illinois State Prison at Stateville, with its distinctive panopticon watchtower carefully memorialized by Hathaway's set-ups in a move that proudly proclaims the film's authenticity. Its story, noticeably devoid of the baroque twists and turns featured in the Chandleresque screenplay for *The Dark Corner*, is based on a magazine article that is slightly fictionalized by the screenwriters, including Jay Dratler again. It traces in a deliberately unmelodramatic fashion the attempt of a newspaper reporter, P.J. McNeal, played in a suitably deglamorized fashion by James Stewart, to free a convict whom, after examining the evidence, he believes to be innocent.

Through McNeal's doggedly persistent efforts, Frank Wiecek (Richard Conte), serving a life sentence for the murder of a policeman, is released. If, in the mode of more action-oriented noir films, *The Dark Corner* climaxes with an unexpected but welcome act of violence, as Cathcart is shot dead by his unfaithful wife, *Call Northside 777* resolves the question of Wiecek's innocence in a much less spectacular fashion, as McNeal is able to provide photographic proof that he could not have done the crime, proof that is made available through a careful enlargement of a photograph dated by the newspaper Wiecek holds in his hand. In part, the realism of the film is best exemplified by its careful toleration of a middle in which the plot seems to stall for some time in violation of Hollywood screenwriting conventions. Only Stewart's intensity as a crusading McNeal, whose reporting puts the case in the news and arouses public attention, holds the two halves of the film together. The crusading reporter is only able to continue the crusade when he convinces a now-reluctant Wiecek that the continuing series of articles he is publishing will lead to a reconsideration of the case, not just to the unwelcome glare of publicity they are bringing upon his ex-wife and son. McNeal's struggles are not with thugs who want to kill him or frame him for murder, but rather with finding, and getting access to, the decades-old records he needs and overcoming the reluctance of the justice system to reconsider a judgment he believes has been rendered in error.

As in the case of Hathaway's two previous semi-noirs, *Call Northside 777* affirms the essential rightness and righteousness of the American system, which is here expanded to include a press that takes its watchdog mission seriously. What is noir about the film is McNeal's navigation of an officialdom that, if not exactly treacherous, is clearly obfuscating and recalcitrant in its self-satisfied impenetrability, and this is the disappointing correlative to a shabby urban underworld that is home to the working-class poor and petty criminals. An inhabitant of this grim environment, Wiecek is in some ways the typical noir protagonist (framed, like Brad Galt, for a crime he did not commit), but the heroic McNeal is essentially a figure from another genre, the social problem picture, whose narrative characteristically centers around the struggles of a heroic, dedicated individual to right an obvious wrong or ameliorate some galling communal ill.

Kiss of Death, in contrast, centers on the struggles of a more morally ambiguous figure to escape from a life of crime and build a respectable life with his family. Unlike Frank Wiecek, Nick Bianco (Victor Mature) goes to prison because he is guilty of participating in a jewelry

Above, the scene Hathaway is directing on page 116: D.A. D'Angelo (Brian Donlevy) visits Widmark's Tommy Udo and Mature's Nick Bianco in their holding cell in *Kiss of Death.*

store robbery and, though pressured by the district attorney Louie D'Angelo (Brian Donlevy) to turn in his comrades in exchange for a lighter sentence, decides to do his time without complaint because his lawyer, Earl Howser (Taylor Holmes), who is deeply connected to the criminal underworld, assures him that his wife and children will be looked after. But his wife commits suicide after one of his erstwhile partners in crime attacks her and his children are then sent to an orphanage, revealing to Bianco that Howser's promises were worthless. He decides to cooperate with the district attorney in order to get a parole and see his children. His information on the jewelry store robbery no longer useful because of the statute of limitations, D'Angelo arranges for his parole on the condition that he get evidence against a murderous thug, Tommy Udo (Richard Widmark), he met in prison. Before his release, Bianco had been visited by a young woman, Nettie (Coleen Gray), and the two soon fall in love. Back home, he decides to marry Nettie and make a new life. But his new role as in effect a double agent is dangerous and nearly fatal. Bianco eventually gets the evidence on Udo that D'Angelo needs, but Udo realizes that he has been betrayed and sets a trap for Bianco, shooting him several times when the police who are supposed to protect their "plant" arrive too late. Against the odds, Bianco survives to build a life with Nettie, having completed a penitential journey that,

Another posed shot of Widmark in silhouette menacing Coleen Gray and Mature, a stylish arrangement that externalizes the emotional core of *Kiss of Death*'s narrative.

so the film seems to argue, erases his criminal past.

Unlike *The Dark Corner*, *Kiss of Death* focuses on the "real" issues that career criminals face. Unfortunately, the film is saddled with a title that misleadingly evokes the connection between sexuality and death that is a persistent theme in the noir series and is arguably more appropriately descriptive of another Hathaway project, *Niagara*. Bianco agrees to participate in the robbery only because he is down and out and needs the money to finance his family's Christmas. Working with a superb script from two of Hollywood's most noted writers, Ben Hecht and Charles Lederer, Hathaway provides a penetrating and nuanced account of the plea bargaining used by law enforcement to identify and convict those they do not have the good fortune to apprehend. Like many a noir protagonist, Bianco is a divided hero who finds himself trapped between two powerful forces: the police and the district attorney who wish to use him as bait; and his fellow criminals, who care nothing about him except when interested in utilizing his considerable talents. Beyond this dangerous world lies the melodramatic prom-

Below, Bianco deliberately walks into Udo's lair at a local restaurant in *Kiss of Death*.

ise of domestic happiness with the woman he loves and the children whose father he would like to be.

Only by risking everything on betraying his erstwhile colleagues, who have failed to keep their bargain with him, and by cooperating with the police, who care little about his eventual survival, does Bianco escape from the trap in which his own weakness and unfortunate circumstances have landed him. Appropriately, he barely survives an encounter that seems to dramatize his acceptance of the punishment that Udo is eager to mete out to him; he does not flee from the man eager to kill him and, in some sense, for good reason, indicating perhaps that as a criminal, however reformed, Bianco accepts the rightness of this judgment since he knowingly violated a moral protocol that earlier he had stoically upheld at considerable personal cost. In the end, however, the film avoids meditating too deeply on Bianco's ethical quandary. Tellingly, he does not have to give up his actual accomplices, except for Howser, whom the police already suspect. Instead he is set the task of helping to put in jail a criminal of whose pure evil the film provides an unforgettable portrayal. Working his now cooperative double agent, D'Angelo has Bianco inform Howser, his lawyer, that Rizzo, one of his partners in the jewel robbery, has revealed Howser's criminal dealings to the police, a move that the district attorney hopes will help the police apprehend Udo. The plans work perfectly after a fashion since Howser hires Udo to murder Rizzo. But there is unfortunate collateral damage as Udo, going to Rizzo's home, finds the man gone and decides instead, for no reason other than pure psychopathic malevolence, to murder his wheelchair-bound mother (Mildred Dunnock) by pushing her down a flight of stairs.

In a sense, Bianco is responsible for her death, but the film does not explore the connection between his morally ambiguous work for the police and the woman's horrific death. Though he only appears more than forty minutes into the film, Widmark makes an indelible impression as the psychopathic murderer with a spine-chilling and quite insane laugh. Always attired in striking outfits that seem to be labeled "gangster wear," Udo overshadows the other characters, who are less expressively drawn and seem at times to be inhabiting a different universe, a credit to Widmark's over the top performance, reportedly carefully coached by the director. Interestingly, Hathaway's camera does not privilege Udo even in the climactic shootout, and the narrative otherwise remains carefully focused on the less spectacular Bianco, thereby leaving the psychopath a barely explored source of evil, a signpost toward a more deeply noir world of violence and emotional extremes whose outlines the film only barely limns.

Though it is a noir romance whose central themes are illicit passion and betrayal, *Niagara* develops a similar contrast and to better effect, demonstrating Hathaway's impressive command of the full range of styles that characterize the noir movement. Set in the proverbial honeymooners' paradise, the narrative traces the connections that develop between two couples staying at the same tourist lodge. Each pair is out of place at the vacation spot since they are hardly newlyweds, but seek instead, at least ostensibly, to renew relationships that have lost their passion. With its script prepared by a screenwriting team headed by Charles Brackett (famed for his several collaborations with director Billy Wilder), *Niagara* is in essence a melodrama in which an "ordinary" couple, Polly and Ray Cutler (Jean Peters and Casey Adams), who are enjoying a postponed honeymoon in the midst of a business trip, find themselves staying in the same motel as the Loomises, George and Rose (Joseph Cotten and Marilyn Monroe), who are deep into marital crisis. Hathaway makes this clear in an early pair of striking scenes (George soliloquizing in voiceover during an early morning visit to the falls, there to regret what has happened to his life; and Rose turning aside with a look of pure revulsion when he returns to their bed, in need of comforting). As George later confesses to the

Marilyn Monroe in *Niagara*.

astounded Cutlers after an outburst of anger, marrying Rose has ruined his life, leading him to fail at business and then enlist in the Army despite being too old for war; he is tortured by jealousy, certain that Rose has taken other lovers. Polly discovers that this is true enough when, on a tour of the falls, she finds Rose in the arms of another man.

Rose, it turns out, is plotting with her current lover to murder George near the falls, making his death seem a suicide, but this plan goes wrong when George kills him instead and sneaks off in the other man's street clothes. The police think that he has in fact killed himself, but soon afterward Polly spots him near the motel, and Rose realizes the truth when summoned to the morgue to identify a body that is ostensibly that of her husband. George thinks first, as he tells Polly when he seeks her out again as she is visiting the falls, that he will go away and start a new life, but he proves unable to escape the past, sets a trap for Rose, then tracks her down and murders her. Now a wanted man, he tries to escape on a small boat that, as melodramatic chance would have it, has Polly on board. The engine fails, and the two are carried relentlessly toward the falls. George goes over, but only after putting Polly ashore on a rocky shoal, from which she is rescued by a police helicopter and re-united with Ray.

With its carefully detailed location work and the appropriate staging of the story in well-known areas of the resort that gives the film its title, including the carillon tower that plays requests for honeymooning couples, *Niagara* recalls Hathaway's fascination with the docu-noir and its melding of documentary and fictional approaches to storytelling. And yet the film does not so much represent its setting as allegorize it, offering a profound meditation on sexuality that rescues it from the deliberate banality of "Niagara" as a cultural construct, a locus of the temporary sexual overindulgence that prepares the way for a marriage to be lived out in a less intently erotic fashion. Hathaway and Brackett transform the falls into an image of relentless, mysterious, and overwhelming naturalness, a view of the "sight" that opens the film, with Loomis' solitary meditation from the woods below, far away from the resort and its motels, about the way in which the "independence" of the falls, its self-sufficient presence, dwarfs his own attempts to create a life of his own. The camera reinforces this theme as it first finds Loomis walking along the shore in a shot that captures the entirety of the falls, but, then, focusing on his figure, reveals him as microbial in comparison. A cut must then take us to a scale where Loomis dominates the scene, where his voice can be heard, where he can be shown to matter. The contrast between the naturalized meaning of the falls (the place where ostensible tourism makes way for the real mission of honeymooning) and its revealed significance as the objective correlative of an immensely powerful naturalness that, lived out in human relationships, elevates and destroys.

Seeking a renewal of an erotic connection, Rose discovers another kind of sexual force that can literally sweep her away into nothingness. Hathaway presents the connection between sex and death in a stylistically brilliant fashion as Rose, lured from her hotel room by Loomis, who has the carillon play the song that reminds her of her lover, realizes that he will not let her be. At the bus station, where she desperately tries to buy a ticket out of town, Loomis blocks her way, and she flees—inevitably it seems—toward the carillon tower, now empty, whose steps she scales to the very top, there to be found by her husband, who strangles her. This act of fulfillment and disengagement is imaged by a succession of shots of the carillon bells, now silent as the romance they are meant to reinforce has come to an end. An overhead shot from the point of view of the carillons shows us the murder in a now abstract set, crossed by swirling shadows, in one of film noir's most effectively expressionistic images. Hathaway, we might say, in this film makes a strong case that among noir directors he is the master of location—its various meanings, to be revealed by the filmmaking process, as well as its multifarious connections to the characters it contains and defines.

Biography

Henry Hathaway was born in Sacramento, California, in 1898, the son of stage actor and theater professional Rhody Hathaway and the daughter of a Belgian aristocrat who acted under the name of Jean Hathaway. Hathaway was introduced to filmmaking as a child and adolescent, appearing in several Allan Dwan films. Military service in World War I interrupted his acting career. Back from overseas, Hathaway re-entered the film business behind the camera, working as an assistant director during the last decade of the silent era, often under prominent professionals like Fred Niblo, Victor Fleming, and Josef von Sternberg. His first film as a director, *Heritage of the Desert* (1932), was a western, and this was a genre in which Hathaway would excel throughout his long career; his exemplary work for the John Wayne vehicle *True Grit* (1969) helped that actor win an Academy Award. Like all directors in the classical studio era, Hathaway labored on many disparate projects, not all of his own choosing, but he was arguably most successful in inaugurating, with *The House on 92nd Street*, what critics have called the noir semi-documentary. Hathaway, sometimes working with de Rochemont, followed up with a number of similar, well-received noir semi-documentaries: *The Dark Corner*, *Kiss of Death*, and, most notably, *Call Northside 777*. All these films are considered key releases of the postwar noir cycle. Additionally, a number of other Hathaway films with modern settings are more or less noir: *13 Rue Madeleine* (a spy espionage film), *Fourteen Hours* (about a disturbed man's suicide attempt), *Niagara*, *The Bottom of the Barrel* (a melodramatic thriller focusing on the conflict between two brothers), and *Diplomatic Courier* (a Cold War spy thriller shot largely in Trieste). Following the fashion in the 1950s for genre revisionism, Hathaway also made several noirish westerns: *Garden of Evil*, *Rawhide*, and *From Hell to Texas*. His *23 Paces to Baker Street* (a British co-production) is an intriguing, noirish remake of Hitchcock's *Rear Window*, with an effective transference of that thriller's Greenwich Village setting to a postwar London of dangerously unstable bombed-out buildings, and shadowy pubs with dark corners where conspiracies are hatched. Hathaway died in 1985 from a heart attack.

Noir Films

The House on 92nd Street (1945)

The Dark Corner (1946)

13 Rue Madeleine (1947)

Kiss of Death (1947)

Call Northside 777 (1948)

Fourteen Hours (1951)

Rawhide (1951)

Diplomatic Courier (1952)

Niagara (1953)

Garden of Evil (1954)

The Bottom of the Bottle (1956)

23 Paces to Baker Street (1956)

From Hell to Texas (1958)

Left, Hathaway's noir Westerns: *Rawhide* and *From Hell to Texas*. Right, directing *Fourteen Hours*.

Alfred Hitchcock directs Henry Fonda in
The Wrong Man.

Alfred Hitchcock

Geoff Fordham

There is considerable debate among film critics and commentators about the extent to which Hitchcock can be considered a noir director, if at all, and therefore which of his movies should be thought of as falling within the noir canon. Some studies view him as a major contributor to the development of noir style, while others merely acknowledge his influence.

Film noir is defined by common stylistic characteristics and common themes, followed, more or less self-consciously by those making a particular type of movie (mainly) in the 1940s and 1950s, (although of course no one at the time was using the label "film noir"). Those movies which are *unambiguously* noir display a regularity and consistency of form and style, characteristic of the studio system. By contrast, Hitchcock, like other directors to whom the label *"auteur"* has been applied (such as Hawks or Welles), enjoyed great autonomy and independence, which meant that none of his films ever completely conformed to any particular style or genre. Certainly, Hitchcock had a reputation for compulsive planning, every detail emphasizing his directorial control, symbolized of course by his cameo appearances. Underlining this, immediately after his appearance at the start of *I Confess* (set in francophone Quebec,) the camera cuts repeatedly, in close-up, to the French traffic sign *"direction."*

Caughie (in his 1981 book *Theories of Authorship,*) summarizes the characteristics of an auteur as "uniqueness of personality, brash individuality, persistence of obsession and originality," characteristics demonstrated in plenty throughout Hitchcock's work. In particular, these are displayed by his constant reliance on a series of stylistic and thematic preoccupations, evident in work predating any of his movies ever considered to be noir (the earliest of which is probably *Rebecca* in 1940, though there are other contenders) and continuing beyond the last (often claimed to be *Psycho* in 1960). This consistency means that his films have more in common with each other than with those of any particular style or genre.

That said, there is very considerable overlap between Hitchcock's distinctive stylistic and thematic obsessions, and those that later came to characterize film noir. In part these overlaps reflect many common influences: Hitchcock often acknowledged his debt to the masters of German Expressionism (he had worked in Germany in 1925-26 in the studios used by Expressionist directors including Fritz Lang and Robert Wiene) and the montage theory of early Soviet directors, and Eisenstein in particular. Thus, chiaroscuro lighting, highly subjective camera work alternating with wide angles, often shot from below, all form part of Hitchcock's visual signature. Similarly, throughout his career he used standard noir devices like voice-over and flashback among his preferred narrative techniques.

Even if presented in his own inimitable style, the thematic obsessions which characterize Hitchcock's film-making also often formed the staple diet of more conventionally noir movies. For example, many of Hitchcock's films explore the hidden similarities between apparent opposites: appearance and reality, suspicion and trust, and above all, guilt and innocence. In Hitchcock as in noir, the boundaries between good and evil are blurred and ambiguous—

there is no clear moral line to be drawn distinguishing the criminal from the forces of law and order. But in a way that is distinctively Hitchcockian, these antitheses are overlaid, not just with a religious, but an explicitly Catholic sensibility, frequently accompanied by a Catholic iconography. So, we see in Hitchcock films stylistic and thematic elements that are also to be observed in noir movies; but none of his films are ever straightforwardly noir: if noir at all, they are noir with a Hitchcockian twist.

Inevitably critics differ about which film was Hitchcock's first noir, though many accord that honor to *Rebecca,* (including the French critic Patrick Brion, in his 1981 book, *Le Film Noir). Rebecca* provides a perfect illustration of the difficulty categorizing the work of a direcor like Hitchcock. There is certainly much about the movie that is distinctly un-noir. The locations are far removed from the mean streets of a Hammett or Chandler, switching largely between Monte Carlo and a grand country mansion in the remote English countryside. There are no dives or speak-easies, no rain swept streets, no gumshoes with hats shielding their hand-rolled cigarettes. Instead what we have is a Gothic romance, with undercurrents of the horror movie or even ghost story.

Rebecca: below, Judith Anderson as the formidable Mrs. Danvers terrorizes the "new" Mrs. de Winter (Joan Fontaine). Opposite, given a certain context even Nigel Bruce as Major Lacy may seem sinister.

Yet there are powerful noir undercurrents, most interestingly in the form of the eponymous heroine. Rebecca is dead at the start of the movie, yet nevertheless her presence haunts it throughout. When we first learn of her, Rebecca appears to be the most wonderful creature who ever lived, beautiful, witty sophisticated and charming—everything her widower's (Laurence Olivier) second wife (Joan Fontaine) is not. But as the film develops and we learn more about her, the details of her selfishness, infidelity and cruelty emerge. As Olivier's Max de Winter says to his mysteriously anonymous second wife, Rebecca's "...shadow has been between us all the time, keeping us from one another." She becomes one of the most destructive femmes fatales never actually to appear in a noir movie.

Beyond that, in *Rebecca* Hitchcock deploys voice-over and flashback to launch the story, de Winter's involvement in Rebecca's death (and therefore his guilt or innocence) remains ambiguous, and we have a case of mistaken identity when another woman conveniently turns up dead the night Rebecca's body is found. But most importantly, the film chronicles the second Mrs. de Winter's loss of identity—a standard Hitchcock trope—as she struggles inadequately to step into her predecessor's shoes, trying to become something she is not nor can ever be.

Perhaps even more than *Rebecca, Shadow of a Doubt* (made in 1943) demonstrates the problems of attaching labels to Hitchcock films. If, as is often claimed, noir movies display a visual homogeneity, then *Shadow of a Doubt* is not noir. It has been suggested that noir

movies often resemble the visual imagery of a Hopper painting. In contrast, *Shadow of a Doubt* resembles the visual imagery of a Norman Rockwell. Largely set and filmed in Santa Rosa in bright sunlight, the story is staged among an all-American mom and pop family, with two cute kids alongside an elder daughter (Charlie), who together with her similarly named uncle is the film's central character.

But as with Rebecca, behind the non-noir exterior, Hitchcock explores those distinctly noir-ish themes which run through many of his pictures, and in particular the dualism of good and evil. Uncle Charlie (a superb performance by Joseph Cotten) displays a split personality, alternating between the charming and genial, idolized by his sister and his niece, the young Charlie; and a psychopathic misogynist serial killer, who seeks out and murders wealthy widows. But there is a similar duality in the relationship between uncle and niece, highlighted by a series of parallel shots: for example, in separate scenes we see uncle and niece stretched out reflectively on their beds, in both cases the camera tracking through the bedroom window. Uncle Charlie comments on how alike they really are, and young Charlie says to him "But we're sort of like twins. Don't you see?" In his long interview with Truffaut, Hitchcock describes the "telepathy" between young Charlie and her uncle.

Below and opposite *Shadow of a Doubt*: the two Charlies and the rest of the Newtons look at a photo album. Outside, the elder Charlie frowns under the afternoon sun.

Much of the film tracks young Charlie's attempts to confirm her suspicions that her uncle is the "Merry Widow killer," but when we learn that another suspect has been arrested, we start to question whether Uncle Charlie really is guilty, or if his niece's suspicions are simply fantasy. However, as he is leaving town, young Charlie extracts a confession, and exacts a kind of retribution, accidentally pushing her uncle from a train, in self-defense.

With most noir films, evil is out in the open, even if the lighting is dark; in *Shadow of a Doubt,* it lurks behind the conventional facades of a small-town America that Hitchcock recruited Thornton Wilder (author of the play *Our Town*) to help create. The Newtons (young Charlie's family) live a comfortable life of home cooking, church socials and parlor games; her father has a running game with the neighbor about how to commit the perfect crime. As well as these two, the two younger children provide some comic relief, not a customary ingredient of noir films (though always an important ingredient for Hitchcock). But as Uncle Charlie says to his niece: "Do you know the world is a foul sty? Do you know if you ripped the fronts off houses you'd find swine?" The respectability is superficial, but the guilt remains hidden; even after his death, the townsfolk turn out respectfully for his funeral, his guilt remaining a secret shared with his niece.

The last two of Hitchcock's noir offerings to be examined in this essay, *I Confess* (1952) and *The Wrong Man* (1957), both focus on a quintessentially Hitchcock theme: an innocent man caught up in a mystery through mistaken identity (also explored in both versions of *The Man Who Knew Too Much* [1934 and 1955], but probably most famously in *North by Northwest* [1959]). This is a standard noir theme as well, but in these two movies they become distinctively Hitchcockian because of the way the director inserts Catholic imagery and theology.

In *I Confess,* a man dressed as a priest is seen leaving a house where a brutally murdered body is found, and Father Logan (played in a haunting performance by Montgomery Clift) is charged. The real killer, Otto Keller (O. E. Hasse), has confessed to the priest, but the sanctity of the Confessional means he cannot break the confidence.

This theme of the transference of guilt is profoundly Christian, reminding us of the biblical account of Christ's sacrifice for the sins of the world, and in *I Confess* Hitchcock reinforces this, not always with great subtlety, with the context of the story, and also with much of the imagery. For example, in one scene we see Father Logan—Christ-like in his willingness to die for another's sins—walking the streets of Quebec. Flanked by two guards in the foreground, Clift is presented in a long shot in the background of which is a statue of Christ carrying the cross. In the play on which the film is based *(Our Two Consciences),* in fact the priest

I Confess: the priest and the man he knows is guilty but cannot implicate.

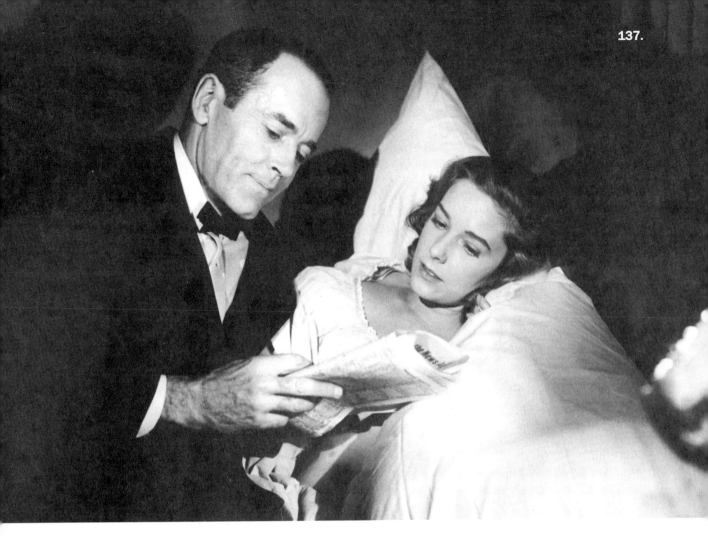

The Wrong Man: Henry Fonda as the title figure comforts his wife (Vera Miles) after the ordeal causes her to suffer a nervous breakdown.

does die at the end, but in Hitchcock's version, Logan is (improbably) found innocent, and it is Keller's wife who dies for her husband's sins. In the last scene, where Keller is shot by the police, (on the stage of a theatre, a characteristic Hitchcock denouement site—*The 39 Steps* as well as both versions of *The Man Who Knew Too Much*), Logan administers the last rites, absolving Keller of his sins.

Compared with other Hitchcock ventures into noir, *The Wrong Man* is closer to conventional noir style: night-time scenes on urban streets, the seedy night-club where the "wronged man" Manny Balestrero (Henry Fonda) works as a musician, dark shadowy lighting, images of prison bars. But as with *I Confess*, *The Wrong Man* is shot through a Catholic prism: when he is arrested, Manny's property is confiscated, but the desk officer returns his rosary. Manny's release from his nightmare is only achieved after, on his mother's instruction, he prays, the camera closing in on a crucifix on the wall. In the next shot an image of Manny miraculously dissolves into a look-alike who turns out to be the real culprit: he is caught red-handed trying to rob a store, and justice is secured.

It's a fine, characteristically dignified performance from Fonda, calmly cooperative, trusting in the integrity of the judicial process, naively believing the police reassurance: "It's nothing for an innocent man to worry about.... If you haven't done anything, you have nothing to fear." But actually, it transpires that an innocent man has plenty to fear, as Manny gets embroiled in an almost Kafkaesque maze of bureaucracy and legal insanity.

The Wrong Man is darker than most Hitchcock fare, as indeed is *I Confess,* and for that reason, Hitchcock was happy with neither. In his long interview with Truffaut he says: "In the mystery and suspense genre, a tongue-in-cheek approach is indispensable. I feel that both *I Confess* and *The Wrong Man* suffer from a lack of humor." And despite what he says—quite correctly—about these two movies, as a rule, this stress on the importance of humor is perhaps the main feature of his work that sets his films apart from the more conventionally noir. Hitchcock pictures typically display a detached amusement, as the director sets elaborate traps to snare innocent victims. While his films contain elements of film noir, they are above all defined by "humeur noir"—black humor.

Hitchcock's own stress on humor and his role as a showman—he described *Psycho* as "a fun picture" which he made with a sense of amusement—have led some critics to question his status as a serious film-maker. For some, like Truffaut (among many more), he is in the front rank of "auteurs" while for others he is a mere technician, more concerned with form and style than content or substance.

As Thomas Leitch has argued (in his 1991 book *Find the Director and Other Hitchcock Games*), there is indeed a strong element of game playing in Hitchcock movies, including those with noir undertones. His characters are engaged in (often highly competitive) games with each other—Uncle Charlie and young Charlie in *Shadow of a Doubt*, or Guy Haines and Bruno Antony in the noir *Strangers on a Train* (1951). He plays often quite cruel games with his characters (the second Mrs. de Winter, Manny in *The Wrong Man*, and quintessentially, Roger Thornhill in *North by Northwest*.) And above all of course, he plays games with us, the audience (among many examples, Norman Bates' alter ego in *Psycho).*

But the games conceal a serious purpose, reflecting a duality in Hitchcock himself, running through all his films, and nowhere more than in those claimed as noir. Partly because of his Jesuit upbringing, Hitchcock embraced a profoundly conservative morality, based on a defense of traditional sources of authority—family, church, police. But he was also deeply conscious of the frailty of those authorities, and keen to show that people are neither as bad nor as good as they initially appear. Through the games he plays in his movies, Hitchcock shows how appearances can be illusory, that apparent identities often conceal something quite different, and that the distinction between guilt and innocence is not clear cut.

Left, *Strangers on a Train*: Bruno Antony (Robert Walker) and Guy Haines (Farley Granger) are two more characters caught up in Hitchcock's narrative games.

Opposite, Hitchcock directs Laurence Oliver and Joan Fontaine in *Rebecca.*

Biography

Alfred Hitchcock was born in London in 1899, the son of a green grocer, and raised as a Catholic, attending St Ignatius, a strict Jesuit school. He began work in his teens as a commercial artist, around 1920 drifting into the film industry, designing the titles for the silent films then being made locally. In 1922 he was invited to finish a film, *Always Tell Your Wife,* when the director fell ill, and from then on he worked full-time in the cinema. He spent a couple of years in the mid-1920s working in Germany, observing the work of Expressionist directors like Murnau and Lang, whose influence he later acknowledged. After a hesitant start, he first achieved recognition with *The Lodger: A Story of the London Fog*, in 1927. In 1929, his *Blackmail* is often thought to be the first British sound feature movie. Throughout the 1930s Hitchcock worked for Michael Balcon at Gaumont-British, making the finest pictures of the British phase of his career, including *The Man Who Knew Too Much* (1934), *The 39 Steps* (1935), and *The Lady Vanishes* (1938). In 1939 he signed a contract with David O. Selznick and moved to Hollywood. His first "American" film was *Rebecca* (1940), winner of the Best Picture Oscar. Hitchcock denied it was truly American as it is set in England, and made with British actors and technicians. He returned briefly to Britain during the war to make a series of propaganda films for the Ministry of Information, resuming his work for Selznick in 1945 to make *Spellbound*, featuring a dream sequence designed by Salvador Dali. In 1948 he broke with Selznick, forming his own, short-lived production company, before joining Warner Brothers, for whom during the 1950s he made *Strangers on a Train* (1951) and *Dial M for Murder* (1954.) In the same year he moved to Paramount, to make *Rear Window* (1954), *To Catch a Thief* (1955), and the re-make of *The Man Who Knew Too Much.* During the late 1950s and '60s he made his best known films, including *North by Northwest* (1959), *Psycho* (1960), and *The Birds* (1963), made for Universal with whom he stayed for the rest of his career. Over the same period, from 1955-65, he introduced 270 shows for TV, called *Alfred Hitchcock Presents.* After that, with his health failing, the volume, and at least for some critics the quality, of his output declined, and he made his last feature film in 1976. He was knighted in 1979, and died in California in 1980.

Noir Films

(Since there is little consensus about which Hitchcock films may be considered noir, the following list is likely to be contentious; noir is in the eye of the beholder.)

Rebecca (1940)
Suspicion (1941)
Shadow of a Doubt (1943)
Spellbound (1945)
Notorious (1948)
Rope (1948)
Strangers on a Train (1951)
I Confess (1952)
Dial M for Murder (1954)
Rear Window (1954)
The Wrong Man (1957)
Vertigo (1958)
North by Northwest (1959)
Psycho (1960)

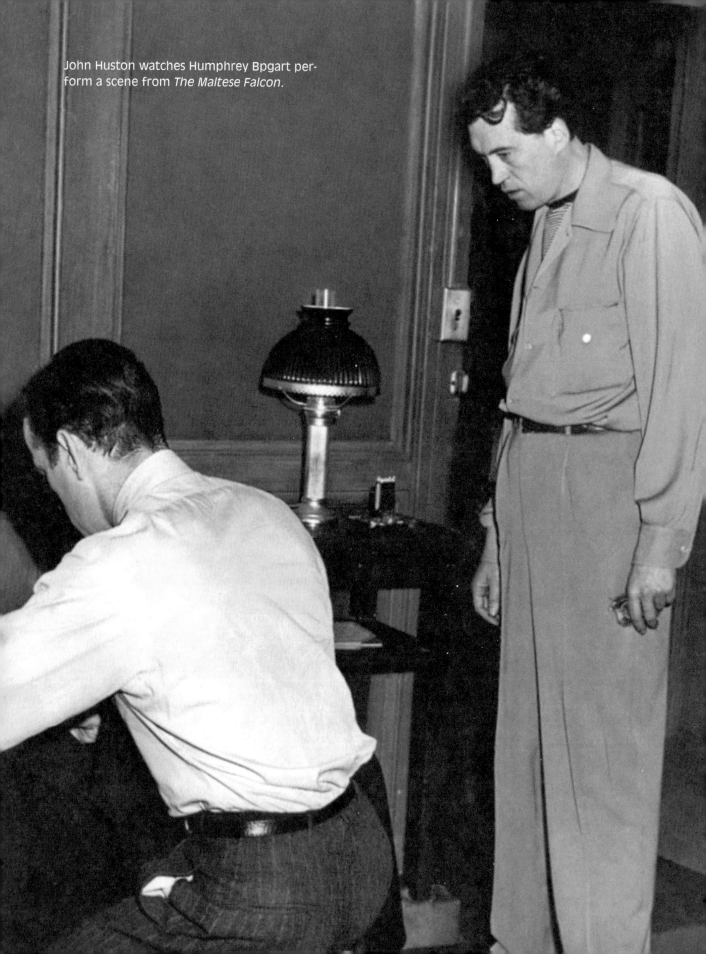

John Huston watches Humphrey Bpgart perform a scene from *The Maltese Falcon*.

John Huston

Willam Covey

A gambler by nature, writer John Huston convinced Warner Brothers to risk letting him direct his first film *The Maltese Falcon* (1941). Much closer to the source novel than the two previous versions made at the studio, Huston's version also benefited from elements he drew from French "poetic realism" films like Marcel Carné's *Le Quai des brumes/Port of Shadows* (1938) and the moodiness of American mystery films which preceded it, like Boris Ingster's *Stranger on the Third Floor* (1940). Huston's film was not only a hit, but has often been hailed as the first Hollywood film noir.

Never strictly a genre director, Huston is better described as a maverick who managed to work both in and out of the Hollywood system on stories about people defeated by illusions. He completed literary adaptations, political, and documentary films such as *The Treasure of the Sierra Madre* (1948), *The Red Badge of Courage* (1951), *Moby Dick* (1956), *The Misfits* (1961), *The Night of the Iguana* (1964), *Wise Blood* (1979), *Under the Volcano* (1984), *We Were Strangers*

Bogart as Sam Spade and Mary Astor as Brigid O'Shaughnessy in *The Maltese Falcon.*

Left, *The Maltese Falcon*: Bogart with the stylized villains portrayed by Peter Lorre and Sydney Greenstreet.

Confronted by the shadowy cops (Ward Bond, left, and Barton MacLane) whose dark foreground figures hem in Spade.

(1949), *Report From the Aleutians* (1943), *The Battle of San Pietro* (1945), and *Let There Be Light* (1946). Despite being rejected by *Cahiers du Cinema* auteurists like Jacques Rivette and Eric Rohmer, André Bazin, in "The Death of Humphrey Bogart," praised Huston, crediting him with inventing the iconic American noir *character* that Bogart first embodied in *The Maltese Falcon* and whom Godard lionizes in *À bout de souffle* (1960).

The lingering influence on American film noir of Bogart's tough, cynical, cigarette-

Right, *The Asphalt Jungle*: as they watch Doc Riefenschneider (Sam Jaffe) check the robbery proceeds, Dix (Sterling Hayden) and Doll (Jean Hagen) make a far more comfortable (and alliterative) couple than Spade and Brigid while sitting on a sofa.

The uniformed cops cannot encircle Dix quite as completely as the detectves did Spade.

smoking, urban loner with a hidden, but strong, moral fiber cannot be overstated. In "The Beam That Fell and Other Crises in *The Maltese Falcon*" Ilsa J. Bick argues that Huston depicted American paranoia and fears of what was happening in Europe during World War II with his "*film-noir*-ish depictions of psychologically divided and tormented men." And, such damaged masculinity continues to be depicted beautifully in post-war noirs like *The Asphalt Jungle* (1950), especially in our sympathy for alienated and damaged criminals like Dix Handley (Sterling Hayden) and Doc Riedenschneider (Sam Jaffe) who, after all, are merely occupied with "a left-handed form of human endeavor."

Huston also created many artful and unforgettable noir scenes such as when just busted criminal Brigid O'Shaughnessy (Mary Astor) in *The Maltese Falcon* is both framed and shadowed in a medium close-up within the metal bars of an elevator door or when elderly Doc in *The Asphalt Jungle* lustfully eyes a teenaged girl gyrating to jukebox music in a diner just before he is caught by the police.

As he had in adapting W.R. Burnett's *High Sierra*, Huston and co-scenarist Ben Maddow underscored the gritty and unglamourous world inhabited by small-timers. Despite being a model for many caper films that followed, *The Asphalt Jungle* is focused on the alienated and desperate characters and not the mechanics of the meticulously planned heist. As with *High Sierra* Burnett's proletarian perspective meshes effectively with the noir perspective, criminals and cops each doing their job and both equally disdainful of Emmerich the crooked lawyer, a

Below, gangsters, moll, and victims, the assembled cast of *Key Largo* questioned by the sheriff.

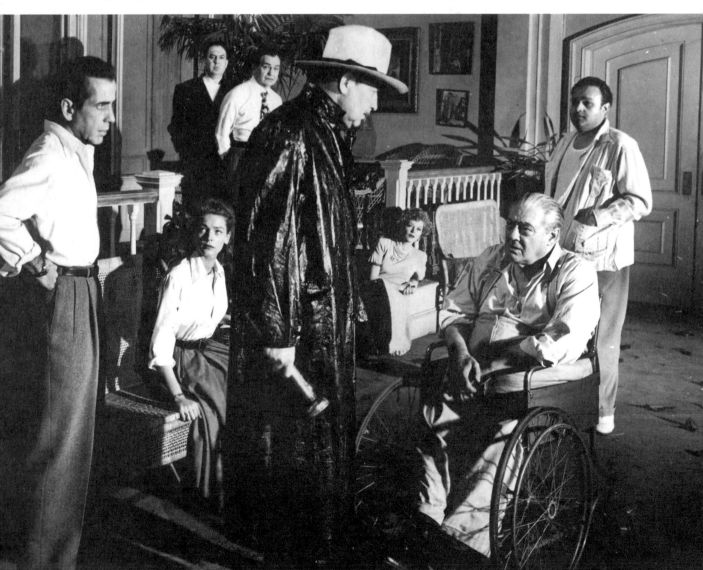

man unlike them who violates the particular code to which he is supposed to be dedicated. Unlike the larger-than-life performances by Bogart as Spade in *The Maltese Falcon* or Edward G. Robinson as Johnny Rocco in *Key Largo*, the core of *The Asphalt Jungle* is naturalistic, in line with the shift in the noir movement from the 1940s to 1950s. All of the criminals are forced to confront their life choices, to ask themselves what they have to show for so many years of trying for a big score. In that

Above, more old grifters: Robert Morley and Bogart in *Beat the Devil.*.

sense, they do share the self-doubt of troubled veteran Frank McCloud (also portrayed by Bogart) in *Key Largo*. What they do not share is his sense of guilt. Like "Mad Dog" Roy Earle in *High Sierra*, Dix Handley leaves the violent milieu suggested in the title and returns to the country to "crash out."

Huston also employs psychological precepts like claustrophobia and isolation underscored by such settings as the cramped offices and hotel rooms in San Francisco and the hurricane-battered lodge to paint a composite of criminals past their prime in both *The Maltese Falcon* and *Key Largo*. While the style of *The Asphalt Jungle* takes elements from both, the oddballs and grotesques are relegated to the periphery, the use of foreground objects and framing still suggest elements in entrapment and predestination.

Huston went on to experiment even more with noir stylistics in spy thrillers like *The Kremlin Letter* and *The Mackintosh Man* or horror films like *Phobia*. Huston infuses dark humor in noir parodies like *Beat the Devil* and *The List of Adrian Messenger*, perhaps best exemplified by the absurd murder attempt sequence on pretentious Harry Chelm (Edward Underdown) in the former film.

This sequence is shot with low-key lighting to create a *chiaroscuro* effect and features various close-ups of struggles and grimaces, all in imitation of film noir stylistics; yet every thrust of the knife and every character's maneuvering is botched to a comic effect that undermines the menace of the scene. Such genre experiments illustrate Huston's interest in criminal situations, the darkness of noir characters, and the various ways that fate—or the stuff that dreams are made of—trip people up. In fact, Andrew Sarris wrote that Huston was expert at illustrating "the universal experience of pointlessness and failure."

Late in his career, and not strictly arriving at the very beginning of the later cycle, Huston's role as Noah Cross in Roman Polanski's *China-town* (1974) remains key to the birth of

Above, wounded noir figures across more than three decades:
Ida Lupino and Bogart in *High Sierra* and Dominique Sanda and
Paul Newman in *The Mackintosh Man*.

neo-noir. Polanski's direction, script, and the nostalgic costumes and settings of the film create a noir homage, but Huston's ability to cheerfully depict an evil patriarch who is involved in sexual proclivities that could only be hinted at in classic noir creates a key character who ensures that this film will help define a new genre. In sum, Huston's life and films follow the multiple interests of an interpretive artist whose cynical detachment and practical joking sometimes mask his close and serious examination of selected evils discovered within humankind. The triumphs and tragedies of his antiheroes who gamble with their lot in the human condition illustrate complex characterizations and thematics.

In an interview with Louise Sweeney in 1973, Huston claims of such characters and themes, "Their defeat is everlasting...and then they recover...It's the fighting heart." Huston's camerawork and mise-en-scène, sometimes employing moving camera, deep focus, or low angles also includes memorable and poetic moments such as when Dix stops to pet his horse in long shot just before he dies of his gunshot wounds at the poignant end of *The Asphalt Jungle*. Though Huston often de-emphasized his own artistic abilities and aspirations, even claiming he had none, he spent the majority of his life, whether in an Irish estate or near the beach at Las Caletas Mexico, reading, writing, painting, and pursuing life adventures that would directly influence his art. In a 1982 PBS interview called

"Creativity with Bill Moyers" the director is asked, "Did you really work hard at studying the techniques of film?" Huston responds. "No, I didn't work at it. just absorbed it....[by] just doing it...I don't think there is a formula. Interest. If your interest is sufficiently alive, you're sufficiently observant." With historical perspective, one sees that, by luck or by plan, Huston was both interested enough and in the right place at the right time, often enough, to create key defining moments in both film noir and neo-noir.

Biography

John Huston was born August 5, 1906 to actor Walter Huston and journalist Rhea (Gore) Huston in Nevada, Missouri. After his parents divorced when he was four years old he became a child vaudeville actor. He was later institutionalized for physical ailments with small hope of leading a healthy life, and yet still managed to sneak out in the evening to strengthen his body through night swimming. He dropped out of high school to pursue a series of passions, including such roles as boxer, beggar, painter, writer, stage actor, and, eventually, successful scriptwriter. Married five times, having survived numerous international adventures, illnesses, and medical procedures, Huston's life story is now legendary, with one era of his adult life even made into a Hollywood film called *White Hunter, Black Heart* (Clint Eastwood, 1990). Suffering from terminal emphysema and a heart condition and working from a wheelchair hooked up to an oxygen tank, Huston died after completing his final film, *The Dead*, on August 28, 1987.

Noir Films

The Maltese Falcon (1941)
Key Largo (1948)
The Asphalt Jungle (1950)

Films with Noir Elements

Beat the Devil (1953)
The List of Adrian Messenger (1963)
The Kremlin Letter (1970)
The Mackintosh Man (1973)
Phobia (1980)

Screenplays

High Sierra (1941)
The Killers (1946, uncredited)
The Stranger (1946, uncredited)

As an Actor

The List of Adrian Messenger (1963)
The Kremlin Letter (1970)
Chinatown (Roman Polanski, 1974)
Breakout (Tom Gries, 1975)
Winter Kills (William Richert, 1979)

Below, Huston with Marilyn Monroe and Lewis Calhern (at right) on the set of *The Asphalt Jungle*.

Fritz Lang with actors Edward G. Robinson and Charles Kemper on the set of *Scarlet Street*.

Fritz Lang

Richard T. Jameson

Would film noir have happened without Fritz Lang? Probably, since so many factors and forces contributed to its flowering. But would it have been as rich and strange, as philosophically provocative and aesthetically exciting? Among the directors associated with film noir, no other possessed a personal vision—both style and worldview—so apt to that cinematic environment.

You could say that Lang had a two-decades-plus head start on noir. During his German Expressionist heyday, from 1921's *Der müde Tod* (*Destiny*) to 1933's *Das Testament des Dr. Mabuse*, he was exploring themes and forms, coining screen language and syntax, and forging an approach to character and ambiguity that would be crucial to the noir world. Perhaps most crucially of all, the power and mystery of Lang's Weimar-era films sprang from a uniquely dynamic symbiosis of narrative and design: story emerged through the recognition of pattern, as character was forged in the struggle against Fate—the ultimate design.

Those films serve as early recon maps of the terrain that would become noir. Most of the major works deal with criminality and shadow societies pervading, underlying, and sometimes flourishing right on the surface of a modern city. Several feature a criminal genius whose powers of disguise and organizational supremacy make him seem ubiquitous, almost supernatural. Sometimes called Dr. Mabuse (though the mastermind in the best of the "Mabusian" films, the 1928 *Spione*, doesn't go by that name), his plots to orchestrate complex capers, undermine national currencies, steal international secrets, and so forth are finally incidental to his primary impulse: to play with the very fabric of contemporary reality. The nature of that reality is suggested by a hallucinatory mise-en-scène in which the décor is at once stark and decadent, a playground for perverse spectacle and gamesmanship, a maze of corridors and doorways and streets where the modern and the Gothic interlayer. There's a pervasive air of paranoia, a nightmare of a world in which chaos and order are opposite sides of the same coin.

Just as striking as the exoticism of these films is the social commentary. Decades before the pop socio-cultural epiphanies of the *Godfather* films in the 1970s, Lang was asserting the essential similarity, even the interchangeability, of the criminal and corporate worlds. *M* (1931) carries out a more extensive dissection of society at large in the course of following the hunt for a serial killer of children. Common organizing principles and parallel behaviors are observed among four

Hallucinatory decor in *Spies.*

Compared to *The Testament of Dr. Mabuse* (left) and *Dr. Mabuse the Gambler* (bottom), the set from *Metropolis* (above) *seems* almost (but not quite) prosaic.

distinct strata of an urban population: the miscellaneous citizenry, the police, the criminal faction, and the shadow army of beggars, peddlers, and street creatures who pass freely among the rest. One night both the police council and the leaders of the underworld hold simultaneous meetings to discuss the crisis; Lang intercuts the two sessions and composes the action so that, say, a question raised by a municipal official is "answered" by a representative of one of the criminal guilds, and a sweeping gesture begun by the chief gangster is completed by the chief of police. Other correspondences are worked into the texture of the film overall. When, in the penultimate reel, enraged members of the underworld's kangaroo court leap on the captured child-murderer in an angular shot and drag him back down a flight of stairs, we recognize the echo of something an hour earlier in screentime: casual passers-by on a city street mistaking a misdemeanor arrest on the top tier of an omnibus for the apprehension of the child-murderer, and swarming the steps in vigilante frenzy. (The criminals give the *Kinder Mörder* a trial; what the ordinary citizens do to their perp is a question left unanswered.)

And yet surely the director's greatest legacy to *noiristes* is stylistic. Lang's style invites voluminous discussion; we'll spotlight two key principles. One of these, unforgettably at play in the early moments of *M*, is something we might call the force of absence or emptiness. More than merely a variation on negative space (of which, to be sure, Lang is also a master), this is an assertive stylistic event, an explicit and at the same time chillingly resonant crystallization of something irretrievably gone missing, or something too awesome to contemplate directly.

M begins with a black screen and the faint sound of a child's singsong voice reciting the nursery rhyme formula whereby one playmate at a time is counted out of a charmed circle. That circle of children is the first thing we see, in an overhead shot of a tenement courtyard—an acceptably realistic yet abstract shot that is portentous even before a mother calls down to protest the grisly chant about the "man in black" who may strike at any time. As the singsong continues nonetheless, that mother returns to her kitchen to await her daughter's return from school. Lang proceeds to intercut shots of the tenement and street scenes in which the daughter is approached by a dark-clad, hatted, effectively faceless figure. He speaks

Peter Lorre in *M*.

to the daughter, buys her candy and a balloon twisted into humanoid form. She is doomed, her death forecast not only by the reward poster about the murderer against which she is tossing her ball, and on which the shadow of the murderer falls as he greets her, but by the way the everyday details of her home environment are presented. The child will not again climb the several flights of stairs to her family's apartment. She will not be there to remove the ring from the napkin her mother has set out in anticipation of the child's afterschool snack. She will not again wear one of the garments drying on the clothesline in an otherwise empty attic. And as her name, called out by her mother, reverberates down those stairs and through that attic space, the child's ball rolls from under some shrubbery, wobbles over a few feet of bumpy ground, and comes to rest. And the balloon, a grotesque simulacrum of life, is seen twitching for a moment under some overhead power lines, then borne off by the wind.

The other principle crucial to Fritz Lang (and much of noir) is the power of the frame, including the motion picture frame itself. Frames trap Lang's characters as his films' plots trap them. In any given shot it is difficult to imagine an actor standing anywhere other than where he stands, relating to camera, movement, architecture, light-and-shadow patterns in any other manner. In the almost entirely studio-created world of Lang's Weimar films, the frame implies an intensely restricted awareness within an intensely restrictive environment. Again,

M affords a definitive example.

Beckert the child-murderer (Peter Lorre) stands on a streetcorner, having just realized that he is being shadowed in the night. Around him, we know from a previous scene, an army of beggars in the service of the underworld are closing the net; but we do not see them in the shot. All we see is Beckert, on the street corner, photographed from a position a few yards down the sidewalk; Beckert stands against the emptiness of an intersection, only the corner of an adjacent building visible at frame right. The whistles of the beggar patrols stab the night as vividly as blades, and with each whistle Beckert leaps a few inches one way or the other, the frame remaining fixed: he can't get out of the shot. Finally he selects a route, in the general direction of the camera, and takes several steps. The camera pans slightly to follow him, bringing into view just a bit more of that nearby wall. Beckert freezes again: there is a man flattened along the wall, watching him. Beckert had already reached the corner; he should have seen someone standing against that wall—should have, by any rule of spatial logic except the one operative here. The motion picture frame is a trap as effective as iron bars or a cordon of pursuers. Within that frame the character is visible, and vulnerable. Just beyond it lurks ... what? The unseen holds power over the seen. And although we in the audience are watchers, although we knew Beckert was being tracked by the beggars before he knew it, we didn't know that that man would be standing precisely *there*. And Beckert's knowledge was not increased until ours was increased.

Images are power; form is power. Elsewhere in *M*, Beckert stands in front of a display window featuring an array of cutlery. A set of blades is arranged in a diamond shape around a diamond-shaped mirror, and as Beckert stares, the mirror frames the face of a schoolgirl also looking in the window. The layers of the spectacle—including the window's own shimmering reflection of the glinting knives—constitute a visual and virtual immersion in the murderer's obsession. It's perfectly realistic and at the same time hallucinatory. This window is a portal of desire, the first of many to come in the cinema of Fritz Lang.

Lang in America

The Fritz Lang who emigrated from Germany after the rise of Hitler forfeited not only national celebrity as a culture hero but also an epic mode of address. *Doktor Mabuse, der Spieler* is in some respects a potboiler, yet its two feature-length parts were respectively subtitled "A Picture of the Time" and "People of the Time." No such pretensions would be made by Lang or any other director of the 1940s and 1950s toiling in the Hollywood vineyards of film noir (even if noir collectively affords a rich and provocative picture of its time and the people congenitally doomed to take one false step in it), and Lang was never to regain anything like the social and professional status he'd enjoyed in Germany. Nevertheless, Lang's personal vision increased in complexity as circumstances forced him to adjust to a new society, a new culture, and a new film industry.

Lang, at far right arriving in America newly signed by MGM, stands next to *David Copperfield* filmmakers: David O. Selznick (producer), Hugh Walpole (screenwriter), and George Cukor (director)

154.

There are resonances to Peter Lorre's performance in *M* in Lang's direction of Spencer Tracy in *Fury*.

The classic noir era was still a decade away when he arrived in Hollywood, yet Lang's first two American productions are indispensable to any accounting of it. *Fury* (1936) introduces a regular American guy (Spencer Tracy as Joe Wilson) who, en route to marry his fiancée (Sylvia Sidney), is detained in a small town on suspicion of being party to an ongoing kidnap-and-ransom plot. The circumstantial evidence is flimsy, but enough to get him locked up for a few hours. Rumors of the capture spread, and soon a motley crowd—local wastrels and upstanding citizens alike—marches on the jail, then sets it afire. From the innocent man's early, first-person sighting of an armed deputy approaching him along the roadside with shotgun extended, through the escalation of the townsfolk's self-righteous bluster to lynch frenzy, to the raucous assault on the jail and then the communal hush at the imminent death of the prisoner, Lang's direction of this whole movement of the film is brilliantly kinetic and unsettling. But it's just the preparation for a still darker second half, when Joe Wilson, having secretly survived the fire and escaped, schemes to have his lynchers put on trial and executed: "They're murderers. That I'm not dead isn't their fault."

Fury was sanctified by reviewers of the day as a work of social consciousness, but its abiding power and interest belongs to the moral symmetry Lang brings to bear and the dynamism of his direction. Joe Wilson's fury is fiercer than the mob passions loosed in the town of Strand, and the most essential drama is internal. The film's structure harks back to Lang's two-part *Die Nibelungen* (1924), with the pure white bride of *Siegfrieds Tod* replaced by/revealed in the increasingly dark, ferociously garbed, lethally vengeful widow in *Kriemhilds Rache*. And just as Kriemhild must destroy most of the visible world in order to purge a past crime, so must Joe lose self and soul in order to regain them. In describing his escape from the jail, he says, "I almost burned my side off. I could smell myself burn." He also speaks of having sat in a newsreel theater and watched himself getting burned alive. In a sense, it's an experience his would-be victims share, horrified to recognize animalistic, freeze-frame portraits of themselves as the prosecutor has newsreel footage of the mob violence projected in the courtroom.

Joe's implacable hatred finally estranges him from even the few loved ones aware of his survival. Wandering alone in empty night streets straight out of *M*, he's haunted by phantom images of the 22 citizens whose death warrants he has signed, and he flees, pursued by phantom footsteps. His ultimate decision to stride into the courtroom and reveal that he is still alive has nothing to do with compassion or forgiveness. He is a walking dead man in that his former idealistic notions of justice and decency, and belief that "my country was different from all the others," have been destroyed. Joe Wilson's declaration to the court is scrupulous in its moral distinctions and unflinching in its bitterness. Despite an infamous, studio-mandated intrusion at this point—which in a matter of seconds shifts Joe's tone to mealymouthed contriteness ("Maybe after I've paid for what I've done...") and tosses in a closing clinch with his fiancée—*Fury*'s insights into human nature and institutional corruption remain on record, unanswered, unalleviated, and primed to resonate through the film noir cycle in years to come.

Lang's next film, *You Only Live Once* (1937), was also taken in some quarters as social-consciousness exemplum, a parable of how ex-convicts can't catch a break from a society that won't let them go straight. The thesis may apply, but Lang's interests, sympathy, and artistry transcend any such agenda. The terms of the film are elemental. The movie abounds in obstructions of vision: bars, shadows, corners and hard angles, smoke, rain, gas, fog stabbed by lights that only emphasize its impenetrability, restrictive frames that open up horribly to increase our knowledge (a caustic newspaper scene that begins on a close-up of an edition announcing the acquittal of a man on trial, pulls back to reveal *three* editions ready to accommodate any jury outcome, and then closes on the conviction headline).

The first scene includes a modest joke in best *Lehrstück* tradition, a viewing instruction for the audience. Joan Graham (Sylvia Sidney), the Public Defender's secretary who's about to marry convict Eddie Taylor (Henry Fonda) when he's freed later that day, opens the door to her boss's inner office and says, "I don't believe it, the District Attorney and the Public Defender holding hands!" Lang pans from her grinning face to the attorneys, and we see that one man is merely lighting the other's cigarette, though from Joan's angle of vision the wisecrack would have made sense. For Lang's purposes the joke is two-pronged—underscoring the collegiality of "the system," for one thing, but also, more importantly and pervasively, keynoting the concept of point of view and its limitations.

Having issued fair warning, Lang proceeds to set a trap. He establishes the decency of Eddie and Joan, enlists sympathy for their dreams of a home and future (much like those of *Fury*'s Joe Wilson and his girl), portrays several examples of prejudice and small-mindedness directed against them, and generally disposes the audience to be so favorable toward the well-meaning ex-con that we become virtual advocates. And so when Eddie, after a series of rude and mostly unwarranted setbacks, bitterly storms offscreen apostrophizing, "And I wanted to go straight!" we sadly accept that he's been forced back into a life of crime. And here Lang stages one of the great set pieces of his career, a bank armored car robbery in the rain. As the camera closes in on an automobile parked near the bank, a window rolls down an inch to reveal two staring eyes; then a hat bearing the monogram "E.T." on the band is laid on the

"One of the bleakest of Lang's films," *You Only Live Once*: a barely perceptible visual irony, Eddie's medal on the dresser. Opposite, the performance of Silvia Sidney and Henry Fonda set the standard for the many fugitive couples of film noir's classic period.

car seat, a hand lifts a gas mask to the occupant's face, and all hell breaks loose. Next thing we see is Eddie, slinking into his own house looking guilty as sin and pulling a gun at the first sound from outside. "The bottom's dropped out of everything," he sobs to Joan, and it's a damn shame because, even though what he did was wrong, we understand what led him to do it. Except that *he didn't do it*. Lang springs his trap: Eddie has been guilty of nothing, the robbery was carried out by his old cellmate, the hat had been stolen and deliberately planted. Like the society that will now try and convict him, we took Eddie's guilt for granted, and there's no consolation in having done so with the best of intentions.

After the process of convicting and imprisoning Eddie—compressed into a montage as strong as a chain—he is locked in a death-row cell, the pinned focus of the alternating rays of harsh light and blackest shadow radiating through the bars. Eddie's lost even his soulmate Joan, who had urged his surrender to the police, and who he believes ignored his single plea, for a gun to aid his escape. He's wrong about that, and will be fatally wrong again when he fails to believe the one man who always kept faith with him, the prison chaplain Father Dolan

(William Gargan). At the very moment of his exoneration—the truth about the armored car robbery having been discovered and the news of a pardon for Eddie Taylor ticking across a black screen somewhere on a narrow white ribbon of tape—Eddie makes a bad call, shooting Father Dolan, and becomes the killer everyone thought he was all along.

You Only Live Once is among the bleakest of Lang's films, but also the most compassionate. Here as never before (apart from a few quasi-pagan gestures in *Metropolis*), the director invokes religious authority and specifically Christian archetype. Father Dolan intercedes twice for the Taylors, first to cover for Joan when the gun she is smuggling to Eddie sets off a metal detector, and then for Eddie himself, trapped in the fog of the prison yard and of his hard-earned cynicism. With his dying breath Dolan calls for the prison gates to swing open, and they do, spectrally. The moment anticipates the film's final image, after the Taylors have fled Bonnie and Clyde–like into the harshest of heartlands, toward a border that can never be reached, only transcended. You only live once.

Lang made four war-related thrillers in the 1940s, beginning in 1941 with *Man Hunt*, a notable critical and commercial success; followed by *Hangmen Also Die* (a collaboration with fellow émigré Bertolt Brecht) and *Ministry of Fear*; and ending with the mostly negligible *Cloak and Dagger* (1946). These present a challenge to the film noir purist. The first three titles abound in danger, atmosphere, stylistic and formal intensity, striking set pieces, and more spiritual and moral ambiguity than customarily found in World War II films of espionage and intrigue—but are they noir? Even prematurely noir (as in "prematurely antifascist")? For the moment, we take the position that only one of them migrates into the psychically precarious and stylistically addictive noir zone.

Much as we love it, that's not *Man Hunt* (1941), a 20th Century–Fox production from Geoffrey Household's hit novel *Rogue Male*, which Lang succeeded in making his own despite the studio's having first assigned the picture to John Ford. Still, there are portents of noir, aspects of theme and narrative worth noting in our present inquiry.

Opening "somewhere in Germany" with a (subjective or objective?) camera insinuating its way through a very primeval-looking forest, the movie follows its protagonist's journey of awareness across pre-war Europe and into his own moral and political soul. The title, applicable to so many Lang pictures, first and last refers to English big-game hunter Alan Thorndike (Walter Pidgeon) stalking Adolf Hitler, and in between—the main body of the film—his own pursuit by sundry Gestapo and fifth-columnists. Thorndike's hunt begins as a "sporting stalk," with the Englishman lining up der Führer in his telescopic sight (recalling the finale of *You Only Live Once*) and pulling the trigger on an empty rifle. Then he realizes that "playing the game" requires that a bullet be in the chamber, with only his civilized restraint between his target and extinction. Jumped at that instant by a Berchtesgaden guard, Thorndike can't convince the resident SS man (George Sanders) that he isn't on assignment from the British Government to assassinate the leader of Germany.

The film is Germanic to the max, with imagery of fierce angularity and rich chiaroscuro, literally underground confrontations, and a scenario rife with doppelgängers and secret selves. The torture of Thorndike at Berchtesgaden, his botched "accidental" death in a landscape reminiscent of *Die Nibelungen*, his escape by ship to England (stowed away while a Gestapo man travels freely above board in his name), cat-and-mouse games in foggy London, consolation and (rejected) love from a gutsy little prostitute (Joan Bennett), and ultimately his becoming a fugitive from the police for his own murder (i.e., that of the Gestapo man using his identification papers)—all lead to Thorndike's accepting the possibility that maybe he did want to pull that trigger in Bavaria after all.

Alan Thorndike (Walter Pidgeon) making his escape from Nazi Germany in *Man Hunt*.

Hangmen Also Die: The grandfatherly Alexander Granach as Gestapo Agent Gruber smiles as he prepares to "interrogate" a trussed-up Jan Horal (Dennis O'Keefe), left, and again as he introduces Hasha Novotny (Anna Lee) and Dr. Svoboda (Brian Donlevy) to a couple of SS troopers.

Lang's next anti-Nazi thriller, *Hangmen Also Die* (1943), likewise cannot be deemed noir, but it's fascinating for the way history was catching up with and emulating Langian archetype. The setting is Prague, Czechoslovakia, where the previous year Czech partisans assassinated Reichsprotektor Reinhard "Hangman" Heydrich and the Gestapo responded with massive reprisals. In a dynamic variation on the urban phantasmagoria of the *Mabuse* films and *Spione* and *M*, the underworld is replaced with the Underground, the occupied people of Czechoslovakia gathered into "a shadow army sworn to haunt [the Nazis] till their blood runs cold." Much of the picture is concerned with how the Underground frames one of their number, a Quisling, for the murder of the Hangman; the man is trapped by the same sort of circumstantial evidence that enmeshed the sympathetic protagonists of *Fury* and *You Only Live Once*. There's a subtle ambivalence tunneling under the movie, which, though unwaveringly on the side of the resistance forces, acknowledges how they agonize over their culpability in jeopardizing hundreds of innocents taken hostage as part of the reprisals. The moral-ethical duality extends to the casting, and audiences' response to it: the "good guys" are mostly ho-hum Central Casting types, while the Nazis, evil incarnate, are juicily portrayed by a passel of German-Jewish émigrés who relish the opportunity to skewer their own oppressors while playing them—and to act up a German Expressionist storm in Hollywood exile.

One of those émigrés is Hans von Twardowski, who had played a murder victim 23 years earlier in *Das Kabinett des Doktor Caligari* and plays another here: Heydrich. Though his time on screen is necessarily brief, his departure is unforgettable—a supreme instance of Lang's genius for narrative negative space. After terrorizing an assembly of Czech toadies, Heydrich intends to do more of the same to the workers at the Skoda factory. As he strides out to climb into the backseat of his open car, the camera is shooting over the rear of the vehicle. Von Twardowski turns his hawklike profile to the camera and barks "Skoda!" As he holds that pose, his escorts rev their motorcycles—and then, as engines rumble, *no one and nothing moves*. After an electrifying suspension, the shot dissolves to a Prague side street where a taxicab quietly idles. In the uncounted interval covered by the dissolve, the shooting of the Hangman has been accomplished. The fare for whom the cabbie waits is the assassin.

With *Ministry of Fear* (begun in 1943 but not released until after *Woman in the Window* early in 1945) we cross the noir frontier. The film follows a traumatized patient, newly released from a mental asylum in the English countryside, into a war-torn world of bombings, intrigues in the dark, multiple identities and multiple betrayals, and the tentative possibility of a new life. The source was Graham Greene's novel of the same name, which Lang had attempted to buy in order to produce a film of it himself. Outbid by Paramount Pictures, he ended up being hired to direct. Irksomely, his contract obliged him not to tinker with the studio-approved script (by Seton I. Miller, who was also the producer). The finished film bears only glancing resemblance to the Greene original that had caught Lang's interest, starting with the exoneration of the film protagonist for what had led to the book protagonist's spending two years in a sanitarium: the mercy killing of his terminally ill wife. But some of what's invented is excitingly apt and flavorful, and hair-raisingly successful in conveying an off-kilter world for the lead character and the audience to move through in something like shell shock.

Knowing the backstory of the production, we can't help but feel amazed at how essentially Langian the movie is. The quaint little country fair Stephen Neale (Ray Milland) visits within moments of leaving the asylum happens to be utterly faithful to the book, yet the director takes possession the instant Neale is greeted at the gate by a blond girl's bouncing ball. A huge hand, also reminiscent of *M*, stands enigmatically outside the fortune-teller's tent, along with a Wheel of Fate. It is Neale's fate to impulsively ask a certain question of the frumpy palm read-

Ray Milland as Stephen Neale with Marjorie Reynolds as Carla in *Ministry of Fear*.

er, and thereby be mistaken for the man who is supposed to be told the winning weight of a cake being raffled off outside. It will be learned, much later, that the cake contains microfilm of British coastal defense secrets. For the moment, it gets Neale stared at by a yard full of quaint English characters who are suddenly standing very still. And a few moments later, it nearly gets him killed in a railway compartment during an air raid, by a blind man Graham Greene never met, but who, like other blind men in the films of Fritz Lang, can see.

Lang's visual penchant for paganism infects the film, most notably during Neale's visit to the London home of Mrs. Bellane the fortuneteller—though she turns out to be another, much more imposing Mrs. Bellane (Hillary Brooke): a dark goddess, framed between two white columns and two black urns surmounted by crescents, who presides over a séance bringing 20-year-old echoes of *Doktor Mabuse, der Spieler*. The aura of something occult, cut-rate or otherwise, entirely displaces Greene's (and Lang's) Catholicism and encourages us to share an almost primitive awe in shapes and forms: the circle of the séance, and dis-

Ministry of Fear: the publicity pose uses the Swastika as political and pagan symbol and also recalls the "crucified" posed of figures in *Metropolis*.

embodied hands luminous in the darkness; the triangular arrangements of candles; the odd translucent window in the door to a dusty detective agency where Neale goes seeking help; the central circular image of that cake, keynoting the film's environment even after it's been blown to bits.

Throughout, Lang rarely brings the camera close to his characters. Get close and you banish space. The entirely soundstage universe of *Ministry of Fear* (even the country fête and the landscape outside the bombed railway train are clearly constructs) is hermetically sealed against vagrant reality, but it does have rooms and corridors and spaces—and people are contained by spaces as much as by corners and frames. Lang's exact judgment about space and camera distance pays off beautifully in two setups in a corridor of the hotel where the movie's climax occurs. When Stephen Neale gets off the elevator, we see enough of the hall that this mundane setting takes on some of the monumentality of the heroic backgrounds in *Die Nibelungen*. And when, attempting to escape a few minutes later, he starts for that elevator, there is enough space around it for us to appreciate the framing UP lights flashing on—a signal that pursuers are on the way, and a throat-grabbing touch whose provenance reaches back to *Metropolis* and the great machine metamorphosing into luminous-eyed Moloch.

And, as ever, there are those many, many doorways, in which people stand and are measured and measure other people and their chances. Lang may have had reservations about the mashed-up story Paramount had given him to tell, but the single greatest argument for Lang's authorship is the thoroughgoing consistency with which he maps the film's itinerary by way of doors—this image, this commonplace fact of life, this link between lives and living-spaces, between the known and the not-yet-suspected, between sanctum and jeopardy, custody and liberty. Consider the introduction of the second- and third-most-important characters in the film, the siblings Hilfe, Carla (Marjorie Reynolds) and Willi (Carl Esmond). European refugees, they operate a wartime charity, the Mothers of the Free Nations; the fête was a project of theirs. Stephen Neale first sees them in high-key through a darker doorway, the two leaning together, incestuously close and secretive, giggling over a shared understanding. Consider that, and the progression to another doorway, one opening out of an absolutely black-dark room, and Willi's last self-confident verbal caress of the dear sister he has by now betrayed. We see him briefly against a rectangle of light, then blackness again; a gunshot: and a single dot of white, off-center on the screen. Decisively, film noir has arrived.

The Woman in the Window (1944) is among Fritz Lang's subtlest films, eschewing epic flourishes in favor of carefully worked texture that suggests everyday reality but is actually quite stylized. Richard Wanley (Edward G. Robinson), a mild-mannered assistant professor of psychology alone in Gotham for a few weeks while his family summers upstate, is pleasantly startled to encounter the flesh-and-blood model for the beautiful portrait on display in the gallery window near his club. Her name is Alice Reed (Joan Bennett) and both of them are agreeable to a platonic late-night drink. When the lady's brutal financier lover shows up unexpectedly at her apartment and attacks them, the professor kills the man in self-defense with a scissors Alice hands him. The innocent assassins resolve never to see each other again, and Richard dumps the corpse in an isolated woods off the northern parkway, hoping that that will be the end of the matter. No. Soon Richard experiences the exquisite torment of being invited along by his best friend Frank (Raymond Massey)—the district attorney!—as an observ-

Woman in the Window: Richard Wanley (Edward G. Robinson), murder weapon in hand, bends over the body of the wealthy lover of Alice Reed (Joan Bennett). At the same time, he is reflected in the mirror by the fireplace.

er on the case. Then the financier's bodyguard (Dan Duryea), as unsavory as his late employer, shows up at Alice's place, raising the specter of blackmail and, beyond that, murder and suicide. That story is grippingly told in the first hour-and-a-half of the movie. What follows in the final few minutes is the revelation that most of it was a dream Wanley had after dining at his club and discussing "the woman in the window" with Frank and another friend. Some viewers and commentators have reflexively denounced this tactic as a cop-out, a way to have a gratuitous happy ending: it's only a dream, so nothing matters and anything goes. That kneejerk criticism is precisely wrong. In this movie, virtually *everything* matters, doubly so *because* it's a dream.

Woman in the Window is full of mirror reflections and Robinson in effect plays his own double. What is remarkable, in the context of Lang's work, is how very unremarkable a guy Richard Wanley is—no compulsive child murderer he; even his aberrant dream-behavior is directly traceable to the most petty and mundane of resentments about the world out there. The dream itself is a suffering/learning experience, with emphasis on minor yet symbolic instances of pain, a more everyday analog of *Fury*'s Joe Wilson watching himself burned alive in a newsreel.

In a bathroom full of reflective surfaces, Reed watches Wanley as he cleans the scissors.

Of course, Lang sees to it that reality is already layered with unreality before the dreaming sets in. Peering at the painting on the way to his club, Wanley joins a long line of Lang dreamers who have looked in display windows and seen the reflection of their desires or their fears. The woman is not a woman but a painting—one man's vision of the woman, now being filtered through the sensibility of a second man. The painting is framed, and it is set apart from Wanley by the further frame of the window. The window reflects Wanley when he looks into it, and when he is viewed from the other side of the glass, the painting is reflected over him.

This is a good movie on first sight and a better one in reflection. On a second viewing we are in a position to appreciate how much and in what terms Wanley is the architect, the director, of his fantasy. Incidental to the suspense plot, Wanley the dreamer awards himself an unlikely academic promotion from assistant professor to chairman of his department. He also promotes himself romantically. He has his D.A. chum theorize that the woman in the case clearly preferred him to the victim (the Mabuse-like magnate of World Enterprises!), as has been demonstrated by her connivance and silence on the killer's behalf. (Edward G. Robinson's registering of this speculation is one of the loveliest moments in the annals of screen acting.)

Yet Wanley—an honest dreamer—manifests a sense of inferiority that is worked out ambivalently. Attacked and overpowered by the large Claude Mazard, Alice's lover, he manages to kill him anyway. He defends Alice, forgives her failures time and again, but he dreams her getting pushed around by Mazard and by the bodyguard. We are shown at

As if in a dream, Wanley first sees Reed reflected in the window, then a wide shot reveals her objectively standing in front of it.

Above, Wanley outside in the rain creates another example of multiple sight lines and distortions in *Woman in the Window*: there are water streaks over his cheek and Reed's reflection looks back at her, while the entire frame is divided into two panels with separate figures. Opposite, Bennett and Robinson locked into another twisted relationship in *Scarlet Street*.

the end that the visual prototypes of Mazard and the bodyguard exist at Wanley's club in the respective forms of Charlie the hatcheck man and Ted the doorman. But why were *they* selected by Wanley to play snarling villains? Both seem to be perfectly nice guys, but they're taller than Wanley, both wear uniforms, and both serve the function of servants. Wanley is frequently menaced by uniformed figures (patrolmen, a toll collector who delays him, a motorcycle cop) and by other "public servants" and private ones.

But the key antagonist in Wanley's waking life appears to be his own best friend, District Attorney Frank Lalor, about whom Richard probably has never had one conscious critical thought. All we see, really, is that Frank is, again, taller than Richard, that he has facetious first claim on their "dream girl" (the painting), and that he embodies that stuffy sense of safety and propriety Richard respects, believes in, even shares, but also ruefully resents. Frank's casually low-angle authority sitting in a club easy chair escalates into the towering, smoke-streaming beacon of justice leaning against the mantel above tiny Richard, and by extension into every God's-eye-view of Wanley that pins him down. Although doubling of first names is not at all uncommon in life, it's a rarity in movies; the pseudonym under which Claude Mazard is first introduced is Frank Howard. Moreover, Mazard wears the same sort of straw boater first seen on Frank Lalor, and subsequently worn by both the bodyguard and a man who interrupts a very interrupted rendezvous tête-à-tête between Richard and Alice.

Of course it's quite possible—inevitable, on first viewing—to watch *Woman in the Window* as straightforward psychological suspense movie and spellbinding film noir. The film does "happen" with absolute cinematic reality, and Prof. Wanley's waking from his dream in no way denies the finality of the dream scenario's grim outcome. But one of many doppelgänger aspects to this movie is that it tells two stories, not one. Lang even has a joke about the game he's playing: Wanley sits at his desk, a warlike statuette poised nearby as if about to spear the wrist he has already twice wounded in the course of the action, while a radio announcer hymns the blessings of a product that will "remedy that tired feeling" that "can affect a person's whole outlook on life."

Scarlet Street (1945) is a movie of such density and interlocking detail, so completely imagined and then fed through a camera and made to come out precisely as it needed to, that watching it you shake your head again and again and wonder how he did it. In fairness, "he" is a collective term here. There's Fritz Lang, but also Dudley Nichols, the John Ford writer with whom Lang had been brought together on *Man Hunt* several years earlier, and who wrote the director the most meticulously developed script he would ever shoot. Add Milton Krasner, who had photographed *Woman in the Window*, its streets silvered with dream rain, and who lights even more memorable streets here. The *Woman in the Window* stars are back, too: Edward G. Robinson, at his absolute peak in 1944-45 (what with the two Langs plus playing

Barton Keyes in Wilder's *Double Indemnity*); Dan Duryea, who had died twice for Lang in *Ministry of Fear* (the second time among a forest of mirrors and on the handiest approximation of a Roman sword); and Joan Bennett, also first paired with Lang on *Man Hunt*, and the wife of producer Walter Wanger, whose civility and supportiveness on *You Only Live Once* Lang so appreciated. It was a good group. Lang, Bennett, and Wanger went so far as to form a production company, Diana (to which Nichols also signed on), and Diana made *Scarlet Street* at Universal-International. It stands as Lang's American masterpiece.

The film centers on the fatal liaison between Christopher Cross (Robinson), an unassuming little man who's been desiccating for 25 years in a cashier's cage, and Kitty March (Bennett), a tawdry wench he saves from a brute (Duryea) late one night on an otherwise deserted street. The brute is, to eyes more worldly than Chris', clearly Kitty's pimp and lover, and he proceeds to orchestrate, mostly from offstage, her milking of the infatuated older man for every buck they can get. They take Chris for a wealthy artist, and it's true that he devotes his Sundays to setting up an easel in his apartment bathroom and painting (to the exasperation of his shrewish wife Adele). He's gifted, too, though he doesn't know it and never signs his work. Eventually, after Kitty has offered to let Chris rent her a Greenwich Village apartment where he can keep his pictures and paint new ones, Johnny leaves some of Chris' "pipe dreams" with a street vendor. Seen in public for the first time, the paintings catch the eye of a celebrity art critic, who tracks down the new genius who created them...which seems to be one Katherine March. As the immediately smitten critic tells Kitty, "Your work is not only original, it has a masculine force!"

Chance encounters lead the characters portrayed by Bennett and Robinson to share a late night drink in both *Woman in the Window* (above) and *Scarlet Street*. The latter venue is a bit more downscale, but the noir narrative is kick started in both movies.

That only begins to suggest the film's reservoir of perverse psychology, the blurrings of gender and identity, the twisted sort of logic that swallows its own tail in the course of one dialog exchange, sometimes a single sentence. (Far from being outraged that his work has been attributed to Kitty, Chris is exultant: "It's just like we were married, only I've taken *your* name! Well, this gives me a little authority around here...") Such a description also omits the element of crime, with Chris stealing from his wife or embezzling from his company's safe, and of course

the growing tensions in the film's two sadomasochistic pairings that will end by destroying three lives. No one ever made a darker noir.

A source of special fascination is that in *Scarlet Street* Lang often seems to be meditating on his own art. Chris explains his untutored method to Kitty: "I just put a line around what I feel when I look at things." Chris misses seeing a lot (he has "a little trouble with perspective"), but it's amazing what he takes in and transforms. The black purse ringed with white dots Kitty is toting when Chris first sees her, the orange slices on the rum Collins drinks she orders for them, even the jewel-like drops of rain arcing out from Chris' umbrella as he twirls it shortly before meeting her, all find their way onto Chris' canvases, transmuted, exalted—and more often that not, with their black-and-white values reversed.

Art is ubiquitous in the movie: genuine art, phony art, accidental art, décor as art/art as décor. As Chris stands in his bathroom atelier painting a flower Kitty gave him and translating it into something otherworldly, he's surrounded by flowered wallpaper of suffocating banality. The Cross family dining room is dominated by a pseudo-painting ("mud," Chris terms it), an enlarged photograph of Adele's first husband—with his for-real posthumous medal for bravery pinned to it. Such attention to art and kitsch at war is intensified in the design of the apartment Chris rents for Kitty. A triumph of Universal-International art director Alexander Golitzen, it's a near-funhouse playground of glass separations (with etched foliage patterns), mirrors, split levels, and outside balcony, with the additional embellishment of rough sketches by the former tenant, a successful commercial artist, still adorning the walls.

"Ubiquitous art": above Johnny (Dan Duryea) wants an appraisal on Chris Cross' work from a disinterested dealer. Below, Johnny instructs Bennett's Kitty to take a brush and sign a canvas,

Below, there are also reflections in *Scarlet Street*: Kitty and her mirror image both laugh at Chris when he announces that he is free to marry her.

Art and reality keep up a free exchange. A shot of Johnny skulking, speckled with leaf shadows, under the porch steps in front of Kitty's apartment dissolves to one of Chris' paintings: the giant serpent twining through the grillwork of the Greenwich Village el train, its scales echoed in the cobblestone street, while Kitty stands angelically in the cone of light from a street lamp (protected as though by Chris' umbrella). This is Chris' flashback rendering of the moment he first saw Kitty and her attacker, but it also prefigures his own moment as a skulker under stairs, after he has consummated his relationship with Kitty the only way he could, by killing his object of obsession. About to leave her building on the fatal night, he takes cover when an angry Johnny comes bursting in, arriving just in time to be blamed for her murder. Johnny elbows a jagged hole in the opaque door glass as he passes, and the door becomes abstract art, the globe of a street lamp revealed within the hole just so.

So much to be said about such a provocative and endlessly ambiguous film. We'll end with this. Deep into his thrall with Kitty, Chris is presented with a way out of his stifling marriage. Homer, Adele's late first husband, proves not to be late after all, and when he suddenly shows up offering to stay away permanently for a few hundred bucks, Chris proposes to let him into their apartment so that he can steal Adele's savings. Although he tells Homer that Adele will be away, Chris knows otherwise, and knows that Adele will catch and keep the husband she wished she hadn't lost. And so he signals to Homer from the window, with a flashlight, up-down and then laterally. This deception is the one work of art he signs. Criss cross.

Below, *Secret Beyond the Door*: newly-wed Mark Lamphere (Michael Redgrave) gets bit a moody when he returns from Mexico with his wife Celia (Joan Bennett). Opposite, in their last collaboration Bennett strikes one last pose before a mirror for Fritz.

Following this chef d'oeuvre, Lang's next excursion into noir was the almost unmitigated disaster *Secret Beyond the Door* (1948), which killed Diana Productions and marked the director's final collaboration with Joan Bennett. Her role, Celia, is that of a slightly aging pre–JetSetter who impetuously "marries a stranger," an architect named Mark (Michael Redgrave) whose path she has crossed in Mexico. She soon discovers him to be a man of many secrets, a widower with a son he neglected to mention and the more-than-eccentric habit of "collecting" rooms where murders took place. It's only a matter of time until Celia learns another has been added along his creepy corridor: a replica of her own bedchamber.

The essential story idea, of a sort it was once allowable to term women's-novelettish, was probably irredeemable from the get-go; Lang's decision that the movie should have an overripe running voiceover by Bennett's character sinks it further. The film is both a specimen and a casualty of the postwar penchant for "Freudian" mysteries susceptible to instant cures for the troubled central character; Lang brazenly emulates Hitchcock's *Spellbound* of several years earlier, borrowing Miklós Rózsa to score and Disney animators to provide some dream imagery à la Salvador Dalí's contributions to the Hitchcock picture. It doesn't help that by far the movie's best scene occurs in the first reel, when Celia becomes mesmerized by a knife fight over a woman in a sun-blasted Mexican bazaar. Here, as throughout the film, cinematographer Stanley Cortez supplies his signature ink-black shadows and milky whites, and Lang adds one of his inimitable touches, a flock of pigeons exploding up from the cobblestones and then settling again as the two men begin circling each other. Quite unexpectedly, one of the men suddenly throws his knife, underhand, and it pins Celia's sleeve to a post. It also pins Mark's gaze on Celia for the first time. Can love be far behind?

The next Lang picture sometimes designated noir, and opportunistically marketed as such in the DVD age, is the *Clash By Night* (1952). This is basically a straightforward drama, set in a maritime community, of the emotional lives of some half-dozen characters—notably those played by Barbara Stanwyck, Paul Douglas, Robert Ryan, and Marilyn Monroe—only one of whom is cursed with an aggressively noir nature. That would be Ryan's, a movie house projectionist whose hostility toward women finds expression in his being a heartless seducer. His love–hate affair with Stanwyck, the wife of his dull-witted fisherman friend Douglas, is the core of the movie, and yes, probably enough justification for hanging out the noir sign if you feel you must.

The picture marked a significant departure for Lang in that he shot much of it on location (in Monterey, California), and loved doing so. Interior soundstage scenes mostly blend seamlessly with the location footage, thanks to the scrupulous work of master RKO cinematographer Nick Musuraca. This film has never been accorded much respect, or attention for that matter, perhaps because it's short on action, devoid of criminal activity, and guilty of being a play adaptation (from Clifford Odets). That's regrettable, because Lang and Musuraca's careful, often integral mapping of movements and spaces, in the domestic scenes especially, results in a mise-en-scène of considerable subtlety and power. The most strikingly noirish image has the drunken Ryan character walking toward the camera position over some distance of ground, to end up staring into the lens in extreme closeup—only half his face, actually, at the right edge of the frame, under an inauspicious moon.

lBelow, *Clash by Night*'s two couples: Stanwyck and Douglas, for whom passion has waned, and Marilyn Monroe with Keith Andes in a more intense relationship.

Lang and Musuraca worked together again on *The Blue Gardenia* (1953), a suspense picture produced on a 20-day schedule for Warner Bros. release. The haste and cheapness show, though these filmmakers are scarcely to be blamed that much. Hollywood production at the time was shifting away from the pearly luster of previous decades and toward the flat functionality of filming for television.

The movie ramps up the inherent ambivalence of male–female relationships addressed in *Clash by Night* (touched on more mildly in the mock-violent courtship caresses of that movie's younger couple, Marilyn Monroe and Keith Andes). The main character, Norah (Anne Baxter), shares an apartment with two other bachelor girls. Well, Crystal (Ann Sothern) has an ex-husband she's now dating; Sally (Jeff Donnell) gets her kicks recounting the violence done to the heroine of the latest "Mickey Mallet" paperback. Norah is waiting faithfully to marry her long-time boyfriend after his Army tour in Korea, but when a "Dear Jane" letter abruptly aborts that future, she impulsively agrees to have dinner with Harry Prebble (Raymond Burr), the priapic sleaze of a sketch artist who's been chasing Crystal. Here, as elsewhere in the movie, women are interchangeable. Dinner and many drinks at the titular Blue Gardenia nightspot lead to tussling with the increasingly insistent seducer at his apartment. Come predawn, Norah awakes from a blackout to stagger home, and soon afterward, Prebble's body is discovered by a cleaning woman, a bloody fireplace poker nearby.

Blue Gardenia: Anne Baxter as Norah Larkin, above with Casey Mayo (Richard Conte) and below with Nat "King" Cole as himself.

Norah and the audience will spend most of the balance of the film under the impression that she killed a man in self-defense. The struggle—on a couch in front of the fireplace, amid deepening shadows and with a shatterable mirror above the mantel—gives Lang a chance to serve up his trademark mayhem in jagged, angular images, and Musuraca the opportunity to remind us of his wizardry in *Cat People* and *Out of the Past*. Otherwise, departures

from the general visual blandness are limited to moments like Norah's listening for news of the killing as she conceals herself and her radio under the bedcovers, her face lit only by the radio dial; or the scene a few minutes later when she slips out to burn an incriminating taffeta dress, the grate of the backyard incinerator glowing in the darkness.

There's one other character implicated in the sexist dynamics of the film. Richard Conte plays Casey Mayo, a stellar newspaper reporter and columnist who seizes on the quest for "Blue Gardenia" as a vehicle to a higher-paying gig. Mayo is a bit of a roving cocksman himself—his "little black book" is the envy of his tag-along photographer—but he progresses from trying to bag the presumed murderess as a trophy, to developing a growing sympathy for her, and finally playing a key role in coaching and exonerating her. (Women are interchangeable: another of Prebble's conquests did him in.) Although the film's finale has Norah making a point of walking away from her savior, she's smiling as she goes, and Casey turns his black book over to his helper.

Only *Scarlet Street* and parts of *Fury* rival *The Big Heat* as the most corrosive of Fritz Lang's films. "The city is being strangled by a gang of thieves...." The City has been Lang's allegorical battleground so often; he owns it as Ford owns Monument Valley. Here the alarm is sounded by an ex-policeman who, a moment later, will set his hands to strangle the woman he's addressing. Elsewhere in the film the socially and politically eminent master criminal will stand against a starry city backdrop, a Master of Metropolis, and advise an impetuous henchman: "Never get the people steamed up—they start doing things." He is a family man who worships the memory of his mother and dotes on his daughter, but he pushes buttons and orders others to "give contracts" on human lives. His empire is threatened by the activity of another family man, the would-be strangler. The moral landscape is as recognizable as the urban.

The grid of cross-references in *The Big Heat* is extraordinarily thorough, making for an intricate architecture of plot, motive, character, and theme. Rarely have so many ambiguously shaded characters been so inextricably bound together by figure of speech, gesture, and behavior. A police detective shoots himself and his widow (Jeanette Nolan) looks dry-eyed on his corpse, immediately setting into motion a plan to provide for herself by blackmailing the semi-respectable underworld kingpin he had worked for. Moments later, she sits before three mirrors, composing her public face; another detective, our protagonist-to-be, knocks at the door, and she crosses the room to assume a grieving widow pose. The camera moves with her, keeping the mirrors in the background of the shot as an index of deceit; and when Dave Bannion (Glenn Ford) enters, he is reflected, fragmented, in two of them. *The Big Heat* is consistently the most fluidly photographed of all Lang's works, and its environment transforms with something like viscosity.

All through the film, characters, too, metaphorically reflect one another. At a glance the good guys and bad guys are easy to separate, but beware of such complacent categories. A good cop can ignore a warning from a bar-girl because she was the married cop's floozy, and when Bannion accuses her of attempting "a shakedown," he has no idea that that is precisely what the respectable widow is perpetrating on crime boss Mike Lagana (Alexander Scourby). Bannion walks out feeling morally superior to the B-girl, but the next day learns that her corpse has been found outside of town. "You saw those cigarette burns on her body?" the morgue attendant asks him. "Yeah, I saw them. Every single one of them." And he savagely grinds out his own cigarette, in conscious or unconscious acknowledgment of his culpability.

The screenplay (from the William P. McGivern novel) is the work of former crime

Opposite, *The Big Heat*: Gloria Grahame as Debby Marsh, the moll whose goal in life is to get a fur coat. How she feels about gunsel Vince Stone (Lee Marvin) should be clear from her expression.

reporter Sydney Boehm, and it cedes pride of place only to the Nichols scripts for *Man Hunt* and *Scarlet Street*. From its firm basis Lang makes forays into his German (and Germanic) past. After Bannion's wife (Jocelyn Brando) is blown away by a car bomb meant for him, the American home Lang has respectfully framed in early scenes of the movie stands empty. A baby carriage he once moved tenderly off the front walk now sits off center but geometrically emphasized in a barren living room. We may think of the never-tenanted dream-houses and dream-windows of *You Only Live Once* and *Fury*. But the image also casts back to the ecstatic extremity of *Spione*, when the heroine who betrayed the master criminal was not only spirited away in the night—her very home was dismantled, stripped of any sign that she had lived there hours before, down to the removal of electric outlets from the walls.

After this, where can a man go when he believes all values have been turned upside down and the authorities, even his former friends and colleagues, are on the take? Well, to a rented room peerlessly summed up by a lady visitor: "Hey, I like this! Early Nothing!" She is gangster's moll Debby Marsh (Gloria Grahame), lately scalded by boiling coffee hurled in her face by boyfriend Vince Stone (Lee Marvin). Precisely half her face covered with gauze, two distinct profiles to present to the world, she is one of the definitive figures in the Lang universe, and she stands sanctified as the most hieratic of Lang's American heroines.

Bannion keeps looking everywhere but at her face in their one intimate scene save the last, until his confession about wanting to kill policeman's widow Bertha Duncan enables him to see her and himself. As he stands at the window, his face ribbed by shadows from the venetian blind (as he was shadowed in the police commissioner's office where he resigned from the police force and from the world), she sits on the other side on the screen, a pattern projected by that same window suggesting a symmetry in their relationship. Debby is about to become Bannion's agent in assassination and unlock the whole ironic trap, but this time he will be without guilt. He leaves her a gun for protection; she decides what to do with it. At the Duncan home Bertha comes down the steps as she came on the night of her husband's suicide, this time to admit two-faced Debby, her "sister under the mink," who shoots her at the same desk where her husband died and—after a breath-holding delay while the symmetry of the situation and the conspicuously unfilled space in the shot register with us—tosses the gun into

the frame. By this time Fate itself, no mere abstract convenience in Lang, has taken over; the very form of the movie calls for and condones this completion. With the second Duncan death "the big heat falls for Lagana, for Stone, and all the rest of the lice," the big heat which burns, torments, but—perhaps—purifies.

Order is apparently restored in the final scene of the film, but it would be a mistake to take the redemption of the city, the police, and Dave Bannion too compla-cently, or to assume that Lang does. There are fresh homicides to handle, and a con-spicuous sign on the wall urges: GIVE BLOOD NOW. And make what you will of Bannion's final word to the house sergeant: "Keep the coffee hot, Hugo!"

The Big Heat was the first of two movies Lang made under a year's contract to Columbia Pictures. *Human Desire* (1954) re-teams the director with stars Glenn Ford and Gloria Grahame and, like *Scarlet Street*, has the distinction of being an adaptation of material (here, Émile Zola's novel *La Bête Humaine*) previously filmed by Jean Renoir. All things considered, it's a disappointing film—and disappointing film noir—that, despite a rising toll of murder or the threat thereof, grows less compelling as it unreels. A late-show item to fall asleep to.

Ford plays a railway engine driver newly returned from military service in Korea. Some effort is made to suggest his experiences have left him troubled, but the intention is never realized, and finally Ford's guy is just a character waiting for someone else's story to ambush him. That story belongs to Grahame and her railroad-er husband Broderick Crawford, who tries to save his job (he has a temper) by sending his wife to charm an executive she once knew. Upon completion of her mission, her

The Big Heat: opposite, Lang adds a layer of pathos to Bannion's quest for revenge by depicting the family together before his wife's murder. Above Bannion turns the disfigured Debby's own desire for revenge to his advantage. Below, Lang immedi-ately re-tearned with Ford and Grahame in *Human Desire*.

husband finds that he's enraged, with the result that he murders the man in a train compart-ment while Ford, unknowing, loiters a few feet away. Things go downhill from there.

Somehow, between the making and release of *The Big Heat* and that of *Human Desire*, standard screen format for mainstream Hollywood releases was widened, and Lang never fully adjusted. That may be part of the reason *Human Desire* only sporadically achieves dramatic or

178.

Opposite, passionate still photo pose of the actors in *The Big Heat* belies Lang's approach which includes the furtive moment aboard the drab passenger train on page 177 or the shot above: unhappy expressions distorted by the rain as was Wanley's on page 166.

kinetic focus—that, and the fact that Burnett Guffey's cinematography, especially of interiors, lacks the snap and strong black-and-white–ness Charles Lang (no relation) brought to *The Big Heat*. However, the opening and closing images of Midwest train tracks rushing on forever, while Ford in his engineer's seat enjoys the only peace he knows, do make one wish for a movie worthy of them.

Lang's final noirs would be made two years later for RKO, a studio soon to cease production. *While the City Sleeps* (1956) is, somewhat surprisingly, one of three films the director named when asked which were his favorites among his work (*M* and *Fury* were the others). It does feature the most all-star cast he ever worked with, and it does begin well: A city skyline, lights reflected in water, a boat passing; the title "New York City...Tonight." A nocturnal street, still moon-bright with rain that has passed. A faceless, silhouetted figure mounting some apartment stairs, the camera in waiting. Games in a doorway, surreptitious gestures, the mirror world of "impulses" rippling into fatal motion. The camera itself moving in on a woman in a bizarrely decorated bathrobe. She screams.

So, another city in the grip of terror. The twisted compulsions that lead the "Lipstick Killer" (John Barrymore, Jr.) to commit his crimes seem less heinous to Lang than the calculated oneupmanship games played by the civilized people who command much more screen time. Most of them are jockeying for position at Kyne News Services, a Hearst-like (or Kane-like) operation whose longtime chief perishes after instructing his trusted TV anchorman (Dana Andrews) to pump up ratings and circulation by keeping every woman in town scared silly. The anchorman does, and though he's nominally "the hero," he's not above setting up his own fiancée (Sally Forrest) as bait for the killer.

The film includes the last chilling visual coup of Lang's American career. A police lieu-

tenant (Howard Duff) answers his telephone and begins to acknowledge, by repeating aloud, the descriptive data being read to him: height, weight, hair color, so forth—the police description of a murdered woman. Lang cuts to a bedroom, and a bed with a woman's figure marked on the dark coverlet, the lieutenant's voice continuing to be heard for several phrases' worth. Here is Lang's force-of-absence principle uncannily effective once more, as the reality of a once-living human being is translated into a hollow outline and a set of statistics.

While the City Sleeps lacks the dynamism of the director's strongest noirs, but there's plenty of juicy character work (the big cast also includes Ida Lupino, Thomas Mitchell, George Sanders, and Vincent Price), a worldly acceptance that homo sapiens is intrinsically and mostly incorrigibly flawed, and one more occasion for Lang to dive into the underground dark— namely, the subway tunnel where the Lipstick Killer is ultimately pursued. This and other scenes are well photographed by Ernest Laszlo, who had shot Aldrich's edge-of-doom thriller *Kiss Me Deadly* shortly before, as well as the SuperScope Western *Vera Cruz*. In the decades since its initial theatrical release, *While the City Sleeps* has been shown in a conventional TV-style format (1.37:1) that rarely did right by the people and places it framed. The 2:1 DVD release in 2011 has rescued the film from visual maladroitness, the last thing of which such a meticulous framer as Lang should be accused.

Restoring the proper SuperScope shape to *Beyond a Reasonable Doubt* (1956) also

leaves that film looking a lot better—but not better enough. Lang's American career ends on a distinct anticlimax, a movie with a fascinating central idea but scarcely a glimmer of style or insight in the realization. Dana Andrews plays a novelist, Tom Garrett, whose future father-in-law Austin Spencer (Sidney Blackmer) is adamantly opposed to capital punishment. The two hatch a plan to create spurious evidence that Garrett has committed a murder, carefully recording all their efforts so that after he is convicted they can go public with

From *Fury* on Lang seamlessly added critiques of social mores, as in top left opposite where Rhonda Fleming and Vincent Price portray a conveniently married power couple in *While the City Sleeps*. Sensationalized TV coverage is part of the narrative in that movie (opposite top right) when the killer watches a newscast and *Beyond a Reasonable Doubt* with a camera in the court room (opposite, bottom left). In his last American noir, Lang staged a variant (above) of the jail scene from *You Only Live Once* (right) with very different emotional context.

what they've done and expose the dangerous flaws in the justice system. Before long, a murder does occur, they swing into action, and Garrett is duly implicated, tried, and convicted. Then, on his way to court with the exonerating evidence, Spencer is killed in a freak motor accident and the relevant documentation destroyed. No one else knew of the plan, and now an innocent man is going to die for a crime he did not commit.

There ensues an urgent attempt, spurred by Garrett's fiancée Susan (Joan Fontaine), to dig up evidence to prove what really happened. The search is successful and Garrett will be freed. Then a chance remark of Garrett's leads Susan to realize that the murder victim was a woman from his past and he had used Spencer's plan to cover for a crime he fully intended to commit. Susan reveals the truth to the authorities and Garrett is returned to the death cell from which he had just been released.

The double whammy structure of the narrative is clever, and Lang was gutsy in leading the audience to accept Andrews' character as a fine fellow for almost the entire length of the film—"and in two minutes," as he said in interview with Peter Bogdanovich, "I show that he is a son-of-a-bitch." However, from moment to moment the movie is pedestrian, talky, and dully lit besides (William Snyder was the cameraman), with some takes running minutes on end for no apparent reason but the director's lack of interest. By this time Lang had become fed up with double-dealing producer Bert Friedlob, and as he told Bogdanovich, "I decided not to make pictures here anymore."

It was, when you get down to it, the end of an era.

Below, in white shirt and pants, Lang got down and dirty to frame a shot for *You Only Live Once.* Opposite, almost twenty years later on the set of *While the City Sleeps* with Ida Lupino and Dana Andrews.

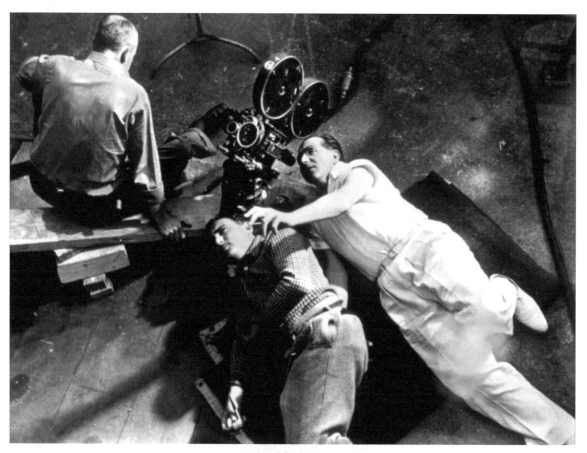

Biography

Fritz Lang was born Friedrich Christian Anton Lang in Vienna on December 5, 1890, to parents of Moravian descent. His father, Anton Lang, was an architect who hoped his son would follow that profession. Mother Paula (née Schlesinger) was born Jewish but embraced Catholicism, the faith in which her son was raised. Before WWI, Lang's interest in art took him to exotic cultures and climes. He studied painting in Paris, but when war came he volunteered for the Austrian army and fought in Russia and Romania. While on medical leave for wounds, he toyed with scenario writing. Following the war, after a brief turn at stage acting in Vienna, he was taken on as a writer by movie producer Erich Pommer. By 1919 he was directing. From 1920 he collaborated exclusively with aristocratic novelist and scenarist Thea von Harbou; they married in 1922. *Der müde Tod* (*Destiny*, 1921) is generally considered the first true Fritz Lang film. From then on, all his Weimar-era films were epic productions; a new Lang film was a major cultural event. Among the high points were the two-part *Die Nibelungen* (1924), the futuristic *Metropolis* (1927), *Spione* (1928), and *M* (1931), his first sound film, generally considered his masterpiece. Lang left the country after Hitler came to power (von Harbou remained). After making one film in France (*Liliom*, 1933), he emigrated to America and resumed his career with *Fury* (1936). He rarely stayed long at one studio, and his reputation as a dictator on set alienated many in Hollywood. Nevertheless, over the next 20 years Lang completed 22 feature films, including some of his best. In the late 1950s he accepted an invitation to return to Germany and revive the classic tradition, his last attempt being *Die 1000 Augen des Dr. Mabuse* (1961). In 1963 he made a memorable appearance playing a German-American director named Fritz Lang in Jean-Luc Godard's *Le Mépris*. He spent his last years in California and died August 2, 1976.

Noir Films

Ministry of Fear (1944)
Woman in the Window (1944)
Scarlet Street (1945)
Secret Beyond the Door (1948)
Clash By Night (1952)
The Blue Gardenia (1953)
The Big Heat (1953)
Human Desire (1954)
While the City Sleeps (1956)
Beyond a Reasonable Doubt (1956)

Pre-Noir

Dr. Mabuse, der Spieler (1922)
Metropolis (1927)
Spione (1928)
M (1931)
Das Tagebuch des Dr. Mabuse (1933)
Fury (1936)
You Only Live Once (1937)
Man Hunt (1941)
Hangmen Also Die (1943)

Joseph H. Lewis
(in white cap)
directs
Glenn Ford in
Undercover Man.

Joseph H. Lewis

Geoff Mayer

A challenge was issued in the Spring 1962 issue of *Film Culture* to investigate the merits of the films directed by Joseph Lewis. However, a warning came with this challenge. It would mean viewing Lewis' early films, including his 1940 output such as *Blazing Six-Shooters, The Man from Tumbleweeds, Texas Stagecoach, The Return of Wild Bill, Boys of the City* and *That Gang of Mine.* In this direction, the critic concluded, "lies madness." In 1971 Paul Schrader, and others, partially accepted this challenge by viewing 12 films directed by Lewis and, aside from *Gun Crazy,* which he described in *Cinema* (Fall, 1971) as "shockingly brilliant," he was disappointed. Others, including myself, have also accepted this challenge and reached a different conclusion after watching all of his films. Lewis' films, aside from *The Return of October* (1948), which was directed in part by Rudolph Maté after Lewis was removed from the film, continually surprise and reward through his ability to breathe dramatic life into potentially unrewarding projects. This included his contribution to the rigidly formulaic series of Westerns he made between 1937 and 1942. To take one film from the 1940s list, *The Return of Wild Bill,* Lewis repeatedly found fresh ways to invigorate numbingly familiar conventions. For example, the film culminates with the villain Matt Kilgore (George Lloyd) struggling with his sister Kate (Luana Walters) for control of a gun. Lewis, unlike virtually every other director in this type of film, chose to focus only on the faces of the protagonists during their struggle and when the shot is heard

from the unseen gun out of frame, the audience is unsure who has been killed. He holds the camera on their faces until Kate, wistfully, looks at her brother before collapsing to the ground. This image predates similar moments in *Double Indemnity* (1944) and *The Strange Love of Martha Ivers* (1946). Lewis used the same technique earlier in the film when Wild Bill Saunders (Bill Elliott) kills Kilgore's brother. He also used it the following year during the climax of *Arizona Cyclone* (1941) and in the MGM melodrama *A Lady Without Passport* (1950) when John Hodiak and Ned Young battle each other over the control of a gun. There is an intelligence, a visceral energy and a sense of aesthetic integrity in his films, whatever their budget or genre. When Columbia insisted that Lewis insert more close-ups of their female star, Iris Meredith, in *The Return of*

Below, tight framing in the proto-noir *Boys of the City*.

Wild Bill, a request that damaged his carefully composed compositions, he quit the studio.

The breakthrough film for Lewis was also his first film noir, *My Name is Julia Ross* (1945). However, his previous film, *The Falcon in San Francisco* (1945), is often overlooked. This film, the eleventh in the thirteen Falcon films produced by RKO between 1941 and 1946, stands out from the others due to its ability to render the normally implacable Falcon (Tom Conway) vulnerable. In an atypical moment for the Falcon, but characteristically typical image from Lewis, the Falcon wakes dishevelled in the apartment of the femme fatale, Doreen Temple (Fay Helm). To heighten his vulnerability, and involve the audience in his torment, Lewis alternates point-of-view images from the Falcon with Temple and her henchmen watching him. This includes a series of out-of-focus shots to convey the Falcon's damaged state following a beating. The sequence concludes with a low angle image of Temple looking down on the hapless Falcon, a recurring image employed by Lewis to signify domination and vulnerability, most notably in *My Name is Julia Ross.* After he refuses to answer her questions, Ricky, her thug, hits the Falcon, sending him flying across the room until he lands behind a chair with wooden bars. Finally, Lewis has orchestrated the image he really wants and he proceeds to continue the scene by alternating shots of the Falcon on the floor with (his) point-of-view images of the villains looking down at him through the bars of the chair. He is now totally trapped and Lewis has choreographed the scene to fully exploit its dramatic potential.

After eight years of low, and almost zero, budget films at Universal, Columbia and Poverty Row studios such as PRC and Monogram, *My Name is Julia Ross* became Lewis' breakthrough film. The cast included talented actors such as Dame May Whitty, who was cast against type as the ruthless matriarch Mrs. Hughes who plans to murder Julia Ross, George Macready as her psychopathic son Ralph, and Nina Foch, in her debut role, as the victim Julia Ross. The dramatic basis of *My Name is Julia Ross* goes back more than 150 years to Gothic fiction and, at least, Ann Radcliffe's 1794 novel *The Mysteries of Udolpho.* Radcliffe's story, involving the imprisonment of the vulnerable heroine Emily St. Aubert by the sinister Montoni in a shadowy castle penetrated by secret chambers is, in broad narrative terms, similar to Lewis' film which is set in London and Cornwall in the 1940s. Both share themes involving morbidity, solitude, psychological disturbance and the threat of sexual violation and death. Based on Anthony Gilbert's (the pseudonym for Lucy Malleson) *The Woman in Red,* Lewis finally had the opportunity to logically employ his depth staging, unusual angles, chiaroscuro lighting and, above all else, his repetitive need to imprison his actors within window frames and door frames criss-crossed by lattice work or vertical bars, steel gates and various physical objects and other devices to highlight their fragile condition within a perilous world.

Consistent with the conventions of Gothic fiction, an unemployed young woman (Julia Ross), with no relatives except for an aunt in America, is drugged by Ralph and his mother and taken to an isolated mansion built on the side of a cliff on the rugged Cornwall coast. Lewis suggests an abnormal world through his opening image, filmed with a tilted camera, of Julia crossing the street in the rain as she returns to her Bloomsbury boarding house after a fruitless search for employment. Thereafter she is drugged, stripped and threatened with the loss of her identity. Lewis, cunningly, allows the audience to speculate what actually took place after she is drugged. We know early in the film that Ralph has aberrant sexual predilections, most notably where he is shown cutting up Julia's underwear with his knife, and Lewis clearly builds on this sequence by showing Julia waking up in Cornwall in a different nightgown, with the letters "M H" (Marion Hughes, Ralph's dead wife) woven into the fabric, to the one she went

Opposite, some Gothic trappings in *My Name is Julia Ross.*

to sleep in.

An earlier scene in *My Name is Julia Ross* shows Julia sleeping in the Hendrique Square apartment as a hand emerges from the left hand side of the frame to steal her handbag. The twin themes of sexual violation and the loss of identity, which underpin most Gothic fiction, are efficiently established during Julia's second night in Cornwall. At 12:02 a.m., the camera pans down her illuminated bed to show her sleeping in a darkened room as a hand appears to stop the clock. This movement causes her to wake and as she peers into the darkness, the hands, rendered in shadow, move over her body to her breasts where they briefly pause before moving on to her throat and chin. Julia screams, tries to turn on the lights, which have been disabled, and then throws an ornament at the eyes peering at her in the dark. This disturbance brings Mrs. Hughes to the room while Ralph also appears. Julia, frightened by the intruder, asks them: "Why did you bring me here? What are you planning to do with me? Are you trying to drive me crazy is that it? Tell me what you are planning to do with me!" She is answered by Lewis cutting to a low angle composition of Hughes and his mother looking down on the vulnerable woman. While this scene crystallizes the theme of sexual violation, a subsequent scene establishes the source of this threat, the phallus, when Ralph erupts, attacking the stuffing in the couch with his knife. He only calms down when his mother takes it out of his hand and places it in a drawer.

Julia makes four attempts to escape, interspersed by Ralph's attempt to kiss her during a walk along the cliff. No one, however, in the village, believes she is sane or that the Hughes family is trying to murder her. Finally Ralph's lust and madness coalesce in a rape attempt on Julia. After she slaps his face, the same action that triggered his attack on his wife, he erupts and only the intervention of a maid saves Julia. That night she cleverly feigns her own suicide, after smuggling a note to boyfriend Dennis Bruce (Roland Varno) in London. The police arrive and shoot Ralph as he attempts to escape along the beach. However, unlike most directors, Lewis is not content to merely wrap up the film with the perfunctory death of the villain. He films Ralph's demise in a series of images showing his body tumbling into the surf. Finally, after his hand lingers in the sand as the waves encroach, a point-of-view shot of the oncoming surf about to engulf Ralph's body provides a satisfactory closure, paralleling how he had tried to consume Julia's body in the Cornwall mansion.

So Dark the Night (1946), one of the great unseen noir films, was directed by Lewis with virtually no budget, no known actors, a short shooting schedule, and no publicity. Understandably, the film virtually disappeared despite the fact that it is one of the great noir films of the 1940s. The plot, classic film noir, concerns a middle aged, respectable man who commits a series of murders after suffering a humiliating rejection from a younger woman.

Left, lighting effects help to mask the minimal budget of *So Dark the Night.*

However, it is much more than a simple reworking of earlier noir films with similar stories such as *Scarlet Street* (1945) and *The Great Flamarion* (1945). Henri Cassin (Steven Geray), the most respected and successful detective at the Paris Sûreté, is also Lewis' first divided protagonist, a psychological and morally divided character that would reappear in different guises in subsequent, and better known films, directed by Lewis such as *Gun Crazy* (1950), *The Big Combo* (1955), *A Lawless Street* (1955) and *The Halliday Brand* (1957).

Cassin, due to fatigue, is despatched to the rural French village of St. Margot by Dr. Manet (Jean Del Val), the Sûreté's doctor, where he falls in love with a young woman, Nanette Michaud (Micheline Cheirel). While Nanette is engaged to a young farmer, Leon Archard (Paul Marion), the prospect of marrying a rich man is attractive to her as she will be able to live in Paris. Lewis cleverly records her real interest in Cassin when he first arrives in the village in a chauffeur driven car through a series of point-of-view shots from Nanette's viewpoint. He cuts between Nanette and various parts of the gleaming vehicle to indicate that she is not interested in Cassin, only what he can offer her. She encourages the detective while deflecting the jealousy of her fiancé by describing Cassin as "an old man." Unconvinced, Leon tells Nanette "I know the way he looks at you, like a hungry dog begging for a favor, and you love it." She calms her fiancé down by stroking his lips although her distracted gaze suggests that her actions are not genuine, a reading that is soon confirmed in a matching scene between Nanette and Henri. After he proposes to her, a similar movement of her eyes reveals her lack of romantic interest in the middle-aged detective as he kisses her fingers.

Mama Michaud's (Ann Codee) delight at the possibility of acquiring a wealthy son-in-law is not shared by her husband Pierre (Eugene Borden) who is repulsed by the prospect of his daughter marrying a man of Henri's age. On the wedding night Pierre tells Henri that a man of his age is not meant for marriage and, to visually emphasise the difference between the young, sexually potent Leon and the middle-aged detective, Lewis places a very large bottle of champagne, with a long neck, in the front and center of the frame when Leon confronts Henri. This sexual metaphor remains the only explanation as to why Nanette reverses her decision to marry Henri. This sexual explanation is reinforced by a subsequent comment from Pierre to Henri that it is not surprising that Nanette has not contacted her family after leaving with Leon as "two people in love on their honeymoon don't take time for letter writing." This only compounds Henri's humiliation.

The failed marriage ceremony in the inn marks a change in the film's imagery, especially in the way Henri is filmed. After Nanette's sudden departure Lewis provides the first visual representation of Henri's alter ego, his repressed murderous side, by inserting an extreme close-up of Cassin, lips clenched, watching his intended bride leave the inn with Leon. Subsequent scenes reinforce this dividedness, in an especially typical Lewis image, filmed from outside of the inn, showing Henri enclosed within a small window frame divided by a single piece of wood. Lewis also employs double lamps shown in the foreground on Henri's desk. There is also the overt suggestion that Henri cannot contain his rage. During the discovery of Mama Michaud's body Lewis positions the detective in the back of the frame with steam from a boiling kettle dominating the foreground.

So Dark the Night is one of the more extreme films in the strong cycle of 1940s amnesiac films, a sub-genre that includes film adaptations of Cornell Woolrich's stories such as *Street of Chance* (1942), *Black Angel* (1946), *Fall Guy* (1947) and *Fear in the Night* (1947), plus other films such as *Crack-Up* (1946) and *High Wall* (1947). While this cycle often focused on the loss of identity and a pervasive sense of alienation, *So Dark the Night* intensifies its fatalistic premise with Henri desperate to expose the killer which means, in effect, destroying himself. Just prior to the film's climax Lewis points to Henri's duality during a scene between the detective and the

Above, Glenn Ford as the conflicted title character in *The Undercover Man*.

Opposite, Peggy Cummins and John Dahl as the fugitive couple in *Gun Crazy*.

Widow Bridelle (Helen Freeman). The actors appear in the foreground while their images appear in a large mirror on the back wall. Finally Henri is shot during an attack on Pierre, the last member of the Michaud family, in the inn. At this point the film's thematic strands coalesce. Henri's image is now divided between the murderer inside the inn and the peaceful, dedicated detective reflected in the window which shows his arrival at St.Margot. Henri destroys the image in the window and the film concludes with his nihilistic declaration: Henri Cassin is no more: "I caught him. I killed him."

The Undercover Man (1949) seemingly belongs to the cycle of "semi-documentary" crime films, such as *T-Men* (1947) and *Naked City* (1948), released in the post-war period. Characterized by an understated style which focused on the dogged determination of police and Federal agents to expose subversive and criminal organizations, this cycle was not conducive to Lewis' characteristic expressive style. Hence *The Undercover Man* focuses not only on the investigation but also on the emotional damage it inflicts on the families—including the Internal Revenue Service agents, led by Frank Warren (Glenn Ford), his long suffering wife Judy (Nina Foch), young Rosa Rocco (Joan Lazer) and her mother Theresa (Angela Clarke), Police Desk Sergeant Shannon (John F. Hamilton), the crooked attorney Edward J, O'Rourke (Barry Kelley) and the adulterous husband Salvatore Rocco (Anthony Caruso).

The film, loosely based on an article by Frank J. Wilson titled "Undercover Man: He Trapped Capone," jettisons specific reference to Capone, who is referred to as the "Big Fellow" throughout the film, and shifts the setting from 1930s Chicago to the post-war period in an unnamed city. Much of the film adheres to the conventions of this cycle, although Lewis includes a number of bravura scenes that rupture the naturalism associated with this type of film.The most sentimental example follows Warren's decision to resign as he is troubled by the periods of long separation from his wife. However, Maria Rocco (Esther Minciotti), as told through her granddaughter Rosa's translation, pleads with Warren and the other agents not to abandon the case. This moment of melodrama gives Lewis the dramatic license to generate strong emotion and he inserts Warren's face into the sequence when Maria warns the men that "these are evil days when people will not speak out against evil men." This scene, in effect, functions as the film's emotional and narrative climax. Warren subsequently commits to the investigation as Maria and Rosa supply the ledger that will bring down the "Big Fellow" and the Syndicate.

The other major set piece concerns the murder of Salvatore Rocco (Anthony Caruso), a bookkeeper for the Syndicate. Salvatore arranges a meeting with his daughter in the street and both father and daughter are delighted that they are finally reunited. However, their euphoria is interrupted when two gunmen appear and chase Salvatore. Lewis, however, keeps the camera on Rosa's horrified reaction and tracks alongside the little girl as she screams for her "Papa." The scene ends with a close-up of the distraught girl looking at her father's body in the street.

Less emphatic, but equally effective, is a scene early in the film when Judy, knowing that she will be again separated from her husband for many months, quietly registers her disappointment when a phone call destroys their last chance for a brief moment of intimacy. Forced to live 200 miles away on a farm, she keeps in touch by letter. As she reads his letter under a tree, her husband is shown working with the other agents in a cramped urban apartment. Lewis highlights their sense of loss via a slow dissolve of Judy reading the letter to the image of Frank in the apartment and he holds the dissolve for an inordinate amount of time so that her image is superimposed over Frank.

A sense of loss and sadness permeates the film. Sergeant Shannon, a former police captain demoted to desk sergeant after organizing a police raid on the "wrong people," accepts his humiliating demotion only because his police pension is two years away and he has a "boy in college." Unable to live with himself, he gives Warren a vital piece of evidence before committing suicide. Similarly the "Big Fellow's" attorney O'Rourke works with the criminals he despises because of his family and his creed seems to sum up the social indifference which allows criminals like the "Big Fellow" to not only survive but enjoy celebrity status: "If anybody cared, men like my client wouldn't exist."

If the semi-documentary conventions of *The Undercover Man* inhibited Lewis, no such restrictions limited his best-known film *Gun Crazy* (1950). While the couple-on-the run film was not new when production of *Gun Crazy* began in 1949, these films, including *You Only Live*

Gun Crazy: above the sideshow exhibition where Bart first meets Annie Laurie Starr. Opposite, seduced into a life of crime.

Once, 1937, and *They Live by Night*, 1948, invariably presented their protagonists as victims of a hostile society within a sentimental framework. *Gun Crazy* is decidedly non-sentimental and rejects any suggestion that its protagonists are victims of society. Instead, the film celebrates their criminal pursuits as a form of sexual foreplay and climax, based around the metaphor of the gun. For Bart Tarre (John Dall), the gun's appeal is metaphysical and beyond rational explanation. Holding it makes him feel good. For Annie Laurie Starr (Peggy Cummins) its appeal is direct and literal. The gun offers excitement and power—and the possibility of inflicting pain and death. As a carnival sharp shooter she is attracted to Bart because he is a better shot. Annie tells the owner of the carnival, Packett (Berry Kroeger), a victim of her sexual attraction and dominance, that Bart is, unlike him, a "real man."

In *Gun Crazy* Lewis pushed the Production Code about as far as it would go during this period. The carnival sequence, where Bart meets Annie, is imbued with sexual excitement and provides the motivation for the rest of the film. The carnal basis of the attraction between Bart and Annie is established by the setting, the illicit atmosphere of a cheap carnival, and the first image, a high angle shot showing Bart and his two boyhood friends looking at the various attractions. This master shot, showing the three men in the background as dancing girls perform on a platform on the left side of the screen, provides the visual motivation for the next shot, the one Lewis really wanted. In the foreground he shows the dancer's twirling legs, which are framed showing only the lower portion of their bodies with legs apart, as the men watch from below. This generalized atmosphere of eroticism is soon made specific when Bart encounters Annie-Laurie. Following Packet's seductive introduction—"so appealing, so dangerous, so lovely to look at"—an empty screen is filled by smoke from her guns followed by a low angle shot of Annie, in a western outfit, as she moves forward to dominate the frame. Smiling, she shoots her gun into the camera. This is followed by the reverse shot of Bart, initially startled, and then increasingly fascinated. Both Clyde and Dave watch Bart's ardour intensify during Annie's act, a process that is reciprocated as she seems to perform just for Bart—especially when she bends over, looks at Bart, and fires her gun between her legs at the target. These "wild animals," as Packett later describes them, circle each other in front of the audience after Bart accepts an invitation to compete with Annie. After she places a crown filled with matches on her head, he playfully asks her if she is afraid he will "shoot too low." *Gun Crazy* eschews any simple psychological explanation for Bart and Annie. An early scene in the film depicts Bart, aged 14, in court for stealing a gun. During the trial, Bart's teacher, Miss Wynn (Virginia Farmer), tells Judge Willoughby (Morris Carnovsky) of an incident when Bart sat in her classroom, surrounded by his classmates, clutching the barrel of a gun with his left hand. Her only explanation is that "it was something he had to have." Lewis, however, extends this aberrant association between Bart's gun and the excitement it incites in others, especially the females, when one of the girls, titillated by the sight of Bart clutching his weapon, asks him "Do you shoot it?"

After Bart and Annie marry and leave the circus, they soon run out of money. Annie, bored by normal life, pressures Bart to embark on a life of crime. Dressed in a bathrobe, she sits on the bed in a motel putting on her stockings while he cleans his guns. Bart, initially hesitant, succumbs and moves over to the bed and a close-up of Annie's reaction anticipates his submission. The sexual basis of his scene is clear and forms part of a recurring metaphor where robbery is depicted as a form of sexual intercourse. This is made explicit when Lewis cuts from a close-up of Annie's mouth, promising sex to Bart, to a bowl of chewing gum violently torn apart by a bullet from Bart's gun during a robbery. This association escalates with each robbery showing Annie's post-coital reaction as she clings to Bart. This includes the celebrated

Hampton robbery sequence, filmed in one unbroken long take, with the camera placed in the back seat of the car while Peggy Cummins and John Dall improvise the dialogue. He robs the local bank while she waits in the car, emerging only to disable an inquisitive policeman. The exception to this pattern occurs during their final robbery, the Armour meat packing plant, where she satisfies herself during the robbery by shooting a female supervisor.

These crimes come at a cost to Bart, another example of Lewis' morally conflicted characters. After stealing a military uniform he tells Annie that he hates wearing it and that nothing appears real to him anymore. When she reassures him that she is real and sexually available, he nods and tells her "you're the only thing that is, Laurie. The rest is a nightmare!" However, his inability to abandon this perverse woman forms the basis of one of Lewis' most exhilarating scenes. After deciding they must part, as the police are searching for a couple, they drive off in different cars in separate directions. However, after going a short distance, both simultaneously stop, look back at each other, and then Bart swings his car around, drives back to Annie, abandons his car in the middle of the road and drives off with her clinging to him. This action, while condemning them to an early death, reiterates Lewis' powerful ability to ingratiate the audience into the criminal lives of this aberrant couple.

Finally, trapped in the mountains by the police, Bart shoots Annie, the only person he kills in the film. The ending is superficially similar to the 1941 film *High Sierra* when Roy Earle (Humphrey Bogart), cornered by the police at the foot of Mt. Whitney, is shot by a police sniper. However, while Earle is presented as the victim of an uncaring society, there is no such sentimental closure in *Gun Crazy.* Instead, Lewis' ending, the antithesis of the earlier sentimental gangster melodrama, is deeply ironic.

Although *The Big Combo* (1955) was not a commercially successful film at the time of its release, it is a highly significant noir film which extended and intensified many of the themes that emerged in the 1940s and early 1950s, involving society, human nature and relationships. In this regard *The Big Combo* is a key 1950s film noir due to its bleak, claustrophobic presentation of a broken society populated by damaged protagonists. The film eschews the exhilarating visual imagery of *Gun Crazy* for a closed world permeated by sexual repression and obsessive, or doomed, people. Lewis also foregrounds the sexual perversity, psychological torment and conflicted protagonists found in his other films such as *Invisible Ghost* (1941), *The Falcon in San Francisco, My Name is Julia Ross, So Dark the Night, Gun Crazy, A Lawless Street* (1955) and *The Halliday Brand* (1957). In *The Big Combo* the neuroses found in the other films bloom and fester.

There are superficial similarities between *The Big* Combo and *The Undercover Man.* Both films feature troubled government agents confronting major criminals. Also, the narrative trajectory of each film details the agent's frustration when leads fail to materialize. However, the similarities end here. In *The Undercover Man* the mobster is brought to justice when a young Italian girl, her mother, and grandmother combine to provide the necessary evidence for the agent. *The Big Combo,* on the other hand, offers no such sentimental moment as its mobster, Mr. Brown (Richard Conte), is only brought to justice after he betrays his loyal hit-men Fante (Lee Van Cleef) and Mingo (Earl Holliman).

Betrayal and obsession dominate the film and its central theme is articulated by Brown's tormented mistress Susan Lowell (Jean Wallace) when she tells the equally tormented cop, Lieutenant Diamond (Cornell Wilde), who is in love with Lowell, that she cannot leave Brown because she lives "in a maze, Mr. Diamond, a strange, blind and backward maze, and all the little twisting paths lead back to Mr. Brown." In accordance with Lowell's explanation, the entire film is presented as a "strange, blind and backward maze" where all vestiges of reality, and normality, are repressed via John Alton's expressive, chiaroscuro lighting, Lewis' unbalanced com-

Above, obsessed Det. Diamond and the showgirl he will sacrifice to get his man in *The Big Combo*.

positions, Philip Yordan's stylized dialogue and David Raksin's jazz score. These master crafts-men combine to present a hermetically sealed universe that allows no sunshine and, corre-spondingly, no hope. There is no polarization between good and evil, only a neurotic battle between two men in love with a masochistic woman. The primal basis of their battle is articu-lated by Brown when he explains that "first is first and second is nobody." The film's "hero," Diamond, covets Brown's power, both sexual and financial.

   The Big Combo begins at a point where the three major protagonists in the film, Brown, Diamond and Susan Lowell, are beginning to psychologically unravel. Lowell's attempted sui-cide is a turning point and during her delirium she murmurs the name "Alicia." This clue, a kind of circuit breaker, leads the detective on a destructive quest. Its victims include Alicia, Brown's

Above, *The Big Combo*: The classic finale in the airplane hangar.

wife (Helen Walker), who hides away in an institution where she feigns insanity to stay alive, the informer Bettini (Ted De Corsia) who wants to die in a squalid room rather than face Brown, the stripper Rita (Helen Stanton), who provides sexual relief for Diamond and who is murdered by Fante and Mingo, and Diamond's loyal colleague, Detective Sam Hill (Jay Adler), who jeopardizes his job, and his life, to assist Diamond. On the other side, Brown repays the devotion and loyalty of the thinly veiled homosexual gunmen Fante and Mingo with betrayal. Ironically, these two sadistic hit men are the only loyal couple in the film.

Along the way Lewis challenged the censorship strictures of the period with his depiction of oral sex as his camera records Susan's rapturous face while Brown slowly moves down her body, and out of the frame. The film also intensified the brutal basis of the 1950s crime film, a trait remarked upon in the 1955 *Variety* review. When Diamond is tortured by Brown, Fante and Mingo place a hearing aid worn by the displaced mob boss Joe McClure (Brian Donlevy) in Diamond's ear while music is played loudly through the earpiece. The excruciating pain suffered by the detective is highlighted in the *Variety* review as one that "will shock the sensibilities and cause near-nausia [sic]." Lewis' determination that the audience share the pain of this brutal world is also made apparent later in the film when Fante and Mingo execute McClure.

After Brown removes McClure's hearing aid, so that the victim will not hear the shots fired into him, Lewis films the sequence without sound via a prolonged point-of-view shot. Alton's cinematography, Yordan's neurotic characters and Lewis' determination to render the battle between Brown and Diamond in a closed, brutal manner elevates *The Big Combo* to the pantheon of 1950s film noir.

Biography

Joseph H. (for Harold) Lewis was born in New York City on April 6, 1907, the son of Russian Jewish immigrants. In 1925 he moved to Hollywood to join his brother Ben who was working at M-G-M. In 1935 Lewis inveigled a job at Mascot Pictures as supervising editor, after Nat Levine mistakenly employed Joe thinking it was Ben Lewis. In 1937 Lewis moved to Grand National where he reshot scenes for *Navy Spy* (1937) after the studio was disappointed with Crane Wilbur's direction. Lewis was hired by producer Trem Carr to direct four low budget westerns, starring Bob Baker, and an espionage film, *The Spy Ring* (1938), starring William Hall and Jane Wyman, for Universal. In 1939 and 1940 he directed five low budget series Westerns, starring Charles Starrett and Bill Elliott, for Columbia before resigning from the studio. He moved further down the Hollywood system when he worked for ultra-low budget producer Sam Katzman on three Bowery Boy films and a horror film, *Invisible Ghost* (1940), starring Bela Lugosi, before returning to series Westerns and another horror film at Universal. Lewis' descent in the Hollywood hierarchy reached its nadir when he joined Poverty Row studio PRC for *Bombs Over Burma* (1942), the exploitation melodrama *Secrets of a Co-Ed* (1943), and the sentimental melodrama *Minstrel Man* (1944). In terms of production values, things improved for Lewis after the Second World War with *The Falcon in San Francisco* (1945) for RKO followed by his breakthrough film *My Name is Julia Ross* (1945) for Columbia. After working on the superb film noir, *So Dark the Night* (1946), which was filmed in twelve days, Lewis spent six months shooting the musical numbers for *The Jolson Story* (1946), starring Larry Parks. Lewis also directed Parks in *The Swordsman,* a visually sumptuous period action film set in 17th Century Scotland and filmed in the High Sierras. Lewis was removed from his next film, his worst, the fantasy comedy *The Return of October* (1948), when he left the set to attend his mother's funeral. He resigned from Columbia after *The Undercover Man* (1949) and then directed his most famous film, *Gun Crazy* (1950), for independent producers, Frank and Maurice King. United Artists released the film as *Deadly Is the Female* on January 26, 1950 and then re-released it as *Gun Crazy* on August 24, 1950. Three films for M-G-M, *A Lady Without Passport* (1950), *Desperate Search* (1952) and *Cry of the Hunted* (1953) and a Korean War film for U.S. Pictures, *Retreat, Hell!* (1952), released through Warner Bros., followed. His last film noir, *The Big Combo* (1955), preceded two Westerns with Randolph Scott, the oddball *A Lawless Street* (1955) and *7th Cavalry* (1956). *The Halliday Brand* (1957), a bleak Western was followed by his last film, fittingly, a low budget Western, *Terror in a Texas Town* (1958), which Lewis directed in ten days as a favor to his friend Ned Young who was blacklisted throughout the 1950s. Lewis worked in television from 1957 to 1968 and died on August 30, 2000.

Noir Films

My Name is Julia Ross (1945)
So Dark the Night (1946)
The Undercover Man (1949)
Gun Crazy (1950)
The Big Combo (1955)

Studio portrait of
Joseph H. Lewis

Joseph Losey

Chris D.

Joseph Losey's prime concerns as director were the struggle for social justice and excavating the damaged psyche of the self. The first, visible in early films and sporadically in later pictures, has to do with the relationship of the self to the outside world; the second, seen over Losey's whole oeuvre, reveals secrets, emotions, the search for the origins of self-loathing and hypocrisy. Losey composed some of the most grueling examples of confessional art in the history of the movies. By nature, these fictionalized confessions are dark—noir.

Some fit into a more traditional definition of noir; some mid-period and later films stretch the boundaries to the breaking point; some non-noir, even a tragic period picture like *The Go-Between* or a melodramatic Tennessee Williams fantasia like *Boom!* position shadows over their characters' lives, ready to suck them into the void.

Losey was not a happy guy; at times, conscientious and generous to a fault; at other times, particularly when he was in his cups, prone to wallow in negativity. The latter proved more of a liability as his life and alcoholism progressed. Despite acclaim, even his most successful pictures never did smash hit business at the box office. The better he became known to a discerning audience, he also developed a reputation as a crotchety, uncompromising filmmaker tackling unpleasant subjects.

One could compare him to Nicholas Ray, who was born in the same town of La Crosse, Wisconsin and whose career, at various points, followed a parallel course. Though they did not know each other that well from La Crosse, they both directed feature films circa 1947 on the RKO lot, became friendly and both were caught (Ray with little damage) in HUAC's feeding frenzy.

Some of Ray's movies have similarities in theme to Losey's. Ray's were often more visceral and emotional, but both men were dyed-in-the-wool romantics. Though both directors were primarily heterosexual, both men dealt with issues regarding their "masculinity" and attractions to the same sex. Both were serial adulterers with a number of wives and both suffered substance abuse problems, though with Losey it was primarily alcohol. Their pictures are often explorations of their own demons by proxy. There are really no other directors of their era, at least American, that took the same kind of private journeys in their films.

For the reader unfamiliar with Losey, hopefully this supplies some context.

The Lawless

Losey's writer friend, Daniel Mainwaring, often wrote under the pseudonym Geoffrey Homes, including the novel on which *Out of the Past* was based and would later go on to write Don Siegel's *Invasion of the Body Snatchers* and Phil Karlson's *The Phenix City Story*. Mainwaring contacted Losey about directing a low budget film he was writing for Paramount's B unit called *The Dividing Line.* The film was to retain that moniker in the UK, but had its title changed to

The Lawless (1950) for America.

Losey's MGM boss, Dore Schary, gave permission to Losey to take the job, but relations between the two cooled.

Losey was happy to be working on a movie dealing with a social justice theme, but did not get along with producers William Pine and William Thomas. They interfered often, most grievously inflicting a music score which slowed the film's pace. It was only through Mainwaring's intervention that Losey wasn't fired.

Losey gave credit for staying on schedule to cinematographer Roy Hunt, an old hand at breaking down and immediately heading for the next set-up. Losey had a talented cast at his disposal, including professional Macdonald Carey, and had the advantage of friend, trailblazing artist, John Hubley, as his production designer.

Carey plays Larry Wilder, a former crusading journalist who is tired of fighting dragons and has settled in a California town as the editor of a small newspaper, *The Union.* He meets Sunny Garcia (Gail Russell), a Mexican American woman who puts out a smaller Spanish language paper, *La Luz*, at a dance for Latino teenagers. The party is interrupted by Anglo boys, led by Joe Ferguson (John Sands), who starts a fight when he makes a pass at the girlfriend of Paul Rodriguez (Lalo Rios). Earlier that day the two boys had had a minor fender bender. A brawl erupts, the police are called, and Paul steals an ice cream truck. He is eventually stopped by the cops, one of whom beats Paul in the back seat. His partner tries to stop him but ends up rolling the car and dying in the accident. Paul goes on the run. Meanwhile, John Ferguson's liberal, rich father, Ed (John Hoyt), pays the other Latino kid's bail, knowing his son is a troublemaker.

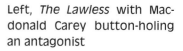

Left, *The Lawless* with Macdonald Carey button-holing an antagonist

Opposite, Van Heflin and Evelyn Keyes in *The Prowler*.

Larry is ashamed to see his reporter Jonas (Herbert Anderson) who strings for a bigger paper, sensationalizing the story.

Paul hides in a barn, and Mildred (Gloria Winters), the girl who finds him, panics, hits her head on a board, claiming later the boy did it. The bigger newspaper, *The Express*, portrays the boy as a dangerous criminal.

Larry and the police chief accompany the posse. Larry goes off on his own, getting ahead, and finds Paul in a drainage culvert. In one of the most exciting sequences in the picture, Losey generates suspense as Larry has the double challenge of calming Paul and keeping the posse from blasting them. Back in town, Larry incurs wrath for editorializing to raise a defense fund. He gets word that a lynch mob, led by Mildred's father, is outside the jail. He leaves Sunny at the paper and helps the police chief spirit Paul away, but the mob attacks two of Paul's friends. One of them, Lope (Maurice Jara), takes refuge with Sunny. The citizens attack the *Union*'s office, destroy the printing press and leave Sunny and Lope unconscious. When the crowd is dispersed, and Larry returns, he is disgusted and ready to leave town. Ed Ferguson pays Paul's bail and tries to convince Larry to stay. Larry gives Paul a ride to his family home, and when Paul gets out of the car, he mentions when Larry found him, Larry reminded him of his big brother who was killed in the war. This changes Larry's mind, and he goes to *La Luz* to ask Sunny to help him put out an edition of *The Union* on their printing press.

The Lawless is fast-moving and gets its message across without too much proselytizing. But the difficulties with the producers and Losey's lack of experience dilute its power. We are never drawn in by the characters' plights. Carey and Russell are fine, but we don't get to know them very well. There are some effective sequences contrasting working class Paul's lifestyle with his upper middle class nemesis, Joe. Still, the focus is never kept on him long enough.

The Prowler

Things were turbulent for Losey in 1951, with HUAC hearings looming.

Made before Losey's *M* remake, but not released until a couple of months later, *The Prowler* (1951) was a startling leap ahead. Losey had a friendship with soon-to-be-blacklisted screenwriters Hugo Butler and Dalton Trumbo, and producer Sam Spiegel (under the pseudonym S. P. Eagle), and *The Prowler* was co-produced by an uncredited John Huston. At the time, Huston's marriage to actress Evelyn Keyes was on the rocks, but Huston wanted to give Keyes a role worthy of her talent.

Losey and artist John Hubley designed the

interiors of the three main sets — the Spanish house of Susan Gilvray (Keyes), the motel and the ghost town building — for maximum ease in camera movement and subliminal visual cues to illustrate the desires and loneliness in Webb Garwood and Susan. Losey also planned the shooting schedule so Van Heflin and Keyes would have two weeks of rehearsal, including blocking for camera angles. Along with Losey's often long takes, it is obvious this had a salutary effect on the pair's extraordinary performances. It was also good for cinematographer Arthur Miller who a reputation for slowness. Helping things run smoothly was assistant director Robert Aldrich.

Policemen Webb (Heflin) and his older partner Bud (John Maxwell), are called to the residence of Susan after she reports a prowler. She's alone because her husband has an all-night radio show. They can't find anyone. It's clear Susan has sparked Webb's interest, and he returns on his way home to check up. Susan offers him coffee. They realize they are from the same town in Indiana and bond.

Through his friendship, Webb whittles away at Susan's resistance, becoming her lover. Susan married her older husband for security, and Webb manipulates her fears, hoping to get her to leave. Unbeknownst to Susan, Webb has discovered the amount of money she would get if he died. Webb devises a plan to draw her husband outside with a noise, then mistaking him for a prowler, shoot him dead. The ploy works, Webb shoots the armed homeowner, then shoots himself in the arm with the husband's gun.

Susan is devastated. At the inquest, she lies about knowing Webb, guilty over their affair, and it's ruled an accident. Afterwards, Susan will have nothing to with Webb, and he gets to her through her brother-in-law. When Webb goes to see her while she's packing to move, he makes her feel guilty for thinking he intentionally killed her husband.

Shortly after, Webb and Susan are married. They honeymoon at the motel they've bought near Victorville, and Susan reveals she's a few months pregnant. Webb is moved, then realizes it's a disaster. Her husband was sterile, and they haven't been married long enough. When the baby is born early, people will know about their affair. Webb convinces her that they should go to a ghost town where his ex-partner and his wife go rock hunting. They can wait out the pregnancy, then fudge the dates. Things degenerate once they're camped in the ruins, Susan taking a turn for the worse, and Webb persuades a nearby doctor to follow him to treat Susan.

Once they arrive, the doctor delivers the premature baby. He leaves Susan and Webb alone, and Susan tells him she realizes he intends to kill the doctor, and that he murdered her husband. A car starts outside, the doctor taking off with the baby. Webb is going to follow, but the doctor has his keys. Susan says that she's told him everything. Panicky Webb admits his guilt, and disgusted Susan throws him the spare keys. Once Webb reaches a narrow pass, where only one car can fit, he runs into his ex-partner and wife who are coincidentally on vacation. Webb spots a highway patrol car approaching and runs back to the ghost town. Moments later, he's shot as he tries to reach the top of a hill. Susan watches despairingly from a dirty window.

Losey and his writers touch on so many issues in *The Prowler*, both personal (sexual, psychological and class anxieties) and social (function of class in building interpersonal relationships and aspirations for materialistic upward mobility) that it is impossible to enumerate them all. Webb's character is not totally unsympathetic, but, in the end, he's beyond redemption. His ambition to grasp at seemingly unattainable "things" like the perfect, but controllable woman, the "easy life" of a property owner, being a potent lover, subverts his ability to achieve those things. He cannot function in the end because of his overcompensation, without regard for others. Susan tries to survive in a male-dominated world where her dreams of being in "show business" have been crushed, and she has done the only thing most women could do in the 1950s, marry for protection and sustenance. When provided with an exciting alternative, she doesn't look far enough ahead to see the disastrous consequences. Her reluctant descent into adultery from a sexless marriage, something she thinks will be worth it because it will result in real love and fulfillment, turns out to be the opposite.

M

Seymour Nebenzal, who produced Fritz Lang's original 1931 version of *M*, had tried to entice Losey several times to helm the remake, always to be rebuffed. Finally Losey caved. Nebenzal had a deal with Columbia, retaining long-term rights, so Losey had a solid support team. He got to hire assistant director Robert Aldrich as well as soon-to-be-blacklisted writer Waldo Salt. He also had cinematographer Ernest Laszlo, fresh from lensing Rudolph Maté's noir indie, *D.O.A.* Losey and Laszlo make evocative use of Los Angeles locations, particularly the now disappeared Bunker Hill neighborhood.

If *The Prowler* is primarily a two person character study, *M* (1951) is a return to the multi-character structure of *The Lawless*.

The title sequence immediately leaps into a nightmare world: A nocturnal shot from the back of the Angels Flight cable car as it goes up a hill, a bundle of newspapers thrown down with the headlines: CHILD KILLER SOUGHT...in daylight, a little girl getting candy from a machine...we see a man's legs appear in the mirror on the machine while anxious music turns to a lullaby...the back of a man watching kids on a merry-go-round...the back of a man watching an Asian girl at a drinking fountain... a man's legs coming into frame as an African-American

Below, the trial of Harrow/M by the criminals of Los Angeles.

Above, *M*: Harrow/M flees Angels Flight with his latest victim

girl kneels on the sidewalk to do a chalk drawing...the back of a man approaching on a beach boardwalk as a little blonde girl takes off her shoes to go running in the sand...he picks up the shoes, then leans on the railing...

After these titles, the straightforward visuals continue...the man getting a shoeshine, watching kids in a crosswalk...we see his face; it is Martin Harrow...he catches a little girl's ball and takes her hand...a mother sets the table...she looks at the clock, worried...Harrow buys a balloon for the girl from a blind balloon seller on Santa Monica Pier...the mother is sewing and looks at the clock again...she hears children running in the hall, but it's only the neighbor kids...she looks over the stair railing, runs down the many flights...a cut to two lonely glasses of milk on the kitchen table...the mother runs down the block screaming her daughter's name...the balloon floats into the sky, telegraphing the little girl's fate...a ball rolls and stops on a pile of debris...

The police are introduced, Inspector Carney (Howard Da Silva) and his lieutenant, Becker (Steve Brodie). A councilman's grandchild is the latest victim, and Carney feels the pressure.

Harrow (David Wayne) lives in an old Victorian house converted to apartments in Bunker Hill. He sits on his bed with his face in the shadows as he twists a shoelace drawstring on a low hanging lamp, shaping it into a ligature and, in a spasm, dousing the light. There's the ticking of a clock. zombie-like, he sits at a desk, breathing heavily as he twists a shoelace around a clay doll's neck, then pulls until the head pops off. He looks at the portrait of his mother.

Carney, Becker and uniformed cops roust a Skid Row saloon where low-lifes congregate. Bidding everyone assemble single file, Carney holds court from the bar as a cop carries a tablecloth filled to overflowing with knives, brass knuckles and other weapons. Carney questions several hoods but lets one go without comment, a disgraced lawyer named Dan Langley (Luther Adler) who is the mouthpiece for Marshall (Martin Gabel), the town's gang boss.

Marshall calls his underbosses together (Norman Lloyd, Raymond Burr and Glenn Anders) and alcoholic lawyer Langley to tell them the manhunt is bad for business, especially with grand jury hearings starting. They must organize to hunt the killer themselves.

Becker returns from a search of former mental patient Harrow's flat. It strikes a chord with Carney. They visit again, finding him still not home but discover a compartment where he has hidden his victims' shoes.

Simultaneously Harrow buys a balloon from the blind vendor for another girl (Janine Perreau). Harrow plays a piccolo, always the same tune, and the vendor recognizes it. He signals one of the delinquents nearby to follow them. There's a suspenseful foot race through the city blocks, with various youths joining the chase. Harrow and the girl duck into the Bradbury Building as the night watchman locks up.

Marshall's underbosses and their brigade of crooks descend with their "Trojan Horse" disguised as a cop, tie up the watchman and systematically comb the structure. Harrow and the girl are in a mannequin-filled studio with a bolted metal door. Losey makes the most of the Bradbury as film location, his framing reminiscent of painters Brueghel and Hieronymous Bosch.

They break in the studio, rescue the girl, but Harrow flees across rooftops before they catch him. In an underground parking garage, Marshall thanks his minions and says their work is done. But the mob wants justice. Marshall gets nervous, ordering the drunken Langley to put on a mock defense of Harrow to dissipate the tension.

Harrow, for the first time, talks. Wayne gives a startling performance: "Mother always told me men were evil...they needed to be punished, whipped and tortured so they'd be good...my father, he should have been punished for the things he did to my mother...once he had a bird with a broken wing and he nursed it back to health but then he knew it would have to fly back into the world of men, a world that wasn't fit for birds or children, so he killed the children, the bird...I know they'd take me to the farm to punish me, that's why I've had to do all these vile things, vile things I didn't want to do, but I couldn't help myself..."

When the crowd still want his blood, Langley answers: "You don't kill someone because he's blind stumbling to find his way...don't you put him in an institution? ...Have we any excuse? What of our guilt? The pennies and nickels and dimes stolen from the poor, children's lunch money that goes into our slot machines, workmen's rent that's bet on horses, how many children have gone hungry because of us?"

Marshall is not amused and threatens Langley to stop. Langley goes on, and Marshall shoots him. Carney and his men appear at the top of the ramp. Langley falls dead as they drag Marshall and Harrow away.

M is without question one of Losey's seminal early films, and one of the best movies of the 1950s. It is criminal that it is currently unavailable. Like *The Prowler*, *M* needs to be the object of a similar restoration crusade.

The start of *The Big Night*: George's birthday party is brutally interrupted by Al Judge and his henchmen.

The Big Night

Losey's final Hollywood picture, *The Big Night* (1951), was his lowest budgeted and, up until that time, his poorest-reviewed. It's severely underrated.

John Drew Barrymore is Georgie, teased as he's coming home from school on his sixteenth birthday. He and his father Andy (Preston Foster) live above their tavern. The local denizens are present as Andy brings out a cake. They bid Georgie blow out the candles and, as he does, intruders barge in. It's tough guy sports columnist Al Judge (Howard St. John) with his bodyguards. Judge commands Andy to strip off his shirt and get down on all fours. Andy reluctantly does as he is told. The small crowd is paralyzed. Georgie can't understand why his tough father is submitting. Judge takes his walking cane and repeatedly beats Andy across the back, then leaves. Andy's business partner Flanagan (Howland Chamberlain) orders everyone out and for Georgie to close up. As Georgie counts cash from the register, he notices his father's gun, which he quickly pockets.

This is the beginning of Georgie's "big night," his journey to manhood. Intending to kill Judge, he tracks him, first through a boxing arena where he's intimidated by a conman (Emile Meyer), then befriended by an inebriated professor, Cooper (Philip Bourneuf) who takes him to a nightclub where Cooper introduces his girlfriend, Julie (Dorothy Comingore). Georgie is confused, alternately tormented by his father's humiliation and bedazzled by adult pleasures, including the Black torch singer, Terry (Mauri Lynn).

Afterwards, when they're waiting for a cab, he drunkenly notices a dog next to him and looks up to see the singer holding the leash. He gushes about her wonderful voice, charming her, then tells her how beautiful she is, "…even if you are —" Immediately, Terry is sad and hurt and Georgie mortified that he has expressed a racist sentiment he doesn't feel. This is one of the many grueling moments where Losey places Georgie in an awkward position of unconsciously doing or saying things, things he's absorbed growing up that are not his true character and spark self-loathing. Losey became expert at revealing these moments of humiliation we all feel; it is one of the key characteristics of his work.

Later, at Julie's apartment, he meets her sister, Marion (Joan Loring), who tries to talk sense to him when she sees his gun.

He runs out, tracking Judge to an apartment that belongs to his father's ex-girlfriend, Frances. When Georgie confronts him, Judge explains that Frances was his sister. She committed suicide because Georgie's father wouldn't marry her. Georgie can't kill him, but Judge tries for the gun, it goes off, and Judge is shot.

Georgie flees back to Marion's, but the hungover Cooper drives him off. Georgie goes to a church, but the priest is rushing out. The boy washes his hands in the holy water and, at last, heads home.

Andy and Flanagan put him to bed as the cops screech to a halt outside. When Georgie comes down, he sees the cops taking Andy away. Georgie tells them he shot Judge and reveals his gun. The cops back him into the bar, telling him Judge survived. Georgie won't give up the gun, even after Andy orders him. Georgie wants to understand why he didn't marry Frances, and his father explains he is still married, Georgie's mother is not dead. She left him for another guy, and he didn't want Georgie to hate her. "Didn't *you*? "No, I loved her. Even after she left me."

Georgie leaves with the cops. It's dawn. *The Big Night* is over.

Before *The Big Night* could get into post-production, Losey got the word HUAC's subpoena was imminent, and he left for a directing job in Italy on a few hours notice. As a result,

he was not happy that the flashback structure he had devised had been scrapped in favor of a chronological one.

Comparable to Ray's *Rebel Without a Cause*, *The Big Night* is waiting to be rediscovered.

Stranger on the Prowl, The Sleeping Tiger, Finger of Guilt and Time Without Pity

Stranger on the Prowl (Imbarco a Mezzanote) (1952) was taken from a story by Noel Calef, who would accrue fame for Louis Malle's adaptation of his *Elevator to the Gallows*. *Stranger* was shot around Tuscany, in largely bombed out ruins. Losey commented later that lead star, Paul Muni, was a "pain in the ass" with his over-elaborate rituals of character immersion.

Muni plays a stowaway discovered while his ship is still docked, and he gets the captain to look the other way for a price, which he then must raise before the midnight embarkation. He tries to sell his gun in town but can't get a decent price. Muni's fate is sealed when he tries to steal bread but is caught by the bakery proprietress, whom he accidentally kills. He flees with citizens in hot pursuit. A boy, Giacomo (Vittorio Manunta), who had stolen a bottle of milk, thinks the crowd is after him, and he joins Muni in flight. The two are thrown together, much to Muni's chagrin, but they develop a bond as they dodge through a carnival, ancient underground tunnels, finally landing in the building of an older teenage girl (Joan Loring) Giacomo knows, one step ahead of the cops. The story ends tragically as Muni escapes over rooftops but goes back to save Giacomo, who is hanging from a roof ledge. Muni flees tear gas, and a sharpshooter cuts him down, causing Muni to fall into the square in front of the girl, Giacomo and his just-arrived mother. Muni is convincing as the starving wanderer, and Losey captures the

Left. George finally confronts Al Judge near the end of *The Big Night*.

Right, Paul Muni in *Stranger on the Prowl*.

Below right, *The Sleeping Tiger*: Alexis Smith with Dirk Bogarde in his first picture with Losey.

feel of early Italian Neo-realism in the stark locations.

This is the hardest of Losey's pictures to find, though well worth a look. Poor quality, grey market DVDs of the butchered-by-twenty-minutes American version can be found by scouring the internet. Many years later, Losey was told by Calef that the elements for the uncut Italian version were destroyed when a remake was planned. It appears that the short version was recently restored by the Cineteca di Bologna.

For the next couple of years, Losey was on the move, traveling to the UK and joined there by fellow exile, producer Carl Foreman, who'd just had a hit with *High Noon* (which Losey was originally in line to direct). Foreman found Losey a London flat, plus TV work.

Plagued by panic attacks at the prospect of having to renew his visa every month, through Foreman's help, Losey was eventually offered a low budget film that would become *The Sleeping Tiger* (1954).

Through fortuitous circumstances, Losey met Dirk Bogarde. Initially, the budget was too low for the actor. But they showed each other their films, *The Prowler* and *The Hunted*, and the two agreed to work things out. Once Bogarde was on board, they were able to attract Alexander Knox, Hugh Griffith and Canadian-American Alexis Smith. Smith, who had coincidentally auditioned for Keyes' role in *The Prowler*, was unaware that Losey was directing, having been told the name of British front, Victor Hanbury; even in the UK, the blacklist was feared. After misgivings, Smith decided to throw caution to the winds.

Frank (Dirk Bogarde) tries to mug psychiatrist Clive (Alexander Knox) on his walk home, but Clive prevails. The next day, Carol (Maxine

Audley), Clive's assistant, explains to Clive's wife Glenda (Alexis Smith) that Frank is staying for six months of therapy, rather than go to prison.

Over the weeks, Clive is away on lecture tours. Frank and Glenda are antagonistic, but an illicit love affair develops. Frank is abusive towards Sally, the maid, and also sneaks out to perpetrate the odd crime. A police inspector (Hugh Griffith) comes to question Clive about Frank, but is reassured Frank is going straight.

Clive pumps Frank about his childhood, to no avail.

Sally quits because of Frank's bullying, and shortly thereafter her fiancé complains to Clive. After a private discussion, the issue is resolved, but Frank discovers Clive paid the man off, and he resents this. He secretly borrows Clive's gun, and holds up a securities office the next day.

The inspector returns to arrest Frank, but Clive gives him an alibi. After the inspector leaves, Clive makes Frank promise to anonymously return the money. Clive at last breaks Frank's shell, Frank admitting he hated his bullying father who had thrown over his mother for a younger woman, and he had wished him dead. A week later his father died of a heart attack, resulting in Frank's guilt complex. Clive takes Frank on a fishing trip and, when Clive returns alone, Glenda is alarmed. She goes to the lodge, ordering Frank to run away with her. Frank is agreeable but unenthusiastic. That night at dinner, after Clive says he is taking Glenda on vacation, Frank announces he is turning himself in for crimes committed while under their roof.

While Frank is packing, Glenda intrudes. Frank says he can't live with himself hurting Clive. Hysterical, she runs to her room and writhes tormented on her bed (viewed by Losey from a ceiling vantage point—please note this overhead bed shot is missing in the British print). Running downstairs, she knocks over a vase of flowers, then bites her hand, drawing blood.

Clive and Carol are in the office, when Glenda, blood on her mouth, bursts in. She blames Frank. Stoic Clive gets his gun, Carol following, shouting "Don't!" Losey cuts to Glenda in the corner, smiling demonically, lit from below like a vampire. She realizes what she's done and runs to the stairs, only to hear a shot. Clive appears, and she asks, "You killed him?" He says "Yes…isn't that what you wanted?" Glenda: "Yes, no, he was leaving…leaving…not you, me…" Clive is playing the experimenter again and tells her that he isn't dead, he's gone.

Glenda races off in the car. Clive and Carol follow. Glenda stops Frank, who is walking to the police station, telling him that Clive wants to kill him. Mystified, Frank gets in, tries to get her to turn around, but she refuses, speeding, until a truck pulls in front of them. They crash through an Esso gasoline billboard with a painting of a huge tiger. Glenda dies, and Frank is only slightly hurt. A crowd gathers as Clive and Carol arrive.

The Sleeping Tiger represents a feverish, entertaining continuation of Losey's obsessions, which would be seen in many later films: surrogate father-son relationships, incompatible marriages, a third party intruder destroying a home, the randomness of fate disintegrating a vulnerable person's psyche, the yin-yang joy/destructiveness of sex, repressed homosexuality, etc. The last eight minutes of the British version were trimmed by 10 or 15 seconds, apparently due to the sequence's intensity.

While *The Sleeping Tiger* is a sleeper in need of rediscovery, *Finger of Guilt (aka The Intimate Stranger)* (1956), is not quite of the same caliber. Sporting an even lower budget than *Tiger*, this programmer was written by fellow blacklistee, Howard Koch.

American film editor Reggie (Richard Basehart) has moved to the UK after an affair with a movie mogul's wife. Somewhat implausibly, he's resurrected himself as a producer at a British studio run by his father-in-law, Ben (Roger Livesy). Out of the blue, he starts receiving letters from a woman named Evelyn (Mary Murphy) who claims they are long-time lovers. Soon he has to tell his wife Leslie (Faith Brook) and his father-in-law, which bewilders them. Reggie's search for Evelyn consumes him. When he finds her, she seems to know every detail of his life, and Leslie begins to doubt his innocence. Leslie and Reggie's actress ex-lover, Kay (Constance Cummings), help Reggie prove he's telling the truth. Evelyn was hired by Ben's right-hand man, Ernie (Mervyn Johns), who resented Reggie's ascendancy to a position he felt was rightfully his. The climactic scene, where Reggie confronts Ernie and Evelyn during a war movie's sound effects dubbing session on a dark soundstage is dynamic, vibrating with the energy seen in Losey's more memorable movies. Otherwise, *Finger of Guilt* has an inconsistent tone, and Losey's direction of the actors is all over the map. Basehart, who had just given phenomenal performances in Fellini's *Il Bidone* and *La Strada*, overacts, and apparently Losey either encouraged him or failed to rein him in. Livesey has little to do. Murphy's scenes are mundane, but it's nice to see her as a femme fatale as opposed to her more familiar, good girl role in *The Wild One.* Cummings, an expatriate American actress known for her British comedies, turns in the most consistent performance. Like *Tiger*, Losey had to sign the film under a pseudonym, this time as Joseph Walton.

Time Without Pity (1957) is a crazy movie, one of Losey's most entertaining, charged with electricity. Adapted by Ben Barzman from an Emlyn Williams' play, Losey dumps the who-done-it element; we see automobile tycoon Roger Stanford (Leo McKern) strangle a young woman in the opening scene. Recovering alcoholic writer David Graham (Michael Redgrave) returns from Canada with only twenty-four hours to save his son, Alec (Alec McCowen), the girl's beau, from hanging for the crime. Clayton (Peter Cushing), Alec's attorney, has gotten two stays of execution but can't do more. Unwilling to accept defeat, the shaky Graham tracks down Stanford at his dealership, encountering Alec's friend and Stanford's adopted son Brian (Paul Daneman) in the showroom. Brian is nervous; to avoid confrontation with his rage-aholic father, he introduces Graham as his tutor. Later, Brian feeds Graham clues.

Graham questions the victim's showgirl sister, Agnes (Joan Plowright), Stanford's former secretary, Vickie (Lois Maxwell) who has just been promoted, Vickie's manipulative mother, Mrs. Harker (Renee Houston), and Stanford's wife, Honor (Ann Todd), who seems inordinately concerned about Alec's welfare. Graham hears of a missing suicide note at the crime scene the police never saw, a letter he thinks was written by Honor.

When Graham shares a visit to Alec with Honor, it becomes clear the two are in love, and he is wrong about her. Alec has no confidence in his father and berates him. Graham gets drunk, not seeing how he can save Alec by the next morning. But more encounters with Stanford, Honor and Brian give Graham new

Leo McKern in *Time without Pity.*

Michael Redgrave in *Time without Pity*.

insight. Stanford is being eaten alive by paranoid megalomania.

Agnes tells Graham her sister had been physically abused, and she thought it was Alec. It dawns on Graham that Stanford was secretly seeing the girl and goes to the magnate's proving grounds at dawn to confront him. Stanford is personally test-driving their new car and takes off when he sees Graham approaching. There is a wild sequence with Graham running across the huge old Restoration estate, through crumbling statues and masonry, trying to flag Stanford down. Stanford comes back, jumps out, elated his car's a success, and he ignores Graham.

Graham follows him to his office. Stanford tries to buy him off. Graham draws a gun, but Stanford doesn't believe Graham will shoot him, knowing it won't save Alec. As the two struggle, Graham turns the gun on himself, telling Stanford he will be charged with the murder of Alec's father. Graham squeezes Stanford's finger, is shot and dies. There is a pounding on the door, and Stanford becomes a terrified child. Honor and Brian break in, seeing Stanford wiping off his prints from the gun and placing it in Graham's palm. Brian phones attorney Clayton at the prison to have the execution stopped.

The director, with designer Richard MacDonald and cinematographer Freddie Francis, go all out with the debut of the fabled Losey baroque, arresting nightmarish visuals—a mirrored elevator that resembles stepping into infinity, Mrs. Harker's drawing room full of nerve-jangling alarm clocks, Stanford's 17th-century ruins of a race track—and frantic performance rhythms. Where Basehart's overacting in *Finger of Guilt* sputtered, Redgrave's and McKern's hits a fever pitch that is convincing. Redgrave was an actor who was ruining himself with drink in real life (though sober on the shoot) and McKern seems like he is going to spontaneously combust. McKern's Stanford, the magnate, is a working class man with ambition on steroids, a sociopathic tin god clawing his way into the upper class. The viewer will either love or hate Redgrave and McKern abusing each other—there is no middle ground.

Chance Meeting (Blind Date), The Concrete Jungle (The Criminal), These Are the Damned (The Damned)

Chance Meeting (1959) was the result of Losey trying to put together a big budget anti-nuclear thriller called *S.O.S. Pacific* with German actor Hardy Kruger. But when producer Sydney Box heard from Columbia, who would be financing, it was a thumbs-down on Losey's participation, Box offered Losey another lower-budgeted film with Kruger with an already-finished script by Eric Ambler. Losey accepted, but wanted it rewritten, so he called in fellow exiles, Ben Barzman and Millard Lampell. For the role of Inspector Morgan, Losey cast Peter O'Toole. But this being pre-*Lawrence*, the casting was nixed. His second choice was Stanley Baker.

Kruger is Jan, a naïve Belgian painter in love with older Jacqueline (Micheline Presle), charged with her murder when he is found in her flat with the body. Morgan is incredulous at Jan's story of not noticing (it had been covered with drapes). Seeing the woman's gaudy apartment, it's clear she was a high-priced call girl. Morgan spends the first third of the film interrogating Jan in the apartment, with the corpse, which Jan can't bring himself to look at.

Jan flashes back to how he met her at his gallery job and how they became lovers. She had been secretive, and this was the first time he'd been invited to her flat.

When working class Morgan is warned not to dig too deeply into the case by his superiors, he knows something's not right and learns Jacqueline was the mistress of high-powered diplomat, Sir Howard Fenton. On a hunch, he takes Jan to the airport to see Fenton arriving with his wife. Jan is bowled over to see Jacqueline coming off the plane. But it's *not* Jacqueline, it's Fenton's wife.

Bringing her in for questioning, Lady Fenton denies knowing Jan. Despairing Jan professes how much he loved her. How could she frame him? Just as she leaves, Jan reaches out to her and she slips, sadly whispering his name, and Morgan realizes Jan has been truthful. It turns out Lady Fenton murdered the real Jacqueline, her spouse's mistress, afraid he was going to ask for a divorce, and she would lose her upper class status.

Losey handles the proceedings well, including the nice, but somewhat implausible twist, with a triumvirate of performances by Kruger, Presle and especially Baker. At times, though, the claustrophobic nature of the enclosed sets and the tightly wound schematics is wearying.

Stanley Baker had already done two pictures for Hammer Films, and he came to Losey with another one of their scripts, a gangster saga written by Jimmy Sangster. Losey hated it, and Baker told Hammer he would only do it if Losey could transform the material. In the process, producer Nat Cohen (*Finger of Guilt*) and his Anglo-Amalgamated took over the project. An underworld friend of Baker, suave "bad man" Albert Dimes, became a consultant, and Losey enlisted Alun Owen to completely rewrite the story. Designer Richard MacDonald was

Right, *Chance Meeting*.

Stanley Baker in *The Criminal.*

brought in again; Losey was coming to depend on him to help visualize his material.

The Criminal (aka The Concrete Jungle, 1960) follows Johnny Bannion (Baker) contradictorily a devout Catholic and a ruthless hoodlum. Refusing to kowtow to sadistic guard captain Barrows (Patrick Magee), he is released from prison in the first fifteen minutes to meet up with Mike Carter (Sam Wanamaker), a smooth weasel of a fixer organizing a racetrack heist. At a homecoming party things go sour when Johnny's ex-girlfriend Maggie (Jill Bennett) gets hysterical. The party fizzles after she's thrown out, and Johnny then finds nude blonde Suzanne (Margit Saad) in his bed.

Conditions for financing the heist are in flux, and Carter proves unreliable. Shortly after the heist, the seen-it-all Inspector Town (Laurence Naismith) arrests Johnny, telling him they got a tip. Johnny won't admit his guilt, and he alone knows where the loot is buried.

Johnny has his share of friends as well as enemies in stir, and Barrows is being paid from outside to make things rough. Suzanne visits. Carter is asking her where the money is. Johnny begs for her to leave town. He gets angry, and storms out before their time is up.

Things turn progressively nasty, with his best friend, borderline schizophrenic Paulie (Brian Phelan) having a knife planted on him. Already claustrophobic, Paulie flips out, and he falls over the tier to die slowly on the floor below as a riot erupts. Safrin (Gregoire Aslan), an Italian gang boss, engineers Johnny's escape for a major slice of the loot, and something happens Johnny doesn't bargain for: he's labeled as a rat, made to look like he's helping the guards quell the riot so he'll be transferred.

Once out on the road, Johnny's transport is overtaken. Two of Johnny's men spirit him away, then knock him unconscious — they've sold out to Carter. He wakes up on Carter's yacht where Suzanne is a hostage, but he gets the drop on them, escaping with her. They head for the now-frozen field where the loot is, but Carter and henchmen arrive, and a gun battle erupts. Johnny kills everyone except Carter, but Johnny is mortally wounded. He screams at Suzanne to leave. Carter ignores her, cradling Johnny, begging him to tell where the money is buried as the dying man recites an act of contrition. Using a helicopter, Losey shoots from overhead; they become small figures, Carter at last grabbing a shovel, and Suzanne walking back up the muddy road.

Losey throws in character-defining bits, utilizing every one of his cast to maximum effect. One example: shortly before convict Paulie's death, the lights go black, and Paulie sits in a stylized halo, giving a monologue how he's not completely crazy, just half crazy; there are several moments like this sprinkled unexpectedly throughout. Losey also works for the first time with jazz composer John Dankworth and his singer wife, Cleo Laine. She croons "Thieving Boy" over the beginning and end titles, as well as when Suzanne pays her prison visit, giving the film a wistful, ballad feel: "...all my sadness and all my joy came from loving a thieving boy."

Released at 97 minutes in the UK, as *Concrete Jungle* in the U.S., it was cut by 11 minutes.

These Are the Damned (aka The Damned) was filmed by Losey for Hammer in 1961, but was not released in the U.S. until 1963, on the second half of a double bill. Losey's original cut was 96 minutes, and was cut to 87 minutes in the UK and 77 minutes in America. The film was restored to its original running time in the late 1990s.

Although Losey brought in screenwriter Evan Jones, most of Losey's crew will be familiar to Hammer aficionados: cinematographer Arthur Grant, production designer Bernard Robinson and composer James Bernard. Also then Hammer regular Oliver Reed appears as the puritanical, sociopath leader of the teddy boys, brother to Joanie (Shirley Anne Field).

A strange amalgam, in some ways the film is a precursor to *A Clockwork Orange*, with its black leather clad gang, then midway through, the mystery of the radioactive children.

Weary of the business grind, American Simon (Macdonald Carey) sails the world in his small yacht, docking at Weymouth. Succumbing to Joanie's wiles, he follows her down a deserted street only to be mugged by King (Reed) and his gang. Simon is helped by plain-clothes military officers (Walter Gotell, James Villiers) into a restaurant where their boss Bernard (Alexander Knox) is having drinks with his bohemian artist mistress, Freya (Viveca Lindfors).

Later Joanie, fed up with King, joins Simon on his yacht. At first, he's unhappy to see her, then realizes she's a lot like him, wanting to escape the status quo. They set sail, escaping from King's gang, who nevertheless follow them down the coast on their motorcycles. Joanie often comes to Freya's carved-from-stone clifftop house while Freya's away, and she and Simon hide there.

That night, they're chased onto the grounds of Bernard's top secret installation above an underground bunker where nine radioactive children are being raised for the aftermath of a nuclear war. Simon and Joanie accidentally run off a cliff, falling

These Are the Damned.

Above, Jeanne Moreau and Stanley Baker in *Eve*.

into the sea, and are rescued by the children. King follows into the cliffside caves and ends up in an uneasy truce with Simon. All three are frightened by the touch of the children's ice-cold skin.

Bernard puts two and two together after catching one of the gang.

When Major Holland (Gotell) descends into the bunker to get the adult fugitives, Simon and King take him prisoner, forcing him to explain. Simon and Joanie claim they need to save the children, but when they take the kids topside, Bernard and his men in protective suits catch them. King escapes with a young boy in Freya's sports car, only to be waylaid by helicopters. He careens away, but already sick from the radiation, crashes off a bridge into the bay.

Bernard lets Simon and Joanie go back to the yacht, knowing they'll soon die. One helicopter follows as they sail off.

Bernard, knowing Freya's disapproval of his work, has never mentioned the children.

He tries to talk sense to her: "You know my secrets now, my children are the buried seeds of life, when that time comes the thing itself will open the door, and my children will go out to inherit the Earth." "What Earth, Bernard?...Is this the extent of your dream? To set nine ice-cold children free in the ashes of the universe? I have no choice, I have no choice at all." "You will refuse to join me?" She shakes her head. "You know what your refusal means?" "Yes...it means you are wasting whatever time I have left."

As the helicopter follows the dying couple out to sea, Bernard shoots Freya, and the camera moves down to the base of the cliff where we hear the once again imprisoned children crying out, "Help us, please, somebody, help us!"

The last ten minutes of the film is chilling, and the impact of the movie only grows with repeated viewings. Whatever Losey's bleak worldview, he always maintained he was a hopeful person; he must be given credit for unflinchingly taking the story's fantastic premise to its logical conclusion.

Eve (Eva)

Eve (Eva) (1962) is noir *amour fou*. No one is out-and-out murdered, but there are other kinds of death, both spiritual and physical, through neglect, mental cruelty and thoughtlessness. This is the quintessence of the confessional Losey, vulnerable and psychically naked, and it would be difficult to do the movie justice in a few paragraphs.

Approached to film a potboiler by James Hadley Chase, with Jeanne Moreau as star, Losey agreed if he was allowed a major rewrite (with Hugo Butler and Evan Jones) and to discard the Hollywood setting.

Stanley Baker is Tyvian Jones, a Welsh novelist who has just had the movie of his best-seller premiere at the Venice Film Festival. The only problem is he is a fraud, having stolen his late brother's manuscript. He can't live with the guilt, so he drinks to excess, is obsessed with Eve (Jeanne Moreau), an emotionally abusive, high-priced courtesan and is unfaithful to his new wife, Francesca (Virna Lisi). After Francesca realizes he is hopeless, she kills herself, crashing her speedboat into a jetty in front of him. Tyvian spirals downwards, tormented by self-loathing and the young Italian producer, Michele (Riccardo Garrone), who was in love with Francesca. By the end, Tyvian is reduced to life as a tour guide and submissively tending house when Eve goes away on trips with high-rolling johns.

Losey always claimed he had exposed himself emotionally in *Eve* more than any other film, and he was devastated—along with Moreau and Baker (both of whom were never better) — when his original 160 minute cut was reduced, first to 119 minutes in Europe, then to 107 for the American market. *Eve* is not for everyone, especially those expecting a straightforward noir. But for those who enjoyed Roman Polanksi's *Bitter Moon* (1992), Frank Perry's *The Swimmer* (1968), Antonioni's *La Notte* (1961) or Losey's other psychodramas like *The Servant*, they will not be disappointed. Shot in luminous black-and-white by Gianni di Venanzo, Losey's and production designer Richard MacDonald's nightmare-skewed vision of a hall of mirrors Venice, filled with decrepit villas and cemeteries, alleys of feral cats, tunnels and stairways to nowhere, rivals Visconti's *Death in Venice* (1971) and Nicholas Roeg's *Don't Look Now* (1973) for creating an ancient landscape of never-ending dread.

The Servant

Based on a novella by Robin Maugham (Somerset's nephew) and adapted by Harold Pinter, *The Servant* (1963) still remains Losey's most well-known movie.

Spoiled, rich young Tony (James Fox) leases a townhouse and hires a nominally obse-

Anove and below, Dirk Bogarde (and Sarah Miles) in *The Servant.*

quious butler named Barrett (Dirk Bogarde). Tony's fiancée Susan finds Barrett repulsive, and Barrett responds, walking in on her and Tony when they are becoming intimate. All the time we're watching Tony and Barrett together, we can see—through Bogarde's subtle expressions—that the servant is taking measure of the master. Barrett asks Tony if he can bring his sister, Vera, up from the boondocks to stay in the house, and she can work as a maid for room and board. Tony reluctantly acquiesces.

When Vera (Sarah Miles) arrives, the below-the-surface sexual tension becomes palpable. Barrett finds reason to leave Vera and Tony alone, and Vera sets on seducing her upper class boss. Losey conjures a memorable scene between them in the kitchen, erotic frissons boiling over to the urgent ring of the telephone and the deafening drip-drip of a faucet, until Tony can no longer stand it and grabs her.

A few nights later, Tony and Susan return from dinner to hear what sounds like Barrett and Vera in Tony's bedroom. Losey spends agonizing minutes, neither Tony nor Susan saying a word. It is an uncomfortable scene to watch, Losey imperceptibly building suspense until Tony explodes, yelling for Barrett. When Barrett appears, his hair is mussed, a cigarette hangs from his lips and he mutters, "Aside from being in your room, I'm well within my rights." Tony: "You bastard. She's your sister." Barrett tells him Vera is not his sister. He lied. She is his fiancée. He calls her down, and Vera haughtily enters, then throws it in Tony's face that he's had

her, too. Susan is devastated and leaves.

Weeks pass and Tony runs into Barrett in a local pub. Both are down in the dumps, and

Barrett is barely getting by. He begs for his job back, and lonely Tony weakens. But their relationship has changed from one of master and servant to two hard-drinking bachelors whiling away their time with weird parlor games. Losey's style becomes darker, reminiscent of Polanki's *Repulsion* (1965), and the film attains a creepy thriller aspect as Tony's personality disintegrates with drink, and Barrett's goes on the ascendant. Working again with designer MacDonald and composer Dankworth and, for the first time, with cinematographer Douglas Slocombe, Losey creates a ticking time bomb. It escalates so gradually, one isn't fully conscious of the depths to which Losey's brought the viewer until they are as ensnared as Tony, and there is no escape.

Secret Ceremony

Losey had collaborated with his friend George Tabori three years before, adapting a short story set in Argentina, hoping to film it with Ingrid Bergman. But there was a holdup with the rights. Once *Boom!* was finished, the rights were clear. Losey and Elizabeth Taylor wanted to work together again, and *Secret Ceremony* seemed the perfect project.

Losey scouted London locations with Richard MacDonald. They settled on a giant mansion that had been taken over by a church to house mentally ill people (ironic, considering the plotline!). The organization had run into financial trouble, so it was available. As Losey made clear with *The Servant*, he often considered a house to be as much a character in a movie as a human being. *Secret Ceremony* (1968) was another such case.

Taylor is Leonora, a sometime prostitute grieving over her recently drowned daughter. She runs into teenage Cenci (Mia Farrow) in the neighborhood near the cemetery and gets sucked into the lonely girl's life. Leonora has mental issues but can tell reality from fantasy. Childlike Cenci slips in and out of schizophrenia and believes Leonora is her returned mother. When Leonora reluctantly stays, she spots a photograph of Cenci's mother — the resemblance is striking. Leonora relishes the size of the house and enjoys the missing mother's luxurious wardrobe but, most of all, there is the unspoken idea Cenci is a surrogate daughter. Leonora learns Cenci's ritualistic daily routine; for a short while, things seem almost normal.

Then Cenci's stepfather, Albert (Robert Mitchum), an American professor, shows up. Things go downhill fast. Albert reintroduces the unhealthy family dynamic that may have triggered Cenci's schizophrenia. He is a profane man who has sexually abused Cenci since she was a child. Leonora and Albert engage in a battle of wits, and Leonora spirits Cenci off to the seaside to escape. But Albert follows. There is an uncomfortable scene where Cenci goes out in the evening, and Leonora is shocked to see her straddling the prone Albert on a deserted beach. When Cenci returns, she has a large belly and claims to be pregnant by Albert, something which causes Leonora to erupt, pulling a pillow from beneath the girl's dress. Back in town, Cenci gets worse. Leonora leaves, and Cenci takes an overdose of pills. Later, with Cenci in her coffin and Albert looking down on her, Leonora comes out of the darkness and stabs him to death. She returns to her lonely apartment to stare at the photo of her dead daughter.

In France, *Secret Ceremony* won Best Foreign Film the year of its release. In the UK and America, most reviews were negative. Sold to American TV, NBC and Universal cut several scenes, then shot bookend sequences of two psychiatrists discussing "the case" without Losey's or producer John Heyman's knowledge. Fortunately that version is history, and the uncut film is out on DVD in the UK and Europe. It continues to enjoy a mixed critical and audience reception. Many now condescend to it as a campy guilty pleasure; entertaining but a "bad movie," in the same category as the flamboyant *Boom!*

Above, Elizabeth Taylor and Mia Farrow in *The Secret Ceremony.* Opposite, *The Assassination of Trotsky.*

Aided immeasurably by Richard Rodney Bennett's eerie score, it remains one of Losey's best, most emotionally unsettling pictures.

The Assassination Of Trotsky

The Assassination of Trotsky (1972) can be seen as penance for the many years Losey spent as a Stalinist, his disillusion stoked in the 1960s when many Soviet communists admitted Stalin's genocidal purges were not just anti-Red propaganda.

When exile Leon Trotsky was killed in 1940 in his compound in Mexico City, many unquestioning Party members, especially those at a once-remove from the Soviet Union in America and Europe, believed Stalin's campaign of lies about him.

One should know some history before viewing this opaque, historical neo-noir. From the very opening with Stalinist demonstrators clashing with a parade of Mexican Trotsky supporters on May Day, Losey expects his audience to be well-schooled in the minutiae of the then current Mexican labor movement. Even a short prologue as a superimposed crawl following the opening credits would have been welcome. But we're thrown into the deep end and expected to sink or swim.

That said, the movie has been unjustly trashed by critics because Losey didn't choose to make it a suspense thriller. A kind of anti-thriller, Losey continually presents sequences in

prolonged takes in either medium or long shot. Losey focuses on assassin Frank Jacson (he spelled his alias without a 'k'). Played by Alain Delon as a tortured loner, he reconnoiters, meets with Stalinist contacts and indulges in masochistic navel-gazing, unable to decide until the last minute if he will go through with his mission. He romances Trotsky's devoted secretary Gita (Romy Schneider) to get an introduction to Trotsky in his guarded compound. Self-obsessed Trotsky (Richard Burton), a man who knows he has changed the course of history, continually pontificates, sometimes idealistically, sometimes ironically, as he writes articles, memoirs, dotes on his loving wife (Valentina Cortese) and tends his pet rabbits. In a series of discussions with Jacson, whom he believes to be an activist writer, Trotsky warms to the shy assassin. Some exteriors shot in Mexico City, with Italian locations filling in for the rest, Losey creates a languid, tropical fever dream of hallucinatory, lazy boat rides on city canals, Rivera murals, giant church bells ringing incessantly as if to drive Jacson mad and an endless, gory bullfight.

After Jacson finds the guts to bury his climber's pick in Trotsky's head, Trotsky loudly erupts from his chair, causing Jacson's capture by Trotsky's guards. Burton is especially effective in these scenes where he's rushed fully conscious to the hospital and takes hours to die. Meanwhile, Gita getting to at last unleash her frustrations and fury at cowering Jacson at police headquarters is as much catharsis as we get.

Mr. Klein

As in Jean-Pierre Melville's *Le Samourai*, Alain Delon was born to play certain stoic roles, and Losey's *Mr. Klein (Monsieur Klein)* (1976) is a prime example.

Penned by Franco Solinas (writer of Pontecorvo's *Kapo, Battle of Algiers* and *Queimada*), *Mr. Klein*'s background is the true story of the collaborationist Vichy government initiating the Vel d'Hiv round-up of French Jews in July 1942.

Delon is Klein, an art speculator who is indifferent to the plight of anyone but himself and is known for buying paintings at a fraction of their worth from Jews trying to flee the country. The film begins with him receiving a Jewish newsletter right after he has completed his latest transaction. Alarmed, he goes to the publisher, who cannot explain how they have him as a subscriber. Klein becomes obsessed with how he got put on the list, eventually finding he has a Jewish namesake who may be active in the Resistance. But the man is an elusive presence whom Klein never seems able to glimpse. In the process, Klein registers on the authorities' radar as a possible Jew. The dismay that envelopes Klein impels him to visit his hypocritical, bourgeois father, quizzing him if he has the birth certificates for all his grandparents.

Alain Delon as
Mr. Klein.

He may have to prove that he has no Jewish ancestors, which his father finds insulting.

There are hints of Kafkaesque paranoia in Losey's other efforts, but in *Mr. Klein* the all powerful bureaucracy of a merciless state is front and center. Klein has numerous chances to leave France but can't conceive his privileged existence is really in jeopardy. His compulsion to find the other Klein leads him to finally make phone contact and schedule a meeting, only to have the man arrested before his very eyes. The arrested man's dog follows Klein, refusing to leave his side. The police confiscate Klein's paintings and valuables. He arranges to leave with a forged passport, breaks off with his mistress and makes it to the train station. It is the morning of the roundup of Jews. Before the train leaves, Klein glimpses a man he thinks is the other Klein and gets off to follow him. His lawyer, who is on the platform, is flabbergasted.

Klein gets caught, then put on a bus to the stadium where they are organizing concentration camp transports but, even on arrival, he compulsively follows his phantom double. Suddenly his lawyer appears in the stadium seats, waving he's got the last birth certificate Klein needed to prove his racial purity. Still, Klein hesitates, hoping to come face to face with his doppelganger. The crush of the crowd carries him into a tunnel, at the end of which is a freight train. Police officials herd the multitude into boxcars. Then he is inside. As the train starts, the boxcar door is slammed in his face.

Mr. Klein moves at a slow, deliberate rhythm, Losey purposely concentrating on Klein's obsessions. It builds unbearable suspense from the character study alone, Losey putting Klein's compulsions under the microscope, and the resultant impact is to an undeniably devastating effect.

Biography

Joseph Walton Losey was born on January 14, 1909 in La Crosse, Wisconsin. His father died in 1925 when Losey was 16. Losey became politicized by 1932, dismayed by the violent suppression by Herbert Hoover of the Veterans March. Losey's sister was friends with Nicholas Ray from La Crosse, but Losey didn't become friends with Ray until Losey moved to New York after his college years. Ray, Elia Kazan and Losey were involved with one of the first Communist collective theaters. Losey made trips to Europe in 1928 and 1931, and to the Soviet Union circa 1935. He gathered momentum directing theater in the late 1930s. At the outset of the U.S. entering WWII, Louis B. Mayer courted Losey, but Losey was drafted. He never went overseas and was at MGM in Hollywood by the end of 1944. Around this time, he helped Bertolt Brecht stage a Los Angeles production of Brecht's *Galileo*, starring Charles Laughton. Losey directed

MGM shorts, most notably an award-winning segment of the *Crime Does Not Pay* series called *A Gun in His Hand* (1945). Dore Schary, a new member of RKO's top brass, offered Losey a contract. The project Losey and producer Adrian Scott developed was a contemporary anti-war fantasy, *The Boy with Green Hair,* Losey's feature debut. In 1947, friends, composer Hans Eisler and Scott, were singled out by HUAC as communists. Midway through *Boy's* shooting, RKO was bought by the ultra-right Howard Hughes. Both Losey and Nicholas Ray turned down Hughes' request to direct *I Was a Communist for the FBI*, a litmus test to weed out "pinko" filmmakers. Losey followed the fed-up Schary back to MGM to the writers' department, working with Daniel Mainwaring. Mainwaring brought Losey onto *The Lawless* at Paramount, Losey's second feature; the rest of Losey's American output—three indie produced noirs—were distributed by United Artists and Columbia. Subpoenaed by HUAC, Losey fled to Italy, then the UK, where he was to live virtually the rest of his life. In the early 1960s, Losey made a critical splash with *The Servant,* his second of five films starring Dirk Bogarde and his first of three Harold Pinter collaborations (*Accident* and *The Go-Between* being the others). Losey's attempts at pop phantasmagoria, *Modesty Blaise* (1966) and *Boom!,* were panned by critics. *Mr. Klein* was his last picture to receive wide critical acclaim. Losey was married four times and had two sons. He died June 22, 1984 in London from cancer.

Noir Films

The Lawless (aka *The Dividing Line*, 1950)

The Prowler (1951)

M (1951)

The Big Night (1951)

Stranger on the Prowl (*Imbarco a Mezzanote*, 1952; as Andrea Forzano)

The Sleeping Tiger (1954; as Victor Hanbury)

Finger of Guilt (aka *The Intimate Stranger*, 1956; as Joseph Walton)

Time Without Pity (1957)

Chance Meeting (aka *Blind Date*, 1959)

Neo-Noir

The Criminal (aka Concrete Jungle) (1960)

These Are the Damned (aka *The Damned*, 1961; released in the U.S., 1963)

Eve (Eva) (1962)

The Servant (1963)

Secret Ceremony (1968)

The Assassination of Trotsky (1972)

Mr. Klein (Monsieur Klein, 1976)

Films with Noir Elements

King and Country (1964)

Accident (1967)

Figures in a Landscape (1970)

The Go-Between (1970)

The Romantic Englishwoman (1975)

Roads to the South (*Les Routes du Sud*, 1978)

Right, Losey directs David Wayne in *M*.

Ida Lupino with actors Edmond O'Brien (left) and William Talman (center) on the set of *The Hitch-Hiker*.

Ida Lupino

Jans B. Wager

Ida Lupino directed, scripted, and produced films during the classical Hollywood period. Scholars sometimes question her usefulness as a feminist icon because as a filmmaker she avoided the appearance of female empowerment. Her films do not typically feature strong, resourceful female characters, but her male characters are equally as confused and buffeted by fate. Even those films not neatly categorized as noir tease at the indeterminate borders of film noir, featuring working class characters trapped by their class, youth, and physical or mental limitations. Her films are remarkable for their complexity. Many noir films rank as B films—low-budget, studio productions utilizing second string cast and crews. Lupino's films were all made by her own production company for less than $160,000 each; they star mostly unknown and inexperienced actors, use minimal sets and costuming, and at least initially, feature an inexperienced director. The crimes in Lupino's movies sound egregious: bigamy, kidnapping, and assault. Compared to the sexy, duplicitous, and self-aware protagonists of most classic film noirs, her criminals are swept away not by passion but by passivity and engage in almost mindless action spurred by their past experiences. Her films reveal post-war noir as a cultural current as much as a film style, and include Neo-realist working class milieus in tune with tight production budgets and the requirements of institutional Hollywood, including the Production Code Administration (PCA). Without the gloss that the studios apply, even to the B output, Lupino achieves a tough and singular noir vision. Her films borrow and quote from classical Hollywood cinema even as each one expands the notion of what might be shown on the screen. Lupino earns iconic status as trailblazing scriptwriter, producer, and director, a woman who brings consistency and humanity into Neo-realist noir.

Before Lupino began directing and producing films, the successful Hollywood actress composed music and wrote a symphony, drafted stories and screenplays, and chafed regularly against the restrictions placed upon her by the studios. After protracted negotiations with Jack Warner, who wanted exclusive rights to her talents, Lupino ended her contract with Warner Bros. late in 1947. She started Arcadia Productions with producer Ben Bogeaus (William Donati, *Ida Lupino: A Biography*, UP Kentucky, 1996, p. 135), a brief association that ended when Lupino became engaged to her second husband, Collier Young. Young was an experienced Hollywood insider, having worked as an agent, story editor, successful script writer, and assistant to Jack Warner and Larry Cohn. Along with Anson Bond, Young and Lupino started Emerald Productions, and in 1949 released their successful first film, *The Judge*, directed by Elmer Clifton. Lupino and Bond agreed to co-produce the next film, a story of unwed motherhood called *Not Wanted* (1949). with Clifton again directing. After *Not Wanted*, Lupino and Young parted ways with Bond, and included Malvin Wald, screenwriter for the remarkable semi-documentary crime drama, *The Naked City* (1948), in their new production company, the Filmakers.

Roberto Rossellini inspired the Filmakers' production aesthetic. Lupino cites the Neo-

Left, exploitation poster for the "Neo-realist" *Not Wanted*. Above, in the highly romanticized French-language poster, it's "a film by Ida Lupino" that "shocked America."

realist film making of *Shoeshine* (De Sica, 1946) and *Rome, Open City* (Rossellini, 1945) as models, and insists her company will make semi-documentaries, and avoid the "lurid sensationalism of some films on controversial subjects" (Bob Thomas, "Life in Hollywood," *San Mateo Times*, Feb. 9, 1949). A year later, she and Young take out a full page in *Variety* to publish a "Declaration of Independents," in part to promote their next film about a dancer stricken with polio, *Never Fear*, but also to publically assert their attempt at autonomy from mainstream Hollywood. In the four paragraph declaration, Young and Lupino express their "admiration for...Stanley Kramer, Robert Rossen and Louis de Rochemont." The declaration asserts "We like independence. It's tough sometimes, but it's good for the initiative. The struggle to do something different is good in itself. We think it is good for our industry as well." Young and Lupino claim they will "explore new themes, try new ideas, [and] discover new creative talents" (*Variety Daily*, 20 Feb. 1950). Independent filmmaking in Hollywood gained ground with the anti-trust Paramount Decree (1948) and the extension of First Amendment rights to film (1952), which substantially reduced the power of the PCA. With doors opening for independent filmmakers, Lupino took full advantage of her fame and popularity as an actress to plunge into producing and directing, becoming the second woman, after Dorothy Arzner, admitted to the Director's Guild of America. Although Lupino and Young's marriage ended in 1951, their Filmaker association continued effectively until 1954, with both partners often writing and producing, while

Lupino also directed and acted. As Annette Kuhn details, "(b)etween 1949 and 1954 Emerald Productions and The Filmakers produced at least twelve feature films. Lupino directed or co-directed six of these, scripted or co-scripted at least five, produced or co-produced at least one, and acted in three" (*Queen of the 'B's: Ida Lupino Behind the Camera*, Praeger, 1995, p. 2). She would also join "forces with fellow actors Dick Powell, Charles Boyer, and David Niven in Four Star Productions, which was responsible for [a]...highly regarded" CBS television series (Kuhn, p. 3). Lupino and her third husband, Howard Duff, would form Bridget Productions, named for their daughter, to produce their Emmy-nominated TV series, *Mr. Adams and Eve*. She proved highly capable as a director and producer of television and film.

Lupino quickly gained experience as a filmmaker. Her first film production presented her with her first directing job. Lupino worked hard to bring *Not Wanted*, which she co-wrote with Paul Jarrico, to the screen. She met with the PCA, which she found "amazingly helpful....They virtually wrote the story for us" (PCA files, Margaret Herrick Library, Academy of Motion Picture Arts and Sciences, Letter from Ida Lupino to Jack Vizzard dated Feb. 11, 1949). She defended the fledgling project about pregnancy out of wedlock against attacks in the press that labeled *Not Wanted* "degenerate." Three days into shooting, director Elmer Clifton suffered a heart attack. Although he retains screen credit, Lupino stepped in and directed the film. *Not Wanted* features a flashback structure much like *Mildred Pierce* (Curtiz, 1945) which places the female protagonist in police custody. But the "poor man's Betty Davis," as Lupino called herself, does not have her lead in a fur coat being questioned by the chief inspector. Instead, the struggling working class young woman, Sally (played by actress Sally Forrest, a Lupino discovery) winds up in a sordid jail cell populated with loud, slovenly women and a natty, slacks-clad dyke. The noir lighting in the police station sequences in *Mildred Pierce* and *Not Wanted* appear remarkably similar, if less vivid in *Not Wanted*, probably due to production costs. The shadows cutting Mildred's (Joan Crawford)

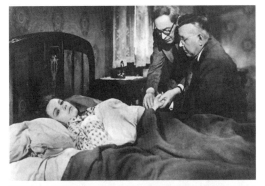

Above, *Not Wanted*: a "sensational" narrative unfolds in the noir visual style.

face point to her duplicity and doubt as she seeks to redirect suspicion for murder from her daughter; in *Not Wanted*, those same shadows reflect how Sally feels about herself, as she asks herself how she wound up in jail. As in *Mildred Pierce*, after the opening gambit at the police station, the flashback introduces a suburban neighborhood of comfortable, if a bit seedier in the later film, bungalows. In *Mildred Pierce*, the home is the site of dissatisfaction and strife between husband and wife. The same is true in *Not Wanted*. The atmosphere in both films seems to suggest that there is no peace or satisfaction to be found in the bounds of married normalcy—only domestic drudgery and economic hardship. For the young protagonist in Lupino's film, her awakening sexuality and youthful vitality find no outlet in the family home and small town life, only containment.

Film noir often presents female characters with the choice of the death of desire in the domestic realm, which requires that female agency and energy be contained, or literal death for transgressing the laws of a society. The femme fatale, beautiful and assertive, wants more than the domestic economy provides, more money, more independence, and often more passion. And she usually dies for her desires. Even the femme fatale is usually peripheral to the noir narrative, which focuses on a male protagonist. Lupino makes the female character central, but with a Neo-realist twist. Beginning with Sally, Lupino's characters are uniformly lower class, less glamorous, and less experienced than those she and other women

Below Keefe Brasselle and Sally Forrest as the young lovers in *Never Fear*.

often play in Hollywood studio productions. Sally seeks to escape her working class domestic milieu through a passionate obsession with a surly but talented and handsome piano player, Steve (Leo Penn, Sean Penn's father). Her punishment is her desperate flight from home, her rejection by Steve, her pregnancy, and her eventual relinquishment of the child to a couple who are "people of your own race and your own religion." Regretting that decision, she kidnaps a baby and that lands her in a jail cell, ending her flashback. Sally winds up in the benevolent hands of the patriarchal judicial system, usually remarkably humane and understanding in Lupino's output, and the kidnapped baby's sympathetic mother drops the charges. Finally, Sally's acceptance of a wounded war veteran (Keefe Brasselle) as her savior and probable husband ensures her redemption and survival, just as Mildred accepts her cheating husband Bert at the end of *Mildred Pierce*. In *Not Wanted*, the extended and heart-wrenching final scene, with Sally running endlessly across bridges and up and down stairs while the good-hearted vet gives chase, dragging his "plastic leg" along, leaves easy her acquiescence to society's demands in question. This melodrama about unwed motherhood reveals noir themes of female desire and dissatisfaction, of the dangers and dreariness of the domestic economy for working class women and for men. Without a hard boiled male protagonist and a duplicitous femme fatale, *Not Wanted* might not qualify as full-fledged film noir. It inaugurates what Carrie Rickey, writing for the *Village Voice*, calls "Lupino noir: a dimly lit, low-budget world where everyone lives sadder-but-wiser ever after" ("Lupino Noir," *The Village Voice*, Oct. 29-Nov. 4,1980, p. 44).

Lupino's second directorial outing, the first for which she takes unmitigated credit, *Never Fear* (1950, aka *The Young Lovers*), features the same two actors as *Not Wanted*, Forrest and Brasselle, as young lovers and struggling dancers (he is also a choreographer). This time the female protagonist is struck by polio on the cusp of their success as a dancing duo. Lupino, who had a brief bout with polio when she first arrived in Hollywood, co-authors the script with Young. She foregoes noir elements in favor of a remarkable Neo-realist reliance on location shooting at the Kabat-Kaiser Rehabilitation Institute in southern California, a facility opened in 1946 primarily to help wounded soldiers and others with neurological problems. Lupino integrates actual patients and workers at the facility into the film, along with the actors. She includes her sister, Rita Lupino, who plays a young wife with polio. The film ends with the couple reunited on the busy street in front of the institute—her cure and their future together, assured. Lupino's capable direction, her sympathetic focus on the struggles of the female protagonist, and her unique Neo-realist use of location shooting and working class characters, become more pronounced.

For *Outrage* (1950), Lupino directs and co-writes a script about an initially carefree young woman whose life is violently changed by a rape, euphemistically called a criminal assault throughout the film. After an opening credit sequence showing a disheveled young woman stumbling through darkened and empty streets, hinting at what will come, the film introduces Ann (Mala Powers, another Lupino discovery) before the attack. Ann works happily as an accountant in a factory, and buys two pieces of chocolate cake from the flirtatious and vaguely threatening man running a lunch truck outside the factory. In a subtle bit of foreshadowing, her footsteps sound as she runs up to the busy stand at noon. Ann ignores the lunch counter man's attempts to engage her. She goes off to meet her future fiancé for lunch on a bench in a crowded park, under the watchful eyes of a middle aged woman. The next day she is engaged to be married, and while she takes a coffee break with a friend, the lunch counter man's hands lurk in the foreground of the shot, drying a cup. Invisible to the women, his presence dominates the shot. Ann and her friend go back to work as another worker, a man, takes their place at the counter. The camera shows the dark-haired, bushy eyebrowed counter man briefly ignore his new customer as he watches the women walk away. Ann works

Above (with Tod Andrews as Rev. Ferguson, another emotionally damaged character), right, and on page 232, Mala Powers as the traumatized rape victim in *Outrage* whose emotions range from apprehension to shame to rage.

late, and when she leaves the factory after dark, he sees her leave, hurriedly closes the counter, and follows her.

In countless films noir, the doomed criminal runs desperately through empty nighttime urban landscapes, seeking to escape the inevitable—his capture and containment. In Lupino's film, an innocent young woman stands in for the criminal; her shoes echo on the unheeding pavement as she runs through factory yards, truck lots, and loading docks. Her eventual and inevitable apprehension by the man who has lurked at the edges of the scene since the beginning of the film is assured. This reworking of the common noir theme of the male doomed by malignant fate to an innocent young woman similarly doomed speaks of the extent to which the post-war malaise infects every aspect of existence for both men and women. Lupino's Neo-realist noir does not insist that the protagonist's anti-social desires for money or success or sex lead to her punishment. Instead, terrible violence and disruption can occur anywhere, to anyone. Noir paranoia infects the realm of the everyday. The film does not show the attack that motivates the narrative. Such techniques explain why, in the 1960s, "Lupino earned the nickname 'the female Hitch' for her…talent at creating suspense" in television programming (Mary Celeste Kearney and James M. Monran, "Ida Lupino as Director of Television," *Queen of the "B"s: Ida Lupino Behind the Camera*, Ed. Annette Kuhn, Praeger, 1995, p. 138). In *Outrage*, she adopts a classic Hitchcock stance towards violence, realizing that what the audience imagines is much worse than what can be shown on screen. Lupino thereby avoids a problem in many filmic rape narratives. She omits any possibility of visual pleasure in

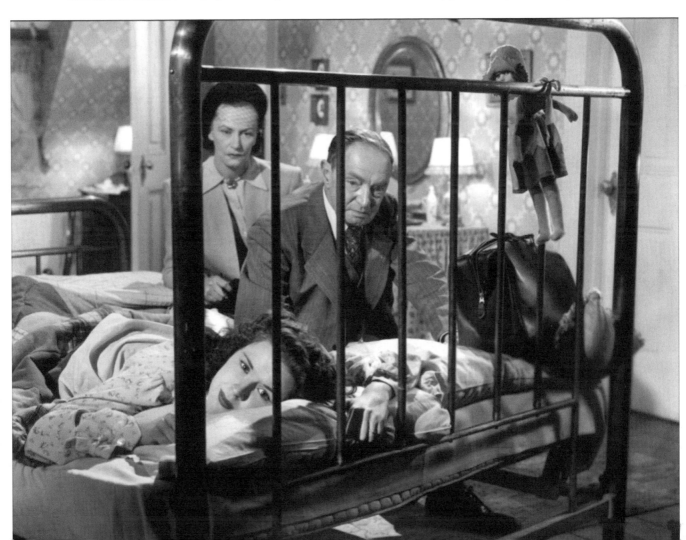

violence by showing only the attacker chasing Ann, and the aftermath of the rape. Here, the PCA restrictions likely informed her choices, which produce a less exploitive text.

The noir elements recede after the rape. Like *Not Wanted* and *Never Fear*, *Outrage* becomes a more standard Hollywood tale of redemption through the return of the woman to the constraints of an eventual heterosexual marriage. The film details the complete disruption of Ann's existence. Subjected to the unwanted attention from the police, her family, her fiancé, co-workers, and neighbors, she takes flight and winds up in rural California. She is taken in by a fruit farmer and his wife, and nurtured by a handsome, kindly pastor. Like Ann, he has been damaged, although by war. He lost a lung, and periodically sucks on an empty pipe. The film inserts actual location shots of an orange packing plant, where Ann works. She slowly begins to heal, thanks to her anonymity and the tender care of the pastor and his friends. Then, at a dance, she almost kills an insistent country suitor. He makes aggressive demands for a kiss, and maligns her handsome savoir; she flashes back to the rape, responding with a savage blow to his head with a huge wrench. As in the earlier films, kindly justice takes control of the situation; a judge drops the criminal charges but insists Ann get psychiatric help. The pastor argues that society has a duty, to Ann and even to her rapist, who was supposedly scarred by his war experiences, to help those in need. The noble pastor cares for Ann and eventually, despite Ann's feelings for him and his for her, puts her on a bus back to her home town, her family, and her waiting fiancé. The film's closing shot does not show her arrival there, but instead watches the bus pulling away from the country stop while the pastor gazes after it, and then walks to his car. The ending leaves the narrative open—it seems Ann will wind up back in the community from which she fled, but the camera does not deliver her there. This slight and implied disruption adds a taste of noir uneasiness of the film's closure.

Hard, Fast and Beautiful (1951), directed by Lupino and produced by Filmakers, also recalls *Mildred Pierce*, but rejects its melodramatic status by foregoing murder. While Mildred devotes herself to her selfish and unremarkable daughter, Veda (Anne Blyth), Millie Farley (Claire Trevor) devotes herself to making sure her talented daughter's tennis exploits are well paid. Mildred Pierce works hard so her daughter will never want for anything, seeking to protect her from the domestic drudgery that Mildred experiences. At first, it seems Millie only wants to protect her daughter, Florence (Sally Forrest, again) from a similar fate. But as the movie proceeds, it becomes clear that Millie uses her daughter's athletic prowess to gain access to a life of luxury, travel, and freedom from the domestic realm for herself, and that Millie manipulates and schemes to keep Florence athletically and economically productive. Set first in a small town, then in fancy hotels and European locales, and including footage from famous tennis matches, *Hard, Fast and Beautiful* ends with Millie sitting alone, rejected by daughter and husband, in an empty sports stadium as the wind blows detritus through the

Above, after winning a tournament in *Hard, Fast and Beautiful*.

empty stands. There is no reintegration into the stable family for Millie. She left behind her husband and sacrificed the happiness of her daughter, but she lives on to scheme again. In addition to her directing projects at this time, Lupino stars in another Filmakers production, *Beware My Lovely* (Harry Horner, 1952). She plays a war widow who hires a psychotic handyman (Robert Ryan) to help around the house. After being trapped in the home as an actor, she escapes to direct a claustrophobic road movie.

The Hitch-Hiker (1953) leaves stable homes, families, wives and mothers safely off screen, except for a woman murdered by the deadly criminal in the opening sequence of the film. Lupino considered *The Hitch-Hiker*, which she directed and co-scripted with her business partner and by now ex-husband Collier Young, her best film. The PCA files indicate that Young and Lupino negotiated doggedly with both James Bennett, the director of the Bureau of

Above, opposite and page 236: three versions of masculinity in *The Hitch-Hiker.*

Prisons in the U.S. Department of Justice, and Joseph Breen at the PCA to bring the story to the screen. The film opens with an on-screen paragraph insisting the story is true; indeed, it is ripped from the headlines in the early 1950s, when a killer named "William Edward Cook Jr., a 22-year-old Missouri ex-convict...killed six people on a murder spree while hitch-hiking in the Southwest" (Paula Rabinowitz, "The Hitch-Hiker," *Queen of the "B"s: Ida Lupino Behind the Camera*, Ed. Annette Kuhn, Praeger, 1995, p. 92). Young and Lupino aroused the ire of Bennett by contacting Cook in jail, via his lawyer, and getting him to sign a release. They initially planned to call their film *The Cook Story*; Breen objected on the grounds that "No picture shall be approved dealing with the life of a notorious criminal" (PCA files, Margaret Herrick Library, Academy of Motion Picture Arts and Sciences, Breen letter dated April 18, 1952). After four months of negotiations and changes to the script, the Filmakers won Breen's (and Bennett's) provisional approval. The script changes the murderous hitch-hiker to Emmett Myers (William Talman, who would go on to play the prosecuting attorney on television's *Perry Mason*). Lupino and Young keep the outline of Cook's crime spree—Cook killed a family of five, Myers murders a couple; Cook kidnaps prospectors and forces them to drive him to the Mexican town of Santa Rosalia, Myers kidnaps two middle-class men on a fishing trip, forcing them to drive him to Santa Rosalia. Breen's provisional approval suggests that "the town of Santa Rosalia be given some other name; again having in mind the necessity to disconnect your story, as much as possible, from the Cook story" (PCA files, Margaret Herrick Library, Academy of Motion Picture Arts and Sciences, Breen letter dated May 21, 1952).

Santa Rosalia remains in the film, as does a remarkably un-stereotypical treatment of the Mexican people, who are helpful, polite, and dutiful, and the Mexican police, who perform a careful investigation and dragnet leading to the arrest of the criminal at the end of the film. In a few sequences, the Mexican actors speak Spanish to one another; despite the extended nature of these conversations, no subtitles are provided. In one scene, a station owner reports the theft of gasoline, and insists he does not care about the gas but only his dog, which Myers shot dead. In another, a young man sees the wanted poster at the post office, and insists to the postal worker that Myers just hired a boat from him, and he calls the police. The Spanish sounds authentic, and these sequences allow the players to reveal their humanity and decency. Such portrayals underscore how Lupino longed to do stories dealing with racism, among other social problems, but Filmakers had partnered with RKO on "production facilities and distribution" (William Donati, *Ida Lupino: A Biography*, UP Kentucky, 1996, p. 167). Eccentric studio head Howard Hughes had story approval and was not interested in racism or "a story about Mexicans" (Donati, p. 173). Despite these hurdles, Lupino manages to include some racial diversity in her films: an Asian woman lives in the home for pregnant mothers, and a Black police

The Hitch-Hiker.

officer assists with the suspect line-up in *Not Wanted*. Her careful representation of non-Whites in the U.S., and of Mexican nationals in *The Hitch-Hiker* allowed her to exert her views regardless of Hughes' control. Nevertheless, producer Young portrays a sleeping Mexican in one scene, perhaps the most stereotypical role in the film.

Despite Lupino's sympathetic treatment of ethnicity, *The Hitch-Hiker*'s thematic focus is not race, but white male subjectivity and post-war masculinity in crisis. In the claustrophobic confines of a car racing across the Mexican desert, three men "race against death." Hitch-hiker Myers kills all his hosts eventually, and the law, and the two men who pick up Myers, know this. The three versions of masculinity offered by the film include Myers, a sadistic murder who takes what he wants and kills without remorse; Gil (Frank Lovejoy), a draftsman and dedicated family man, and Roy (Edmond O'Brien), a garage owner. After the opening that shows only the dusty feet of a hitch-hiker getting into various cars, apparently killing the driver and occupants and rifling through wallets and pocketbooks, the film introduces the two kidnap victims. Setting off on a fishing trip, their first since they both married and had kids, the men reminisce about the freedom they once enjoyed as single men. But the film explicitly answers their longings with Myers, a brutal and cruel version of masculinity without the social constraints that Gil and Roy have accepted. Myers tortures the men mentally and physically. He forces Gil, a skilled sharpshooter from his war days, to shoot a can from Roy's hand. Most Hollywood movies would not include that bit of plot without allowing Gil to later use the skill to catch or kill the criminal. Here, however, it seems only to point to Gil's and Mye''s parallel abilities and the total emasculation of Gil. Myers can also sharpshoot. The hitch-hiker goads both men, but especially Roy, who is particularly susceptible to the relentless cruelty. Roy takes Myers' taunts about his blue collar job (as a mechanic, although he owns the garage) and middle-class life personally, eventually breaking down. At one point, the more self-controlled Gil punches Roy to prevent him from attacking Myers, thereby saving Roy from almost certain death.

Noir films often portray contrasting female archetypes, the dangerous and desiring femme fatale and the *femme attrapée*, a woman content to marry and have children. Masculinity gets similar treatment in classic noir, with two archetypes of masculinity—the *homme fatal* who wants more than legal occupations offer him and often a dangerous dame as well, and the *homme attrapé*, a man content to obey society's rules and rule in his home. Here, the two versions of masculinity appear on screen together, battling it out for dominance. The asocial Myers, self-centered, murderous, and autonomous, contrasts with the quietly competent Gil, skilled with a gun and at work, as well as a family man, and Roy, who perhaps occupies a place somewhere between the two. For Ronnie Scheib, Roy, "is caught between the compromising caution of the petit bourgeoisies [Gil] and the petty vengeance of the dispossessed [Myers]," ("Ida Lupino: Auteuress," *Film Comment 16:1* (1980) p. 63). One odd sequence has the two kidnap victims rolled up into blankets on one side of a creek, while Myers dozes with one eye fixed on his captives. The men almost look like larval forms, wrapped in black blankets with only their heads visible in the inky darkness. The odd, off balance framing, stark nighttime lighting, and bleak hopelessness of the immobilized figures suggest something unspeakably brutal about the situation in which the men find themselves. At the end of the film, the competent Mexican police handcuff Myers, who suddenly realizes he is trapped and struggles, only to be punched in the head by Roy. The police separate the men, and take Myers away. Gil puts his arm around his friend, telling him "It's alright," and they walk into the darkness. Their middle-class lives, disrupted by the extreme form of autonomous masculinity both men longed for briefly at the beginning of the film, have been reinstated. Yet the vision of their own helpless, immobilized masculinity remains in the darkness at the edges of the frame.

The Bigamist (1953) is another "Lupino noir." Like *The Hitch-Hiker*, *The Bigamist* features three people trapped in an intimate situation. Rather than *Mildred Pierce*, the film self-consciously evokes *Double Indemnity* (1944), with numerous allusions to the earlier noir, and various jokes in casting and dialogue spicing up the rather plodding plot, at least for those in the know. Instead of Edward G. Robinson playing the dedicated and indigestion plagued insurance

Below, Edmond O'Brien as the title character in *The Bigamist* with Lupino as one wife and Joan Fontaine as another.

Deglamourized over a decade:

Bottom left, *The Man I love*, Lupino as the chanteuse Petey for Raoul Walsh, one of her directing mentors, in 1946.

Left, Lupino as she presents herself in *The Bigamist*.

Below, portraying a more debased character for director Don Siegel in *Private Hell 36*.

investigator, *The Bigamist* features Edmund Gwenn, known to moviegoers as Kris Kringle from *Miracle on 34th Street* (1947), as adoption investigator Mr. Jordan. Jordan pops little pills to assist with his stomach troubles, and acknowledges his dedication to making sure adoptive parents are worthy stems from the fact that "If you had made a mistake once, you wouldn't want to ever let it happen again. Not when a child is involved." So the Santa Claus-like investigator starts to dig, his indigestion telling him something is not quite right with the husband in a prospective adoptive San Francisco couple. The wife, Eve (Joan Fontaine) seems perfect: beautiful, successful, and desirous of a child. The husband, Harry (Edmond O'Brien) seems secretive and needlessly churlish. Jordan's digging brings him by taxi right to the front door of a small southern California bungalow, complete with a baby carriage, toys, and crying child. Harry has another wife, Phyllis (Lupino), and a child, in Los Angeles.

With her part in *The Bigamist*, Lupino becomes the first woman in classical Hollywood to direct herself in a starring role. Much was made of the casting for the film in the trade and publicity press of the time. Although still business partners in the Filmakers, producer Young and Lupino had by now divorced, and Joan Fontaine, Young's new wife, plays Eve, the first wife of the bigamist. Fontaine's mother (Lillian Fontaine) plays the supportive Miss Higgins, owner of the boarding house where Lupino's character, Phyllis lives. Young himself appears briefly as a glowering, scarred barfly, eying Harry when he stops in to see Phyllis at the Chinese restaurant where she works as a waitress. The camera lingers on Young as he looks at Harry threateningly; for a moment, it seems a different film noir will take up the narrative thread. Instead, Phyllis ushers Harry into dinner, and *The Bigamist* continues. The script, authored by Young, points numerous times to Gwenn's Santa Claus status, referring to the character as Claus-like, and the actor's name and presumably his house are featured on the itinerary of the bus tour of the stars where Harry and Phyllis first meet in Hollywood. This element of intimate fun sparks the film, with its milquetoast criminal protagonist who seems to fall benignly into a second marriage, unable to act to extricate himself until the benevolent investigator forces his hand. Even then, he manages to avoid confrontation with both women, leaving a note for one, and the other with no explanation. He leaves that to the courts.

Harry's voiceover begins when Jordan tracks him to his cluttered and harried domestic life with Phyllis. As the investigator picks up the phone to call the police, Harry seeks to explain how he wound up married to two women. The hard-boiled male protagonist in film noir often cannot see clearly into the criminal and murky situations in which he finds himself; Harry seems to know all too well how he wound up with a wife in both Los Angeles and San Francisco, but his criminality results from passivity, not activity. As Scheib astutely notes, for Lupino, passivity is "unwanted, restless, anxious, impotent....[h]er characters are sleepwalkers, their subjectivity condemned to incompleteness, their faces swept by emotions that happen to them but never belong to them" ("Ida Lupino: Auteuress," *Film Comment* 16:1 (1980) p. 54). Harry matches this description perfectly. Eve, the beautiful, sophisticated wife in San Francisco could not have a child and so devoted herself successfully to their deep freezer business. Feeling unneeded and having difficulty turning her attention to his personal needs as opposed to their joint business concerns, Harry uses a business trip to southern California to strike up a conversation, and then a relationship with the lower class Phyllis. Phyllis seems like any number of Lupino dames, tough talking but tenderhearted. Although Harry's voiceover indicates he is wracked with guilt about his affair, he and Phyllis wind up celebrating his birthday in Acapulco, and as in *Not Wanted*, one night of intimacy leads to Phyllis' pregnancy. Three months later, in town to make a clean break with Phyllis, he discovers her pregnancy and instead proposes marriage.

Harry's inability to do the right thing, by society's measure, almost stops the film's narrative in its tracks over and over again. He is buffeted by circumstances that he instigates, but does not seem to control. He stumbles helplessly into a friendship, a love affair, fatherhood, a marriage with Phyllis, and finally into admitting his duplicity. As in *Not Wanted* and *Outrage*, benevolent justice interprets the crime for the two women in the courtroom as well as the cinematic audience, asserting Harry's basic decency. Steeped in film noir and Neo-realism, Lupino looks forward to the French New Wave, ending the film with a freeze frame of Eve in the door of the courtroom. All the characters survive the narrative, "sadder but wiser ever after" (Rickey, p. 44).

Not all the characters survive *Private Hell 36* (1954), the final film Lupino stars in, co-produces and co-writes for the Filmakers. Directed by Don Siegel, and utilizing Sam Peckinpah (as David Peckinpah) as dialog director, *Private Hell 36* has all the trappings of film noir—two working stiff detectives, a sultry lounge singer, a briefcase full of money, a fatherly police chief, location shooting, and a dénouement so soaked in inky darkness that the characters all but disappear in the hell of their own making. Two struggling middle class police detectives, an odd couple in terms of habits and morality, engage in a protracted hunt for a thief passing hot money at a race track, taking along the lounge singer, Lilli Marlowe (Lupino) who received a fifty-dollar tip from him and can identify the perpetrator. The extended race track sequences show Lilli and the two detectives watching the crowd, watching people bet and lose and win huge amounts of money, and watching drivers leave the lot at the end of the race day, apparently day after day. Shot on location, these scenes both vibrate with the energy of the huge crowds and express the ennui of the boring, interminable, and seeming hopeless aspects of the search. Lilli falls for one of the detectives, dandy and ladies man Bruner (Steve Cochran). The other, Farnham (Howard Duff, Lupino's husband at the time) although struggling financially, is happily married with a wife (Dorothy Malone) and child (Bridget Duff, Duff and Lupino's daughter). When Lilli finally spots the man who gave her the marked money, the detectives give chase. The criminal drives off the road and into a ravine, dying in the accident—and the two men cannot resist the briefcase full of cash they find near the car. This begins the "private hell"—36 is the number of the trailer where Bruner hides the money—for Farnham, who is immediately guilt-ridden.

The fatherly police chief sets up his detectives, suspecting that they stole the money from the bust. The antagonism between the two men grows, "a lover's spat" as Lilli calls it, with Bruner deciding to leave town with Lilli and the money, and Farhham wanting to turn in the money and himself into their superior. In the final scene, Bruner shoots his partner rather than allow him to ruin their hopes of escaping their middle class struggles. He then dies in a hail of gunfire; instead of meeting a blackmailer who is after his share of the money, the chief is there to catch his own men in their deception. Unlike the Lupino-directed films, paternalistic justice does not set the surviving, guilt-ridden detective free. Instead, he lies wounded in the dark trailer park, his arrest and incarceration ensured.

Lupino's output, as director, producer, and screenwriter, and of course, as actor, ensures her place in noir's canon. The noir films she created are bleak, realist documents that hold fast to the tenants of masculinity, femininity, and criminality set up by classical Hollywood cinema and the PCA. At the same time, these films exhibit a unique vision, extending the noir sensibility into the low-budget milieu where domesticity and criminality co-exist as two sides of the same narrative. Lupino's Neo-realist focus on working class women and men, on issues such as rape and teen pregnancy, on the social implications of the post-war condition, on locations such as packing plants, rehabilitation centers, and homes for unwed mothers, mark her tremendous contribution to film noir and Hollywood's output during the noir years. Her icon status is assured.

Biography

Hollywood and other sources claim that Ida Lupino was born in London in 1918, and that the talented and artistic family had performed for European royalty since the 1800s. Lupino's first movie acting reportedly came at the expense of her mother, who had taken her young teenage daughter along to an audition and lost the job to her. Subsequent film roles in England, Hollywood contracts with Paramount, and then Warner Bros. led to Lupino calling herself the "poor man's Bette Davis," as she often played roles Davis, also contracted to Warner's, refused. She excelled at portraying tough, damaged, hard-boiled dames with a heart, in films such as *High Sierra* (Raoul Walsh, 1941), *Road House* (Jean Negulesco, 1947), and *Private Hell* 36 (Don Siegel, 1954). In 1948, Lupino married her second husband, Hollywood insider Collier Young, became a U.S. citizen, and with Young started Emerald Productions. They changed its name to The Filmakers in 1950, and in the next five years, the independent production company made twelve films. Lupino directed, produced, screenwrote, and performed in Filmakers films; she simultaneously acted in other Hollywood productions, such as On *Dangerous Ground* (Nicholas Ray, 1952). Her film projects include female melodramas featuring a rape victim, a scheming mother, and a polio-stricken dancer, and male melodramas of passivity including *The Bigamist* and *The Hitch-Hiker*, all of which function at some level as film noir. From the mid-1950s until the late 1960s, Lupino devoted her prodigious energies to television. She directed and acted in a TV series with her third husband, Howard Duff, who also produced the show. She directed episodes of *Have Gun, Will Travel; Alfred Hitchcock Presents; The Rifleman; Thriller; The Fugitive; Gilligan's Island; Bewitched; The Twilight Zone* and many other successful series. Lupino returned to directing for Hollywood in 1966 with *The Trouble with Angels*, and continued to play roles on television screens into the mid-1970s. Ida Lupino died in 1995.

Noir Films

Not Wanted (1949).
Never Fear (1950)
Outrage (1950)
Hard, Fast and Beautiful (1951)
The Hitch-Hiker (1953)
The Bigamist (1953)

Anthony Mann (seated) is flanked by star James Stewart and cinematographer William Daniels (standing far right) on location for *Winchester '73.*

Anthony Mann

Susan White and Homer Pettey

Dr. Broadway (1942)

Having worked with some success as an actor, stage manager and set designer on Broadway, and finally as production manager for the Theater Guild, Anthony Mann made his move to Hollywood in 1939. He worked as a talent scout for David O. Selznick, and directed screen tests for projects including *Gone with the Wind* and *Rebecca*. Moving over to Paramount, Mann worked as assistant director for several years, for directors including Preston Sturges (see Jeanine Basinger, *Anthony Mann* [Middletown, CT: Wesleyan University Press, 2007, pp. 2-3]). His directorial debut, *Dr. Broadway*, was made possible with the help of his friend, Macdonald Carey, who starred in the film. On the credits the director's name reads "Anton Mann," a name he had used in his theatrical career.

Dr. Broadway is an agreeable B-picture, based on a story by Borden Chase, who became a frequent Mann collaborator. Mann's beginnings as a director of noir films are easily discernible in this minor thriller. The plot centers on "Dr. Broadway," Dr. Timothy Kane (Madonald Carey), a cheerful young physician who treats the inhabitants of the Broadway neighborhood, from charwoman to judge—often "on the cuff." The setting provides the opportunity to introduce any number of colorful characters, including newsies, gangsters, and B-girls. As Jeanine Basinger observes, the characters and situations depicted with humor in *Dr. Broadway* "would later materialize in their more realistic and seedy forms" (p. 21). Rear-projected stock footage supplements the sets, creating an occasionally "Weegee"-like atmosphere. The film frequently features bold compositions and lighting. Near the beginning, a young woman stands on a ledge, threatening to jump. The camera's low angle and high contrast lighting—police klieg lights and photographers' flashbulbs—as well as curved buttresses and an enormous neon "S" on the side of the building, dramatize the woman's plight. The crowd response and policemen's dialogue render the scene strangely humorous, something that makes sense when we learn that her cry about being "out of this world" is actually a disguised advertisement for "Hambone Harris and His Harlem Hot Shots." Dr. Broadway convinces the attractive blonde, Connie Madigan (Jean Phillips), to come off the ledge, and tries to help her hide the advertising ruse. When the police get wise to her act, she goes before a judge, who happens to be the doctor's friend. Charges are dropped, especially since Connie's crime was "strictly from hunger," but Connie must pay for her bad behavior by going to work as the doctor's receptionist and eventual operative. The story becomes more convoluted, as gangster Vic Telli (Eduardo Ciannelli) whom the doctor had helped to put in jail, is released. Far from wanting to kill him, as is widely assumed, Telli actually wants the doctor to act as intermediary for the one good action of the killer's life: giving $100,000 to his estranged daughter. Telli's death in the doctor's office throws suspicion on Dr. Kane. Hide-and-seek with the police, amateur sleuthing, the appearance of a false and then the real daughter of the gangster, bring the film to its obligatory romantic ending.

Dr. Broadway

Basinger notes (p. 20) that the emotional linking of villain and hero at work in this film will become one of Mann's most characteristic themes. Set design and cinematography reinforce that link. Although Dr. Kane, as played by Carey, is irrepressibly pleasant, he inhabits a noir world of stage doors, nightclubs, pool halls, boxing gyms, and dark streets. The ceilinged sets, producing a sense of claustrophobia, are explored by means of tracking shots, and their darkness often conceals deadly threats. One of the most visually interesting and ambiguous moments in the film occurs when Telli comes to the doctor's office to make his request for help. Fearing for the gangster's health, Dr. Kane sets up a sunlamp, whose hard top lighting creates an eerie atmosphere, reminiscent of police interrogation lights or the bare light bulbs hanging over countless noir sets. Stranger still are the goggles Telli dons, which enhance the scene's grotesque mood. As short and underplayed as this scene is, it is typical of the way that Mann will come to manipulate objects, character, and cinematography in the interest of revealing the dark side of human nature.

Strangers in the Night (1944)

In this film Mann worked with veteran cinematographer Reggie Lanning—who photographed

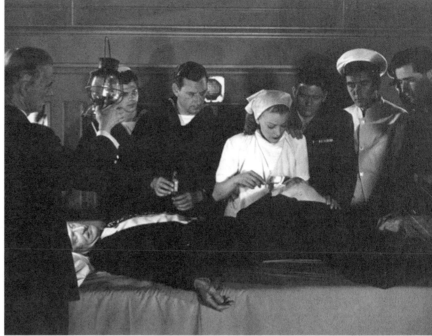

many B-pictures and films as diverse as Keaton's *The Cameraman* (1928) and Allan Dwan's John Wayne vehicle *The Sands of Iwo Jima* (1949)— and began to experiment with the Expressionistic visual style that would continue through the rest of his noir films.

The film's plot is convoluted. In it a wounded veteran, Johnny Meadows (William Terry), returns stateside to meet Rosemary Blake to whom he wrote after finding her address in a novel, *A Shropshire Lad*, that she had donated to the military hospital. Having been comforted and sustained during his convalescence by Rosemary's letters, Johnny is determined to meet Rosemary and express his love. On the train to California, where Rosemary lives with her mother in Monteflores, Meadows encounters Dr. Leslie Ross (Virginia Grey) who is en route to the same small town to set up a medical practice. Leslie happens to be reading a copy of *A Shropshire Lad*, making him wonder momentarily if she is Rosemary—a "doubling"

Strangers in the Night: above, Virginia Grey as Dr. Leslie Ross.

Right, an early exampe of Mann's staging in depth with Mrs. Blake (Helen Thimig) on the telphone in the foreground.

that is never explained. Upon arrival, Johnny encounters Rosemany's strange mother, Hilda Blake (Helen Thimig), whom Leslie has already met and found unpleasant. When Mrs. Blake realizes that Leslie and Johnny know one another, she becomes suspicious. Like Mrs. Danvers in *Rebecca*, Mother Hilda shows Johnny Rosemary's room, while commenting on the beauty of her clothes and the smell of her perfume; but in a home dominated by her portrait, Rosemary herself remains mysteriously absent. Hilda's secret is that she invented her daughter out of loneliness. To maintain that ruse Hilda eventually murders her companion Ivy and tries to do likewise to Johnny and Leslie but fails. When confronted by them, an unhinged Hilda begs Rosemary's portrait for help. It answers her plea by falling over and killing her.

Basinger describes a number of scenes that establish *Strangers in the Night*, despite its low production values, as an important learning experience for Mann. Using a fish-eye lens, "deep focus, daring camera angles, exaggerated close-ups and deeply shadowed environments...the collaborators miss almost no opportunity to use photography to improve the

Erich von Stroheim and Mary Beth Hughes in *The Great Flamarion*.

quality of the film" (p. 22). In one particularly disturbing scene, the crazy villainess insists on toasting Rosemary's birthday by candlelight. "The firelight casts a flickering light over the faces of the two women, and the lack of direct illumination engulfs the large, handsomely appointed room in ominous shadows." The eerie quality of the scene is intensified by Mrs. Blake's fanatical worship of her "daughter." Thimig's performance is baroque, but not without skill. When she finally admits that Rosemary is a fiction, the camera slowly tracks in on her face. In a grotesque close-up, she tells Johnny the truth: "You were loving me." Rather like Norman Bates in *Psycho*, she will do anything to keep the myth of her loved one "alive." The film's ending—Mrs. Blake's bizarre death—is inadvertently funny.

This film is an amalgamation of many plots, but its impact derives from an ancient narrative device, the "loathly lady" of medieval literature. But whereas the hideous old woman in those tales could be turned into a young beauty, *Strangers in the Night* reverses the tradition, creating the horrifying image of a young woman who lures the man into her web only to reveal her true hideousness. And yet this "villainess" is by far the most interesting character in the film, and reveals the divided nature of many future Mann heroes.

The Great Flamarion (1945)

An eccentric but fascinating little noir, *The Great Flamarion* is a study of sexual obsession, told in voiceover flashback by a dying man, as in *D.O.A.* or, with some variation, *Sunset Boulevard* (1950), which also features von Stroheim. As with many another noir, *The Great Flamarion* may have been inspired by the previous year's *Double Indemnity*, especially considering that it was produced by W. Lee Wilder, director Billy Wilder's brother. Erich von Stroheim is the Great Flamarion, a sharpshooter in a vaudeville act. His perfectionism as a marksman, rigid upright posture, Germanic diction, and steely gaze, conceal a heart broken some time in the past by a mysterious woman. His act is a weird microcosm of the classic noir triangle, in which his character comes home to find his "wife," Connie Wallace (Mary Beth Hughes), in the arms of another man, Connie's real-life husband, Al Wallace (Dan Duryea). The likably sleazy Duryea, who would play another such character later that year in *Scarlet Street*, gives what James Ursini, in *The Film Noir Encyclopedia*, terms "another stellar rendering of a weak noir male." An alcoholic also besotted by his wife, he is clearly ill suited to his work dodging bullets in the act. This is especially true since Connie is an expert manipulator, even as femmes fatales go.

The film opens in Mexico City, where a comic vaudeville act is interrupted by the sound of bullets and a woman's scream. The police clear the crowd, but up in the darkened rafters a man lies bleeding. He falls behind the curtain and one of the vaudevillians offers to seek help. But Flamarion knows that he's doomed, and wants only to tell his miserable tale. The flashback reveals Flamarion at the top of his game, precision firing at the "illicit" couple onstage. Connie, cool and collected under fire, has plenty of ammunition herself—and she doesn't hesitate to use it on any attractive man in her vicinity, wishing to rid herself of her inconvenient husband in order to run off with another vaudeville performer.

The obvious solution to her dilemma is to seduce Flamarion and convince him to kill Al "accidentally" during their act. Flamarion's professionalism finally fails him in the face of her persistent seduction. Giddy with love, Flamarion commits the deed, only to be left waiting in their previously arranged meeting place, a hotel room he has lavishly filled with flowers. The sharpshooter slowly sinks into degradation, spending his fortune in search of the faithless Connie, who has married another performer and fled to Mexico. When Flamarion, now broke and dressed like a tramp, finally catches up with her, Connie has yet another man waiting in the wings. The story comes full circle, with the femme fatale and the ill-fated Flamarion having met their demise.

Vaudeville is an unusual but effective noir setting. Flamarion's act and its cynical performers bring to mind the setting of Carné's magisterial French Poetic-Realist film, *Le Jour se lève* (1939). In that film, dogs are trained to perform by means of hot irons, the ultimate symbol of the manipulations, entrapment, and torture of their human counterparts. The shift from the U.S. to Mexico redoubles *The Great Flamarion*'s surrealistic atmosphere, already established by the footlights of the stage and the strange costumes of the ultimately hapless performers.

Strange Impersonation (1946)

Mann's *Strange Impersonation* relies upon a noir narrative convention of the protagonist undergoing a drug-induced hallucinatory moment, used for the first time in Edward Dmytryk's *Murder, My Sweet* (1944). Typically, this convention reveals the underlying psychological state of the entrapped noir hero, often moving through several, rapidly occurring emotional stages from acute anxiety to delusional paranoia. Directors employ visual distortions, superimposed faces, and surrealistic imagery to achieve these experimental, dream-like effects. In *Strange Impersonation*, Mann expands upon this nightmare technique so that the film itself is an

Strange Impersonation: Above, Mann uses superimposition for expressionist effect. Brenda Marshall as chemist Nora Goodrich with Hillary Brooke, below; accused at bottom left; and with her disfigurement veiled, bottom right.

extended exploration of the feminine psyche and its discontents. What appears at first to be a B-grade melodrama becomes a hard-boiled account of psychopathological revenge. Mann also complicates the role of the femme fatale so that both women in the love triangle express fatal intentions.

Film noir often experimented with film techniques, such as shooting entirely from Marlowe's (Robert Montgomery) point-of-view in *Lady in the Lake* (1947) or the Ray Milland vehicle *The Thief* (1952), in which not one word of dialogue is spoken. Since Mann's *Strange Impersonation* is almost entirely a hallucination, its plot is further complicated, because the events are only the psychological projections of the heroine. Like the heroine's dual roles, there are two plots, the simple events and the complicated nightmare.

As a career-minded chemist, Nora Goodrich (Brenda Marshall) chooses to develop a new, powerful anesthetic over the desires of her fiancé, Dr. Stephen Lindstrom (William Gargan). This new drug requires exacting portions; otherwise, the solution becomes volatile and incendiary. In order to test its effects, Nora invites her assistant, Arline Cole (Hillary Brooke), to her apartment to observe the self-experimentation Nora will perform. On her way home, Nora bumps her car into an inebriated Jane Karaski (Ruth Ford), who stumbled and caused the minor accident. Still, J. W. Rinse (George Chandler), factotum for an ambulance-chasing attorney, witnesses the accident and tries unsuccessfully to persuade Jane to seek legal advice. Nora takes Jane to a tenement apartment, where Jane obstinately refuses her financial help.

Back at her apartment, Stephen proposes marriage for the very next day, but Nora cannot contemplate settling down until the experiment is complete. She offers her engagement ring back to Stephen, but he still holds out hope. Arline arrives and the experiment begins when Nora injects herself with the anesthetic. Nora drifts off as the screen blurs then fades to Arline smirking over the unconscious Nora. Arline mixes the chemicals incorrectly and steps back as Stephen enters the apartment, just in time to witness the explosion and Nora set on fire. Nora, covered in facial bandages, awakens in the hospital with Stephen professing his love, as all the while, the treacherous Arline schemes to keep the lovers apart and to make Stephen her own. Nora recovers, but remains physically disfigured and emotionally scarred, believing that Stephen no longer wants her. Jane Karaski returns, steals Nora's purse and engagement ring at gunpoint, but is shot in a struggle with Nora on the balcony and plummets to her death, landing on her face!

Because Jane's body is mistaken for her own, Nora assumes Jane's identity and flies to Los Angeles, where she undergoes months of intensive and successful plastic surgery to transforms her hideous facial scars. Nora discovers that Arline has married Stephen, so she returns to New York to work again at the Wilmotte Institute, this time in the guise of a longtime friend of the supposedly dead Nora. As Stephen's chemical assistant, she reverses Arline's duplicity, making Stephen fall in love with her instead. Confronting Arline about the fire, Nora threatens to shoot her if she refuses to give Stephen up. When she acquires a passport, the police match Nora's fingerprints to the murder weapon. In a noir third-degree harshly lit scene, Nora is accused of killing Nora Goodrich. Superimposed faces accuse the frightened Nora of murder, until she faints under the pressure. The screen blurs again and then fades to Nora back in her apartment, awakened by Stephen, whom Nora now asks to marry her. It was all a nightmare.

Strange Impersonation requires a retrospective review of the plot and its meaning. Freud is not needed to understand that Nora's split personality represents her struggles between being a career woman and a fiancée. The fire that burns her is a visual metaphor for both her sexual desires and her secret jealousy of Arline. Her disfigurement is an attempt to efface her involvement in the sterile, scientific world. Nora, not Arline, is the real femme fatale, but fatal only to her professional self. Nora murders herself in order to kill off the career chemist and to transform into a new identity, the domesticated female.

Desperate (1947)

Newlywed Steve Randall (Steve Brody) is suckered into acting as the wheel man for a warehouse robbery masterminded by a childhood friend, Walt Radak (Raymond Burr). A cop is killed during the heist. A novice at crime, Walt's brother Al (Larry Nunn) is injured falling from a landing, picked up by the police, tried, and sentenced to death. Steve manages to escape both the gangsters and the police to get his pregnant wife Anne (Audrey Long) away to the country where she can stay on her Czech relatives' farm. Scared off the train when Steve believes a man recognizes him (the man actually "recognizes" them as honeymooners), they find themselves again and again in incriminating circumstances. Steve "steals" a car that he has in fact purchased from an unscrupulous dealer, and drives away in the smashed-up car of a sheriff who tries to arrest them. Once he is sure that his wife is safe, Steve approaches Lt. Ferrari (Jason Robards), an ironic detective who early on believed in Steve's guilt, to confess to the crime. But Ferrari now realizes that Steve is innocent and that only he can lead police to the real killers. Back on the farm, Uncle Jan (Paul E. Burns), and Aunt Klara (Ilka Gruning) are adorably old-country, and insist that the young couple have the church wedding they hadn't been able to afford. During the wedding, a crooked private investigator Pete (Douglas Fowley) insinuates

Desperate: above, heavy shadows and sharp contrast as Steve (Steve Brodie) raises a fist.

Left, Raymond Burr as the sadistic Walt Radak with his robber cronies.

Opposite, the image of Hugh Beaumont as Ferguson in *Railroaded* is heavily constricted.

himself into the folksy affair, just as Anne says that she finally feels safe. As the clock counts down for Al's execution, Steve is taken prisoner by Walt, who wants to kill Steve at the stroke of midnight in revenge for the death of his younger brother. A timely interruption makes it possible for Steve to break free and kill Walt just at the stroke of midnight. Ferrari ends by giving his regards to Steve's family.

Like Mann's later *Side Street* (1950) and *They Live by Night* (Ray, 1948, photographed by George E. Diskant as is *Desperate*), this is interesting as a couple-on-the-run film. But *Desperate* is especially intriguing in its depiction of a "double desperation," on the part of both hero and villain. While Raymond Burr brilliantly incarnates a sadistic killer, he shows as much or more emotional complexity as the "hero." His love for his brother betrays an obsessive protectiveness. Reluctant to let Al (Larry Nunn) take part in the warehouse job, Walt turns tender as he relents. It's an uneasy moment when he gives his brother a gun, smiling dotingly. The film's visuals alternate between the bright spaces of the Randalls' kitchen and of Uncle Jan's and Aunt Klara's farm and the dark space of Radak's hideout. While the film is replete with noir effects, including the lattice shadows thrown on the gaunt face of Radak's sidekick Reynolds (William Challee) in Steve's truck, and the rain-slicked street outside the warehouse. Most intriguing is the space of the hideout, which features the classic hard overhead lamp swinging wildly in scenes of torture and conflict, picking out human faces like a searchlight and throwing shadows on the walls. Low lighting from an unseen source reinforces the sense of the grotesque. Point-of-view shots from Steve's perspective register the threat of a fist and a broken bottle, hinting at the brutality of which Walt is capable. But not only is Walt trapped in his hideout as he awaits word of Steve from his crooked private detective, he is also psychologically trapped by the countdown to midnight as he awaits his brother's execution. The attempt to avenge that punishment by executing Steve at the same time is thwarted by a knock on the door by a friendly neighbor woman, offering cake from her dinner. (The four-month "anniversary" cake that goes uneaten at the beginning of the film metaphorically reappears to save the day.) Driven out into the corkscrew stairwell, Walt is killed by a single bullet fired by Steve from the gun of Lt. Ferrari. In this way Steve is doubly redeemed: he has destroyed the menace to his family and he has been symbolically united with the law in that destruction.

Railroaded (1947)

Critics have overlooked *Railroaded* (1947) among Mann's noirs and in the canon of the genre, primarily because of its low-budget, B-film status. Just three years before the release of this film, *Murder, My Sweet* (1944) ushered in many of the aesthetic conventions for film noir. Interspersing of light and dark spaces accentuates the noir mood of portentous doom and expressions of fear. Oblique camera angles and foregrounded objects contribute to a sense of disorientation in the noir world of moral ambiguity. Chiaroscuro techniques and inventive camerawork express the alienation imposed by this noir society, as well as alienating personalities of both the protagonists and villains. These standard features for noir are exaggerated to the extreme in Mann's *Railroaded*, which violates even the experimental conventions of this new film style. In particular, Mann relies upon the excessive power of blackness, at times the absence of light, to convey its crucial scenes of violence. More than any other early noir, this film visually casts a black pall over interior spaces in order to reveal the psychological fixations of its characters, all of whom

Above, source lighting used to motivate heavy contrast in *Railroaded*. Below, a sullen Duke Martin (John Ireland) in a nightclub with Rosie Ryan (Sheila Ryan), the sister of the man he framed.

are possessed with a type of monomania. Mann took these visually compelling, aesthetic risks with *Railroaded* in order to portray the dark moods of fetishism that typify the modern world.

The opening sequence of *Railroaded* establishes its noir aesthetic and how that aesthetic form sustains the thematic content of the film. An elderly patron emerges from the shadowy exterior of Clara Calhoun's (Jane Randolph) beauty shop. She asks about her hair style "How do you like it?" to which Clara outrageously responds, "Honey, I just hope you get home safely." The innuendo of sexual aggression suggests a pervasive concern in the film with women and violence. (Later, at the Club Bombay, owner and underworld boss, Jackland Ainsworth [Roy Gordon] quotes from Oscar Wilde, "Women should be struck regularly like gongs.") Through foreground objections of domed hair dryers and hanging electric curlers, the camera pans as Clara moves back through an extremely dark salon to an off-track gambling parlor in the back. The desire for money, for illicit profits, is a fetish that dominates the criminal psyche in the film. Clara shoos the women gamblers out with the line "Ain't I got a right to a date?" and then asks Marie Weston (Peggy Converse) to close up after the women depart. In retrospect, Clara's comment ironically reveals her obsessive need for attention from her sadistic lover, Duke Martin (John Ireland).

Clara opens the back door and signals into a pitch-black alley, out of whose darkness emerge two armed men, Duke Martin and Cowie Kowalski (Keefe Brasselle), their faces obscured by scarves. The sawed-off-shotgun-toting Kowalski herds Marie into the front of the parlor and as he hears veteran patrolman O'Hara checking the shop locks on the street, he forces Marie back. Mann uses two zooming, extreme close-ups in shot-reverse-shot sequence to reveal Marie's frightened face and Kowalski's phallic shotgun barrel. Marie screams and faints. O'Hara's silhouette with his gun drawn moves across the frosted salon window. Kowalski fires two shots at the window, the white-hot blaze of the blasts is the only illumination Mann provides. Through the broken glass of the salon's door, O'Hara shoots Kowalski, but Duke fires upon the policeman, who crashes through the door into the pitch blackness of the shop, his feet remaining in the broken glass frame. Duke grabs Kowalski and marches him into the blackened alley and into a laundry truck for their getaway. Mann cuts to an exterior street shot in front of a physician's house. Mottled, entangled shadows from tree limbs and leaves allow for very little light and represent the predicament for the two robbers. In the interior of the truck, faint light illuminates only part of Duke's face as he tells Kowalski to frame Steve Ryan (Ed Kelly) as his accomplice, since it is Ryan's laundry truck that was used for the escape.

From here, the film moves to the fixations of police, who will stop at nothing to convict the framed Steve Ryan. Mickey Ferguson (Hugh Beaumont), who enacts the seething rage against the murder of O'Hara, leads the criminal investigation with fixed intensity in his pursuit. Rosie Ryan (Shelia Ryan) serves as Ferguson's feminine counterpart and seeks to exonerate her brother Steve by any means necessary, even spending time with the verbally abusive Duke at the Club Bombay. To secure a true alibi for her brother, Rosie confronts a drunken Clara in her apartment. Duke has already slapped her around for being an alcoholic. Rosie accuses Clara of lying, which produces a drawn-out, vicious fight between the two women, all done in semi-darkness as Duke watches with a smirk on his face from the shadows of the bedroom door frame.

Duke's obsessive, compulsive ritual of polishing his bullets and Dixon .38 special revolver with a perfumed handkerchief epitomizes the fetishistic desires of the modern world for materialism and for vengeance. His penchant for homicide escalates with the killing of Marie; the only evidence left is the bullet hole in her purse. Not able to trust Clara, whom he has sequestered in a dingy waterfront hotel, Duke sadistically shoots her in the belly. As she dies, she grabs the breast pocket handkerchief, which Ferguson later acquires, along with the

Mary Meade in a posed shot for
T-Men that fully refects the noir
visual style.

bullet as evidence against Duke. Methodically rubbing his revolver, Duke then confronts Ainsworth at the Bombay Club, whom he also gut-shoots.

In the final scene, Duke sits in almost complete darkness, obsessively stroking his piece, as Rosie arrives, her face barely visible in the contours of upturned chair legs of the afterhours nightclub. From his hip, Duke slowly raises his weapon, as he calmly accuses Rosie of double-crossing him. In a repetition of the opening scene, Ferguson arrives at the Club and smashes through the glass doors, as a gun flash bursts into the frame with Rosie hit by Duke's bullet. The ensuing shoot-out among overturned chairs and tables in extreme darkness exemplifies noir visual techniques from this early period.

Mann's innovative noir sculpting with shadows, not light and his portrayal of obsessions with blackness, not gray scales, sets this film apart from other noir films for the next decade. Clearly, *Railroaded* deserves a critical re-assessment for its ultramodern experimentation with noir visual and thematic content.

T-Men (1947)

T-Men, directed by Mann for Eagle-Lion in 1947, was his first collaboration with cinematographer John Alton, and, with *Raw Deal*, one of two Mann films starring Dennis O'Keefe. Jeanine Basinger describes *T-Men* as Mann's first "fully realized project," technically and thematically speaking. Like some of Mann's other films, it is a police procedural. The story of Treasury Department agents infiltrating a counterfeit money ring in Los Angeles, *T-Men*'s title obviously refers to *G-Men*, a 1935 anti-gangster Cagney vehicle. Like other police procedurals, *T-Men* foregrounds the police investigation, giving the film a semi-documentary feel. Its narrative space is split into two distinctive parts, with high-key-lit scenes at the Treasury Department alternating with scenes in the criminal underworld. Mann's and Alton's depiction of urban gangland features some of the most distinctive stylistics of the film noir movement. Its split narrative seems to offer an unassailable boundary between the criminal and law-enforcement environments. A solemn voiceover (by Reed Hadley) and an appearance by the Chief Coordinator of Law Enforcement for the Treasury Department (Elmer Lincoln Irey) serve to reassure the film viewer that the law will prevail. However, the extremely dark nature of visuals and content throughout the film seriously undermine that guarantee

Treasury agents Dennis O'Brien (O'Keefe) and Tony Genaro (Alfred Ryder) are chosen to infiltrate a large counterfeiting ring based in Los Angeles. The two agents go to Detroit to acquire mob credentials before heading out to the Coast. Male interactions in the film are already marked by violence, and the violence escalates rapidly. The men embrace their new identities, backed by phony wanted posters planted by other Treasury agents. O'Brien (now Harrigan) and Genaro (now Galvani) befriend Pasquale (Tito Vuolo), the mobbed-up owner of a seedy hotel. Tony impresses Pasquale with his vernacular Italian, so the agents manage to learn enough about the defunct River Gang to stand up under interrogation. They are put through the test right away when gangster boss Vantucci (Anton Kosta) questions them closely. Although emphasis is placed again and again on the difficulty

From *T-Men*, an early example of one of Mann's visual motifs: apprehensive characters unseen by each other but both visible to the audience.

Mann's early noirs did not back away from graphic and sometimes shockingly (for the time) graphic violence: Moxie (Charles McGraw) prepares to administer a beating to "Vannie Harrigan," the assumed identity of Agent O'Brien (Dennis O'Keefe) in *T-Men*. Opposite, the Schemer (Wallace Ford) with "Harrigan" and about to die at the hands of Moxie in the steam room.

with which O'Brien and Genaro acquire their criminal veneer, the hard top-lighting, diagonal compositions, and wide angles—as well as their casually hard-bitten diction and flashy garb—confirm them in their criminal roles as they move deeper undercover. Vantucci's suspicions allayed, he "hires" them to work in the liquor warehouse he controls. In a stark locker room, the men get an important lead. Noting that a pair of overalls assigned him are short and wide, O'Brien learns that they belonged to the "Schemer"(Wallace Ford), a fat, fiftyish con artist on the outs with the Detroit mob. O'Brien heads to L.A. to find the Schemer, whose habit of chewing "Chinese dragon liver herb medicine" (a detail noted in the scientifically managed Treasury files) puts the agent hot on his trail. Back in Detroit, in a particularly claustrophobic scene, Vantucci's boys knock Tony around under the ubiquitous harsh, interrogation-style lighting, Tony hangs tough, earning Vantucci's respect.

A montage sequence ensues, as O'Brien combs Chinatown looking for an herbalist who might know the Schemer. O'Brien's racial and cultural alienation reaches its apex, as image after image of Chinese shopkeepers and their wares inundate the screen. Film noir's familiar association between the "Orient" and degradation or perversion is doubly impressed upon the viewer, who has already been informed that this fictional investigation is based in part on the real-life "Shanghai paper case." O'Brien picks up information that will lead him on another quest, through the steam baths of Los Angeles, where he finally recognizes the Schemer by a scar on his shoulder. A darkened steam bath provides an ideal noir setting, and O'Brien's casing of the two-bit hood is now marked by the disturbing eroticism implied by semi-nudity and low lights. In a chiaroscuro pool hall, O'Brien gets the Schemer's attention by passing a phony bill. Beaten bloody by the other gamblers, O'Brien smiles with pleasure as he lies in the dark alley. He has accomplished his purpose. A confrontation in the Schemer's apartment is another visually stylish set piece. Extreme low-angle shots exposing bare bulbs are motivated by the men's scrutiny of each other's counterfeit. Deep focus, reflective surfaces and frames within frames characterize O'Brien's movement from a glitzy nightclub into the heart of the gang whose boss, curiously in this male-dominated film, turns out to be a woman (Jane Randolph, *Railroaded*'s Clara).

As O'Brien grows closer to the secret of the Chinese paper, the bodies around him continue to fall. Charles McGraw (Moxie) looms large as the film's major heavy. He expertly tortures O'Brien, giving O'Keefe another opportunity to display the agonized facial expressions characteristic of the Mann protagonist under duress. One of the most brilliant and memorable sequences in the film takes place when Moxie dispatches the Schemer in the steam bath. Dressed only in a towel and sweating profusely, the physically imposing actor McGraw backs the smaller Ford into a corner in an intimate, low-angle two-shot. Soft light pours through the steam room window behind Moxie's head. Then the latter makes his move, locking the Schemer in a steamy death trap, smiling sadistically as he listens to the Schemer's screams. Shortly thereafter, Tony's poignant death scene takes place. The death of a man to whom the protagonist is somehow bound by profession, blood, love, or hatred is another Mann staple. Tony has been unmasked as a Treasury agent, but he toughs it out to the end, throwing the crooks off O'Brien's identity even as he is put to death. Like a curtain falling over his face, the shadow of mourning follows the brim of O'Brien's hat as he lowers his head in grief. The amusing theatrics of the agents "passing" as hoods have turned to tragedy.

The penultimate scene plays out powerfully in the space of a men's room, the second such space in the film and hosting a mise-en-scène of threat and violence. While Moxie shaves in hard focus, O'Brien, in wide angle, attempts to recover his counterfeit bill from under the sink. A tear-gas-filled ship where the fake currency is being manufactured reiterates the visuals of the steam room, as the Treasury agents route the gang from its lair. The U.S. government triumphs; high-key lighting and official order close the frame narrative. But the effects of the violence witnessed by the viewer (and protested by the Production Code authorities) lingers subliminally, eradicating the comfort offered by an impersonal and methodical bureaucracy.

Raw Deal (1948)

Raw Deal (1948) is another of Mann's daring film noir experiments. One convention often

employed in noir is use the voiceover and flashback narrative. In *Murder, My Sweet* (1944), Philip Marlowe (Dick Powell) frames the entire plot of the film through his first person, subjective retelling to the police as he sits with bandages on his recently scorched eyes. In *Double Indemnity* (1944), Walter Neff (Fred MacMurray) confesses the insurance fraud murder scheme to Keyes (Edward G. Robinson) in the form of an office memorandum via the Dictaphone, all the while, bleeding from his lover's gunshot. In *Sunset Boulevard* (1950), Joe Gillis (William Holden) recounts his sordid relationship with the forgotten silent screen star Norma Desmond (Gloria Swanson) as his corpse floats in her Hollywood swimming pool. Two common noir features attend these voiceovers: all are male perspectives and all recount the past. *Raw Deal* takes a bolder approach to its narrative by having much of the film told from a female perspective and in the present moment as events occur. As the film's prison break and criminal love triangle plots unfold, Pat's (Claire Trevor) voiceover commentary adds existential depth and emotional tension to the narrative. Pat's voice intrudes upon the narrative to represent her consciousness as she faces the perils of a police dragnet and observes her escaped convict lover Joe Sullivan (Dennis O'Keefe) falling in love with their kidnap victim Ann (Marsha Hunt). In doing so, Mann has given the psychosexual dimensions of noir a feminine point of view.

   With eerie, otherworldly music that expresses her anticipation and desperation, Pat begins her apprehensive, emotional narrative: "This is the day. This is the day. The last time I

Raw Deal: opposite, laced-veiled narrator Pat Cameron (Claire Trevor) with the man she loves, Joe Sullivan (Dennis O'Keefe). Above, Sullivan with the woman he loves, Ann Martin (Marsha Hunt). Right, another example of the ironic motif where the viewer sees what the characters cannot.

shall drive up to these gates, these iron bars that keep the man I love locked away from me. Tonight he breaks out of these walls. It's all set." In quick edits of Pat walking to the State Prison entrance, Mann shifts the camera from objective to subjective and then back to objective point of view, a sly visual maneuver that corresponds to the film's interspersing its plot with Pat's voiceover. Cut to Pat walking away from the harsh exterior light that envelops the prison hallway in long, barred shadows, as though they both convey her emotional entrapment and portend her dismal future. She must wait to see Joe Sullivan, who has another visitor, the smitten social worker Ann, who also wants Joe out of prison, but on parole. As Ann leaves, Joe tells her not to wear *that* perfume because it "doesn't help a guy's good behavior." The close-up of Ann's face is a perfect noir, chiaroscuro portrait with the exception of a small, bright star of light in the corner of her eye. When Pat enters the dark visitors' room, that same starburst of light flashes in the corner of her eye. This visual cue establishes a feminine symbol that represents the film's emotional plot. Joe will kidnap Ann as an excuse to get through roadblocks, but the amorous undercurrent and female rivalry are evident. This tiny glimmer of light also signals the noir aesthetic for the love-triangle narrative, which Mann will film almost exclusively in a world of night and shadows.

The scene shifts to Corkscrew Alley to the candlelit interior of mobster Rick Coyle (Raymond Burr), who has greased the guards to enable Joe's prison break, because the odds are so stacked against it. When a henchman questions the feasibility of the plan, Rick uses a cigarette lighter to burn his ear, clear evidence of Rick's sadism and pyromania. In *Raw Deal*, fire is the primal light, representing the most primitive, bestial impulses in man. Unlike the shadow world of the love-triangle, Rick's world is always brightly illuminated. The flicker of amorous light for Pat and Ann stands in opposition to Rick's destructive, masculine flames. Clearly, Mann has created a leitmotif that associates types of illumination with masculine and feminine views of the world.

To celebrate his birthday, a waiter presents Rick with a dessert in a chafing dish, to which he adds extra Courvoisier, and with relish, sets it ablaze. When Rick learns that Joe has beat the million-to-one odds and that he will have to meet him in Crescent City with $50,000,

Raw Deal: another posed shot in the noir style with low fill to throw banister shadows on the back and a high kicker to rim light foreground faces.

Rick's reaction is one of the most startling moments of violence in the history of film noir. He throws the flaming dessert into the face of his girlfriend, which Mann stages off-screen in order to intensify the shock and violence.

Rick sends Fantail (John Ireland) to kill Joe. In Crescent City, Joe and Ann arrive at "Catskinner" Grimshaw's place, a seaside fishing and hunting supply store, where Joe expects to receive his share of the loot. In the dimly-lit backroom, surrounded by antler trophies and taxidermies, including a large standing black bear, Fantail double-crosses Joe. He taunts Joe by asking Catskinner (Tom Fadden) how much it would cost to mount Joe's head. Joe takes on both Catskinner and Fantail. Mann shoots this lengthy, primitive struggle in low-angles and in deep shadows produced by window frame bars and through the meshing of nets. Joe tries to impale Fantail on horns mounted on the wall, but Catskinner intercedes, as Ann bursts into the room. Catskinner, then, tries to impale Joe with a fishing spike, as Fantail moves in to bludgeon him with an iron bar. A close-up of Ann's face reveals that glint of starburst in her eyes fades as she exchanges that light for masculine gunfire. She shoots Fantail, but not fatally. She runs off down the beach, pursued by the now victorious Joe, whom she embraces and declares her love with tears in her eyes. She has been seduced into the world of the *homme fatal*.

Joe sends Ann away only to have Rick kidnap her. When Rick's henchman telephones Pat with information about Ann's plight, she withholds it from Joe so that they can sail away to South America Aboard the mist-enshrouded freighter, Joe proposes to Pat as Mann shoots her reflection in a clock's face. As the eerie music of the film's opening returns, Pat's voiceover discloses her emotional turmoil, "The lyrics were his all right, but the music...Ann's. Suddenly, I saw that every time he kissed me, he'd be kissing Ann." Pat shouts unconsciously Ann's name and then confesses that Ann is being held by Rick, as the glimmer of light leaves her eye.

In the final conflict in Corkscrew Alley, Joe fights through the ambush of henchmen. Rick, believing his plan has worked, indulges his fetish by lighting three candles. With the lighting of the third symbolic candle, Joe enters and fittingly asks, "Where's Ann?" Rick responds by shooting Joe, who returns two shots, causing Rick to knock over the candelabra, which set his curtains ablaze. Rick tries to force Joe into the inferno, but Joe dispatches him by pushing him through the ring of fire of the window. As Joe and Ann emerge from Rick's building into the gloom of night, Pat arrives handcuffed to a policeman. Joe topples down the steps and dies in Ann's, not Pat's arms. The eerie music once again returns as Pat's voiceover expresses her resignation to loneliness and as the camera pans upward through the fog-covered street, which is illuminated by the blaze in the window and an isolated street lamp.

Raw Deal is a testament to Mann's innovations with film noir. With this film, Mann gave voice to the modern, feminine consciousness, one that expresses as much world-weary acquiescence and despair as any hard-boiled detective's voice. Mann also created a gendered aesthetic to correspond to this new noir sensibility, one that opened up new perspectives and commentary on the sordid and fatalistic world of noir.

He Walked By Night (1948)

Noir aficionados often revere *He Walked by Night* for exhibiting the quintessential visual style of the genre. Although uncredited, Mann directed most of the movie before leaving Eagle-Lion for MGM and his work is evident throughout, particularly in the experimental use of oblique angles, the depth of shadows within crucial scenes of violence, and the exemplary noir ending. Additionally, *He Walked by Night* establishes many conventions for police procedurals that influenced later films and television, such as *Dragnet*. In fact, Jack Webb, *Dragnet*'s creator, portrays Lee, the efficient, amiable police technician, who creates a facial recognition method for the LAPD that enables victims to identify the culprit without mug shots or line-ups. Mann's semi-documentary *T-Men* (1947) already established many of the detailed technical operations of the police procedural, but *He Walked By Night* takes this sub-genre into the marginal world of the criminal. Unlike psycho-sociological film analyses, such as the portrayal of Oedipally-challenged Cody Jarrett (James Cagney) in Raoul Walsh's *White Heat* (1949), this film refrains from superficial Freudian depictions of criminal behavior. Instead, the "He" of the film's title remains enigmatic, not easily categorized, and seemingly without apparent motives. The noir aesthetic of his shadow world corresponds to the inscrutable nature of this criminal, whose

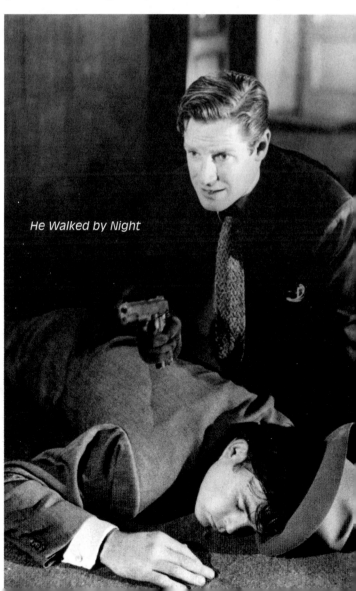

He Walked by Night

actions occur without explanation. In the world of *He Walked by Night*, evil simply *is*.

Violence in this noir world occurs only at night, among deep, ominous shadows and darkened, threatening spaces. Along a mist-shrouded street, irregularly lit by intermittent, harsh street lamps, Morgan (Richard Basehart) walks away from an electronics store that he just attempted to break into. A car approaches with a policeman driving, who follows Morgan, stops him, and asks for identification, which the half-smiling Morgan produces, his "Army discharge," three bullets to the chest. During this homicide, Morgan's face, shot from a low-angle POV of the police officer's car window, remains in shadows, except for the band of light across his intense, eerie eyes. Those eyes will be the key to the facial recognition system later in the film.

The LAPD later discovers a trunkload of guns and Navy electronics that Morgan left behind, indicating that the criminal is both vicious and intelligent. Certainly, Morgan is a clever criminal, creating his own police scanner and changing licenses and car registrations as easily as he does his appearance. His living is earned through theft, minor alterations, and renting out electronic equipment to a gullible Reeves (Whit Bissell), owner of Electronics Laboratories that specializes in sound equipment, radio, public addresses, and radar, the very technologies employed by both the police and Morgan. When Morgan tries to pass off a television projector as his own creation, the inventor confronts Reeves with the police.

Morgan is the noir alter ego of society—the psychotic loner, the existential stranger, the marginal figure, the sociopathic outlier, the underground man—who cannot interact with others except through deceit and violence. The first trap is set by the police at the Reeves' company that night. Morgan skulks his way into the locked offices earlier than expected, catching the two LAPD detective sergeants, Chuck Jones (Jimmy Cardwell) and Marty Brennan (Scott Brady), and the witless Reeves off guard. The offices at night are cast in low-key lighting, with Morgan's barely half-lit close-up in the shadows. Through long shots of dimly lit archways and corridors, the detectives try to surround Morgan, who often appears in low-angle shots that set him against shadows of window bars in classic noir entrapment style. This scene is a prelude to cornering Morgan in the film's iconic finale. A shoot-out ensues and both Morgan and Sgt. Jones are shot. Morgan runs off down into the blackness of an alley. Cut to a sweaty, grimacing, and gasping Morgan operating upon himself, using instruments from a foreground obstructing sterilizing pan, to extract the bullet. When Morgan takes the forceps, Mann shoots him in extreme close-up, lighting half of his face, in order to sustain the strain of his anguished moans.

After recovering from his operation, Morgan changes his modus operandi by wearing disguises and holding up liquor stores. His escape route is through a street gutter into the vast, seven hundred mile long Los Angeles storm drain system. Mann's noir direction can be discerned in these flashlight-only lit tunnels and the diegetic sounds of footstep echoing off the concrete surfaces in the two underground scenes. One year later, Carol Reed's *The Third Man* (1949) would employ similar lighting and sound design for his now iconic chase of Harry Lime (Orson Welles) through the sewers of Vienna. However, Morgan's subterfuge does not succeed, because Lee (Jack Webb) matches bullet casings from the policeman's murder to the liquor holdups and then creates the facial recognition slides that confirm Morgan's appearance.

From the moment the LAPD surround Morgan's bungalow at night until his death, Mann creates a textbook for noir elements in the film's final ten minutes. Morgan's sense of entrapment is intensified by the shadows made by the Venetian blinds in his bungalow. He escapes across the roof and dives into a gutter on a newly rained street, lit only by a harsh street lamp in rising steam and mist. The illumination of flashlights in the tunnels, the echoing and sound-bridges of footsteps, the conical light filtered from tunnel openings, the wet surfaces reflecting streams of irregular light, the low angle of pursuers and quarry, the long shots of tunnels with circular beams of flashlights in the distance, and the intricate cross cuts of police, blackened tunnels, and culprit—all demonstrate Mann's masterful noir aesthetic.

He Walked By Night: opposite, in a manner typical of police procedural narrative technique, lead detectives Brennan (Scott Brady, center left) and Breen (Roy Roberts) in a manner now commonplace for police procedurals go over the plan for their man hunt.

Right, Richard Basehart as Roy Morgan, "the noir alter ego of society—the psychotic loner, the existential stranger, the marginal figure, the sociopathic outlier, the underground man," and one of the earliest serial criminals/killers portrayed in film noir.

Reign of Terror (The Black Book) (1949)

This period piece is set in the violent aftermath of the French Revolution, when Maximilien Robespierre and his cronies were in control of the country. King Louis XVI and his family are dead, but Robespierre continues his ideological purges, arresting and beheading Frenchmen on any pretext. Basinger describes this Eagle-Lion/Walter Wanger film as having almost a campy quality whose exaggerated "baroque horror...will be put to good use" (p. 61).

A montage of revolutionaries' faces against a background of flames opens the film. The voiceover narrator sets the scene: "Paris, July 26, 1794...anarchy, misery, murder, arson, fear. These are the weapons of dictatorship." Robert Cummings stars as Charles d'Aubigny who holds it in his power to save France. By killing and then impersonating a notoriously bloody Strasbourg prosecutor (Duval), Charles plans to infiltrate Robespierre's inner circle. Robespierre, who wishes to be appointed dictator, has lost his infamous black book. It contains the names of those slated, by the all-powerful leader of the Committee of Public Safety, to die on the guillotine. Its publication would undermine Robespierre's power and even end his reign of terror, since many of the names in the book are those of his own committee members. If they knew they were on his list, they might join forces to unseat (and "unhead") him. "Duval" is to search for the book, and given power even over the police to carry out his quest. Meanwhile, Robespierre's plans are also being foiled because François Barras (Richard Hart), the only man who can nominate him for dictator before the National Convention, has refused and gone into hiding.

Below and opposite, shadow play in *Reign of Terror*.

As played by Richard Basehart (*He Walked by Night*), Robespierre is neurotic, obsessive, and meticulous. In an early scene he delicately kisses pigeons, but later refuses to shake hands with Charles/Duval because it's "unsanitary." Fouché (Arnold Moss) is lugubrious and comical, seeming to savor his role as a backstabbing boogeyman. Early scenes set up the compositions in depth, racking focus, *Caligari*-esque distorted sets, and extreme low- and high-angle shots characterizing the film. When Danton (Wade Crosby) is sentenced to death, he appears in close-up in the facial plane, while the Convention mob crowds into the stands behind him, calling out for his death. A racking shot throws the crowd into soft focus, and Danton's noble face into crisp clarity in the foreground. The death of this liberal ally is a mark of Robespierre's growing fanaticism, and is appropriately emphasized by cinematography.

D'Aubigny first meets the film's heroine, Madelon (Arlene Dahl), in a darkened inn. As it turns out, they already know one another, having been star-crossed lovers sometime in the past. The two stand in front of a mirror, a site of revelations, but again a racking focus impacts the meaning of the scene. The images in the mirror go from hard to soft focus as the couple exchanges bitter words. In most of Mann's films, the doubling effect of the mirror would probably have been emphasized by deep focus. In this case, the fact that the lovers no longer know each other, or are meeting again after a hazy past, is emphasized by the soft focus reflections. (Later mirror scenes reflect both the potential treachery of the woman, when Madelon, distrustful of Charles, seats herself before a large one, and Robespierre's vanity, as he has his hair powdered in front of a small ornate mirror.)

As is the case for the agents in both *T-Men* and *Border Incident*, Charles is immediately called upon to deflect suspicions about his identity. In the same inn, he aggressively bluffs the innkeeper who believes (correctly) that Duval's appearance has changed. Charles enacts a credible performance as the ruthless executioner whose identity he has stolen. The scene is played out in front of the suspicious Fouché, who doesn't hesitate to add black humor to every situation, calling Robespierre "Max" to the latter's great displeasure, and from time to time forcing the aspiring dictator to admit his own villainy. (The film hints at Robespierre's homosexuality when, in a later scene, St. Just [Jesse Barker] mentions that the dictator doesn't like women.) As Fouché and the false Duval ride across Paris, someone throws a torch into their carriage. After some frantic fussing, Fouché (who is also Napoleon's future secret police chief) wryly comments, "One thing about Paris—never dull." He smiles.

Another typically bizarre scene takes place in Robespierre's headquarters, a small room in the back of a bakery. Walking by the flickering fire of the oven, Charles (as Duval) and Fouché grab a bun on the way through, and enter a small but well-appointed armory/torture chamber/office. With crossed rifles, bayonets, a bare-chested man hanging by his arms in the background, and a Great Dane's head in the extreme foreground, Robespierre drinks wine and presses fruit with a powerful hand as he fastidiously writes out his nefarious orders. The use of shadows in this scene and in the film as a whole is phenomenally complex. Candles, fires and other lighting sources cast shadows in every direction, creating a maze through which the characters must move. Cummings continues to play the role of the executioner with bravado, pretending to relish the sadism of the aspiring dictator and his men. Robespierre's commitment to cruelty is made clear in a shot-

reverse-shot opposite the tough-talking Charles. The latter is framed in medium shot in an undistorted low angle, while Robespierre, sitting below him, is framed in a wide-angle close-up that has the ironic effect of a decapitation. The parallel lines of bayonets create shadows behind his wigged head in this unusual shot, which leaves more space above the character's head than would a normal close-up, thus creating the severed head effect.

Using the power he has been given over everyone in France save Robespierre, Charles continues his investigation. He goes to meet Madelon in a low-ceilinged but merry café/dancehall, but is intercepted by St. Just, who insinuatingly mentions, as he looms over Charles, that being in bed is not safe in Paris. So many are killed in bed. While in this dancehall both St. Just and Barras again test "Duval's" identity. Bravado and confrontational banter again get him through the tests, but not before he is thrown to the floor in a dark backroom of the dancehall. With his head very close to the ground-level camera, Charles resembles O'Brien in *T-Men*, who is framed in just such a shot when he is thrown in an alley while undercover. The brutalization is engineered by Madelon, who inhabits a sumptuously furnished room above the dancehall. As in a Max Ophuls film, translucent fabrics hang between the camera and the characters. Madelon pulls Charles into a passionate kiss. In extreme close-up, with pin lights creating stars in Madelon's eyes, they discuss the four years that have gone by. Charles, angry and jealous, but admitting his lingering obsession with her, does not melt. Barras emerges from behind the curtains and declares his trust in Charles. Fouché's arrival forces Charles to "arrest" Barras and to turn him over to St. Just. Charles manages to visit Barras in prison. Again, the multiple planes of the image are used to create a rich and variegated setting, with the prison bars and their shadows, Gothic arches, torchlight, black dungeons, and the sounds of sobs

economically conveys a world of horror. Charles again convinces Barras that he is not Duval. Together they deduce that Robespierre has not really lost the book.

St. Just arrives just in time to lock Charles in Barras' cell, burning the document that had bestowed Robespierre's borrowed power. He announces, in a menacing wide angle, that Duval's wife (Mary Currier) has come to Paris. Another potential femme fatale who may expose Charles as an imposter? No—she, too, is a spy for Barras, and greets her "husband" with passionate kisses. The real Madame Duval appears soon thereafter at the prison gates, and a chase over the Paris cobblestones and out of the city ensues. But Charles brazenly goes by Robespierre's headquarters before leaving town. The ever-duplicitous Fouché intercepts him, but expresses a willingness to hand over the book if he can share power with Barras. Robespierre's inner sanctum is a dark cave under a pool of light. But the room holds hundreds of black books: the men frantically leaf through them in search of their prize. (In another suspenseful but light moment, Robespierre's Great Dane slowly pushes open the door.) After they discover Fouché's name in the black book, he tries to stab Charles, who barely escapes with his life. Madelon and Charles assume yet another disguise, provided by a farmer and his wife sympathetic to their cause. (They sell cabbages and artichokes—the cabbages wittily reminiscent of severed heads.) The perennial henchman, Charles McGraw, amusingly attired in a tall fur hat, like that of a hussar, and a soldier's uniform, moves in to torture them.

The couple manages to escape Paris into the bright countryside, arriving at dusk at a friendly cottage. But St. Just is right behind them, and tries to bribe a young boy to tell him that the couple has been there. Just in time, St. Just commits the atrocity of kicking a kitten, and the boy retreats in disgust. Madelon's and Charles's race through the dark forest is, however, to no avail. Madelon is soon a captive in Robespierre's torture chamber, her hands tied above her as were those of the prisoner in an earlier scene, but to much more erotic effect. Fouché offers Charles the choice of getting hold of the book or rescuing Madelon. As Barras is placed on trial before the Convention, and Robespierre demands the role of dictator, the book is circulated among the public. A montage of angry faces repeats the visuals of the scene of Danton's condemnation, except that it is now Robespierre and his cronies who are under attack. In a scene made up of bits and pieces of extreme expressionism, Robespierre attempts to hypnotize the crowd. Just as he is beginning

Reign of Terror: above, wedges of light across detailed set dressing and costuming of various shades capture Fouché (Arnold Moss, left), Charles d'Aubigny (Robert Cummings, center) and Robespierre (Richard Basehart).

Opposite from top, distortions via low, wide-angle lens and background shadows; frames constricted with rearground and foreground clutter.

Below, surreal effect of Fouché and Robespierre enveloped by wisps.

Above *Reign of Terror*: left, the foreground prisoner and line of bayoneted muskets brackets the inquisitors. Right, the stylized landscape of large mill and silhouetted rider.

Opposite, *Follow Me Quietly*: Detectives Grant (William Lundigan) and Collins (Jeff Corey) sit on either side of the silhouetted figure that represents the judge.

to succeed, he is shot grotesquely in the chin, the shadow of a flag waving on the wall behind him. Robespierre lies bleeding on the floor, his jaw shot off, and cannot tell Charles where to find Madelon. Off he goes to the guillotine. Fortunately for Madelon, her captor, the disheveled soldier played by Charles McGraw, is drunk, and Charles manages to track them down in yet another dramatically lit secret chamber. Madelon is saved; Robepierre is beheaded as thunder and the crowd roar. Fouché discusses the execution with a "mere soldier" shown only from the back. "My name is Napoleon, Napoleon Bonaparte." France's future is foreshadowed. Madelon and Charles join in an embrace; and fireworks light up the night sky, celebrating the death of Robespierre to the sound of the "Marseillaise."

Producer and (uncredited) art director William Cameron Menzies was probably an important influence on the look of this astonishing film, with its sweeping panoramas and montages in tight close-up. The film's story and script are by Phillip Yordan, who worked with Mann on four films. With John Alton as cinematographer, Mann had an expert crew able to produce a visually compelling document with few resources.

Follow Me Quietly (1949)

Follow Me Quietly is a police procedural with a romantic twist, but its powerfully uncanny elements take it from noir to the edge of horror. The story was co-written by Mann when he was at RKO. Good reviews of *He Walked by Night*, which Mann directed for Eagle-Lion after leaving RKO, convinced studio officials to put the story into production, with Richard Fleisher (*Armored Car Robbery* [1950] and *The Narrow Margin* [1952]) directing. In terms of both the narrative and certain visual details, Mann's mark is clearly on the film.

A killer known only as "The Judge" is strangling those he considers "evil." At the site of each murder he leaves a note spelling out his verdict. The police have many clues, but no real description of the murderer. The film's protagonist, Detective Grant (William Lundigan), devises an unusual plan of attack. Gathering the bits and pieces of the Judge's identity left at crime scenes, another interesting detail typical of Mann's use of props, they create a dummy in his likeness, hoping that a witness will come forward. But the Judge himself learns of the ruse, and infiltrates the very office where the faceless dummy sits by the window. Grant is shadowed by a girl reporter Ann (Dorothy Patrick) who works for a sub-yellow-journalist paper. She is hot on the case and uses underhanded means to find out more. They quarrel when she writes a story revealing too much to the public, but screwball comedy conventions dictate that they will end up as a couple. Acting on a tip, Grant and his partner Collins (Jeff Corey) trace the Judge to his neighborhood, but the criminal takes off running when he realizes he has been made. They chase him to a refinery where, after a bitter struggle, the Judge falls to his death.

In *The Film Noir Encyclopedia*, James Ursini points out that *Follow Me Quietly* is an early example of a popular subgenre of contemporary neo-noir, the "serial killer" film. The Judge's habit of striking only at night and in the rain creates a chilling atmosphere. The horror component of the film is rendered visually by cinematographer Robert de Grasse, who photographed *The Body Snatcher* in 1945. As Ursini notes, at one moment in the film Ann paces back and forth, "her high heels splashing" in a pool of water where the neon lights of surrounding buildings are reflected, as "the ominous score fills the soundtrack." In the final sequence set in an oil refinery, Grant finally manages to handcuff the Judge, and the water motif returns as the liquid rains down from bullet-riddled pipes.

The film emphasizes the possibility that anyone around us may be an insane killer. Grant's partner often ribs him that he is going crazy, and in the Judge's room they find a book entitled *Law and the Insane*. While the Judge himself turns out to be a weak-chinned, owly little man, the real horror in the film lies in the viewer's imagination—as projected onto the blank face of the "Judge" mannequin.

As it pours rain outside the window of the police precinct (weather in which the Judge is prone to strike), Grant pours out his frustration about the case to the mannequin, which is facing the window. It is slightly unnerving when his partner, standing off-screen behind him, answers Grant's odd request for a "blind date" with the Judge. But when Grant leaves the room, the dummy suddenly stands up: it is the Judge himself, rising up like some Golem come to life (Ursini, 112). The dummy itself sometimes seems alive, as when "he" stands in a lineup, or is posed reading a magazine for the witness who finally identifies him. As the woman blurts out the Judge's real name, the cops (in a touch anticipating the ending of *Psycho*) turn the dummy around, the camera rapidly tracking and optically zooming in to reveal his blank face. After this, the Judge himself can only be a disappointment, so the filmmakers, with ingenious irony, choose to make him as physically unimposing as possible.

Border Incident: Agent Jack Bearnes (George Murphy) is menaced by renegade braceros Zopilote (Arnold Moss, who looks a bit like a "vulture") and Cuchillo (Alfonso Bedoya).

Border Incident (1949)

The modest but distinct critical and box-office success of *T-Men* and some of their other Eagle-Lion films drew the director-cinematographer team to the attention of MGM, where Mann and Alton began work in 1949. Their first film for MGM was something of a remake of *T-Men*, with the action shifted to the California-Mexico border, immigration agents playing the part of the earlier film's T-men. The film is a genre hybrid, anticipating the treatment of landscapes and themes in Mann's Westerns (Jonathan Auerbach, "Noir Citizenship: Anthony Mann's *Border Incident*," *Cinema Journal* 47, no. 4, 102). With its use of deep focus indoors and out under the sky, compositions that dramatically draw the eye from foreground to background, and bright lights tunneling into the dark of desert or field, *Border Incident* is like a Western carved out of a piece of coal. As is hinted at in *The Great Flamarion*, Mexico has represented refuge, lawlessness, nightmare, and dream world in film noir. In Tourneur's *Out of the Past* (1947), it's a locus of slowed-down time and soft, dusky light—a place where even the femme fatale can give way to honest sensuality. Like Welles' masterful *Touch of Evil*, (1958) *Border Incident* situates the events of the film where Mexico and the United States meet, both geographically and psychologically. Both films represent American fantasies about our southern border, but Mann's film colors those phantasms with the bitter reality of human exploitation, vividly rendering visible the cost of maintaining U.S. prosperity at the expense of the most desperate.

The politically liberal Dore Schary, who had executive-produced such "social problem" films as *Crossfire* (1947) for RKO, acquired the screenplay from Eagle-Lion and was responsible for bringing Mann over to MGM. Mann brought Alton along. Schary produced the film, while John C. Higgins wrote *Border Incident*'s story and screenplay with co-writer George Zuckerman, a film noir mainstay. The smooth transition between the films' plots and style reflects this collaborative continuity. The dichotomies between cultures (Chinese, Italian, American) hinted at in *T-Men* lie at the crux of *Border Incident*'s complex treatment of Mexican and American differences and similarities. Whereas *T*-Men is concerned with smuggling Chinese paper into the U.S., *Border Incident* (whose working title was "Wetback") describes the plight of humans being smuggled into the U.S. by coyotes. The plot device of the paper trail remains a constant between the two films: the immigration agents from both sides of the border are trying to crack open a ring illegally trafficking in Mexican laborers, and will use the lure of "stolen" work permits to bait the criminal ringleaders.

Historically speaking, these laborers are collateral damage of the Bracero Program (1942-1964), an emergency initiative put in place early in World War II to provide desperately needed agricultural workers. By 1947, the abuses of that system were well, if not widely, known. The film's narrative and visuals send a double message about the possibility of resolving these abuses, on the one hand presenting the Mexican labor situation as overwhelming (men massed at the border seeking work permits), and on the other offering a tentative solution through the cooperation of the two nations in policing the Bracero Program. Interestingly, posters for the film seem to have been altered before or during release. The tag line on the banner diagonally displaced on the poster initially read "The Shame of Two Nations." Afterwards, a strip of paper was placed over it, calling the film "powerful and true."

Like *T-Men*, *Border Incident* features a frame narrative with an authoritative voiceover narration (by Knox Manning), in true semi-documentary style, and as in the earlier film, events are described as a "composite" of real cases. Within the first six minutes of the film, the basic structure of the narrative has been dramatically established. After credits over a backdrop of dark desert, a helicopter or airplane shot introduces us to the "all-American canal," a man-made and rigorously linear body of water serving to "feed the vast farm empire of the [redundantly] Imperial Valley of Southern California." Crosscutting moves the setting to a dark and narrow

Border Incident: above, Latino agent Rodriguez (Ricardo Montalban, center) is interrogated by Ulrich (Sig Ruman) while Cuchillo and Zopilote watch.

Opposite, Bearnes is in a literal and figurative chess game with Parker (Howard Da Silva) and his crony Amboy (Charles McGraw, center).

passage south of the border, the "Valle de Muerte," whose obscurity matches that of the urban canyons photographed by Alton in other films. This is the treacherous route returning braceros must take. Clearly, the "all-American" canal is the property of the U.S. alone: the Mexican borderland is almost barren. The coyotes (three Mexicans and a White American), cogs in the vast machine smuggling workers into the U.S., are here to strip the men of their hard-earned money. Strangely, in this parched land, the greatest natural hazard is the quicksand that, with the help of the coyotes, swallows the braceros after they have been robbed. (Continuing this play on water and desert, bad-guy Jeff Amboy [Charles McGraw] ironically proposes to drown some inconvenient "wets" in the shallow Salton Sea.)

The film now cuts abruptly to the police procedural element of its plot. Ricardo Montalban, as Mexican agent Pablo Rodriguez, and George Murphy, as American agent Jack Bearnes are introduced in parallel scenes, flying on airplanes as they make their way to their Mexicali meeting point. The government office where they meet is high-key-lit, as is typical of the police procedural. The equality of the Mexican and American agents is again emphasized by their symmetrical placement at the reflective-surfaced table and by their friendly banter. Nevertheless, we have already seen that this symmetry is troubled, both in the representation of nations and the treatment of its two stars. Not only is Montalban the more compelling actor, but his character also takes the role of witness to his American partner's gruesome death, one reserved for the Anglo partner in *T-Men* and one more likely to inspire audience identification with Montalban. The fact that the Anglo partner rather than his "ethnic" counterpart is sacrificed in the film is unusual. Jeanine Basinger notes that "it is practically a generic axiom that the likeable minority figure in movies such as *Border Incident* must be killed in some horrible way, allowing the WASP figure to rescue the situation and pontificate on the sacrifice" (p. 55). That the clues about Pablo's imminent demise are actually red herrings intensifies the shock effect of *Border Incident*'s climax, leaving the spectator reeling. Further, American agents cannot ride to the rescue at the end of the film, which takes place in Mexico.

Right away, the agents go undercover, Bearnes posing as a trafficker of stolen work documents, Rodriguez as a bracero. Pablo immediately joins the crowd at the border, and befriends a peasant, Juan Garcia, (James Mitchell), hoping to work legally in the U.S. The emphasis, as in *T-Men*, is on the men "passing"—Bearnes by donning a bright shirt deemed handsome by the Mexican characters, Pablo with some difficulty passing as a farm worker, because of his soft hands. Garcia's wife, Maria (Teresa Celli), has accompanied him to the border. They say goodbye in a stereotypical and dramatically lit church. One of the few female characters in *T-Men* is Genaro's wife, played by June Lockhart. Her inadvertent encounter with her husband at the L.A. Farmer's Market in that film triggers her husband's discovery and death. Maria is a less "fatal" woman, but her very presence reminds the viewer that it is the need to support a family that drives men over the border in search of work.

Curiously, the issue of nationality becomes even quirkier as the film progresses. The coyote boss on the Mexican side of the border is a German, Hugo Wolfgang Ulrich (Sig Ruman).

It seems natural to include German villains in films made so soon after WWII, but Ulrich also functions as a subliminal scapegoat, drawing attention away from the Mexican and American bad guys. Ulrich's head henchman on the American side of the border is a jodhpured Howard Da Silva as Owen Parkson. Like many mob bosses in film, Parkson surrounds himself with trinkets that symbolize his power (including a revolver-shaped cigarette lighter that fascinates "Cuchillo," a bandito stereotype played by Alfonso Bedoya). Wide-angle close-ups and chiaroscuro treatment of such props help to sustain the eeriness of the material world in which the characters find themselves. In a conversation between Ulrich and Parkson, braceros are referred to as bundles of curios, Immigration officials as duck hunters, and work permits as hunting permits. During a conversation in his office, Parkson shoots an air gun at a target, while Bearnes stands in front of his desk, reflected in a mirror. At a certain point, Bearnes takes the gun and, looking at the reflected target, shoots over his shoulder and hits it. This inspires Parkson to challenge him to a game of chess.

The point is made. Not only are the agents themselves "clay pigeons," as Bearnes remarked earlier, the braceros are sitting ducks, and the whole enterprise is a twisted game to Parkson and his cronies. The eeriness and solemnity of objects pervading the film extends to the many motorized vehicles, the literal machines that menace the lives of agents and workers. Having, along with Juan, gained entry to the U.S., Pablo is transported in a dark truck stacked full of other Mexicans. In a *Grapes of Wrath*-like moment, an old man dies in the crush of bodies and is callously thrown out by the side of the road by Ulrich's men. All Pablo, Juan and the others can do is pray. Later in the film, Pablo himself drives a truck wrested from the control of Parkson's man (Jack Lambert), whose grimacing face is framed by the window until Pablo offhandedly shoves him off.

As mentioned, the most vivid demonstration of human cruelty in *T*-Men is inflicted not on an undocumented bracero, but on the Anglo agent, Jack Bearnes, who is subjected to one of the most brutal deaths in film history. Having gained and lost Ulrich's confidence, Bearnes is locked (ironically) in a water tower, from whose shadowy depths Rodriguez releases him. Earlier in the film, Ulrich, with Zopilote (Arnold Moss), Cuchillo, and Pocoloco (José Torvay) tor-

Left, smug conspirators Cuchillo, Zopilote and Parkson in *Border Incident*.

Opposite, a pregnant Ellen Norson (Cathy O'Donnell) ponders the future with her mother (Esther Somers) in *Side Street*.

tured Bearnes by wiring him up to a truck battery and revving the engine. The hard eyes of the truck's headlights and close-ups of the screaming but defiant Bearnes created a scene already at the limits of "acceptable" violence according to the Production Code authorities. But Bearnes' subsequent death in the field is on another order of magnitude. His real identity revealed, the agent is force-marched across a dark lettuce field. Pablo and Juan arrive in the commandeered truck "just in time," but, despite their efforts, can only witness the horrible spectacle at a distance. Making a run for it, Bearnes is shot and then clubbed with Amboy's rifle butt.

On the ground, crawling feebly, Bearnes sees Amboy start up a tractor pulling a rotating disc. The film's dynamic editing throughout culminates in point-of-view shots in which Pablo and Juan watch the tractor move toward Bearnes, and Bearnes himself sees the monstrous machine move inexorably toward him. High-angle point of view shots from the tractor imply Amboy's merciless gaze. Amboy's sidekick, Clayton Nordell (Arthur Hunnicutt), looks on impassively, then turns away. The tractor's headlights create an "otherworldly" light, as the mute Bearnes watches its underbelly roll toward him, its sharpened discs slowly coming into view. A cutaway to Pablo and Juan, hiding their eyes, spares the viewer from the horrendous sight of Jack Bearnes being plowed into the earth.

The remainder of the film includes Pablo's dramatic rescue from the quicksand, and a return to the representatives of the two governments, who pay their respects to the fallen agent, but it is obvious that, as in the case of *T-Men*, we have seen too much to be reassured that international cooperation can heal the wounds inflicted by injustice.

Side Street (1949)

Side Street is Mann's cinematic response to Jules Dassin's *The Naked City* (1948) of the previous year. Both films rely upon semi-documentary style, location shooting, particularly of lower Manhattan, and voice-over narration. Both films begin and end with fly-over shots of New York City that foreground the Empire State Building as framing devices. Both begin with montages of the city's urban landscape and the daily routines of its eight million inhabitants. Both films

Side Street: veteran Joe Norson (Farley Granger) ponders what to do with the money stolen from crooked lawyer Victor Backett.

employ elements of the police procedural plot and conclude with an elaborate, lengthy chase through New York. Mann replaces the voice-of-God documentary narration of *The Naked City* with the omniscient voice of Captain Walter Anderson (Paul Kelly), who, as lead homicide detective, begins by commenting upon "New York City, an architectural jungle where fabulous wealth and the deepest squalor live side by side," "the sum of its people, with their frailties, hopes, fears, dreams." That summation, however, is more economic frustration than aspiration. Whereas *The Naked City* focuses upon professional police work to restore balance and order to the city, Mann reveals the confusion and despair of the *other* city, where the American dream has failed.

As with so many noir films, *Side Street* critiques post-war American life, particularly as its protagonists face financial hardships that call for desperate acts. Joe Norson (Farley Granger), a WWII veteran with a menial, part-time job as a postal carrier, longs to elevate his status, to take his wife Ellen (Cathy O'Donnell) to Europe, to buy her a fur coat, and to have a financially secure future for theie soon-be-born baby. The symbolic meaning of the birth is not renewal, but rather a death-in-life existence for Joe Norson. He steals a cache of $30,000 by forcing open a file cabinet belonging to a shyster lawyer Victor Backett (Edmon Ryan). The money is the result of Backett's blackmailing of Emil Lorrison (Paul Harvey) in a trumped up sex scandal with Lucille Colner (Adele Jergens). Lucille's body is later found in the East River strangled to death, leading the police to investigate Lorrison and Beckett. *Side Street* establishes a pattern of money as death as its major plot points.

The ill-gotten money is tainted and contaminates Norson, who begins to weave a series of lies to his wife. Claiming a better job in Schenectady, Joe moves into a sleazy hotel in the wharf district, after having left the money in a package, supposedly a negligee for his wife, with his bartender friend Nick Drumman (Ed Max). Because of his obsession with the money, Norson misses the birth of his son. When he visits his wife in the hospital ward, Norson's guilt consumes him.

Deciding to return the cash, Norson meets opposition from the untrusting Backett, who sends his partner-in-crime Georgie Garsell (James Craig) to retrieve the package. Ironically, all that the package now contains is a negligee. Obviously, barman Drumman has taken the money. Garsell kills Drumman and the police blame Norson, who must search for Garsell in Greenwich Village among seedy nightclubs. As Norson moves through lower Manhattan, Mann allows the night to envelop him, with each scene becoming increasingly more dark. Fittingly, Mann has Joe descend into the darkness of the underworld of the nightclub, where he finds Garsell's old flame, a boozy torch singer Harriet Stinton (Jean Hagen). Harriet lures Norson into a rundown, darkened side street to a sleazy tenement. As she leads Norson up the nearly pitch-black stairwell, Harriet remarks with noir foreboding, "Some night somebody's going to get killed on these steps and then it'll cost 'em plenty." In an effort to win Garsell back, she betrays Joe to him, but Garsell strangles Harriet in the same manner that he did Lucille Colner. Garsell's deadly, materialistic relationships with Lucille and Harriet are the obverse reflection of Joe and Ellen's marriage.

With the help of his cabbie accomplice (Harry Bellaver), Garsell takes Norson on a hair-raising drive to the East River, where he plans to kill Joe and dispose of both corpses. A labyrinthine police chase ensues with the most dramatic noir shot sequences in the film: long panning shots of the cab careening around corners and under trolley tracks; head-on, tail-on quick cuts of the pursuit through desolate urban alleyways; and startling, high-angle, eye-of-God shots of the cab speeding through narrow streets cast in perpetual shadows by tall buildings. Garsell shoots the fleeing cabbie and forces Norson to take the wheel. The chase ends with the taxi overturning in front of George Washington's statue before Federal Hall on Wall

Side Street: Norson tries to reason with Backett (Edmon Ryan) and his violent associate Garsell (James Craig).

Street. Literally, a Wall Street Crash! A failed, dashed American Dream culminates at the birth-place of both American capitalism and federalism, the site of Washington's first inauguration. An ironic ending, indeed.

As the bells of Trinity Church ring out, Ellen watches, her head literally haloed by reflected light, as Joe is taken away in an ambulance. This heavy-handed and almost Calvinist ending points to the death of sin now bringing about moral rebirth. The reassuring voiceover of Captain Anderson claims, "He's going to be all right." The iconic image of the Empire State Building that began the film now returns, reinforcing the film's ironic commentary on the Naked City 's reclaiming of the American Dream.

Devil's Doorway (1950)

Anthony Mann called Gary Trosper's script for *Devil's Doorway* "the best" he had ever read. In "The Ache for Home in Anthony Mann's *Devil's Doorway* (*Film and History*, 33:1, 2003, p. 19), Joanna Hearne notes that the script underwent radical alterations between 1946 and 1949, from a Western "that pits a drifter against a big cattleman to a re-activation of the silent era's sympathetic and reformist Indian Western sub-genre." In the various versions of the script, the hero, Lance Poole (Robert Taylor) goes from White man to full-blooded Shoshone. Poole is a Civil War veteran, decorated with the Medal of Honor, who returns home to Wyoming to claim his ancestral land, Sweet Meadows. *Devil's Doorway* is a true noir Western whose power and integrity are not diminished even today. It depicts events taking place after the Civil War and as the all-out war on Western tribes is escalating.

The film opens with a lone horseman, Poole, riding into the town of Medicine Bow. Handsome and upright in his Union Army Cavalry uniform, he stops off at the Big Horn Saloon.

There, the town's old-timers, including Zeke Carmody (Edgar Buchanan) a life-long friend of Lance's father, lift a glass in his honor. But racist insults emanate from the shadowy end of the bar. Lance is startled into awareness of the antagonist who will destroy his life, attorney Verne Coolan (Louis Calhern). When the other men congratulate Poole on his rank of sergeant major, Coolan, who is shot in wide angle as well as darkness, comments, "When I was in the army—the regular army—we were a little particular who wore those stripes." After Lance leaves to meet his father, the lawyer continues: "You notice how sour the air got? You can always smell 'em."

Lance's struggle to live in both the White and the Indian worlds has been succinctly set up in less than two minutes of film. His father (Fritz Lieber) is dressed traditionally, and as the film continues Lance himself will be more and more visually identifiable as an Indian. While Taylor is obviously in brown face and speaks little Shoshone, his gravitas in the role lends him credibility. James Mitchell, who played a Mexican peasant in *Border Incident*, is also credible in the role of Red Rock, Lance's Shoshone companion.

As Verne Coolan says of Sweet Meadows later in the film, it is "what all men dream of when they ache for home," a verdant valley surrounded by mountains. Horses run in the tall grass, and the log house is welcoming, though tenebrous inside. While Lance describes his dream of Sweet Meadows as a refuge of peace and plenty for both Red and White men, his father smokes a pipe, framed in a low-angle, chiaroscuro shot. His only response to his son's speech about how racism and war are things of the past is: "You are home. You are again an

Civil War veteran and American Indian Lance Poole (Robert Taylor) confronts cigar-smoking, racist rancher Verne Coolan (Louis Calhern) in *Devil's Doorway.*

Poole and his attorney/love interest Orrie Masters (Paula Raymond) in *Devil's Doorway*.

Indian." Soon thereafter, Mr. Poole lies dying. A close-up of his ravaged features fills the moment with evil portent. "Now my spirit is dead. Even my eyes are dead. We will die. We will never go back to the reservation." No dramatic embroidery of the moment is necessary. The old man has spoken the stark truth.

Five years pass. Sweet Meadows has grown into a profitable cattle ranch, and Lance comes to town to deposit $18,000 in the bank. He enters the saloon to buy a drink for Zeke, who is now sheriff, but discovers that radical changes made when Wyoming became a territory make it illegal for him to drink alcohol. Zeke, shamefaced, admits that he himself posted the sign in the saloon forbidding liquor to Indians. Coolan is once again at the end of the bar, now accompanied by his hired gun, who mockingly fires off rounds in Lance's vicinity. A fistfight ensues, with Coolan looking on with almost lascivious interest as lightning occasionally flashes in the darkness of the saloon, and thunder rumbles menacingly outside. The saloon is no longer a space of friendship, but one of entrapment and claustrophobia.

Lance soon discovers that the Homestead Act, which came into effect with territorial law, will permit land-hungry sheepherders to lay legal claim to his land. Neither can he buy it from homesteaders. He immediately engages a lawyer, A. Masters, who, to his surprise, turns out to be a woman (Paula Raymond). The parallel between their situations is not lost on Lance and Orrie: she is in a man's profession; he is in a White man's world. Orrie holds the place of both good girl and femme fatale in the film. She is young and lovely, and has a sweet mother (Spring Byington). However, at a pivotal point in the film, Orrie is the one who calls the cavalry to prevent the settlers from wiping out the Shoshone. Her action instead guarantees the end of Lance and the men of his tribe. As Hearne says, "At the heart of *Devil's Doorway* is Lance's divided identity as an assimilated, successful returned cavalryman and a traditional Shoshone. He is also positioned betwixt and between his elderly dying father and his young nephew Jimmy. As he returns home for the first time, Lance lifts Jimmy in the air just as his father falters and falls on the porch step, the first indication of his illness. Lance's choices will be crucial for future generations" (p. 25).

The climax of the film comes soon after a large group of Shoshone takes refuge at Sweet Meadows. They have left the reservation, which they consider a concentration camp, and would rather face death than return. Meanwhile, Coolan has gathered a posse of sheepherders, traditional enemies of the cattlemen. The vigilante mob gathers outside the dark, smoke-filled cabin, and a battle ensues. Lance is seriously wounded. Orrie's call to the cavalry is finally answered. They appear in time to take the reluctant women and children back to the reservation. Lance emerges from the cabin, now wearing his cavalry jacket with his Indian headband and silver belt. Indians and Whites (including Zeke) lie scattered on the meadow. Lance walks proudly toward Orrie and a cavalry officer who asks him, "Where are the others?" Lance replies, "We are all gone," and falls dead at their feet. Orrie's response seems completely inadequate: "It would be too bad if we ever forgot."

Devil's Doorway is a superior contribution to the liberal Westerns of the 1940s and '50s, in comparison to, for example, the better known *Broken Arrow* (Delmer Daves, 1950). The latter was one of the year's seven top-grossing films for Fox, and as a Technicolor star vehicle for James Stewart overshadowed the black-and-white *Devil's Doorway*. Mann's film was actually made before *Broken Arrow*, but had been shelved until after that film's success. It was perceived as a low-budget knockoff of the Daves film. *Broken Arrow*'s plot supports both the treaty and reservation systems. It also features an interracial marriage between a 16-year-old Indian girl and the James Stewart character. The much more problematic idea of a Native American man becoming sexually involved with a White woman is broached in *Devil's Doorway*, but the characters themselves, who come close to a kiss at one moment, know perfectly well that this is impossible. In a beautifully sculpted scene in the smoky cabin, when Orrie attempts to mediate a ceasefire, she and Lance have their final conversation. "A hundred years from now it might have worked," Lance says both tenderly and with finality.

Devil's Doorway is an obvious allegory for the civil rights movement in which African Americans were attempting to assert their right to live as equal citizens in the U.S. But the film was also made in the context of changing policies toward Native Americans: the forced boarding schools, assimilation, and de-tribalization practices in the America of the 1940s and 1950s. While *Devil's Doorway* also critiques the reservation system, it advocates for the integrity of tribes and warns that assimilation continues to be problematic.

Winchester '73 (1950)

When he shifted from modern noirs to the Western, Mann enlivened the oldest American genre with a new visual aesthetic and modern thematic perspective. Mann's *Winchester '73*, was scripted by the extraordinary writing team of Borden Chase (*Red River*, 1948), Robert L. Richards (*Act of Violence*, 1948), and Stuart N. Lake (*My Darling Clementine*, 1950). The first of five Mann-Stewart Westerns, it not only maintains the visual techniques, contemporary cynicism, and dark irony of his urban noirs, but also their psychological and allegorical conflicts. In doing so, Mann ushers in a new era for the Western.

Lin McAdam (James Stewart) and his cowpoke pal High Spade (Millard Mitchell) arrive in Dodge City on the Fourth of July, 1876, barely two weeks after the Sioux retaliatory massacre of the 7th Cavalry at Little Bighorn. Lin steps in to help a saloon gal, Lola (Shelley Winters), who is being forced to leave town, but Wyatt Earp (Will Geer) prevents him. As with all men in town, Lin and High Spade must give up their sidearms to Marshall Earp, but old instincts die hard. When they enter the saloon, Lin's eyes meet those of Dutch Henry Brown (Stephen McNally) and both men slap at their pant legs as though quick-drawing their six-shooters. They are dark mirroring reflections of one another's hatred. Here, the traditional shoot-out is replaced by a contest of marksmanship. The Centennial Celebration for a perfect, one-in-a-thousand Winchester '73 repeating rifle will climax with McAdam and Brown facing off. In an extraordinary display of shooting, Lin wins the match, but before he can leave town to track down the despised Brown, he is ambushed in this hotel room by Dutch Henry Brown and his gang.

At this moment, the film's cinematography changes from a Western to a noir aesthetic. The ambush is shot at low angle as a gang member pulls down a shade, which then converts the struggle over the rifle into a series of chiaroscuro close-ups of the murderous intent in the

Below, the first confrontation between Lin McAdam (James Stewart in white hat) and Dutch Henry Brown (Stephen McNally) is refereed by Wyatt Earp (Will Geer, left) in *Winchester '73*.

Opposite, McAdam listens while his colorful companion "High Spade" Frankie Wilson (Millard Mitchell) speaks to the woman they have rescued, Lola Manners (Shelley Winters).

faces of McAdam and Dutch Henry Brown. Brown nearly kills McAdam with the rifle, but upon hearing Wyatt Earp and High Spade clamoring up the stairs, he leaves through the window with the Winchester '73, his body framed briefly in shadowy bars.

After a two-day ride, the outlaws arrive at the outpost hotel and bar of Jack Riker (John Alexander), where Brown gambles for arms with an Indian gun-trader, Joe Lamont (John McIntire). The claustrophobic poker game between Brown and Lamont employs a glaring, stark overhead lamp in order to deepen the shadows and facial contours of the card players. An ominous sense of death pervades this scene. This shot will become a classic noir convention used for criminal meetings, such as in John Huston's *Asphalt Jungle* (1950) and in Stanley Kubrick's *The Killing* (1956). The game concludes when a full-house of aces and eights, nearly Wild Bill Hickok's dead man's hand, costs Dutch Henry Brown the stolen Winchester '73.

In a harsh, backlit sunset, Lamont meets with Young Bull (Rock Hudson) and his tribe. For Young Bull to obtain the firearms that Crazy Horse used at Little Bighorn, he kills, then scalps Lamont for the Winchester '73. Now, the plot and subplot converge. While talking of their new domestic life to come, Lola and her fiancé Steve Miller (Charles Drake) spy Young Bull's band riding down on them. Steve jumps from the buggy to his horse and rides off, leaving his intended to face the warriors alone. He returns for her, but only after discovering a military wagon in the valley below. Later that night, Lin and High Spade barely flee from the marauding war party into an encampment of the pinned-down U.S. cavalry recruits overseen by a grizzled Sgt. Wilkes (Jay C. Flippen). Mann shoots the night scenes with one light source, the blazing campfire, which casts the figures in shifting silhouettes and shadows, emphasizing the deathly fear that pervades the camp. Of course, Young Bull and his war-painted tribe represent Sitting Bull and the Sioux. In the morning, this ragtag cavalry symbolically re-enacts and wins the Little Bighorn battle with the help of Lin McAdam's repeating rifle. This moment establishes the first of several classic regenerations through violence in the film.

As they ride off in their buggy for the Jameson place, Lola remains still wary of Steve's cowardice, even though Sgt. Wilkes has awarded him for his courage the Winchester '73 found near the dead body of Young Bull by trooper Doan (Anthony Curtis, *before* he became Tony). At the ranch, a gang of outlaws invades the peaceful home as a posse bears down on them. Their leader, Waco Johnny Dean (Dan Duryea), is a psychotic, leering villain devoid of empathy, who guns down Steve in order to obtain both the Winchester '73 and Lola. The scene soon shifts from a Western to a gangster film shoot-out. Moreover, the noir penchant for disrupting domesticity is evident when the posse burns down the ranch house, as Waco Johnny rides away with Lola.

When they meet up with Dutch Henry's gang at the hideout just outside Tascosa, a fearful Waco Johnny hands over the Winchester '73 to a menacing Brown. Inside the hideout, Lola discovers a photograph of three men, a seated old man, and two young men standing behind him, Lin and Dutch. At this point, it can be surmised that McAdam and Dutch are brothers. Here, too, the film switches to a noir allegorical plot, with McAdam ("son of Adam") contending against his brother in an Old Testament sibling struggle akin to the Abel-Cain killing. Additionally, Dutch, the prodigal son, has returned, not with repentance, for he murders his own father. In this modern allegory, the deity is not an omniscient Yahweh, but the new technology that conquers the West, symbolized by the Winchester '73.

Winchester '73: McAdam easily subdues gunslinger Waco Johnnie Dean, portrayed by iconic noir villain Dan Duryea.

In Tascosa, at Jenkins' Bar, Lin and High Spade arrive to discover Lola at the piano. Mann creates the film's most memorable moment when Lin attacks Waco Johnny in order to find out the whereabouts of Dutch Henry. Lola has warned Lin about Waco Johnny's left hand, which can reach for a hidden pistol. In a low-angle, medium shot, Lin grabs Waco Johnny's arm, twisting it around his back; then, Mann cuts to a sustained close-up of Lin's face that reveals the same murderous intensity that occurred in the hotel ambush in Dodge City. The ensuing shoot-out in the streets kills Waco Johnny, foils the gold robbery, and sends Dutch Henry fleeing with Lin in hot pursuit.

The final standoff between the two brothers allows for final regeneration through violence, with McAdam avenging the fallen father. The film's final moment returns all to order. McAdam holds both the prized Winchester '73 and newly won Lola. With *Winchester '73*, Mann recasts the Western idiom by fusing it with noir content and style. And the Western would never be the same.

The Furies (1950)

Made after *Winchester '73*, *The Furies* seems closer in many respects to *Devil's Doorway* than to the latter film. It is a hard-bitten Western, with an unusual emphasis on the plight of the strong woman and on racial injustice. In the New Mexico territory of the 1870s, a cattle baron, T.C. Jeffords (Walter Huston), reigns over the land as far as the eye can see. His enormous ranch "The Furies," is rich in cattle, but T.C. is cash poor. He issues his own currency ("T.C.'s") and lives life with the vigor of a self-made man. T.C.'s daughter Vance (Barbara Stanwyck) is the only person who matches her father in toughness and vitality. Her brother Clay (John Bromfield) is a pale shadow of the old man. The ranch is also inhabited by Mexican "squatters," the most prominent among them being the Herrera family. Their handsome and noble-looking oldest son, Juan (Gilbert Roland) is Vance's lifelong friend. Together they ride the range, racing to the top of hills and mesas, and ritualistically breaking bread each time they meet. In tight two-shots, Juan or Vance pulls out a piece of bread brought along for the occasion, take a bite, and repeat their mantra: "Until our eyes next meet." "Until then."

The film makes clear that "ownership" of the Furies is an historically complex matter. The Hererras have been on the land for many generations, and feel that they have the right not only to live there, but to

In *The Furies* Mann applies noir style to the Western as he did to the period drama *Reign of Terror*: below top, Vance Jeffords (Barbara Stanwyck) threatens her father T.C. and Flo Burnett (Walter Huston and Judith Anderson reflected in the mirror). Bottom, a stylized landscape that recalls the one pictured on page 268.

The Furies: Vance watches T.C. burn the currency that bears his name.

cull a cow or horse from the ranch's stock when needed. Like *Red River* (1948, co-written, like this film, by Charles Schnee), *The Furies* aggrandizes the role of "the men who created kingdoms out of land and cattle...and ruled their empires like feudal lords," as the scrolling text at the beginning of the film reads. Both films present their power-mongering patriarchs ambivalently. But *The Furies*' representation of Mexican claims to the territories of the Southwest stands in contrast to *Red River*'s more elegiac treatment of the White man's acquisition of immense amounts of terrain from Mexican land barons. Among T.C.'s enemies is Rip Darrow (Wendell Corey), owner of the local saloon, the "Legal Tender." The name of the saloon is obviously ironic, considering that T.C.'s homemade currency pushes the bounds of legality. The Darrows' conflict with T.C. goes back at least a generation, when the Darrow Strip, the most beautiful part of the ranch, was appropriated by Jeffords.

The film's conflict begins early in the film, when Clay returns to the Furies at night, gazing at the full-length portrait of his father in the foyer before finding his sister in their dead mother's room. Lance and Clay quarrel, the sister ridiculing her brother for allowing T.C. to get the best of him. In fact, Lance is risking her father's anger at that very moment. She is trying on one of her mother's dresses to wear to Clay's wedding, even though the room itself, much less the clothes, are off limits. A few minutes later, however, she proves her point. Horse hooves outside and his loud voice signal T.C.'s return from a long trip to San Francisco. As her father stands in front of his own portrait, he gazes at his daughter who stands, radiant, on the staircase. "You were in her room?" he asks, almost angrily. Then T.C. smiles: "The gown befits you." She flies to him and they kiss one another on the mouth.

In Greek mythology, the Furies pursue Orestes for having committed matricide (in revenge for the death of his father, Agamemnon, at his mother's hands). It's already clear that Oedipus and Elektra, from the Freudian perspective, are hard at work in Vance's relationship with her father. Both men and women exude complex sexual energies and lust for land in *The Furies*. But it's appropriate that the Furies are female avengers, for the daughter's love and hate are at the heart of the film. As Jeanine Basinger notes, "The characters themselves are archetypes—The father, The jealous brother, The spoiled daughter, The stepmother, etc. Above all, it is a story of fate and of a house of proud people who lack humility" (76).

Landscapes in *The Furies* strongly prefigure their visualization in Mann's later Westerns, particularly *The Naked Spur*. Several scenes in the earlier film anticipate powerful moments in the latter, in particular two in which giant boulders rain down from a fortress-like position atop a mesa. The Jeffords forces attack the Herreras stronghold, and are greeted with giant rocks. They are attacked by the Jeffords forces (minus Vance), with the matriarchal harridan (Blanche Yurka) cackling as she pushes the giant rocks down the mountainside. Like Catherine and Heathcliff in *Wuthering Heights*, Vance and Juan represent the alliance of the light woman with the dark man, and with a rugged landscape that reflects the force of their relationship. But Vance does not love Juan as he loves her. Instead she is pulled as by a magnetic force to her father's enemy, Rip Darrow, who is also tied to the land—to a forested strip rather than a barren crag, as befits his Anglo background. But Darrow, though powerfully attracted to Vance, as well, is as hard-bitten as the Jeffords father and daughter. He accepts $50,000 from T.C. to break off his relationship with Vance, to her utter humiliation.

T.C.'s sins against his daughter are compounded when he brings home a widow woman, Flo Burnett (Judith Anderson), whose manipulative nature is both obvious and fascinating. When Flo takes tea in the former Mrs. Jeffords' room, and makes it clear to Vance that she intends to marry her father, admitting that it is in part for the money, a killing fury possesses the younger woman. An extraordinary scene ensues. As Flo and T.C. announce their engagement to Vance, and Flo condescendingly invites Vance to visit them, the three stand in front of a mirror. The noir doppelganger times three is laid out before us. Behind her back Vance clutches reflexively at a pair of scissors, and with deadly accuracy hurls them at Flo's face. T.C. bellows that if she dies, he will kill his daughter. Flo is mutilated for life.

Soon thereafter, under the embittered Flo's influence, T.C. has decided to get rid of the Herreras once and for all. Ostensibly, this is because the ranch is encumbered with debt. The provision for borrowing enough from a San Francisco bank for T.C. to remain solvent is that the squatters must be removed. But this provision has been in effect for some time, and Vance until now has successfully protected the Herreras. Dynamited out of their strong-

Vance steps between her father T.C. and her swain Rip Darrow (Wendell Corey) in *The Furies*.

hold, the Herreras descend, T.C. promising amnesty. T.C.'s man El Tigre (Thomas Gomez) points out that no amnesty was promised for horse thieves, and that Juan has admitted taking horses—although he does not regard that as theft. The scene's brutality escalates, as the Jeffords clan becomes a lynching party, despite Vance's furious entreaties. The hanging takes place off-screen, but wide angles and low-key lighting emphasize the power and horror of the moment. Juan accepts his fate almost cheerfully, refusing to beg for his life—knowing that T.C. would kill him in any case. Mother Herrera screams; Vance kisses Juan and rides to sit, backlit, facing her father on horseback. She spits her words out with hatred: "Take a good long look at me, T.C. You won't see me again until I take your world away from you!"

And so Vance methodically formulates and executes a plan to ensure her success. While T.C. amicably breaks off with the scarred but philosophical Flo, Vance travels the country buying up the "T.C.'s"—the I.O.U.s that will break the old man's empire. As in *T-Men*, *Border Incident*, *Winchester '73*, and other Mann films, objects in circulation—whether paper, rifles, men, or banknotes—follow the trajectory of human greed and hatred. Having tricked her father into selling 20,000 head of cattle for valueless T.C.'s, Vance, now romantically linked to Rip, realizes that hatred disguised her consuming love for her father. T.C. has become a legend. A ballad to his epic durability is sung by one of the cowboys on the epic roundup, and when someone calls an un-captured bull the "king" of the Furies, T.C. wrestles it to the ground. Tracked and shot down by the Herrera matriarch, T.C. dies in Vance's arms in the middle of the street. But Rip and Vance vow to continue the Jeffords legacy by naming a son T.C.

As radical as are some aspects of *The Furies*, it allows itself nostalgia for the defeated patriarch. In *Devil's Doorway*, the ethnic "other" is expunged, but at the end of *The Furies* T.C.

Above the entire cast of characters thrown together in the Western noir *The Naked Spur* (from left): Jesse Tate (Millard Mitchell), Ben Vandergroat (Robert Ryan), Lina Patch (Janet Leigh), Roy Anderson (Ralph Meeker) and Howard Kemp (James Stewart).

is afforded a luxury that may have been denied Lance Poole: he will, in fact, be remembered.

The Naked Spur (1953)

The Naked Spur relies upon the journey motif to explore the abnormal facets of human social and psychological behavior. In fact, the basic plot relies upon the Ship of Fools journey narrative, in which the voyagers, representing dangerous fixations and types of madness, set out for their fools' paradise. Here, the bounty hunter pursuing the outlaw becomes an allegory of the man's confrontation with deadly sins that plague him.

At first, classifying *The Naked Spur* as a noir might seem odd, since it is filmed in Technicolor, but it should be remembered that *Leave Her to Heaven* (1945) was the first Technicolor noir. Both films examine the human psyche and obsessions that lead to moral destruction, a common theme of noir films. Both films express inner emotional turmoil through shifts from light to shadow as visual representations of man's succumbing to dark temptations. Both films are Expressionist experiments in the truest sense: the emphasis is placed upon presenting primal emotional angst by the use of a dynamic color palette and distortions of aesthetic conventions. For *The Naked Spur*, the shifting landscape, from placid aspens and calm streams to jagged mountains and impassable rapids, reflects the inner psychological states of characters.

The characters in this Western represent the obsessions that forged the American West. Howard Kemp (James Stewart) is a bounty hunter whose desire for money reduces all others to a financial calculation. The films opens with him getting the drop on an inept, unlucky prospector, Jesse Tate (Millard Mitchell), whose obsession for gold blinds him to moral codes of conduct. After discovering that Tate has seen the remains of a campfire in the hills, Kemp pays for his services as a guide. Tate believes that Kemp is a lawman, a false assumption that Kemp does not correct. Kemp even shows Tate a wanted poster for murder, from which he has conveniently and deceptively torn off the reward. When they ride to an impassable crag, they meet with deadly, man-produced rockslides that pin them down. Hearing their rifle reports as they fire at the outlaw, Lt. Roy Anderson (Ralph Meeker), a self-proclaimed "Indian fighter extraordinary," arrives, newly dishonorably discharged for being "morally unstable." Specifically, Anderson has raped the daughter of an Indian chief. After Kemp burns his hands on a rope trying to scale the crag, Anderson replaces him, succeeds in reaching the top, and then holds at gunpoint the murderous outlaw, Ben Vandergroat (Robert Ryan), whose first response, typical of the his sociopathic demeanor, is not fear or dismay, but demonic laughter. Lina Patch (Janet Leigh) sneaks up on ex-Lt. Anderson, bites his hand, forcing his pistol to the ground and giving Ben time to attack. During their struggle, Ben continues his disturbing, demented laughter. Kemp and Tate now arrive atop the cliff and stop the gleeful Ben from killing Anderson. Ben soon informs the assembled fellow travelers that Kemp is no sheriff, but a bounty hunter, showing them a complete wanted poster with the $5,000 reward for him, "Dead or Alive." Tate and ex-Lt. Anderson decide to split the reward three ways.

From this point, the film enacts a series of shifting loyalties and multiple deceptions. The group's moral center disintegrates. All the while, Ben, riding atop an ass, entices each character to embrace their worst desires. Each character represents loss: Kemp was betrayed by Mary, his bride-to-be, who sold his ranch out from under him; Tate has lost human contact in the pursuit of gold; Anderson has no station in life and no future; Lina, the orphan, has no family. Their losses are also what they hopelessly desire.

Most poignantly, Kemp and Lina are joined through mutual need for affection. Kemp is wounded in the leg by an Indian bullet during a siege caused by Anderson's unscrupulous ambush. Unable to continue, Kemp falls from his horse, a symbolic moment of transformation.

Lina nurses Howard in *The Naked Spur*.

The film then cuts to the shadows of night and Kemp suddenly rising up and shrieking in almost inhuman agony, perhaps the most chilling moment in the film. Kemp's delirium is also his salvation, for it begins the process of exorcising his internal demons. Lina nurses him through his ordeal and she becomes a surrogate for his lost fiancée. For the scenes between Kemp and Lina, the film's score modifies Stephen Foster's "Beautiful Dreamer" to harmonize with their new love and, in a minor key, to express their discordant desires: Kemp's material-ism, treating Ben as "a sack of money"; Lina's misguided devotion to her surrogate parent, Ben. Both must break free from their pasts in order to survive.

The climax of the film occurs after a series of betrayals. Tate, envisioning Ben's sup-posed gold mine, helps Ben escape with Lina. Of course, Ben kills Tate, who exclaims before he dies: "I got it comin'. Do business with the Devil and you get it every time!" The film's initial rock crag scene is then repeated. As Kemp climbs the rockface above the cauldron of rapids, he uses his naked spur as a makeshift piton. Ben slithers over to the edge to kill him, but Kemp hurls the spur into his face, causing Ben to stand as Anderson pumps lead into him. Kemp falls into the rapids and Anderson loses his life trying to extract Ben's body in order to claim the reward. Kemp manages to pull Ben's body out of the seething waters and loads his corpse onto his horse. Lina tries to stop him, but Kemp bellows "Money, that's all I've ever cared about . . .That's the way I am!" She dissuades him with "I'll marry you." As Kemp relents, forsaking prof-it for love, and buries Ben, the strains of "Beautiful Dreamer" take over the scene and the cam-era moves heavenward as though to recall the famous lines that conclude the song: "Then will all clouds of sorrow depart/Beautiful dreamer, awake unto me!"

As with many noir films, in *The Naked Spur* the crimes of the villain reveal the hero's foibles and make him as culpable as the criminal. As with all of Mann's noir Westerns, *The Naked Spur* ushers in a new type of psychological plot and visual aesthetic to correspond to it. These new elements will become a standard for Sergio Leone's and Clint Eastwood's later allegorical Westerns, for the psychological studies in violence and obsession in the masterworks of Sam Peckinpah, and for the new experiments with the Western, such as HBO's *Deadwood*, that owe much to Mann's melding of noir expressions with Western settings.

Biography

Anthony Mann was born Emil Anton Bundmann to Austrian-immigrant parents on June 30, 1906 in San Diego, California. As a child Mann began acting in local theaters and, when the family moved to New York in 1917, off-Broadway. After the death of his teacher father, Mann quit high school and found factory work to support his family. At night, he continued to pursue his acting career and eventually became a director on Broadway. In 1938, he returned to Southern California to find work in Hollywood. Initially he was a casting director and talent scout at Selznick International, where he directed screen tests for *Rebecca* and *Gone with the Wind*. He moved to Paramount and was assistant director on *Sullivan's Travels* to Preston Sturges, who advised him that "It's better to have done something bad than to have done nothing." In 1942, Mann launched his own film-directing career in low-budget movies, beginning with such minor noir classics as *Dr. Broadway* and *The Great Flamarion*. In less than a decade, Mann's output of noir films made him one of the most important figures in the cycle, and he transitioned to B- then A-budget studio productions on the films listed below, often photographed by his frequent collaborator John Alton. In 1951 Mann began a series of noirish Westerns starring James Stewart (*Winchester '73*, *The Naked Spur*) that ended his participation in the classic period. Shortly after being replaced on *Spartacus*, Mann left the United States to work on large budget European epics for producer Samuel Bronson: *El Cid* (1961) and *The Fall of the Roman Empire* (1964). Mann died on April 29, 1967 in the midst of shooting his final movie, *A Dandy in Aspic.*

Noir Films

Dr. Broadway (1942)
Strangers in the Night (1944)
The Great Flamarion (1945)
Strange Impersonation (1946)
Desperate (1947)
Railroaded (1947)
T-Men (1947)
Raw Deal (1948)
He Walked By Night (1948, uncredited with Alfred Werker)
Reign of Terror (aka *The Black Book*, 1949)
Follow Me Quietly (1949, story only)
Border Incident (1949)
Side Street (1949)
Devil's Doorway (1950)
Winchester '73 (1950)
The Furies (1950)
The Naked Spur (1953)

Mann shows Barbara Stanwyck some footage on the set of *The Furies.*

Max Ophuls takes his lunch break while sitting on a camera crane.

Max Ophuls

Susan White, Alain Silver, James Ursini

In 1948 Max Ophuls ("Opuls" on the credits of some of his American films), a German-Jewish émigré driven from Europe by the war, had worked on two period pictures, one for Howard Hughes and Preston Sturges at Cal-Pix, *Vendetta* (1950) which Ophuls started filming in 1946, and the second for Douglas Fairbanks, Jr., at International Pictures (*The Exile*, 1947). His next project, adapted by Howard Koch from Stefan Zweig's 1922 novella and produced by William Dozier and John Houseman for Rampart/Universal International, was also period: *Letter from an Unknown Woman* (1948). It features Joan Fontaine as a young girl, Lisa Berndle, who falls obsessively in love with her apartment-building neighbor, pianist Stefan Brand (Louis Jourdan). The setting of the film is written onscreen at the beginning of the film: "Vienna, 1900, the Vienna of Freud." The film, although it has generally been categorized as a "woman's picture," like works including *Mildred Pierce* (1945) and Sirk's flamboyant melodramas, is heavily tinged with noir mood and conventions. The flashback structure and emotional intensity of its "unknown woman," as well as the film's powerful use of chiaroscuro lighting, bring the movie emphatically under the broad shadow of film noir.

The film opens on Stefan, a burnt-out but extremely handsome bon vivant, who must decide whether or not to face a duel the next morning. It seems clear from his jaunty insouciance, as he addresses his fellow carousers, that he will choose to flee rather than fight. As he enters his home, his mute valet John (Art Smith) presents him with a thick envelope. The letter opens, in a voiceover elegantly enunciated by a woman: "By the time you read this I may be dead.... You will know how I became yours...without you even knowing it." These dramatic words prompt a flashback that will constitute most of the narrative. (The allusion to a dead narrator who may already be dead—or is certainly dying—is of course reminiscent of such films as *D.O.A.* and *Sunset Boulevard*.)

Letter opens with Lisa as a teenager watching movers lug into their apartment house the belongings, including a piano, of a mysterious new neighbor. Stefan's looks, piano playing and brooding mien inspire something more than a girlish infatuation in Lisa. When he finally notices and greets her pleasantly, she writes, "From that moment I was in

Below, Joan Fontaine as the young Lisa in *Letter from an Unknown Woman.*

love with you...I began to prepare myself for you." The details of the preparation are revealed in a montage of her dance lessons, music study, and her surreptitious, sublime moments listening to Stefan's music through the transom.

Ophuls' camera angles, notably in the repeated low-key-lit staircase scenes when Lisa observes Stefan's amorous activities, reinforce the film's noir undercurrent. The film's narrative is also characteristic of noir as is reflected in the power of Lisa's obsession with Stefan Brandt. Like many a noir protagonist, she allows passion to rule her life even to the point of destroying her. When Lisa's mother remarries and informs her that they are moving away to a conservative garrison town (Linz, Hitler's birthplace, in fact—an ironic note added by Ophuls), Lisa runs away briefly, hoping to be able declare her love for Stefan, only to be met with another of his giggling women friends at the apartment building. Lisa temporarily accepts her role as obedient daughter.

Within the highly melodramatic context, Ophuls' visualization to some degree idealizes

Below, Joan Fontaine as Lisa and Louis Jourdan as Stefan. Opposite, Stefan reads the letter of the title.

the period environment, but never without touches of irony. The garrison town of Linz and the people Lisa meets there are, for example, nothing short of absurd. When her parents try to arrange a marriage to a young lieutenant, Lisa retreats into a fantasy world and tells her suitor that she is already engaged...to Stefan. While the film still reads primarily as melodrama, Lisa's flight from the stifling bourgeois town and back to the urban world of Vienna, her explicit and emotional rejection of social norms reintroduces the undercurrent of noir.

As will Leonora Eames in *Caught*, Lisa gets work as a model and begins again to stalk Stefan, which results in renewed acquaintance. While Stefan initially treats Lisa like any other pretty woman he has plans of seducing, Lisa intrigues him with discussions of music and insights into his preferences: "You like mystery." Despite this, Lisa is (willingly) seduced and abandoned like the other women. After she gives birth to a son in a Catholic charity hospital, Lisa marries a rich, older military man to secure a future for her child.

The second half of Lisa's story begins in a semi-objective mode. Lisa and her husband join a crowd of operagoers while Ophuls's camera singles them out, following them in a long, unbroken mobile tracking shot. "The course of our lives can be changed by such little things," Lisa says in voiceover, "I know now that nothing happens by chance. Every moment is measured." It may not be exactly the tone of the hapless Al Roberts in *Detour* or the doomed Steve Thompson in *Criss Cross*, but the deterministic pull of the camerawork underscores the narration just as powerfully. When there is a cut, it is, of course, to another who happens to be attending: Stefan, who has given up the piano for a life of pleasant hedonism.

As was the sight of Anna for Steve Thompson, the rush of feeling that hurtles out of the past, obliterates rationality. Again under the pull of her adolescent obsession, Lisa considers leaving her husband and child-to-be for a man who barely remembers her, an unforgivable crime for a woman in that period. "I've had no will but his ever," she tells her husband. His angry reply is typical of all the repressive realists and is repeated in many of Ophuls' films, "That is romantic nonsense."

Lisa's hope is renewed after a brief but dramatic conversation with Stefan outside the opera house, in which he notices that she is strangely familiar, and tries to penetrate her mystery. But when he begins treating her like any other conquest, she realizes she can never recapture the initial rapture. A devastating high-angle (and unusually still) shot observes Lisa walk slowly, under the dimly lit midnight sky, across a desolate square, as the voiceover enunciates her despair. Away at school, Lisa's son is dying of typhus, and she contracts the same deadly disease. Before dying she mails the letter to Stefan.

By embracing film noir's visual style, Ophuls and cameraman Franz Planer reveal the dark underworld of the fin-de-siècle, presaged at the beginning of the film by the indirect reference to "Freud's Vienna." In this context of unconscious drives and obsession, that overlay of darkness becomes more heavily ironic. In the frame narrative (the night before the duel), a disturbed Stefan finally realizes for himself that the course of his life can be changed by such a small thing as a letter from an unknown woman. He decides to face the offended party, who is, of course, Lisa's husband, a skilled marksman. Expecting to be killed, Stefan puts a white

Letter from an Unknown Woman: Lisa with her son and husband. As with all the women in Ophuls' noir films, obligations to the family influence decisions.

rose—taken from the one of the bouquets that (the unknown) Lisa has sent to him every year—in his lapel, and leaves for his rendezvous. In a romantically oneiric flashback, he sees the figure of Lisa as a young girl, smiling at him in the doorway.This flashback works as both narrative truth and tautology, the inexorable replaying of the past prototypical to noir. Neither the viewer nor Stefan questions the veracity of the letter or the existence of Lisa, the unknown woman who exists only on the hand-written pages read during the darkness of night. In a final transference that is also part of the noir schema, Stefan accepts and then mirrors Lisa's obsession, validates and embraces it by going to his death over it.

Despite its complicated production circumstances, *Caught* (1949) is a film firmly marked by Ophuls' directorial stamp, particularly in what concerns the mobile long take (often, in this film, using the newly devised crab dolly), a technique that allowed very efficient filming as well as interesting visual effects well suited to the noir genre. As Lutz Bacher notes in *Max Ophuls in the Hollywood Studios* (New Brunswick, N.J.: Rutgers University Press, 2000, p. 217), Ophuls' good relationship with extraordinary cinematographer Lee Garmes also contributed to the visual interest of the film. Produced by Wolfgang Reinhardt (Max Reinhardt's son) for Enterprise Productions, and adapted from the Libbie Bloch novel, *Wild Calendar*, the script went through a number of writers, with Arthur Laurents finally taking screen credit. The film tells the story of Leonora (formerly Maude) Ames (Barbara Bel Geddes), an aspiring model from an impoverished background, who marries an extremely wealthy but abusive millionaire (Robert Ryan as Smith Ohlrig). As Ohlrig's behavior becomes more cruel, Leonora leaves him to take a position as receptionist for the young Dr. Quinada (James Mason, in his first American film), a rather down-at-the-heels physician devoted to his work with the poor. At first considering Leonora a spoiled young woman from a privileged background, Quinada soon learns that Leonora is capable of compassion and sacrifice for his patients. They fall in love, but a brief reunion with her husband leaves Leonora pregnant. The reunion with Ohlrig proves disastrous, and having miscarried her child, Leonora leaves her husband for a middle-class life with Quinada.

Among the truly noir elements of the film is Robert Ryan's simultaneously enraged and pathetic performance as Smith Olhrig (a thinly veiled reference to the idiosyncrasies of Howard Hughes and perhaps Preston Sturges). The paranoia Ohlrig expresses during a session with his psychiatrist (Art Smith) reiterate and anticipate Ryan's purely noir performances in films such as *Act of Violence* (1948), *Crossfire* (1947) and *On Dangerous Ground* (1952). His dark eyes glint in the chiaroscuro and low-key-lit scene, such as the one on the dock when he first meets Leonora, and his face is as tightly closed as a fist when jealousy or professional frustration dominate his emotions. The woman's film elements of *Caught* are often harsh, not unlike the dark undercurrents of Hitchcock's *Rebecca* (1940), which also features an ill-fated pregnancy.

The titles and then the narrative itself open on Leonora and her roommate, Maxime (Ruth Brady), leafing through a glamor magazine, identifying the outfits and jewelry that they like, a decidedly "woman's film" opening. Leonora even soaks her feet, which hurt as a result of her work as a carhop. We see, as the camera pulls back, that the apartment is shabby. Soon Leonora, by pinching pennies, saves enough to attend charm school (sequences filmed by John Berry when Ophuls was ill with the shingles). Her naïve dreams will be put to the test immediately when, as she models a mink (a significant metonymy in the film already mentioned in the opening scene) in a department store, where two customers (one is Barbara Billingsley) "womanhandle" her while discussing whether one's husbands can afford a new mink. Thus the mink pops up again in the narrative. Soon, a "slimy" little man, Franzi (Curt Bois), asks her to show him the mink's lining, as an excuse to look over her body. Pleased, he invites

her to a party on what will turn out to be Ohlrig's yacht.

After scrambling for something appropriate to wear (including her neighbor's ratty fur stole), Leonora presents herself at a darkened pier, hard light emanating from lamps above her. A boat, which she believes will take her to the yacht, arrives. As events unfold, Leonora learns that the brusque man dressed all in black who descends from the boat is Smith Ohlrig, the kind of millionaire about whom the roommates had been fantasizing in the first scene of the film. Leonora is impressed—and is immediately drawn into his strange life, accompanying him to one of his warehouses at midnight instead of going to the yacht party, sleeping in the car while cast shadows cross the warehouse wall and the black-clad Ohlrig disappears into the dark. As a "nice girl" from Denver, however, she refuses to enter Ohlrig's home that night. In the scene with his psychiatrist, the latter baits Ohlrig about the nature of what Ohlrig calls his "heart attacks," which the doctor believes to be a "nervous reaction"—an inner voice saying "I'm not all powerful; I'm weak; take pity; give me what I want." "I must destroy everyone I can't own." Although Ohlrig does admit that he is afraid that all anyone wants is his money, the conversation triggers an impulsive marriage proposal to Leonora.

Caught: opposite Leonora (Barbara Bel Geddes) looms over a fallen Ohlrig (Robert Ryan). Below, an anxious Leonora with her employer and would-be protector Dr. Larry Quinada (James Mason).

Above the high-key (and sterile) atmosphere of Quinada's office. Opposite, the dark panelled den where Ohlrig's hides from the world prompts Quinada's palpable unease when he comes searching for Leonora.

At this point the film enters truly noir territory, as Leonora waits up night after night for her husband to come home. At almost three one morning, she sits with Franzi (whose character might be read as stereotypically gay) in the game room, where the latter is playing the piano. Franzi plays a Viennese waltz; snow falls outside the window behind him. On the other side of the room, Leonora, dressed in an evening gown, complains about her husband's neglect. They seem, for the moment, to be in entirely different spaces. Franzi, whom Ohlrig later calls a "dirty little parasite" (the script reads "refugee," rather than "parasite," emphasizing the possibility of Franzi's Jewishness—Curt Bois was in fact a Jewish refugee), repeats to her again and again in his wonderfully "Continental" accent: "Take a pill, dahling"; "Tough, buy yourself a new hat. Tough, dahling, tough." When he accuses her of being greedy, Leonora slaps his face, but is immediately sorry. Franzi remarks that he is paid to take slaps for Ohlrig, who arrives immediately thereafter. Leonora hurries to fix herself up, with Franzi's help, for his arrival.

One of the most interesting scenes in the film, both visually and thematically, is the one taking place immediately thereafter, when Ohlrig projects for his employees an industrial film in his private screening room. Just as Ohlrig's image appears in that film, Leonora's laugh is heard. She is merely laughing at something a man has said, but Ohlrig uses the opportunity to humiliate her publically. His confrontation with his wife is shot in depth, with first Ryan and then Bel Geddes in the extreme foreground, using unusual 180 degree shot-reverse shots to depict the two sitting across from each other in the vast room (reminiscent of the use of space in *Citizen Kane* [1941]).

After the employees are dismissed, smoke lingers in the air, lit by the beam of light emanating from the projector. Leonora leaves the room angrily, only to return moments later to shout (with reverberations sounding in the large room) at her husband that she won't remain to be treated in such a way. He asks her to stop shouting, and moves from the window to the pool table, where he faces the camera in a low, wide angle, pushing balls toward the camera, at the bottom of the screen, expressing his contained violence and revealing his sense of domination of the playing field. (The pool table is used to similar effect in Stanley Kubrick's *Eyes Wide Shut*, when Tom Cruise and Sydney Pollack act out their final confrontation.) As Leonora walks out on him, the camera tracks in for a dramatic low-angle shot, while Ohlrig fumbles for his heart pills.

As she had threatened, Leonora finds a job, as a receptionist for Dr. Quinada. Early scenes in the office are high-key lit, signaling our entry into the familiar world of the woman's

The Reckless Moment: Lucia Harper (Joan Bennett) recoils but watches intently as Martin Donnelly (James Mason, far right) fights (against his own best interest) to protect her.

film. Will Leonora make good and prove herself to be worthy of Quinada's admiration—even love? After some scenes where Quinada chastises Leonora (Lee, as he comes to call her) for her society lady manners, the two become close. A night spent treating a child's botulism case in the home of the immigrant Rudeckis will seal their love, though the swinging overhead hard light in the Rudecki's kitchen, and the somewhat noir atmosphere of the bar in the next scene hint to us that all is not yet sweetness and light. (In the bar/dance hall scene, there is even an intervention by a B-girl who asks Quinada for a light, returning three times, and addressing him as "sweetie.") Noticing that she is lightly clad, Quinada buys Leonora a coat and presents it to her the next morning, unconsciously showing her that her need for minks is in the past. But Leonora is pregnant and returns—temporarily—to Smith Ohlrig.

Once again noir style and iconography dominate the film. Leonora is held virtually a prisoner in the mansion. Larry Quinada, not understanding that Lee is actually married to Ohlrig, seeks her out. A stiff conversation leads to Quinada's departure, while Ohlrig expresses rage by playing pinball with violent body English. Leonora calls Quinada out into the garage and explains her situation. Ohlrig arrives, and a scene is played out under strategically placed lights and with cast shadows, ending in Quinada's departure.

At the foot of the grand staircase, Ohlrig tells his wife that all he cares about is breaking her, and if he has to use the child to do it he will. Having placed himself in the role of villain, Ohlrig can expect to be defeated at his own game. Franzi, horrified by Ohlrig's treatment of Leonora, quits him, preferring to return to being a headwaiter. Leonora lies in her bed of pain in her low-key-lit room. Forced to come downstairs, she walks dramatically toward Smith Ohlrig, looking toward the back tracking camera. Her defiance causes Ohlrig to collapse, caught under his pinball machine, hard light shining on the side of his face as Leonora leaves him begging for water. Despite appearances, Leonora doesn't leave Smith to die. The next scene shows the house filled with doctors, while Leonora sits in her dark bedroom, raving that she has killed her husband. Quinada arrives in time to administer a drink, and then to call an ambulance as Leonora begins to miscarry.

The last scenes of the film, in the ambulance and the hospital, are strangely mixed in tone. "Your child will die, and that's a terrible thing, but you will be free to start living," Quinada tells her. Lee is in labor and sweating heavily, mourning the baby who will be born dead, and smiling her love at Larry simultaneously. The final scene is a conversation between Larry and his partner, who has delivered the dead child. As Larry rushes in to see Leonora, Dr. Hoffman (Frank Ferguson) lets the nurse know that Leonora's mink coat will no longer be needed. The nurse walks down the hall, carrying it out of their lives.

The Reckless Moment is quite distinct within the noir cycle. The film was an independent Walter Wanger production for Columbia, starring Wanger's wife, Joan Bennett. An adaptation of the Elizabeth Sanxay Holding novel, The Blank Wall, by Mel Dinelli and Robert E. Kent, the story shows similarities to the plots of Woman in the Window and Detour (both 1945): in each an attempt to conceal a death results in blackmail. The crucial difference, of course, is that while its protagonist is as morally innocent as the male characters in those earlier films, the person enmeshed by circumstances in The Reckless Moment is a woman, a woman whose husband is away in Berlin on business, and who must deal with a catastrophe alone. Certainly there are many female protagonists in film noir, but when fate slaps them in the face few are compelled to grapple with it alone. For the most part without a male figure of equal prominence there is no story, without a man to destroy there is no femme fatale. Ophuls was well aware of the history of the noir cycle, and interested in Italian Neo-realism. With this film, he wanted to work the noir angle even more strongly than before, all the while making a truly American film.

Noir title characters such as *Nora Prentiss* (1947) and *Gilda* (1946) are performers. Nora and Gilda are also victims of a society that can both empower and enslave chanteuses and sirens. Ophuls' own characters, Lisa Berndle and Leonora Eames, are young and attractive enough to find work as models. Unlike any of them, Lucia Harper in *The Reckless Moment* does not perform in nightclubs, marry a wealthy man, travel to exotic locales, or even step out on Saturday nights. She cooks dinner at home and has no shady past. She lives in a comfortable home in upscale Balboa, California with her husband, children, father-in-law, housekeeper, and pets, until a large problem lands on her doorstep: the body of a blackmailer killed by her daughter, Bea (Geraldine Brooks), who, at seventeen, has been seeking Bohemian thrills among Los Angeles lowlifes, including her blackmailer, Ted Darby (Shepperd Strudwick). The blackmail involves letters sent to Darby by the naïve Bea.

After Darby's accidental death (a fall from the Harpers' boathouse onto an anchor; his body disposed of by Lucia), two other blackmailers get their hands on the letters: one is the mysterious Nagel (Roy Roberts); the other is the front man, a handsome Irishman, Martin Donnelly, played by top-billed James Mason, in his second film for Ophuls. As the plot unfolds, Lucia is forced, in the absence of her husband, to deal with these blackmailers, becoming emotionally entangled (without crossing boundaries into an illicit relationship) with Donnelly. In a strange twist, Donnelly will ultimately sacrifice himself so that Lucia can continue her unremarkable suburban family life.

As Lucia Harper, Joan Bennett, who happens to be the femme fatale of both *Woman in the Window* and *Scarlet Street* (1945), is as an ordinary woman, neither glamorous nor cunning. Somewhat like the women in *Mildred Pierce* (1945) or *The Accused* (1949), the irony of her situation is not her innocence but that her middle-class values give her no pause before her decision to conceal a death by misadventure. Unlike Mildred Pierce, who protects her daughter Veda despite knowing that she has become a merciless and murderous schemer, Bea is an ostensibly normal if impressionable and rather bratty teenager and her involvement with Darby seems to be a youthful error. Lucia's decision to try to shield her own family is parental instinct and perfectly "normal." As compared to the ruthless ambition of Mildred Pierce, in which she sacrifices her marriage for the sake of business success and the social advancement of her daughter, or the sexual paranoia of Wilma Tuttle in *The Accused*, who lives an inculcated life as a prim academic, Lucia is entirely ordinary.

Ophuls' visual style (assisted by cinematographer Burnett Guffey) stresses the commonplace aspects of Lucia's milieu. Unlike the dark corners of Ohlrig's mansion that swallowed the hapless Leonora, the Harper house is well lit, compact, tidy, and filled with lived-in furnishings. Lucia's outfits, light-colored suits and dresses, are fashionable but quite different from Alice Reed's elegant evening gown and dark shawl when she suddenly appears to Dr. Wanley reflected as *The Woman in the Window*. With short hair, simple make-up, and lighting that leaves her face free of shadows, Bennett is neither mysterious nor ominous.

The film opens on a bright establishing shot of the harbor in bedroom community Balboa, described in voiceover as a "charming community." The time frame is the week before Christmas of "last year." Quickly we are thrown out of the general into the specific: Mrs. Harper is driving her white sedan from Balboa (past her always inadequately dressed son, fishing in the harbor, who calls out "Mother, where are you going?"—one of the many times a demanding voice from the domestic front urges itself upon Lucia) to Los Angeles, by means of the freeway. Cars and telephones, designed to offer freedoms to the consumer, will prove to be part of the suburban trap in which the Lucias of the world are caught. The voiceover breaks off suddenly. The score is both sprightly and slightly anxious, as close-ups of Lucia show her looking furtively over her shoulder, wearing sunglasses as she drives. From the sunny outdoors of the parking lot in midtown, barely two minutes into the film, Lucia enters a run-down and rather gloomy hotel. A dame in a fur jostles Lucia at the front desk, saying, "Excuse me, honey." The sour man behind the desk tells Lucia that Darby, about whom she inquired, wants her to meet him in the bar. "The bar?" she asks, as if she had never heard of such a thing. A tracking shot takes her past the usual suspects, men talking about hiring a singer, gambling, etc. The bar itself is a prototypical noir setting. Although there is a bartender, the bar is closed and dark, with chairs stacked on the tables. The bartender assures Lucia that it's only ten minutes until he can serve her a drink. She has already established her noir identity, following in the footsteps of her adventurous daughter. Darby appears, fulfilling Lucia's expectations in appearance, manner, and, of course, his proposition to quit seeing Bea for money. Although Lucia believes that Darby's request will alienate Bea, the teenager is determined to continue to see him, as she announces, half-hidden behind an easel where one of her art school creations is underway. (It was Ophuls' wont to place objects in front of characters, defying the viewer's expectation of easy visual access to actors.)

Lucia's only communication with her husband takes place in increasingly deceptive and

Below, Lucia and Donnelly find themselves in a non-reckless, domestic moment.

ironic telephone calls, and in a heartfelt letter declaring her need for male assistance in her life, which she destroys and replaces with a cheerful note. The film heads further into noir country as Bea sneaks into the boathouse to meet Darby and comes to understand that he really is a blackmailer. After an accidental blow on his head during their brief scuffle, he falls to his death. Bea confesses to her mother who moves through one low-key-lit set after another. Only Sybyl (Frances Williams), her African-American housekeeper, will sense and finally help Lucia in her troubles. In a long, almost silent sequence, other than the noise of the boat engine, Lucia struggles with Darby's body, pulling it into the boat and dumps it into the harbor.

Family members, including her father-in-law, continue to harass Lucia in the ways a family will, and the demands of Christmas mount up. Soon Donnelly appears, invading the living room of the Harper home. The house seems literally divided into dark and light halves, as Donnelly closes the shutters to block out light and visibility from other rooms. He has the letters and will be paid, as he tells her in his soft, "Irish" accent.

Donnelly meets the family members as a "friend" of the absent Tom, but only Bea and Sybyl know the truth. The work on the contrast between high and low key lighting, the absence or presence of shadows within the house itself, continues to be of interest throughout the film. Donnelly becomes more and more the spectator of Lucia's harried life. He

The Reckless Moment: meeting family members as a friend.

reproaches her for smoking too much (too much like a noir heroine) and, on an outing to the drugstore that rings both menacing and domestic, even buys her filters advertising "less nicotine and less tobacco stain" for her. But both Donnelly and Lucia are prisoners—as the former says, "You have your family; I have my Nagel." Lucia, who now cringes at the sounds of sirens, comes to realize more and more that as a woman she has no financial resources of her own. Refusing to contact her husband, she attempts to take out a loan (a scene interestingly framed with glass panes and reflections), only to be humiliated by her own lack of knowledge and power. Walking the city streets, she tries a pawn shop—at the end of her resources. But the telephone and their other conversations now bring Donnelly's voice to her as that of a friend, a connection made by two people trying to escape from those prisons.

The film ends with two contrasting scenes. After he kills the sinister Nagle in the chiaroscuro boathouse, despite Lucia's offer to tell everything to the police, the wounded Donnelly drives wildly away, hoping to save Lucia once again from becoming irredeemably sucked into the dark side of the justice system. Lucia follows behind, with Sibyl, her confidant, riding with her. Sybil's pronouncement, "I like Mr. Donnelly," beomes a fitting epitaph for the self-sacrificing Irishman. Lucia tries to save Donnelly, who is trapped beneath the car, but Donnelly insists on sacrificing himself for her. She returns (with Sybil taking the unusual role as the driver) to her "cheerful" home, only to answer a call from her overseas husband, "We are going to have a blue Christmas tree... .Everything's fine." But the spectator knows that nothing will ever be really "fine" again.

Biography

On May 6, 1902, Max Ophuls (somestimes credited as Ophüls or Opuls) was born Maximillian Oppenheimer in Saarbrücken, Germany. He declined to enter the family industry (clothes manufacturing) and decided to be a theater performer. He adopted his pseudonym, and after a brief career as a stage actor, Ophuls began directing plays in 1923 and mounted productions of Shakespeare, Molière, Shaw, and Schiller with companies in Stuttgart, Vienna, Frankfurt, and Berlin. After ten years of theatre, he began work as an assistant to director Anatole Litvak. With his extensive stage experience, Ophuls was soon directing "talkies"; but in 1933 after a half dozen features, the Jewish Ophuls, like Robert Siodmak and Billy Wilder, left Nazi Germany for France. Between 1933 and 1940 Ophuls directed 10 feature-length films in France, Italy and Holland and even became a French citizen and joined the French army. In 1940 the German occupation forced him to flee again, first to Switzerland and then to the United States when Preston Sturges hired him to direct *Vendetta* for Howard Hughes, then fired him (the project had five directors including Sturges before it was finally released in 1950). His next two pictures were at Universal with his colleague from Germany, Franz Planer, as cinematograper: *The Exile* (1947) and *Letter from an Unknown Woman* (1948). *Caught* and *The Reckless Moment* (both 1949) were Ophuls' last two American pictures, and he returned to France where he directed his last four films: *La Ronde* (1950), *Le Plaisir* (1951), *The Earrings of Madame de...* (1953), and *Lola Montes* (1955). If Ophuls's reputation as stylist was ever in doubt, these final films dispelled that and carried him to the peak of critical acclaim in Europe. He had just begun work on *Les Amants de Montparnasse* when he died in Hamburg on March 25, 1957.

Noir Films

Letter from an Unknown Woman (1948)
Caught (1949)
The Reckless Moment (1949)

Ophuls with Joan Fontaine while shooting *Letter from an Unknown Woman.*

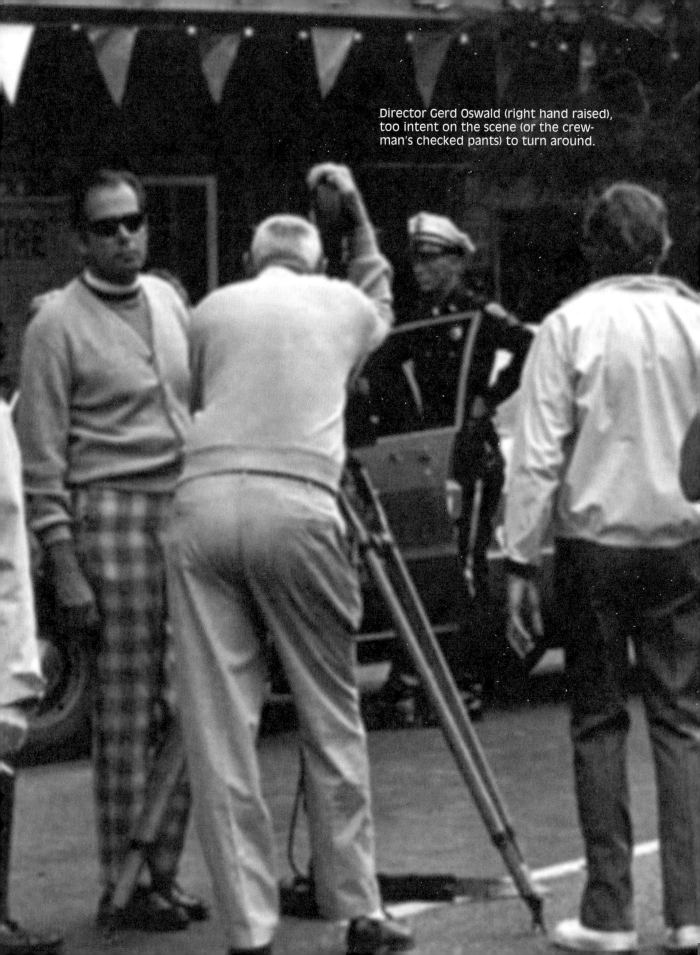

Director Gerd Oswald (right hand raised), too intent on the scene (or the crew-man's checked pants) to turn around.

Gerd Oswald

James Ursini

The Brass Legend (1956) is the first of Oswald's trio of noir revisionist Westerns (which includes *Valerie* and *Fury at Showdown*) in the vein of *High Noon* and *Shane*. The protagonist is a melancholic and conflicted sheriff—Wade Adams (played by Hugh O'Brian, fresh from his television series *The Life and Legend of Wyatt Earp*). Unable to fully commit to settling down with his surrogate family—the Gipsons, which include a crusty father figure, an idolizing young boy, and a lovestruck young girl, Adams has given up his lawman's job several times in the past, only to return to the lure of the "tin badge."

The film opens on a wanted poster for Tris Hatten (Raymond Burr, who will later take Oswald over with him to his successful television series *Perry Mason*), the brass legend of the title, a tarnished sadistic criminal who, particularly in noir icon Burr's hands, exhibits a panache which has won him a following. The camera pans as the face of the criminal is riddled with bullets from the rifle of the youngest Gipson—Clay (Donald MacDonald)—who is learning his craft from Adams.

When riding his new horse, Clay spots the outlaw Hatten in a rendezvous with the saloon girl Millie (Rebecca Welles as Reba Tassell) and returns to tell his mentor. Adams surprises the couple in flagrante delicto and captures Hatten, pistol whipping him as he tries to escape while handcuffed. Back in the town, Millie spreads the news that Adams refused to face down Hatten fairly.

Raymond Burr (left) and Hugh O'Brian (right) in *The Brass Legend.*

The town now splits down the middle, some siding with Adams and others with Hatten. The situation becomes even worse for Adams when the newspaper editor prints a story implying that Adams took credit for the capture and did not mention the help of the young boy in order to collect the bounty. When the alcoholic Shorty (Eddie Firestone), slavishly devoted to Millie (who for her part dismisses his advances with disdain), guns down Clay to show his bravery to Millie, Adams goes into overdrive. He takes on all three of the outlaws who have come into town to free Hatten

and kills two of them.

As for Hatten, he sits quietly in jail, reading the newspaper and biding his time. Oswald and Burr manage to add a patina of sympathy to the characterization of the killer in several ways. His almost preternatural calm under fire, his expressed admiration for the young boy who led to his capture, and, in particular, the final showdown—all garner audience empathy. The showdown is fairly unique in Westerns as it is staged like a medieval joust, thereby invoking the ideal of chivalry. Both men meet in the mountains and in a series of intercuts ride towards each other and shoot until one or the other falls. After Adams is first wounded and unhorsed and then Hatten, the two men roll in the dirt, the camera at their eye level on the ground. Hatten asks Adams if he wounded him and Adams returns the courtesy by asking about his wound. Hatten smiles and tells him it is serious enough that he won't need to be hanged. With that he expires.

Above, the lawman suspected of unfair play in *The Brass Legend*. Below and opposite top (with Joanne Woodward), Robert Wagner as the American Psycho prototype in *A Kiss Before Dying*.

A Kiss before Dying (1956) might be better titled "American Psycho" (apologies to author Bret Easton Ellis). The protagonist , Bud Corliss (Robert Wagner), is a cold-blooded psychopath who sees those around him as objects to be used in his attempt to grab the "American dream" of wealth and status. Shot in Cinemascope and gaudy Technicolor, the film sets Corliss in his 1950s milieu, eschewing closer shots for long shots which emphasize the lush upper middle class settings of the film.

Corliss, twenty-five years old and still living at home while attending college, expresses his dissatisfaction with his life to his mother early in the film as he paces his small bedroom in his mother's lower middle class abode. He then takes out a series of pamphlets from the Kingship mining empire which he studies. Through that scene the audience learns that Corliss is not simply interested in the demure coed Dorothy Kingship (Joanne Woodward) for her beauty and submissive nature but also for her wealth.

When Dorothy informs Bud that she is pregnant, Corliss does not react. Like any true psychopath he has absolute control of his emotions and affect. So while he pretends to be supportive (even though slipping into thinly veiled sarcasms every so often like "love conquers all"), he is plotting her death as her father will disown her if he finds out about the pregnancy. This would, of course, throw a monkey wrench into Bud's dream of marrying into wealth and privilege. Luring her to the top of a building, he kisses her, telling her that he loves her. His performance is so convincing that the audience for a moment might think that he has changed his mind. But shockingly and suddenly he pushes her off the edge and stands there for a few seconds, his arms outstretched in victory.

In Horaltio Alger fashion the murder does not stop Bud in his plans to enter into the Kingston empire. Evidencing a sense of invulnerability and arrogance common to psychopaths, he moves to the city where Kingston mines are located and begins dating Dorothy's sister Ellen (Virginia Leith)—the family had never been introduced to Bud or even known his name. Soon Ellen also falls under his suave spell and becomes engaged to him. But before she can marry him, a bookish detective, Gordon Grant (Jeffrey Hunter), uncovers Bud's identity and his link to Dorothy.

Ellen confronts Bud on a drive to visit the mines he hopes to own one day. Before Grant can arrive to rescue her, Bud pushes her in front of an oncoming truck. However, the truck driver swerves and instead hits Bud whose body flies over the cliff and into the mine pits he so wished to own. And so the American Dream, as often happens in American literature and history, turns into the American Nightmare.

Fury at Showdown (1957) remains remarkable for its use of deep focus and painterly compositions (credit must be given to noir veteran cinematographer Joseph LaShelle who will also photograph Oswald's *Crime of Passion*) to enhance the story of a "mad dog killer" (as the antagonist calls him) who tries to reform his life. In almost every scene foreground objects or parts of bodies as well as similar background clutter frame the main action of the scene. Not only does this contribute to the pictorial virtues of the film but also externalizes the feelings of entrapment which the protagonist—gunfighter Brock Mitchell (John Derek)—owns up to during the film.

Mitchell, after being released from jail, returns to his hometown to help his brother Tracy (Nick Adams) run their ranch. As soon as he enters the town he is threatened on all sides.

Above, John Derek as the angst-ridden and rebellious young gunfighter faces down the capitalist Deasy (Gage Clarke) in *Fury at Sundown*.

The capitalist brother—Deasy (Gage Clarke)—of the man he killed in a gunfight hires a bodyguard and then taunts him to attack him. A young man who is courting Brock's ex-girlfriend—Ginny (Carolyn Craig)—begs him not to kill him for dating her. This triggers Brock's trip-wire temper and he proceeds to beat the boy.

Brock's attempts to control the psychotic elements of his personality become the core of the film. In a scene with his brother—the only stabilizing influence in his life, Brock confesses his fears—fear of loneliness, darkness, and rage. Brock's final test comes after his brother is killed by Deasy's bodyguard. Although tempted he refuses to strap on his guns, keeping his vow to his beloved brother. When the bodyguard takes Ginny as a hostage, he walks out into the street to face him, "gutless and gunless" as the bodyguard calls him. The bodyguard opens fire and, in order to defend Ginny, Brock picks up a discarded gun and shoots the bodyguard, unable once again to keep his vow.

Oswald's *Crime of Passion* (1957) is a mordant critique of the stultifying 1950s, particularly the suburban lifestyle valorized by government, industry, and media during the repressive Eisenhower decade. Kathy Ferguson (Stanwyck), a successful San Francisco journalist, falls passionately in lust with a malleable cop—Los Angeles police detective Bill Doyle (Sterling

Hayden). Against her better judgment, she tries to assimilate into the suburban ethos of the San Fernando Valley where Doyle makes his home. But after a brief period of sexual bliss, implied by her pose at the bedroom door of their home and by Kathy's comment that she will not need any clothes for a while, Kathy finds herself suffocated by the mundane details of her new life. In a memorable party scene, Kathy moves back and forth between the clearly demarcated worlds of men playing poker in the kitchen and women gossiping in the dining room until a montage of diffused close ups and overlapping inane dialogue externalizes her frustration as she runs from the room to the refuge of her bedroom.

In order to counteract this deepening sense of alienation, Kathy begins an affair with another "outsider," the erudite police inspector Tony Pope (Raymond Burr), another unique individual who has repressed his more creative interests (symbolized by a file which he keeps on crimes of passion) in favor of the comfortable suburban life. As their relationship develops, Kathy decides to use her influence over Pope to advance the career of her easy-going husband. Eventually the illicit relationship begins to implode due to the illness of Pope's wife. As a result, the inspector reneges on his promise to name Doyle as his replacement when he retires. Like any self-respecting noir femme fatale, Kathy first tries seduction and when that fails turns to violence. She shoots Pope, hoping that his death will lead to her husband's promotion. It does not and she is arrested by her own husband.

Hooking up with Amazon sex symbol Anita Ekberg, Oswald produced a notable trio of films which

Above and below, Barbara Stanwyck as the stifled and unfaithful wife of Sterling Hayden in *Crime of Passion*

Above, Oswald's last noir Western, *Valerie*. Opposite, *Brainwashed*.: Von Basil (Curd Jürgens) imprisoned in a hotel room.

helped develop the goddess image of Ekberg and which led directly to her becoming one of director Federico Fellini's muses as well as the star of the director's *La Dolce Vita* and *Boccaccio '70*. *Valerie* (1957) is a Rashomon-style Western which tells the story of immigrant Valerie Horvat (Ekberg) and her marriage to war hero John Garth (Sterling Hayden) from three points of view, each presenting "the truth" or some part of it from a different perspective. In the erudite Reverend Blake's (Anthony Steel) version, Valerie symbolizes the beauty and grace of the old world, a goddess trapped in a marriage to a jealous bully who takes his revenge on Valerie for perceived infidelities by murdering her parents and wounding, almost fatally, Valerie herself. In Garth's version of the story, he is the long-suffering husband of a grasping, oversexed succubus who, when she finds out he is not as wealthy as he first implied, refuses to consummate their marriage. Instead she takes lovers, including Reverend Blake and Garth's own brother.

In the final retelling of events, Valerie presents herself as the victim. She is raped by her husband repeatedly, tortured with techniques he learned as an interrogator of prisoners during the Civil War (which includes burning her with lit cigars), and generally terrorizing her psychologically in order to make her a compliant wife. When she becomes pregnant, he even tries to abort the child. Valerie's testimony and the shocking revelation of the cigar burns on her white flesh turns the sympathies of the court towards her. As Garth tries to escape with Valerie as his hostage, he is shot down by his own brother.

In Oswald's *Paris Holiday* (1958), the second film of the triad made with Ekberg, Ekberg plays the seductive double agent Zara in this Bob Hope/Fernandel romp through Paris. Ekberg utilizes her body as well as her intelligence to confuse the Hope character but in the end turns out to be his savior.

The final film in the trio, *Screaming Mimi* (1958), is considered by many critics as a *film maudit*. Cut heavily before release because of its daring content, the film stands out because of Ekberg's subtle performance as well as the story's perverse sexuality. In many ways *Screaming Mimi*, like *Valerie,* is a meditation on the ambiguities of the femme fatale as epitomized by Ekberg. The traumatized, murderous, and sexually irresistible Virginia sleepwalks through the movie like the somnambulist Cesar in the German Expressionistic classic *The Cabinet of Dr. Caligari*. She is a femme fatale without even trying, a semi-conscious Gilda. Dr. Greenwood, her psychiatrist, is mesmerized the minute he sees her, peeping in on her at night through the window of her room, even taking her to his house to see her perform one of the

two blatantly erotic dances in the movie (the other is the bondage number in the club). Violating his ethics and tossing away his career, he takes on the menial job of her manager when she becomes the exotic dancer Yolanda.

The reporter Sweeney is her second "victim," who becomes emotionally enmeshed when he watches her performing her bondage number at the club and then visits her in her dressing room, dropping his tough guy façade as she displays her legs, almost unconsciously, to him. The final and most perverse obsessive male is Virginia/Yolanda's stepbrother who kills the man who attacks his sister in the shower and then obsessively works on statues of her nude and screaming (the "Screaming Mimi" statues), hinting at his quasi-incestuous desire for her. All three men circle in one way or another this semi-catatonic femme, trying alternately to save her and control her. But like the chains she breaks during her performance onstage, Virginia/Yolanda is an uncontrollable force. She leaves Greenwood dead on the sidewalk, her stepbrother in despair as he destroys one of his "Screaming Mimi" statues, and Sweeney distraught as he watches his lover being transported back to the mental hospital.

Working again in Germany, Oswald co-wrote and directed an adaptation of Stefan Zweig's novella *The Royal Game*. *Brainwashed*, as the film was called, centers on the mental and

Above Anita Ekberg in *Screamng Mimi* displaying her seductive "weapons."

emotional deterioration of a man—Werner von Basil (Curd Jürgens)— tortured by the Gestapo in occupied Vienna. The film opens with the broken and paranoid man being transported by a representative of the Catholic Church who has secured his release and transport out of the country. Basil sits hunched over in the back seat, frightened and paranoid—convinced each delay in the trip is only part of a Nazi plan to re-arrest him.

When Basil finally boards the ship his friends have booked for him, his paranoia continues. He shuns people, hides out in his cabin, reacting to the smallest sound and movement. What finally brings Basil out of his paranoid shell is the sight of a chess game being played by an arrogant world champion against several passengers. With dexterity he advises the passengers on their next moves and even predicts the end of the game to the amazement of the chess champion. When asked where he has played chess, he tells them he has never touched a chess piece before, pushing the pieces over as he says this and triggering the film into flashback mode.

The anti-Nazi Basil is arrested for information he has about art he has helped the Catholic Church smuggle out of Austria to protect it from the rapacious Nazis. The cocksure and pretentious Gestapo head—Berger (Hansjorg Felmy)—brags about how he will break the seemingly confident Basil. Berger imprisons Basil in a dingy room in a hotel the Nazis have occupied. There a mute servant delivers soup and bread to the isolated man while a faucet drips water without cessation and rain pours outside his grated window (all the sounds are amplified to subjectify Basil's experience for the audience). In addition, all reading or writing materials are forbidden to him as is any communication with loved ones or friends.

Gradually, Basil begins to crack: peeling the wallpaper away to read an old newspaper used as backing on the wall; hysterically attacking "Moonface," the name he gives the mute servant; and talking to himself as a form of comfort. Finally, in order to maintain his sanity, Berger steals a book while he is being interrogated. But to his disappointment it is a book on master chess games, a subject he has no interest in. Gradually, out of desperation, he begins to memorize the games in the book and then acts them out, using small pieces of bread as chess pieces and his checkerboard bedspread as a board.

Playing himself over and over again, he becomes obsessed with the "royal game." And even when Berger finds the book and makeshift chess pieces and has them confiscated along with his bedspread, Basil uses the shadow of the grate on his window, reflected on the ceiling, to continue his fantasy games.

Refusing to give information even when broken emotionally, the Gestapo releases Basil and sends him off to an uncertain future. As the flashback ends, Basil leaves the game with the chess champion, refusing to finish to the amazement of his rival. For he has seen the ballerina—Irene (Claire Bloom)—who has followed him on board the ship and who helped in his release. Together they walk off to stroll the deck of the ship in this the final entry in Oswald's film noir oeuvre.

Biography

Gerd Oswald was born in Berlin on June 9,1919. He was the son of famed German director Richard Oswald with whom he worked before the Jewish family fled Europe after the rise of Nazism. In the United States Gerd entered the film industry in the late 1930s as an assistant director. In 1955 Gerd was given the opportunity to direct an episode of the Fox television series *The 20th Century-Fox Hour* and then his first major film project in 1956, *A Kiss Before Dying*. This film established his credentials as an up and coming director of noir thrillers, especially low-budget ones. Like many of the directors in this study, he moved into television and became a prestigious director of sci-fi/mystery series like *The Outer Limits* and *The Fugitive*. Oswald eventually returned to Germany to make films. He died in Los Angeles on May 22, 1989.

Noir Films

A Kiss Before Dying (1956)
The Brass Legend (1956)
Crime of Passion (1957)
Fury at Showdown (1957)
Valerie (1957)
Screaming Mimi (1958)
Brainwashed (1960)

Otto Preminger watches intently from his ladder perch.

Otto Preminger

Chris D.

Noir as Theater—The Path to *Laura*

Paradoxical personality dynamics and a strategically pliable yet uncompromising nature enabled Otto Preminger to not only survive but get a second chance as a director after a nearly five-year exile imposed on him by Darryl F. Zanuck, head of 20th Century-Fox. [See Preminger biography on page 341.]

Zanuck decamped into the Army at the outset of WWII, supervising propaganda films and had left William Goetz, Louis Mayer's son-in-law, to run the studio.

While Preminger played a Nazi villain in *The Pied Piper*, he was respectful of Fox studio personnel, hoping for a rapprochement. Done with his bit, he got a call saying Fox wanted him to reprise his Broadway *Margin for Error* Nazi role on celluloid. Knowing Goetz would relish taking action independent of Zanuck, he convinced Goetz to also let him direct (he had directed the play). Preminger collaborated with a young, still-in-the-Army Samuel Fuller on the screen adaptation. *Margin* led to Fox re-signing Preminger as a contract director in 1943.

Two more properties piqued Preminger's curiosity; one of them was *Laura*. Preminger had encountered the story a few years earlier as a play that author Vera Caspary was trying to

To the astonishment of Det. McPherson (Dana Andrews) the dead Laura (Gene Tierney) returns home.

get financed. At his original meeting with Caspary, the two took an instant dislike to each other. The uneasy collaboration sputtered. Caspary never did find theatrical backing and turned the material into two novels, *Ring Twice for Laura* and *Laura.* Fox bought the rights.

It was an original idea: a talented artist named Laura rockets to success in advertising with the patronage of sharp-tongued columnist Waldo Lydecker. Thrown into high society, Laura is seemingly murdered by a shotgun blast when she opens her apartment door, only to return a couple of days later unaware of the crime and generating a new mystery: who is the now-unidentified victim? Laura becomes one of the suspects.

Preminger's interest was reignited. His employers, not Caspary, now held the high card. Goetz gave the director the green light. Preminger worked on a first draft screenplay with writers Jay Dratler (author of the novel *Pitfall*, later filmed by Andre de Toth), Samuel Hoffenstein and Betty Reinhardt. Then potential disaster struck: Zanuck returned from the Army. Preminger's anxiety proved groundless, though Zanuck told him he could only produce *Laura* (1944), not direct it. Preminger counted his blessings.

Zanuck assigned the picture to Fox's B unit, so Preminger had to answer to unit head Bryan Foy. Foy encouraged Zanuck to shelve the story, despite Preminger's protests. Foy would later work on many worthy noirs, including *He Walked by Night, T-Men, Highway 301, Crime Wave* and the popular Vincent Price thriller, *House of Wax*. With *Laura*, he underestimated the story's potential. Not only was Preminger committed, Zanuck brought it up to A-status, personally supervising the production.

According to *Laura* author Caspary, the director saw the story as a conventional mystery, and she saw it as a psychological study. She did not like Preminger's removal of the novel's multiple character viewpoints and the discarding of Lydecker's shotgun murder

weapon disguised as a walking cane. From Preminger's perspective the cane shotgun was a gimmick inconsistent with Waldo's fastidious character. Caspary also reportedly had to disabuse Preminger that Laura was nothing better than a high class whore. Caspary did not see the second draft by an uncredited Ring Lardner, Jr., who reportedly came up with the most memorable lines.

Preminger had larger issues than Caspary. He and Zanuck were having problems finding an A-list director. Lewis Milestone was approached, but he declined, recommending Preminger direct it himself. To be fair to Zanuck, Preminger's previous three movies had not set fires at the box office. It was a risk Zanuck wasn't prepared to take after the fiasco on *Kidnapped* [see Biography].

Director Rouben Mamoulian signed on, but friction with Preminger proved problematic. Zanuck was not happy with the initial footage and discussed the issues with both men. An indignant Mamoulian responded with more inferior dailies, was removed, and Zanuck relented, allowing Preminger to direct.

Once he saw the completed film, Zanuck felt the ending didn't work. His decision to reshoot the final third, making it all a dream of Lydecker's, was not enthusiastically received by Preminger, but the director acquiesced. Inviting columnist Walter Winchell to a preview screening, Zanuck was anxious to know the opinion-shaper's reaction. Winchell loved it except for the reshot climax, which he didn't get. Knowing he'd missed the mark, Zanuck asked if the director wanted to reinstate the picture's original ending. He did.

It is a tribute to Preminger that *Laura* emerges as such a seamless confection; the production was a contest of patience, near misses and meddling powers-that-be; it could easily have ended up as a mishmash with confusing tonal shifts.

Though not on the same plane as 1940s classics like *Casablanca* and *The Treasure of the Sierra Madre*, *Laura* is equal to the pantheon stature of other then-contemporary noirs like *The Big Sleep* and *Mildred Pierce*. It *is* a grand entertainment throughout 90% of its running time, from its David Raksin theme to its dialogue and cast of indelible characters to its melancholy romanticism, tainted with hints of sexual perversity.

Preminger's depiction of the backstabbing and unsavory desires just under the surface of carefree New York high society is one of the strengths of the movie. Everyone except Laura (Gene Tierney) and police detective Mark McPherson (Dana Andrews) are venomous creatures, unhappy with life. Columnist Lydecker (Clifton Webb) has a lavish apartment full of antique bric-a-brac that he neurotically guards. The second twist of the film, coming at the climax, is centered on two identical antique clocks. The

Left, McPherson questions Lydecker (Clifton Webb)

Opposite, Laura with Ann Treadwell (Judith Anderson).

McPherson questions the sneering Shelby Carpenter (Vincent Price) in *Laura*.

baroque, gingerbread grandfather timepieces are right out of a Viennese fairy tale and a worthy substitute for Caspary's walking cane shotgun. Lydecker possesses one, and the other he has given to Laura. Near the end, Mark guesses that they have secret compartments and, when he opens Laura's, he finds the murder weapon.

Preminger does a skillful job of supplying red herring suspects, even disarming us by giving Lydecker a flash-back/monologue to throw us off the track. This is the one lackluster sequence; one idealized scene after another of Laura is paraded before us, Lydecker regaling detective Mark about how he had made her his protégé. The purely platonic relationship Waldo describes is a chore to sit through, as boring as Waldo's neutered aesthete's idea of a perfect relationship.

Two more players are Laura's spineless fiancé, Shelby Carpenter (Vincent Price), and her rich aunt, Ann Treadwell (Judith Anderson). Shelby is the reason Waldo has gone sour on Laura, doing everything he can to break them up, including hiring a detective to reveal Shelby's infidelities. It is Shelby's secret dalliance with Diane Redfern in Laura's apartment while Laura is out of town, ironically mulling over whether she should marry Shelby, that saves Laura's life. It places the unfortunate model in the wrong place at the wrong time. To make matters worse, Laura's aunt Ann is in love with Shelby, knowing he's a heel but not giving a damn.

The one weak narrative link in this chain of egocentric fools is Laura, a character who just happens to be strong-willed, idealistic, talented, intelligent, honest, kind *and* beautiful. If one has to assign a flaw to her, it would be that she is a blank slate as well as a horrible judge of character. Gene Tierney was reportedly not happy about taking the role. She has little to do, her character having no depth. She is certainly an independent role model for women in 1940s films; otherwise she is the most boring character. The only plausible reason it seems detective Mark has for falling for Laura—whom he believes is dead — is her bewitching portrait and Lydecker's rapturous description.

Dana Andrews, portraying the soft-spoken, tough detective, already had a string of B-pictures behind him and supporting roles in two A-movies, but *Laura* was his first crack at top-tier, leading man status. He delivers an assured performance, giving hints of the more cynical, melancholy yet sensitive persona he was to later exhibit in *The Best Years of Our Lives*.

Likewise, Vincent Price and Judith Anderson excel in their roles, but *Laura* belongs to Clifton Webb as Lydecker. Preminger instinctively knew that the primary focus needed to be more on Lydecker than Laura, and this had been another objection from author Caspary. As with many of Preminger's most acclaimed movies, part of the secret of *Laura's* success is the casting. Zanuck and Mamoulian had both wanted contract player Laird Cregar, fresh from playing Jack the Ripper in Fox's *The Lodger*. Zanuck also considered Webb too gay, conversely one of the reasons Preminger wanted him. Preminger had to fight for Webb, knowing Cregar as Lydecker would tip off viewers early on to the murderer's identity. Webb could deliver the waspish dialogue with the appropriate caustic tone. And Webb most assuredly does deliver lines like "I hope you both will be very happy in what promises to be a disgustingly earthy relationship" as the drawing-blood zingers that they are.

Is *Laura* perfect? No. But it is an impressive balancing act, making a convoluted storyline into a fascinating tapestry of believable characters in a milieu that was foreign to most of the ticket-buying audience. Coming from a privileged family in Austria, and known as a champion party schmoozer, Preminger was intimately familiar with the high society phoniness he put on display. That, and the dialogue are the main reasons it remains so damn watchable.

Fallen Angel, Whirlpool, and Where The Sidewalk Ends

After *Laura*, Preminger was back in Zanuck's good graces. But this did not automatically translate into extraordinary assignments. Preminger played hopscotch with his next few movies, delivering anemic period pieces or fizzling comedies when not helming accomplished noirs.

Desiring a hit and learning the system of repeating proven formulas, Preminger found the *Fallen Angel* (1945) property and got a go-ahead from Zanuck. After *Fallen Angel,* a box office success, Preminger did five more movies before his next "true" noir, *Whirlpool* (1949). Three of them were flops. Preminger's next two successful films came in 1948: *Forever Amber*, adapted from a trashy bestseller set in Restoration-era England, and *Daisy Kenyon*, a soap opera love triangle shot in noir style.

Fallen Angel stars one of Preminger's favorites, Dana Andrews, an actor who was punctual, always knew his lines and how to approach a role—he required minimal direction. Andrews amplified what was to become his default noir persona and was to continue in this vein in two noirs by Fritz Lang: *While the City Sleeps* and *Beyond a Reasonable Doubt* (both 1956).

Fallen Angel begins with destitute con man Eric Stanton (Andrews) being kicked off a bus in Walton, a California coastal town. It's night, and he gravitates to an open café on a waterfront cul-de-sac. It's an atmospheric beginning.

Spending his last dollar on a hamburger he never gets—missing-for-days waitress Stella (Linda Darnell) grabs it upon her return — Stanton leaves. Spotting a poster for a spiritualist show in a hotel window, he says he knows the soon-to-arrive Professor Madley (John Carradine), talking the clerk out of the Professor's room key. Madley's advance man Joe (Olin Howland) is miffed but softens when Stanton guarantees ticket sales to the yokels. Joe is having trouble because rich spinster, Clara (Anne Revere), disapproves and has put the word out.

The next day, Stanton pours on the charm all over town but comes up empty. He makes the case directly to Clara, but she is immune, previously jilted by a charismatic hustler.

Fallen Angel: Markedly different reactions to different women.

Linda Darnell in *Fallen Angel*.

Frustrated, Stanton approaches June (Alice Faye), Clara's younger sister, and he whittles away at her skepticism, appealing to her sense of fair play. Spiritualist Madley (John Carradine) meets with Joe and Stanton at the café and is delighted that Stanton's hit pay dirt. He instructs Joe to dig up info on the sisters, since the pair have agreed to come to the show. Eavesdropping from a neighboring stool is retired New York police detective, Judd (Charles Bickford). Stanton invites hardboiled waitress Stella to the show.

The show is a success, but the sisters flee in a huff when Madley, in a "trance," channels their dead father, revealing family financial difficulties. The next morning, Stanton doesn't depart with Madley and Joe, telling Stella he can't leave town without her. She is incensed at his presumption; she's not putting out for anyone unwilling to get married. Stanton schemes to seduce vulnerable June, marry her, then abscond with her money. He extracts a promise from Stella to wait until he raises the dough. June falls for him, and they do get married, despite Clara's warning. On the wedding night, Stanton spies Stella dropped off from a date with Dave Atkins (Bruce Cabot), a chiseler who services jukeboxes. Jealous Stanton and Stella quarrel. When Stanton returns home, the disappointed June is asleep.

The next day, he discovers Stella has been murdered. Ex-cop Judd takes over the case from the mild-mannered sheriff, questioning both Atkins and Stanton in the dead girl's apartment. While Stanton waits, Judd takes Atkins in the kitchen, putting on his gloves, sadistically beating him, trying to extract a confession. The camera roves through the apartment to rest on Stanton's expression as he listens to the raised voices, the sounds of Judd's fists smashing into Atkins' face. Atkins doesn't break and has an alibi, and when it's Stanton's turn, Judd does not resort to brutality. But he tells Stanton not to leave town. But Stanton heads for San Francisco, June with him. They stay at a cheap hotel, Stanton tells June about his past, and the two grow closer.

The next day, June is picked up by the cops when she goes to her San Francisco bank. Watching from across the street, Stanton is powerless. He returns one night to the café in Walton to confront Judd. Unbeknownst to Judd, Stanton has done some digging, learning that Judd had not retired willingly from the NYPD, but had been forced out because of his brutality. Judd had also promised he'd marry Stella once he could convince his wife to give him a divorce. Seeing her fraternize with both Atkins and Stanton, Judd became jealous and killed her. Judd draws his gun when told the San Francisco cops are outside, but Pops (Percy Kilbride), the café owner, wrestles the gun away. Judd is hauled off as June arrives to meet Stanton, and the two go home together.

Despite the contrived elements in the narrative, Preminger and screenwriter Harry Kleiner create a believable chain of events, and the dialogue is convincingly hardboiled. The interplay between Stanton, Madley and Joe especially has a realistic feel for the grifter persona. Despite her mercenary demeanor, Preminger and Kleiner manage to maintain some sympathy for Stella, as they do with Stanton's equally amoral character. Both emerge as more than one-dimensional persons.

Alice Faye is a natural as the sexually repressed, small town spinster. It was her first non-musical straight part and a return to the screen after two years. She projects a personality withering on the vine of small town life, blossoming when she falls in love — an earthy, intelligent, compassionate presence. And Stanton is finally vulnerable enough to accept her love at face value, which proves his redemption. It is a shame Faye reportedly left the first studio screening, angry enough to not accept any movie roles for over a decade. She was rumored to be unhappy that her singing along with David Raksin's theme "Slowly" playing on a car radio was excised and that her best scenes were cut to give Darnell, who Fox was grooming for stardom, more screen time.

Above and right, *Whirlpool.*

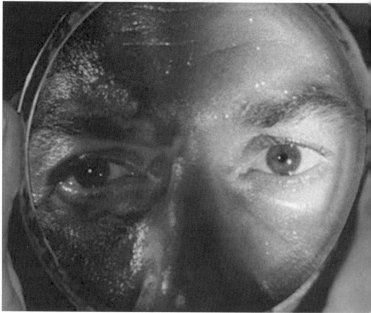

Other sequences were cut as well. Noir expert Eddie Muller asserts photos exist with Stanton in conversation with Judd's estranged wife and another set showing Stanton in a fistfight with Judd on a cliff overlooking the ocean. The ending — Stanton appearing back in town at the café to confront Judd — is too rushed for the scenes we'd just witnessed. Stanton's investigation into Judd's past deserved at least a few minutes exposition, and the idea of a violent confrontation on a clifftop promises a more exciting conclusion. Despite a slightly flawed ending, *Fallen Angel* fulfills the potential promised in *Laura*, adding more atmospheric camerawork by *Laura* veteran Joseph LaShelle and credible integration of both on-location scenes (lensed in Orange, California) and studio interiors.

Preminger reunited with *Laura*'s Gene Tierney in *Whirlpool* (1949), an adaptation written by Ben Hecht and Andrew Solt from a novel by Guy Endore. Tierney is Ann Sutton, the wife of successful Los Angeles psychiatrist William Sutton (Richard Conte) but a closet kleptomaniac. When a store detective catches her shoplifting, sociopathic social climber David Korvo (Jose Ferrer) rescues her from prosecution. Unbeknownst to unstable Ann, Korvo is using her for his own purposes.

A hypnotist adept at conning lonely women, Korvo has made it a point to become a guest at high society parties. He takes control of Ann's life through hypnotherapy, ostensibly to cure Ann's neurosis. He also has recently broken with socialite Theresa Randolph (Barbara O'Neill), whom he has bilked out of a huge sum. At a party where Ann is Korvo's date, Randolph warns Ann that Korvo is no good. Randolph also phones Korvo, threatening him to pay her back.

Ann's marriage is stagnant. Husband William, though affectionate, is busy and too close to see that his wife is heading toward a breakdown. Ann represses her symptoms, afraid she'll lose his love. Orchestrating so he can be seen in public with Ann, Korvo sets her up as a patsy in Theresa Randolph's murder. Randolph's psychiatrist is Ann's husband, and Korvo knows Randolph has mentioned him threatening her, a problem because William records his sessions.

Korvo hypnotizes Ann, orders her to steal Randolph's disc from her husband's safe, then go to Randolph's house and hide it in a foyer closet. Ann comes out of her trance staring at Randolph's body. The police walk in and arrest her. Investigating cop Lt. Colton (Charles Bickford) summons William back from a conference. William knows his wife is incapable of murder. Colton believes the motive was Ann's jealousy of Randolph since they were both Korvo's lovers—another wrinkle William cannot accept. He is convinced Korvo murdered Randolph and tells Colton about the disc. When the two men go to his office, the record is missing. William wants to confront Korvo, but he is shaken when Colton shows him Korvo is recuperating from a gall bladder operation, his alibi.

William later explains to Colton that Korvo hypnotized himself to feel no pain, left his hospital bed, killed Randolph, then returned. William is convinced the record is hidden in Randolph's house. Colton reluctantly agrees to test William's theory.

They have Korvo's nurse casually mention that the police are hunting for a recording disc. Once she's gone, Korvo hypnotizes himself again. Losing blood, he arrives at the Randolph house, retrieves the disc, puts it on the record player to listen, when headlights pull into the drive.

He hides as William, Ann and Colton enter, hoping to spark Ann's memory. They're successful, but the two men can't find the disc. Ann remains in the living room while the two are searching, and Korvo appears beside her with his gun, whispering to tell them the disc is upstairs, so he can escape. But Ann tells them Korvo is there. Korvo races to the door with his gun drawn, arrogantly putting the record back on the player for them to listen to as he leaves. Bleeding from his opened incision, he struggles up the steps, collapses, the gun goes off shattering the record, and he lands on the floor dead.

Preminger and his writers open up the empty lives of married women who don't work and have nothing better to do than go shopping or to luncheons. Tierney's character Ann has a double whammy as she had a rich domineering father and husband William had forbade her to take any of her family's money once married. Ann started stealing in high school, rebelling against her father and continuing when her husband replaced him as a male authority figure.

William realizes his mistakes and the need for the attention that may help Ann heal.

How many women in *Whirlpool*'s original audience might have identified with Ann? Illustrating the neurosis as a thriller, one wonders whether there was any liberating effect, helping to change attitudes about gender roles.

Ferrer, though not above hamfisted flourishes, is perfect as Korvo, and his exaggerated portrayal accentuates Korvo's narcissistic overreaching that leads to his death. Conte's psychiatrist role was undoubtedly a relief to an actor who was typecast as a tough soldier or slum hoodlum. He projects intelligence and, after only a few minutes, one comes to accept him in the part. Throughout the movie, Preminger none too subtly dresses William in a bow tie. In some psychiatric texts, wearing a bow tie is indicative of a fear of castration. It is perfect for the character since he is powerless to protect his spouse or have any insight into her condition until tragedy strikes.

Tierney reprises the kind of nuanced intensity that she had shown in the earlier *Leave Her to Heaven* (1945). However, Tierney's Ann shows a willingness to do something about her mental illness rather than revel in it as her in-denial Ellen character does in director John Stahl's film.

Tierney returns to work with Preminger in *Where the Sidewalk Ends* (1950), though as secondary lead. Primary focus is on Tierney's *Laura* co-star, Dana Andrews, playing Mark Dixon, a chip-on-his-shoulder cop whose hatred for hoods is based on shame over his late criminal father.

The film begins as Dixon and his partner Paul (Bert Freed) return to their precinct, their superior, Inspector Foley, introducing them to by-the-book Lt. Thomas (Karl Malden). Privately, Foley warns Dixon he's had twelve brutality complaints, and he's being busted to second grade detective. If he doesn't shape up, Dixon will be pounding a beat.

At local mob boss Scalise's (Gary Merrill) hotel a high stakes dice game is going down, Texas high roller Morrison (Harry Von Zell) winning big when he decides to leave. The couple he's with, Ken Paine (Craig Stevens) and Morgan Taylor (Gene Tierney), argue. Paine is abusive, telling her he has to keep Morrison there because he brought him — Scalise needs to win back

his dough. Morgan is disgusted. Paine slaps her, Morrison sees it, the two come to blows, and Paine knocks Morrison out. Paine and Morgan leave.

Dixon and Paul get called to Scalise's hotel about a murder. Morrison has been stabbed. Lt. Thomas arrives. Scalise implies Paine may have killed him, but he never saw a knife. Dixon grabs Scalise's address book, finds Paine's address, and Thomas orders him to check it out.

When Dixon walks into Paine's fleabag room without knocking, Paine is on the phone, drunker than before, leaving a message for Morrison. Dixon tells him that Morrison is dead, and Scalise pinned it on him; he needs to come to the station. Paine doesn't believe him and takes a swing at the detective. Dixon decks him, and Paine does not get up. Dixon realizes he's dead. The phone rings. It's Dixon's partner, telling him not to get rough on Paine as he's a war hero fallen on hard times. Dixon decides to get rid of the body, but first calls a cab, packs Paine's suitcase and, disguised as Paine, takes it to the train station to be checked under Paine's name. When he gets back to the room, partner Paul is there but hasn't yet found Paine's body. They question the landlady, who says she saw Paine leave, then Dixon drops Paul off at headquarters. Dixon returns to finish with Paine, but is carting the body into the hall when someone else arrives, and he hides himself and the corpse under the stairway. It's Morgan's angry taxi driver father, Jiggs. When Jiggs gets no response, he leaves in a huff. Dixon dumps the body in the river and returns to the precinct where he and his partner are ordered to get some rest.

Tormented, Dixon can't sleep. The next day, Paine's body is hauled out of the river and, despite Dixon trying to convince Lt. Thomas that Scalise is responsible, Thomas is sure it was Morgan's father. Paine had had a metal plate in his skull from a war injury, and it is that fluke circumstance that made his death unavoidable from a minor blow. Dixon watches as Jiggs and Morgan are brought to the murder scene and grilled. After proving the landlady was mistaken, and the person she saw was the disguised killer, Thomas arrests Jiggs. Dixon is fond of Morgan and is thrown into a pressure cooker to clear her innocent father. He confronts Scalise at a steambath, hoping to get him to confess to Morrison's murder, but Scalise's hoods pummel him into unconsciousness. Coming to, he deliriously makes his way to Morgan's doorstep. She nurses him with a drink and insists he stay there to sleep.

Dixon borrows money from his partner to get Jiggs the best lawyer in New York. But the attor-

Where the Sidewalk Ends: opposite Dana Andrews and Gene Tierney. Right, Andrews with Gary Merrill as Scalise.

ney turns Morgan down, and Dixon feels the need to reassure Morgan, with whom he is falling in love, that her father will soon be proven innocent. She tells him he can't know what it's like to have a father in jail, and he quietly reveals his own father was a thief shot trying to escape. While she falls asleep, Dixon writes a letter of confession addressed to Foley to be opened in the event of his death. He pressures a parolee, one of Scalise's men, to take him to the mobster.

Once in Scalise's hideout in a huge parking garage, Dixon is held hostage. Moments from Scalise killing the tied-up Dixon, the police arrive, causing the gang to run. Dixon frees himself and cuts the power to the car elevators, trapping Scalise and his gang. Back at the precinct, Foley congratulates him and returns his unopened letter. The chastened Dixon has a perfect out. But with Morgan beside him, he hands back his confession letter. After reading it, Foley is impressed with Dixon's honesty but has to arrest him for Paine's murder. The film closes on a downbeat but hopeful note as Morgan tells him she'll stand by him.

Dana Andrews continues to develop his stoic-on-the-surface, seething-on-the-inside image, and his role as Dixon is one of his most intense performances. Gene Tierney brings depth to a role that is not much meatier than *Laura*, her character representing redemptive faith and love to Dixon who otherwise seems to be residing in a cold, unforgiving universe. Preminger and screenwriter Ben Hecht focus not only on Dixon's descent into a hell of guilt

The 13th Letter

and coincidence, precipitated by accident, but also his dawning realization he has paved the way by his reputation as a callous lawman.

As his career progressed, Preminger became adamant about shooting on location. He shot *Where the Sidewalk Ends* in New York City, although there aren't any sequences that could not have been convincingly faked in Hollywood. Considering this, it's unusual so many scenes are indoors, not using any recognizable landmarks: there's a night scene with an elevated train in the distance, some views from a car window into Times Square and the climactic scene of the cavernous interior of the parking garage. Although it doesn't take away merit from the film, not using more exteriors seems to have been a missed opportunity. In comparison, Henry Hathaway's noir classic, *Kiss of Death* (1947) was shot all over New York and New Jersey and looks it.

The 13th Letter and *Angel Face*

Discussion of location filming brings us to Preminger's next film and one of his hardest to see.

The 13th Letter is a remake of Henri-Georges Clouzot's *Le Corbeau* (1943), made when France was occupied by the Germans. Although containing elements of sexual jealousy, it is an allegory about collaboration with the enemy through anonymous, poison-pen letters.

For *The 13th Letter*, Preminger insisted the picture be shot in Quebec. Zanuck had grown to respect Preminger, agreeing to his latest contract's terms and gave him the green light. This time Preminger, along with art directors Lyle Wheeler and Maurice Ransford, took full advantage of the strange, vintage architecture of their settings, both inside and out. *The 13th Letter* is one of Preminger's best-looking, most atmospheric films, and it is a shame that the picture seems to be in a legal limbo.

Preminger is not interested in pursuing the political ramifications of a story originally set in an occupied country. He sets it in the contemporary time period of 1950, concentrating on a toxic environment of sexually frustrated people.

Dr. Pearson (Michael Rennie), who immigrated from England and works at the village hospital, starts receiving poison pen letters accusing him of an affair with Cora (Constance Smith), the wife of hospital psychiatrist Dr. Laurent (Charles Boyer). Cora and two other staff doctors have also received letters, accusing them of their own indiscretions. The letters are signed "The Raven." News of the letters spreads and becomes hot gossip. Pearson and Laurent discuss the situation in a clinical way, with Laurent's views fueled by misanthropic humor.

Simultaneously, Denise (Linda Darnell), a beautiful, club-footed girl who lives in the giant house where Pearson rents a room, has her own designs on the doctor. She feigns illness to see him, which he sees through.

The Raven's letters continue, and people conjecture on the author's identity. Cora's elder sister, Marie (Judith Evelyn), a nurse, was originally to have married Dr. Laurent, but when the older Laurent met Cora, he became infatuated with her. Many people think it's Marie, still bitter about losing her fiancé to her younger sibling.

One of Pearson's patients, a soldier with an over-protective mother, receives a Raven letter saying he has cancer and the doctors aren't telling him. He commits suicide, and his mother swears revenge on the letter writer. Suddenly the town takes the letters seriously. Some think it is Pearson, and the doctor starts losing patients.

Pearson reveals to Denise, who he is now seeing, why he decided to leave London. Married, his wife became lonely due to his schedule, and left him for someone else. When the affair ended, she asked Pearson to take her back. When he had refused, she killed herself.

The mayor and other public officials investigate the letters. One Sunday, a letter from the Raven floats down from the church choir loft in front of the congregation. The police round up everyone in the loft, including Denise and Cora. Laurent and the mayor make them copy the Raven's letters, hoping to deduce guilt from the handwriting. Laurent decides the results are inconclusive. For a short while it's believed Denise is writing the letters, but Pearson discovers it is Cora, trying to frame Denise.

Cora is put in a mental ward, and Pearson gets the full story. She had had a crush on Pearson and had written the first letter herself. Her elderly husband, Laurent, had found out, then made her continue writing, deciding it would be an interesting social experiment. Pearson goes to confront Laurent, with the police not far behind. Laurent is found with his throat cut, interrupted while writing a confession. Pearson looks out open windows and sees the dead soldier's mother walking away. Pearson and Denise end up together.

While Preminger and writer Howard Koch lift some scenes almost verbatim from Clouzot's original, Preminger shoots everything in a slicker, though much darker palette. Clouzot's film does not have the same nightmarish atmosphere, has a faster pace, is angrier and less mysterious. One might call its characters, in some ways, less human. As in Clouzot's film, there is a corrosive pettiness ingrained in the town's inhabitants. Preminger makes the town a character itself; the architecture of the church, hospital and houses, full of twisted pas-

Angel Face: doomed lovers Robert Mitchum and Jean Simmons.

sages and dark corners leading nowhere or back in on themselves, cast a claustrophobic spell. There is also an aura of madness covering everyone, including Pearson and Denise, the most sympathetic characters. Pearson jealously guards his privacy, and his room is a model of obsessive compulsive disorder, filled with antique clocks. In another scene, when the two are alone, Laurent suggests to Pearson that good and evil in everyone shifts like light and shadow, and he pushes a hanging lamp back and forth to illustrate.

On completion of his most famous Nazi acting role in Billy Wilder's *Stalag 17*, Preminger was surprised to learn that Zanuck had promised him to Howard Hughes for a one picture deal at RKO. Hughes was obsessed with young British Jean Simmons, and had bought out her UK-based contract, a development that made Simmons furious. It was obvious that Hughes was infatuated, his primary interest in seducing the young star.

Preminger hated the script called *Murder Story* and refused the assignment. Shortly after, a desperate call from Hughes promising Preminger complete control, with his choice of writers, convinced the director. He worked first with Oscar Millard, then with John Ford veteran Frank Nugent and an uncredited Ben Hecht, to whip the scenario into shape. The title was changed to *Angel Face*.

Former race car driver, Frank Jessup (Robert Mitchum), now an ambulance jockey and his partner Bill (Kenneth Tobey) arrive at an emergency call at the hilltop mansion of the wealthy Tremayne family. Catherine Tremayne (Barbara O'Neill) has nearly asphyxiated when her fireplace gas outlet was left on. Her husband Charles (Herbert Marshall) and a doctor believe she does not need to go to the hospital. As Frank and Bill leave, Frank stops in the foyer, intrigued by a young woman playing the piano, Charles' daughter, Diane (Jean Simmons). She strikes up a conversation and suddenly gets so hysterical Frank has to slap her. The slap makes a big impression.

Back at the hospital, Frank and Bill get off work, Frank planning on dining with his nurse girlfriend, Mary (Mona Freeman). Frank calls her from the local café but gets a busy signal. Suddenly, Diane materializes. Intrigued, Frank engages in a flirtation and, when Mary puts in a call to him, Frank says he's too tired to get together. Frank is already in Diane's web.

Unbeknownst to Frank, Diane has lunch with Mary to tell her what happened and to offer her and Frank financial help in Frank's plans to open up a sports car repair shop. Mary is dumbfounded, and politely declines, letting Diane know she won't let herself be manipulated.

That night, Frank goes out with Mary and puts his foot in his mouth, saying, "I was so beat I hit the sack as soon as I got in" to which Mary huffily and suggestively replies, "That, I can believe."

On the outs with Mary, Frank takes a job as Diane's stepmother's chauffeur, moving into an apartment over the estate's garage. Diane explains how her father, a widowed writer, has squandered his talent marrying into the comfortable life with rich Catherine. Diane hates Catherine, who she feels constantly humiliates her father.

Diane has an idea to ask Catherine to invest in Frank's sports car garage. Frank meets with Catherine, who is receptive, though she can't immediately consult with her attorney. Frank is under the impression the deal is done but, later, Diane shows Frank a crumpled page of numbers that represents their investment discussion, proof to Diane that Catherine led him on. Frank takes Diane's judgment at face value.

Frank drops in on Mary, but she's about to leave on a date with Bill. She asks him about his new job, and he tells her he's thinking of quitting, that the family "is a strange outfit."

The next day, Frank is going to leave, but Diane has packed her bag, too, determined to go with him. He tells her he can't keep up with her, but she convinces him to give her another chance.

Frank has the afternoon off, and Catherine decides to drive herself to her bridge game. At the last minute, Charles decides to get a ride into Beverly Hills. Catherine starts the engine, puts the gear into drive, and the car rockets into reverse instead, tumbling down the cliff and killing the two.

Diane suffers a nervous breakdown when she realizes her father was in the car. Frank is called in for questioning. The police think there is something funny about the accident, and he is charged with murder after Diane's packed suitcase is found in his room.

The Tremayne family attorney hires one of L.A.'s slickest defense lawyers, Fred Barrett (Leon Ames), a master at playing on a jury's emotions. He cooks up a scheme to have Frank and Diane married in the hospital jail ward, where Diane is recuperating, supplying tabloid headlines about two innocents in love. Frank goes along, scared of being convicted on his own. But he now wants nothing to do with Diane.

D.A. Judson (Jim Backus) brings in the car's mangled motor and drive shaft to demonstrate his theory how the transmission was jimmied to stay in reverse. Reasonable doubt, supplied by Barrett, causes the couple's acquittal.

Returning to the mansion, Frank informs Diane he'll go visit Mary to see if she'll take him back. If she won't, he'll travel to Mexico. Diane is devastated and, in desperation, makes him an offer. She'll loan him her Jaguar to go see Mary. If Mary takes him back, he can keep the car. If not, he'll bring the car back.

Diane believes she'll never see him again. She goes to Barrett's office, wanting to confess, and Barrett reluctantly agrees to take her statement. Diane details how she got Frank to show her how the transmission in her stepmother's car worked when he was giving it a tune-up. Unbeknownst to Frank, she rigged it to stay in reverse. Her plan backfired when her father was killed. Barrett tells her that she can't be prosecuted again because of double jeopardy. Genuinely hoping to expiate her guilt, she feels thwarted. Returning home to the empty mansion, Dimitri Tiomkin's dark romantic score swells, seeming to swirl around Diane as the camera leads her drifting, bereft with grief, through the halls and rooms.

Below, *Angel Face*: the sports car as emblem of the passion and despair, from idyllic tryst (left) to champagne before self-immolation.

Diane's hopes are rekindled when Frank returns. Mary has rejected him, preferring the stability of his ex-partner Bill, and Frank is leaving for Mexico. She pleads to go with him. He says no. Even though he's called a cab, he decides to let her drive him to the bus station. They get in the Jaguar, and Diane brings champagne and two glasses. He pours it as she starts the engine. Then looking at him, she floors the car in reverse and shoots them down the hill, the car disintegrating into twisted wreckage.

A few minutes later, the cab arrives.

One of the big achievements of Preminger, his writers, his cast and composer, Tiomkin, is to create a tone of amour fou in *Angel Face* that is realistic, poignant, delirious and suspenseful in equal doses. Frank is not the smartest guy, but he's not a dummy, either. His lackadaisical attitude about life is embodied in Mitchum's languid body language. Slow on the uptake about how dangerous Diane is, his problem is one of the noir anti-hero's most common: thinking with his balls and not his brains. *If* he hadn't given Diane a second chance; *if* Mary had taken him back; and *if* he'd realized Diane was willing to sacrifice her own life to be with him. A lot of *ifs*. Frank is always a half-beat behind trying to get in rhythm, and he pays for it dearly. Preminger actually generates some sympathy for Diane when she tries to make up for the murders by confessing, only to realize the state will never punish her. Barrett's assertion she may end up institutionalized if she presses the issue is more unpalatable to her than the gas chamber. When she comes home before seeing Frank for the final time, the romantic delirium builds to fever pitch, culminating in a bittersweet shot of her curled up in the shadows in Frank's room, Frank's coat wrapped around her. It is one of the most moving sequences in any Preminger film, and the character is completely self-aware of her own psychosis. *Angel Face* is Preminger's finest noir.

The Man with the Golden Arm

Preminger was intent on pushing the bounds of the Motion Picture Production Code. He had already done this with his first indie production, *The Moon is Blue* (1953), a tame sex comedy that was adapted from the stage. He had continued with his adaptation of the fiery, contemporary all-Black opera *Carmen Jones*. But Preminger still felt the need to go further.

John Garfield had purchased the rights to Nelson Algren's controversial novel about Chicago slumdwellers. However, in 1951, when he was told about the Production Code's ban on drug addiction subject matter, Garfield had abandoned the project. Preminger's brother, Ingo, had given Otto the novel in 1950, and after Garfield's death in 1952, Ingo snapped up the rights.

Other Preminger pictures such as *Daisy Kenyon* and *Anatomy of a Murder* are sometimes classified as noir, but are not discussed in depth here. In some respects, *The Man with the Golden Arm* (1956) is in the same boat. Nelson Algren's original bestseller is folkloric, classic Americana spun from what must have seemed degrading elements to many a suburban reader in the early 1950s. It's an uneven book, swinging from wild flights of fancy, bravura descriptive passages, stinging social satire disguised as urban tall tale and genuine poetry to maudlin scenes and frequently cornball dialogue. Though Algren was livid at the liberties Preminger took, the film actually captures the feel of the characters. The novel, *The Man with the Golden Arm*, for all its brilliance, is not an unqualified masterpiece. Algren *would* write a masterpiece, *A Walk on the Wild Side* later (which had its own more problematic movie adaptation).

Preminger wanted to film on Chicago streets, which would have amped up the realism, but limited resources prohibited it. He and art director Joe Wright whip up a decent recreation of a few grimy Chicago city blocks. Preminger's inability to create a natural rhythm

Frank Sinatra and Kim Novak in *The Man with the Golden Arm*.

for the film is partly a liability of studio sets standing in for real locations.

Frank Sinatra is Army veteran, card dealer and drug addict Frankie Machine. Frankie returns from taking the cure in Lexington, Kentucky, site of the only hospital to detox heroin and morphine addicts at the time. He's optimistic, having taken up drums. First, he runs into his pal Sparrow (Arnold Stang), an inept grifter and thief. He then reunites with his invalid wife Zosh (Eleanor Parker), who is wheelchair-bound from a car accident that he caused while drunk. Zosh guilt-trips Frankie about neglecting her. Frankie has a lead on a job playing drums for a big band but has to wait until he's called, a potential problem because they rely on the pay phone downstairs. Frankie runs into first floor neighbor Molly (Kim Novak), a girl who works as a cashier at a burlesque club. They have an unspoken bond. Frankie is also being pursued by gambler Schweifka (Robert Strauss) because he is such a good card dealer. However, Frankie is determined to give up the scene, knowing it will throw him into the company of dope dealer Louie (Darren McGavin). But Zosh's demands, Frankie's yearning for Molly, the whittling away at his will power by both Schweifka and Louie and the suspense of waiting for his audition, make him crack. He shoots up in Louie's pad, then agrees to deal a big card game to make money. Things fall apart. When it's time for his audition, he hasn't slept and is jonesing. He humiliates himself in front of the orchestra. Hooking up with Molly, she agrees to help him kick by locking him in her apartment, and he goes through withdrawals in one night, over the worst of it the next morning—one of the movie's most egregiously unrealistic premises. In the meantime, Louie has come looking for Frankie and stumbles in on Zosh walking. He is amused at her taking advantage of Frankie by her cripple act. Panicking, Zosh pushes Louie over the landing to his death. The head detective on the beat (Emile Meyer) comes looking for Frankie at Molly's. The film ends in frantic fashion as Zosh is caught in her lies, runs out of the apartment with everyone chasing her, and she jumps off a back stair landing to her death. At the end, Frankie and Molly walk off together.

The book has a considerably more downbeat ending; if Preminger had faithfully followed it, it's possible the movie would have been more artistically successful but the public would have stayed away in droves. Frankie is the one who kills Louie halfway through the novel, then spirals gradually downwards, finally fleeing and killing himself. The novel ends with an autopsy report filled out for Frankie.

Bunny Lake Is Missing and The Human Factor

In *Bunny Lake Is Missing* (1965). American Ann Lake (Carol Lynley) arrives in London with her young daughter, Bunny, to move in with Ann's journalist brother Stephen (Keir Dullea). She's distressed to find Bunny missing when she goes to pick her up her first day at school. No one seems to have heard of her, and Ann's angry panic creates a mood of distrust with the people in charge. Ann calls her brother as well as the police. A number of red herrings are introduced, including retired headmistress, Ada (Martita Hunt), who seems to have an intuitive understanding of children's motivations, which are seized on by Stephen. There's also Ann's new landlord, Wilson (Noel Coward) a perpetually drunk radio actor who has made lewd propositions. Police inspector Newhouse (Laurence Olivier) tries to eliminate the possibilities of what may have happened, including the theory Ann is a delusional hysteric.

When things look darkest, Ann remembers how she can prove Bunny exists: retrieve Bunny's doll from the toy repairman. No one points out to her that she could easily have bought a real doll for an imaginary daughter, and this is one of the premise spoilers that introduces questionable logic. She goes to the doll "hospital" owned by an elderly dollmaker (Finlay Currie), shot in a real, antique doll museum. One of the creepiest sequences, it is also where we realize Stephen is off his rocker. He arrives after Ann comes downstairs from talking to the dollmaker, doll in hand, and Stephen knocks her out, takes the doll and sets it on fire. Taking Ann to a local clinic, he claims she's fallen and hit her head. When Ann wakes up, she realizes Stephen has Bunny, and she may have only hours to live. Preminger handles her escape from the hospital in atmospheric fashion, steering Ann down empty corridors and through kitchens filled with shadows. Ann guesses Stephen has gone to an old house from their childhood. In the meantime, Stephen has retrieved a drugged Bunny from the trunk of his car and carries her to a grave on the grounds of the house. Ann arrives, reverting to her childhood persona

Bunny Lake Is Missing.

Nicol Williamson and Iman in *The Human Factor*.

to distract Stephen. He goes back to his child self, wanting to play. Ann realizes Stephen has always resented that she had been to bed with a man, Bunny's father. Bunny is a constant reminder of Ann's loss of innocence. He playfully pushes Ann on a swing until Newhouse and his men arrive, taking Stephen into custody, and Ann is happily reunited with her groggy daughter.

Preminger puts much into the visual look and times the suspense fairly well, at least until the final scene where it falters. It's an engrossing watch for the performances by Olivier and Coward. But Preminger does little with Ann and Stephen. They are all surface with no inner life. Unlike Preminger's masterpiece *Angel Face* and earlier noirs, there are no characters that move us to care about them.

Preminger's not just final noir, but final picture, *The Human Factor* (1979), is his most unjustly forgotten film. Not a complete success, it eschews the thriller mise-en-scène of *Bunny Lake*. But it has something more: a well-written story with believable characters. Based on Graham Greene's espionage novel, with a screenplay by Tom Stoppard, it is a tale of amoral, mercenary interests, of competing nations and their ideologies, with two recognizable, vulnerable humans caught in the middle.

Maurice Castle (Nicol Williamson) is a London agent in MI6, previously stationed in South Africa, whose office partner Davis (Derek Jacobi) comes under suspicion of being a leak. Castle, who is a family man, is seen as a less likely risk, even though his wife Sarah (Iman) is a Black South African and her son was fathered by a murdered activist. Richard Attenborough plays Colonel Daintry, new head of MI6 Security who is taken aback by the cold-blooded discussion of risk liabilities (i.e. human lives) to be quietly disposed of, by his superiors Hargreaves (Richard Vernon) and the cheerfully ghoulish Dr. Percival (Robert Morley).

Castle tries to steer Davis away from poor choices that will make him more of a target. Ironically, no one, including Castle, ever directly informs Davis. Because Davis is hopelessly in love with a girl from the office, he starts behaving out of character, something which perks the antenna of Dr. Percival. Davis is given "routine check-ups," creating a false history of non-existent heart problems, so that in the eventuality they have to poison him, the death will seem a heart attack. Which is what happens.

Simultaneous to Davis' death, Castle has to meet with his nemesis from South Africa, Cornelius Muller, a white supremacist police official, with whom MI6 are working against a Black Communist uprising. Castle is determined not to send any more communiqués to his Soviet handlers, but when he discovers that MI6 and Muller, with blessings from America, are discussing tactical use of nuclear weapons, he has to alert his Soviet contact, hoping the plan can be exposed.

Seeing Muller brings up memories of meeting his wife, Sarah, and how Muller persecuted them under miscegenation laws. A white human rights attorney, who happened to be Communist and one of Castle's contacts there, had helped Castle smuggle Sarah out of the country. Out of gratitude, Castle had misguidedly become a double agent. Sarah has remained ignorant of this.

Muller becomes suspicious, and Hargreaves realizes they've disposed of the wrong man. Castle sends Sarah and son to stay with his mother (Ann Todd). Shortly after, Castle's contact and Soviet superior (Martin Benson) whisks Castle to Moscow, promising they'll bring Sarah and the boy later. Once Castle is gone, Percival invites Sarah to lunch, which turns frosty as Percival pumps her for info. Sarah tells him off. The final scene is a confrontation between Sarah and Castle's mother, who believes her son should be dealt with as a traitor. Right then, Castle calls from Moscow. His mother refuses to speak to him and hands the receiver to Sarah. The two lovers talk of being reunited, but the connection goes dead. A despairing Castle is left with the receiver dangling, wondering if he'll ever see his wife again.

The Human Factor was a problematic shoot. Preminger's previous film *Rosebud* had been a flop, and Preminger secured partial funding from some Arab businessmen, but they dropped the ball on Nairobi location work. Preminger delayed the production for days while selling paintings and securing second mortgages. The lead, Nicol Williamson, like Robert Mitchum, who'd been fired from *Rosebud*, and Peter O'Toole, Mitchum's replacement, was an alcoholic and had also been fired from his last film. Williamson, though sober during the shoot and deferential to Preminger, was abusive to his colleagues behind the camera. Iman had only worked as a model, with no previous acting experience. That lack and her still heavy Somali accent gives her performance an uneven quality. In some scenes, she's awkward; in others, particularly her argument with Castle's mother, she's powerful. The film moves at a slow pace, more a character study than a thriller. There is little violence and no artificial building of suspense. But real dread and tension are generated through narrative and personality conflicts. Preminger makes us feel for Castle, Sarah, Davis and even Daintry, and terrifies us with the casual cold-bloodedness of Muller, Hargreaves and Percival.

Films with Noir Elements

Preminger's *Daisy Kenyon* (1947), follows an independent fashion designer's (Joan Crawford) plight with her two lovers, a veteran (Henry Fonda) suffering from PTSD, whom she weds, and a married lawyer (Dana Andrews). The triangle never reaches the level of fatal tragedy or psychopathic behavior to be true noir. Its happy resolution is also uncharacteristic. Preminger gets close, first, with Fonda's wartime nightmares on a stormy night and, a second time, when Andrews divorces his wife, hoping to marry Daisy, only to discover his spouse has been beating their two daughters. Although well-handled, neither of these subplots are developed enough to give the film noir credentials.

Carmen Jones (1954), Preminger's CinemaScope, Technicolor, modern Black opera, based on Bizet's original, has scorching femme fatale action courtesy of Dorothy Dandridge, a destroyer of men, but it is a stretch to label the movie noir.

Likewise, the excellent *Bonjour Tristesse* (1958), though flitting back and forth between a noirish black and white Paris in the present to a color-drenched, sunny, coastal Nice in the past, is a tragic tale of the callousness of youth, innocence lost and an upper class reveling in pleasure, fearful of real emotions. It has more in common with Fellini's *La Dolce Vita.*

Anatomy of a Murder (1959) comes close to noir, not only for its stark look, but its subject. Yet it emerges as just a good courtroom drama, the kind of saga picture with countless characters that became Preminger's province in the 1960s. The focus is on a lovable defense attorney, James Stewart, instead of the warped relationship of the G.I. murder suspect, Ben Gazzara, and his flirtatious, rape victim wife, Lee Remick.

Advise and Consent (1962), one of Preminger's most fascinating pictures, is one of the best movies about behind-the-scenes American politics. The all American senator (Don Murray) who investigates a Secretary of State nominee (Henry Fonda) for former Communist ties, is a noirish character, giving rise to a subplot of another senator blackmailing Murray, threatening to reveal a homosexual incident during WWII if he delivers a negative appraisal of the nominee. It causes Murray to descend into a nightmare netherworld, unable to reconcile the hurt it will cause his family and his unshakable sense of duty, resulting in his suicide.

Hurry Sundown (1967) is an unevenly realized epic about race relations in post-WWII Georgia. With scenes veering from poignant to overblown TV movie melodrama, there are still memorable moments. A White farmer and a Black farmer (John Philip Law, Robert Hooks) band together to fight a rich landowner (Michael Caine) and his wife (Jane Fonda) from taking over their land. The subplot dealing with Caine and Fonda's severely autistic son has some tragic noir touches. When Caine becomes determined to steal Law's and Hook's farms by any means, Fonda leaves him. Caine dynamites a levee, and in the process, Caine's beloved son is killed.

Rosebud (1975) is a thriller which follows a reporter (Peter O'Toole) working for the CIA to free five rich girls kidnapped by Palestinian terrorists. Fraught with production problems, the movie received terrible reviews. There are some borderline noirish subplots.

Preminger remains most at home trying to achieve a balance between controversial material of social relevance and tempering it with theatrical melodrama to keep audiences entertained. Despite the restriction of the Hays code, his most rewarding movies, at least in terms of defining noir, were his earliest at Fox and his one film at RKO, *Angel Face*, productions of hardboiled stories with downbeat themes, Preminger managing his uncompromising sensibility with a discipline (enforced by budget and studio), subtlety and character detail, traits that did not disappear, but became less consistent in his later work.

Biography

Otto Ludwig Preminger was born on December 5, 1905, in Wisnitz, Austria-Hungary (now part of Ukraine). His family relocated to Vienna when he was still young, and he became pre-occupied with the theater from the time he was a boy.

While directing theater in Vienna, Preminger impressed visiting 20th Century-Fox's Joe Schenck, which led to his first Hollywood job. Fox's creative head Darryl F. Zanuck instructed Preminger to study other contract directors. He was assigned his debut *Under Your Spell* (1936) after eight months. A comedy called *Danger :Love at Work* (1937) followed. Preminger argued with Zanuck about period adventure *Kidnapped* and was removed from the picture. Thinking things would blow over, he was shocked when he found himself frozen out of life at the studio for nearly five years. Though Zanuck attempted a buyout on Preminger's contract, Preminger refused. Making a New York pilgrimage, he enjoyed several popular successes on Broadway. One of them was directing Claire Boothe Luce's anti-isolationist dramedy, *Margin for Error*. Midway through the original run, the German actor portraying the Nazi villain absconded. Having trouble finding a suitable replacement, Preminger took the part himself. This led to a role as a Nazi officer in writer/producer Nunnally Johnson's *The Pied Piper* shooting at none other than Preminger's former studio. Preminger reprised his *Margin for Error* role on film in 1943 (also for Fox), and he convinced acting Fox head William Goetz to let him direct, which led to a new contract. Zanuck was briefly in the Army, supervising propaganda films for the U.S. war effort. Once back at Fox, Zanuck buried the hatchet, and Preminger soon hit his stride with the smash successes, *Laura* (1944) and *Forever Amber* (1948). Preminger directed off and on for Fox through *River of No Return* (1954), as well as for the Broadway stage. In 1953, Preminger began his independent film career that bucked the Production Code in such films as *The Moon is Blue* (1953) and *The Man with the Golden Arm* (1955). That same year also saw Preminger helm the first of his all-star epics, *Anatomy of a Murder*, continuing with *Exodus* (1960), *Advise and Consent* (1962), *The Cardinal* (1963), *In Harm's Way* (1965) and *Hurry Sundown* (1967). Most of these were distributed by United Artists, MGM or Columbia, then later, Paramount, and utilized the graphic skills of Saul Bass in their title sequences and marketing campaigns. After his counterculture comedy *Skidoo* (1968) flopped, Preminger pulled back on the scale of his pictures. As the 1970s progressed, he had a harder time financing his productions. His last was *The Human Factor* (1979). He died of Alzheimer's disease on April 23, 1986 in New York City.

Noir Films

Laura (1944)
Fallen Angel (1945)
Whirlpool (1949)
Where the Sidewalk Ends (1950)
The 13th Letter (1950)
Angel Face (1952)
The Man with the Golden Arm (1955)

Neo Noir

Bunny Lake is Missing (1965)
The Human Factor (1979)

Films with Noir Elements

Daisy Kenyon (1947)
Carmen Jones (1954)
Bonjour Tristesse (1958)
Anatomy of a Murder (1959)
Advise and Consent (1962)
Hurry Sundown (1967)
Rosebud (1975)

Preminger directs Kim Novak in *The Man with the Golden Arm*.

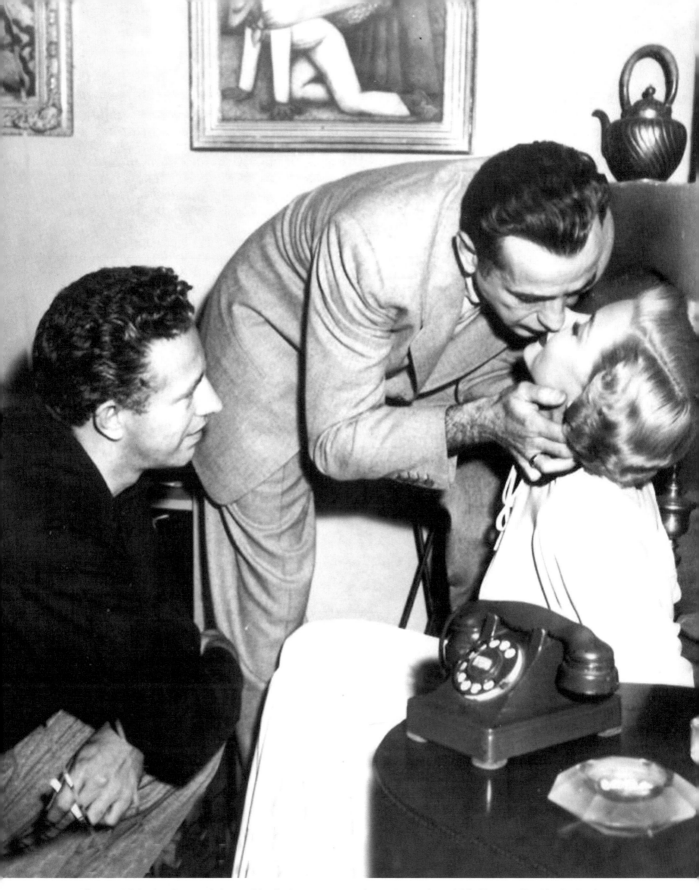

Above, Nicholas Ray watches a kiss between Humphrey Bogart and his then-wife Gloria Grahame.

Nicholas Ray

Jesse Schlotterbeck

They Live By Night

They Live By Night features a compelling mix of elements familiar and unusual to the noir film. It tells the story of hardened criminals, contains scenes of sadism and violence, and has a bold orchestral score. At the same time, it has many brightly lit scenes, is often set in rural locations, and features an unusually innocent romance between two protagonists in the their early twenties, Bowie (Farley Granger) and Keechie (Cathy O'Donnell). Foster Hirsch identifies the romantic plot of the film as unusual. He describes *They Live By Night* as "a genre rarity, a sentimental noir." These lead characters are poor and unskilled and have apparently few options for profit. Bowie, like many crime film characters before him, hopes to begin a new life in earnest following a final heist, but Keechie recognizes the contradictions in this plan and foresees their eventual demise.

More typical to a noir film, the young lovers' attempt to escape from their life of crime is doomed. Still, *They Live By Night* remains a less dark film (both literally and figuratively) than most noir films. Discussing the film's conclusion, Janey Place writes that the "[T]he young lovers are doomed, but the possibility of their love transcends and redeems them both..." In the final

The criminal "family" in *They Live By Night.*

sequence, Bowie returns to see Keechie at a roadside motel. His criminal involvement, a constant threat to his survival, finally catches up to him just as he appears to have reached his lover safely. The final scene suffused as much with romance as violence calls *Bonnie and Clyde* to mind. Just as Bowie reaches Keechie's doorstep, the police gun him down. However, where many noir films would end here or mail in the romantic conclusion, Ray emphasizes Keechie's sadness and resolve. In a series of soft-focus close-ups, she reads his final note to her in a tender voice. Already, she appears more sustained by his love than traumatized by this loss. The care given this finale makes the film ultimately romantic.

In a Lonely Place

From the first shot of *In a Lonely Place* (1950), it is clear that this film is not a typical Humphrey Bogart movie. While this actor had previously played suave and unflappable characters such as Rick in *Casablanca* (1942) and Philip Marlowe in *The Big Sleep* (1946), *In a Lonely Place*'s Dix Steele is frustrated, angry, and out of control. The opening scene shows Dix driving to a bar already tense and in a terrible mood. He nearly picks a fight with another driver before getting into a brawl at the bar.

This character is a typical Ray protagonist. In his summary of *The Films of Nicholas Ray*, Geoff Andrew writes that Ray's film evinces a consistent "disillusionment, both with American life in general and with the American movie establishment in particular." "Pain, anxiety, uncertainty, violence and loneliness" typify the Ray character. This description is, not coincidentally, similar to Etienne Chaumeton and Raymond Borde's characterization of the noir genre as broadly characterized by qualities atypical to popular filmmaking such as ambivalence and cruelty. We encounter Bogart, usually more cool and masculine, with similar surprise here.

Below (with Martha Stewart as the "hat check girl") and opposite (with Gloria Grahame), Bogart as troubled screenwriter Dixon Steele in reflective poses with different women. Ray's staging reveals a more open and less alienated posture for Steele with Grahame's character, Laurel Gray.

In a Lonely Place is also characterized by the expressive style of film noirs. Ray makes full use of the dynamic possibilities of lighting, using shifts from low to high-key lighting to mark dramatic contrasts in mood. Dix's erratic moods are matched with lighting changes. A light dinner party turns morbid as Dix imagines too well how a murder may have taken place. His angry, performative face in this scene is harshly and brightly lit, emphasizing his morbid fascination. A beach party's light atmosphere is broken by the news that Dix is still under investigation for this crime. As the writer rushes away from the party, this evenly lit scene becomes much more dark.

Dix remains an ambivalent character, often more interested in confusing those around him than communicating and remains unapologetically interested in the subject of murder intellectually but not emotionally. He remains completely unshaken that a hat check girl who had just read him a script was murdered just a few hours after leaving his company.

At the same time, Dix remains a more self-aware character than many others. He calls out the hypocritical and moralizing aspects of his surrounding cast: he accuses his agent and another screenwriter of being more interested in profit than art. He also accurately challenges the police when their questioning veers more towards questions of common decorum and morality than towards factual information.

Ray leaves us with the suggestion that an angry, restless screenwriter who "'has killed dozens of people before...in my pictures" may well be a far more actualized and ethical person than most of the more conventional characters who surround and frequently misjudge him.

Born to Be Bad

Born to Be Bad makes the poor moral character of its lead, Cristobel (Joan Fontaine), clear from the start. The film begins as she finds housing with another woman, Donna (Joan Leslie). Shortly thereafter, protected by an innocent and well-wishing façade, Cristobel sets out to undermine Donna and take what is hers for herself; she sets her sights, in particular, on Donna's plans to marry a wealthy suitor, Curtis (Zachary Scott).

While Cristobel is obviously set up as the film's villain, there are moments typical to a Ray film that extend ambivalent characterization to the other protagonists as well. For example, the apparently perfect couple whose lives Cristobel aims to disrupt hide their contemptuous assessments of one another in plain sight. Curtis judges Donna "both domestic and beautiful," while she introduces him to guests as "the man I'm marrying for his money." Here, Ray exposes the cold this-for-that premises of the conventional marriage in the starkest terms.

Born to Be Bad also features a character similar to Bogart's Dix in *In a Lonely Place*. Novelist Nick Bradley (Robert Ryan) has a compelling rapport with Cristobel. Though he has a cruel and controlling streak, Nick (with his author's imagination) understands Cristobel well. Cristobel's attraction to both Donna and Nick is the central conflict of the film. Where Donna represents the appeal of the conventional and the stable, Nick represents the more countercultural and imaginative possibility of life. However, like Dix and Ryan's Wilson in *On Dangerous Ground*, it is unclear whether Nick is unusually insightful or simply irresponsible.

Nick successfully seduces Cristobel by speculating about her conflicted impulses. He pushes her to recognize her two sides, public and private (or conscious and subconscious). Though Cristobel protests verbally, it is clear that this sparks the basis of a strong attraction. Their link, both dark and deep, continues when she reads Nick's violent novel. When Cristobel objects to the presence of a "brutal character" in his story, he retorts, "If you ever draw an honest breath, I want to be there to see it...I've never seen anybody choke to death." Cristobel,

Two faces of Robert Ryan over consecutive movies: Opposite, wealthy writer Nick Bradley in *Born to Be Bad* (with Joan Fontaine) and violent cop Jim Wilson (with Cleo Moore) in *On Dangerous Ground* above.

also an abusive personality, finds a kindred spirit in Nick.

In the guise of being helpful, Cristobel systematically undermines Donna and Curtis' relationship. In a series of conniving tests, she convinces Curtis that Donna is only interested in his money. She has him give her the most expensive necklace at a shop while showing that she is happy with the most modest one. Later, she convinces him to "test" Donna by suggesting she forego all rights to his estate before marriage. While Donna sees through Cristobel's conniving, all the other characters in the film sympathize with her. Her inability to choose between Nick and Curtis is her final undoing. Even though she succeeds in wresting Curtis from Donna, and even marrying him, she quickly grows tired of Curtis and longs for Nick. By this time, Nick too has tired of Cristobel's indecisiveness.

In terms of character design and plot, *Born to Be Bad* may well be the most disturbing of Ray's film noirs. The lead character, Cristobel, is brutally sociopathic. It is also well-scripted and acted. Its style, however, is resolutely classical. *Born to Be Bad* is a well-made, classical style film, but not particularly notable or exceptional in its use of visual style or sound.

On Dangerous Ground (with Ward Bond and Ida Lupino)

On Dangerous Ground

On Dangerous Ground (1951) continues to treat the themes established in *In a Lonely Place* and *They Live By Night*. Robert Ryan plays a character much like Bogart's Dix. Wilson (Ryan), a patrol officer, is alienated and unstable. Like Dix, he offers some insight into the limitations of his profession, yet he is also too entangled with his own demons. Thus, his capacity for feeling and insight become weaknesses: tired of the violence that the policeman confronts, he assaults and abuses suspects with even greater verve. Wilson's instability is represented with dynamic cinematic style. Ray uses an unusual mobile, shaky frame to capture Wilson's overenthusiastic and violent pursuit of a suspect. Nearly half the urban scenes in *On Dangerous Ground* take place in cars. Shots of the bewilderingly busy and chaotic city dominate the first portion of the film.

Yet, as in *They Live By Night*, there is the possibility of redemption. Wilson's instability has jeopardized his place on the police force and his supervisor sends him to upstate New York both to investigate a murder and to regain composure. The rural landscape becomes the site of numerous dramatic sequences for the continued criminal investigation. The disoriented policeman's navigation of this new space is effectively conveyed by sequences featuring fast-paced editing and unstable axises.

In contrast to *They Live By Night* and the possibility of the most frightening rural passages, Wilson finds equanimity and kindness in the country. While on this assignment, Wilson meets Mary Walden (Ida Lupino), a blind woman who lives a secluded life miles away from the already isolated upstate community. After the conclusion of Wilson's investigation, he returns to be with Mary. They passionately kiss in close-up, cueing an exuberant orchestral score as "The End" appears over a slow tracking shot of a beautiful, snow covered landscape.

This is in contrast to Ray's wishes. The director wanted a more pessimistic ending. Andrew Dickos reports that "Ray wanted to end the film on the ambivalent image of Jim Wilson returning to the bleak city," after he had restored order upstate.

Party Girl

As a Technicolor film, the style of *Party Girl* (1953) is not as recognizably noir as some of Ray's earlier features but character interactions quickly establish that it may be appropriately considered as such. The film stars Cyd Charisse as nightclub dancer Vicki. In an early scene, she attends a party run by the mob and adeptly manipulates the male patrons. She leads on a highroller at the craps table and bilks hundreds of dollars from him in exchange for nothing, then convinces the party's most prominent guest, lawyer Farrell, to take her home.

Farrell initially helps Vicki only as a caring father figure, dryly and patronizingly lecturing her about pursuing dance at a more respectable forum than a gentleman's club. When his interest shifts from a paternalistic to a

more romantic one this is signaled by film style alone. In this mostly evenly lit Technicolor film, a glance of Farrell's accompanied by a saxophone score and high-contrast lighting suggests that his fatherly interest in Vicki has shifted to the dangerous and dark intrigue.

Vicki challenges Farrell's professionalism and paternalism. As the mob's lawyer, she challenges him on the notion that his work is any more honorable than hers but that, merely, "your pride sells higher than mine." The theme of moral ambiguity continues to inform the film, as Farrell emerges as a more complex character than Vicki.

A boyhood injury left Farrell crippled and envious of more healthy boys. This sense of inferiority is overcome, sort of, by becoming such a successful lawyer, yet the fact that he works for unabashed criminals makes this success a very partial kind of redemption if not an obvious and morbid kind of overcompensation for his inferior sense of masculinity. Vicki gives him the chance to right this decision; eventually, he does. This happy ending places *Party Girl*, like other marginally noir titles such as *Mildred Pierce*, debatably more in the melodrama genre than in the noir category.

Nevertheless, if the visual style of the film is sometimes too colorful and stately to seem noir, the persistent representation of selfishness, violence, sadism, and struggle between the sexes suggest a consistent thematic link to the noir movement.

Biography

Famed American filmmaker Nicholas Ray explored an astonishingly wide range of art forms and media before settling on filmmaking in the late 1940s. As an undergraduate at the University of Wisconsin, Nicholas Ray studied under dramatist Thornton Wilder and architect Frank Lloyd Wright. After college, he produced radio programs on American folk music. In 1946, he directed Duke Ellington's *Beggar's Holiday*. The next year he began work on *They Live By Night*, starting a Hollywood film career that would span from 1947 to 1963.

Though Ray directed six noir films, *Rebel Without a Cause* (1955), starring James Dean at the height of his career, remains his best known film. More recently, *Bigger than Life* (1956), in which James Mason plays a family man gone mad on prescription drugs, has been reissued by Criterion. Thus, Ray likely will remain most associated with the Technicolor melodrama. Like most Hollywood directors, Ray directed in numerous other genres (including adventure films and war films). He also directed numerous westerns, most notably *Johnny Guitar* (1954).

Ray had a relatively short career in Hollywood, retiring in 1963 after directing 20 films in 15 years. Following his dismissal from *55 Days at Peking* (1963), Ray relocated to Europe. For seven years, he planned numerous projects which were never completed. In the last years of his life, he taught courses in film and acting at New York area colleges, and collaborated with a new generation of filmmakers, most notably Wim Wenders and Jim Jarmusch. Shortly after collaborating with Wenders on *Lightning Over Water*, Ray died in 1979. He was 67.

Noir Films

They Live By Night (1948)
Knock On Any Door (1949)
In a Lonely Place (1950)
Born to Be Bad (1950)
On Dangerous Ground (1951)
Party Girl (1958)

Opposite and page 350, Robert Taylor and title figure Cyd Charisse in *Party Girl.*

Right, Ray with producer Dore Schary on the set of *Born to Be Bad*

Don Siegel checks the sun o̶ the set of *Dirty Harry*.

Don Siegel

Ronald Wilson

"Most of my pictures, I'm sorry to say, are about nothing. Because I'm a whore, I work for money. It's the American way."

Don Siegel[1]

"Doomed Peculiarity": Narrative Space and Movement in Don Siegel's Noir Films

Don Siegel's work has been sorely neglected in film scholarship. Other than his autobiography posthumously published in 1993, and a monograph published in 1975, there are no book length studies of the film director. One reason is that most of his films fall under the category of action films and cross many genres, including noir. Another is that he is often seen as a journeyman "professional" filmmaker rather than an auteur director. Siegel's career transitioned from the studio era into post-war independent production and back into a corporate studio environment. This resulted in an inconsistency in style. However, Siegel's noir films have often been discussed in terms of one distinct characteristic–the outcast protagonist.

In a "Postface" to *A Panorama of American Film Noir*, Raymond Borde and Etienne Chaumeton describe a fundamental change occurring in current (circa 1979) film noirs:

> What has changed is the way of perceiving the characters. A sort of derision—a distance, in any event—is introduced between character and act. The old series gave the impression of a no-holds barred fight against death and chaos. The new series announces itself through far more nuanced states of mind. Freudian analyses, furtive relationships in which time and introspection are to play a preponderant role. The putrescence overwhelms human beings whose main concern is to survive, not to fight back. Machiavellianism takes precedence over a brute strength that will only burst forth in the last resort, with lightning speed.[2]

This shift towards character is particularly relevant to the work of Don Siegel whose most notable noir films feature a central male protagonist, often referred to as the antisocial outcast. Film critic Andrew Sarris argues that Don Siegel's emphasis on character in his most "successful films express the doomed peculiarity of the antisocial outcast."[3] And Alan Lovell maintains that any "account of Siegel's films must begin with a basic situation of the man outside society."[4] Throughout his noir films Siegel characterizes his outcast protagonists through their relationship to surroundings. This objectification of character through spatial relationships, what I shall refer to as internal and external space, is an essential visual characteristic of Siegel's noir films. In addition, the outcast and his environmental space also mirrors the director's own career trajectory in the motion picture industry.

Siegel's noir protagonist, "the man outside society," has several distinct characteristics. Typically he is a loner with no family and few friends. His personal relationships are generally tenuous and fleeting. He is also a non-conformist with a disdain for any type of authority—bureaucracy is anathema to him. Siegel's police noir protagonists in *Madigan* (1968) and *Dirty*

Above, Siegel's noir protagonists over three decades from the locked-room thriller, *The Verdict*, to the last of the independents *Charley Varrick*. Opposite, *The Big Steal* with noir icons Robert Mitchum and Jane Greer.

Harry (1971) also display a contemptuous, anti-authoritarian attitude. These police detectives work more efficiently in meting out justice outside the system by their own means. Siegel's outsider protagonist is either a lawbreaker or a law enforcer. Critic Alan Lovell notes that once Siegel's outsider "heroes" reject society they can "express themselves either through the law or through crime since [their] world only exists in terms of these two blocks."[5] Thus the outsider gains a freedom of mobility once he has rejected society. The outsider can now "express" himself through movement rather than the restraint of societal laws and values. A distinguishing characteristic of the outsider antihero in Siegel's work is their spatial relationship to their surroundings. Particularly important is their mobility within those surroundings.

Narrative space in Siegel's films can be categorized as either internal or external.[6] Both relate to the protagonist's psychological and physical relationship to his surroundings and offers insight into the society that he rejects. One of the most recognized components of a Siegel film is action, particularly violent action. Action is directly related to narrative space and becomes a particularly salient feature of Siegel's use of internal/external space and the spatial relationship with the outsider protagonist within his films. In terms of composition Siegel prefers realistic settings that utilize a naturalistic visual style. Seemingly antithetical to more expressionistic noir visual styles, this approach creates a more complex mise-en-scène that concentrates specifically on character and spatial relationships.

Internal space consists of any enclosed surroundings that the outsider finds himself in. These surroundings may be small as in either an office space or an apartment, or more expansive public spaces such as an amusement arcade, a poolroom, or a large house. What becomes important in these internal environments is that the outsider is *constricted in his mobility*. Internal space in Siegel's noir films is related to social mobility, domestic or societal. These spaces are often claustrophobic and threatening to the outsider resulting in a sense of uncertainty and paranoia. The outsider feels less in control and is vulnerable within internal surroundings. This environment is also constrictive because it represents dependence, especially if it is an office or domestic setting that is ambivalent to the outsider's sense of independence.

Frequently, in a Siegel film noir internal spaces feature acts of violence.

By contrast external spaces express mobility and freedom to the outsider. These are open, exterior surroundings where the outsider has physical mobility. Many of Siegel's outsider protagonists are locomotive and are continually moving from place to place. Emblematic of their independence, they have no real home. The realistic surroundings in external space contribute to the outsider's sense of security within an urban or rural setting: an environmental stability based on mobility and freedom. Movement then is a key element of external space and is evidenced by action sequences such as car chases and dramatic confrontations. A Siegel noir film creates a tension between the two spaces because of the outcast protagonist's desire for individual choice rather than conformity.

We can see three phases in Siegel's career that are useful in tracing the development of the outsider protagonist and his use of narrative space. From Warner Bros. in the 1940s to Universal-MCA in the 1960s, Siegel was able to adapt the outsider to different narrative situations that reflect the character's relationship to his environment and to society. In addition, Siegel's focus on the outsider as the primary protagonist in his film noirs and the use of internal and external space that is developed within these films, mirror the director's own contested relationship to the post-war motion picture industry. An understanding of Siegel's sympathy with the outsider protagonist results by following the character's development from the studio system through independent film production into the corporate studio era. And Siegel's use of narrative space within these films as a reflection on his own circumstances within the industry provides additional insight into his film noirs.

Studio and Post-Studio Era Years (1946-1954): The Exploratory Phase

The first phase of Don Siegel's directorial career is characterized by the seismic shift that occurred in the motion picture industry during the post-war years. The move from studio era to independent production created a need for low-budget films to replace the B product that the studios used as their "bread-and-butter." Siegel was able to transition into this phase with

Riot in Cell Block 11 (left) and *Private Hell 36:* space that reflects tortured relationships.

his first film, *The Verdict* (1946), a locked-room mystery thriller set in Victorian London and made at Warner Bros. It is especially noteworthy because it provides an early example of the outsider protagonist, though the character is not fully developed. The studio-bound sets illustrate how constricted Siegel is working within the studio system. *The Big Steal* (1949), made at RKO, showcases the naturalistic environment that would become a trademark of Siegel's visual style. Basically a heist chase film Siegel utilizes location photography in Mexico, along with studio sets in a fashion that anticipates later spatial/character relationships. The opening scene and the climax are particularly relevant as they are internalized spaces that contain violent action sequences. The move to independent production and a more individual directorial style is reflected in two film noirs Siegel made in 1954 for independent producers—Walter Wanger and Filmmakers Production, Inc.

Both *Riot in Cell Block 11* and *Private Hell 36* utilize internal and external space as a means of visualizing the outsider's psychological relationship to society. This relationship is most clearly defined by the character's mobility within that space. Siegel's visual form begins to develop more succinctly during the later part of this phase and provides commentary on the director's own relationship with the film industry.

The prison setting of *Riot in Cell Block 11* provides an example of the dichotomy of space based on the relationship between Dunn (Neville Brand) and the riotous inmates and the prison's bureaucratic environment. Though this is an almost sole representation of internal space (the prison) the spatial relationships within the prison are well defined. Once the prisoners have revolted and taken over the cellblock that space becomes associated with limited freedom. Yet, it is still an internalized space of instability and chaos. Physically the space is characterized by a darkly lighted corridor and imposing walls—a frequent visual motif in Siegel's noir films. Though the prisoners have more mobility within the cellblock, that mobility is confined. The frequency of acts of violence on fellow prisoners and on Dunn himself, provide evidence of the chaotic and confined elements of internalized space. By contrast is another example of internalized space, the Warden's office. Here the space is stable and orderly and represents the bureaucratic organization of society. The space is well lit and clearly defined. It is within this space that the Warden communicates to the outside world and to guards within the prison. The prison yard is an internal contested space for negotiation between the Warden and Dunn. When the prisoners from another cellblock revolt they attempt to take over the prison yard and are stopped by the state police. These spaces provide a compositional palette for Siegel to work with in regard to his character's spatial relationships.

Private Hell 36 also showcases Siegel's use of internal and external space. Two sequences in particular illustrate this spatial relationship: the opening robbery and the racetrack sequence. In each of these the outsider is psychologically characterized by his mobility within the space. Los Angeles police Detective Cal Bruner (Steve Cochran) prevents a late night drug store robbery in the opening sequence. The darkly lit interior space is confined by shadows and the ill-fated robbery results in violence. More importantly the setting accentuates the consumerism that ultimately motivates Bruner to commit robbery by keeping a portion of recovered stolen money from another heist. Bruner becomes romantically involved with Lilli Marlowe (Ida Lupino) and his desire is further motivated by her materialistic needs. The opening sequence thus begins the theme of materialism that develops Bruner's psychological motivation. This is best exemplified during the racetrack sequence, where Bruner and his partner, are trying to locate the suspect who passed a "hot" fifty-dollar bill at the drug store. The promise of easy riches at the racetrack provides the impetus for Bruner to keep $100,000 of the $300,000 stolen money once they have located it. The racetrack itself is an external space that allows Bruner to consider the freedom available to him with the right amount of money. The horse race itself, with its promise of cash winnings, anticipates the car chase sequence that follows, and the recovery of the heist money.

This exploratory stage in Siegel's development allowed him to begin to experiment with compositional space in regard to his protagonist hero—the outsider. In addition it can also be seen as a parallel to Siegel's emergence from the constraints of the studio system to independence as a director of action genres. The next phase in his career is notable because it contains his most representative films utilizing compositional spatial relationships and his outsider protagonist.

Independent Production (1956-1958): The Descriptive Phase

Invasion of the Body Snatchers (1956), although recognized as an iconic science fiction film, also contains several noir characteristics such as a flashback frame narrative, voiceover narration, and noir lighting techniques. This film inaugurates Siegel's descriptive phase of development where the parameters of spatial relationships become more defined. During this period the director refines his narrative style and the use of internal and external space becomes more efficient and meaningful with regard to the outcast protagonist. This is the most creative phase of Siegel's career and produces his most significant work.

Dr. Miles Bennell (Kevin McCarthy) becomes an outcast within the film because he does not want to be a part of the "pod society" that has taken over the townspeople of Santa Mira. He and Betty Driscoll (Dana Wynter) resist the emotionless conformity that the pod people represent. Siegel uses internal space to illustrate the incursion of the alien spores within domes-

Opposite and above, *Invasion of the Body Snatchers*.

tic space throughout the film. As in most Siegel films domesticity is transient and unstable. The alien seedpods are introduced into domestic space and create the initial "medical" problem for Dr. Bennell. "Uncle Ira" is no longer Uncle Ira and the traumatic young boy no longer recognizes his mother. The aliens are also physically introduced in domestic settings—the imprint of a "body" on the pool table and the body double of Betty in the basement of her home. External space becomes a means of escape for both Miles and Betty as they attempt to warn others of the eminent invasion. Finally, the womb-like cavern that the fleeing couple seek refuge in spawns the alien "Betty" when she falls asleep and succumbs to the pod society. Siegel utilizes internal and external space throughout the film to show both the "normalcy" of the citizens of Santa Mira, as well as its paranoid other.

The gangster protagonists in *Baby Face Nelson* (1957) and *The Lineup* (1958) are defined by their mobility. The use of external space is dominant in these films where the outcast is literally apart from society. The gangster outsider lives on the road and is dependent on mobility to achieve his aims. Therefore, when the character encounters internal space he becomes unstable and often resorts to violence. Siegel's use of narrative space in these films creates a tension between the characters because of this conflict between mobility and stability.

Lester Gillis, aka "Baby Face" Nelson (Mickey Rooney), and his moll Sue (Carolyn Jones) are an outlaw couple on the run and their few scenes of domesticity are fleeting as they are continually on the move. Nelson is a sociopath with a trigger finger whose outbursts of violence are unexpected. Two scenes in particularly illustrate Siegel's use of internal space to represent instability. The first occurs early in the film when Nelson is waiting for Sue to arrive at his apartment. The police arrive instead and Nelson is fingered for a hit on a labor leader. The closed space of the apartment creates tension, as Nelson realizes that he is the fall guy for racketeer Lou Rocca (Ted de Corsia). Another example of internal space occurs when Nelson kills

Left, Mickey Rooney as the titled figure *Baby Face Nelson*.

Right, *The Lineup*: Dancer (Eli Wallach) has trouble concealing his silenced revolver in a steam room.

Rocca and his associates as they are ascending the stairs to their office. The darkly lit stairway provides compositional tension as, gun in hand, Nelson waits for them. Nelson is depicted as larger than life, a contrast to his diminutive size, as he looms at the head of the stairway and begins shooting. Internal space in the film creates psychological tension based on Nelson's explosive personality.

The most effective use of internal space during this phase of Siegel's career can be seen in *The Lineup*. Three key sequences are directly associated with the quest for smuggled drugs. The first occurs in the steam room of the Seaman's Club, where Dancer (Eli Wallach) shoots the seaman, Warner, once he has revealed the location of the statue containing the heroin. The second use of internal space is when Dancer visits the Sanders mansion to find imported flatware containing the smuggled heroin. Staircases and mirrors fracture the vast inner space within the mansion. This constricted space results in the shooting death of the servant as Dancer becomes more agitated within its confined framework. The final sequence takes place in the Bradshaws' apartment where Dancer and Julian are in pursuit of an Oriental doll containing heroin. The domestic environment where mother and daughter live is soon shattered as Dancer becomes frustrated at not finding the smuggled drugs and traumatizes the girl by tearing the doll apart.

Corporate Studio Years (1964-1973): The Critical Phase

The third phase in Siegel's career marks a return to a corporate-controlled studio system. The films made during this period have larger budgets, are in color, and have more name stars than his independent films. There is also a distinct anti-bureaucratic critique developed in several films, particularly Siegel's police noirs. Likewise, there is a shift from the criminal outcast to law enforcement during the late 1960s. The use of internal and external space during this phase becomes more critical of the status quo, with the antisocial outcast protagonist achieving heroic status in two films: *Dirty Harry* and *Charley Varrick*.

Critics and scholars often concentrate on the two eponymous hit men in *The Killers* (1964), little realizing that the film was originally titled, *Johnny North*. North (John Cassavetes) is the outcast protagonist in the film and the narrative, told in several flashbacks, that relate his eventual demise following an ill-fated armored car robbery. North is murdered early in the film and the killers, Charlie (Lee Marvin) and Lee (Clu Gulager), try to find out why he was so submissive to his own death. The school for the blind where Johnny works as an auto mechanics instructor is a fitting metaphor for his own circumstance—he was blind to the machinations of Sheila Farr (Angie Dickinson) and Browning (Ronald Reagan). The film's use of internal space relates directly to Charlie's and Lee's investigation and to the subsequent flashbacks: the school for the blind, the mechanic's shop, Sheila Farr's apartment, the gym, and Browning's

hideout. External space is applied specifically to Johnny North's character and visualizes his freedom (as a race car driver) and eventual entrapment in the heist scheme. The racetrack scenes, where Johnny displays his prowess to Sheila, and the armored car robbery, where he is effectively emasculated, provide clear examples of Siegel's use of external space in relation to his outsider protagonist.

The urban police noir was developed by Siegel in three films: *Madigan* (1968), *Coogan's Bluff* (1968), and *Dirty Harry* (1971). The primary tension in these films is created by the police detective's individualism clashing with civic bureaucracy (society). In this regard, the detective becomes another example of the antisocial outcast in Siegel's work. Siegel's use of internal/external space within these films is much more pronounced and defined. Simply put the outcast detective works best in external space where he is less inhibited by police bureaucracy. Internal space becomes problematic and is typically associated with the quotidian tasks of police work and bureaucracy itself. Domestic internal space further reveals the lonely existence of the outcast protagonists in these films. For Dan Madigan (Richard Widmark) the domestic space of home life is lonely because of his job and results in a sexually frustrated wife

Below, *Madigan*. Opposite, Dirty Harry Callahan in his prototypical pose.

and an equally frustrated mistress. Walt Coogan is a fish out-of-water as an Arizona sheriff sent to New York to extradite an escaped killer. And Harry Callahan is an iconoclastic throwback to Western justice in a contemporary San Francisco ridden by liberalist laws and ideology. External space in these films reflects their respective crime-infested urban centers where violence is an everyday occurrence. *Dirty Harry* is the most representative example of Siegel's use of external/internal space in relation to the outcast protagonist in his urban police noirs.

Harry Callahan functions as a one-man police force dispensing justice with his .45 Magnum revolver. Called "Dirty Harry" by his colleagues he is continually fighting police headquarters and City Hall bureaucratic practices, even dismissive of the length of his hair. When he is partnered with another detective it typically results in the other's hospitalization. Callahan is also a widower, whose wife was killed by a drunk driver. He is the prototypical antihero/antisocial outcast in Siegel's police films. Callahan thrives in external space where his Hobbesian view of justice is unfettered by liberal laws and legalities. But equally problematic to the film's narrative space is that it contains another antisocial outcast: the serial killer Scorpio. Both Callahan and Scorpio share the external space of San Francisco. The internal space in the film is primarily centered in City Hall and police headquarters where Callahan is confronted by the bureaucratic system and rampant liberalism. Siegel often juxtaposes external space with internal space throughout the film to make evident the antagonism between ideologies. The best example is when Callahan apprehends Scorpio in Kezar Stadium after torturing a confession from him. Immediately following is an imposing wide-angle shot of City Hall where Callahan is made aware that liberal laws will protect the rights of the criminal.

Siegel returns to the criminal outcast with *Charley Varrick* (1973). Varrick (Walter Matthau) is a crop duster-turned-bank robber who resorts to con games in order to survive. When we first see him he is disguised as an elderly man wearing a leg cast. The old age make-up and cast are quickly removed after the ill-fated heist. Other forms of trickery that he uses include switching dental x-rays so that, when the time comes, he will appear to be dead and faking an injury in order to trick the mob's hit man Molly (Joe Don Baker), who has been sent to recover the stolen money. This trickster image can be considered a form of mobility as it allows him freedom to outwit both society and the mob throughout the film. Varrick's mobility in external space is also visualized by his dependence on cars and an airplane. Varrick even lives in a trailer that is itself a mobile environment. Siegel shot the film in Nevada and the open space adds to Varrick's sense of "independence." The climactic confrontation between Molly and Varrick is a masterfully edited chase sequence between car and plane, as Varrick seemingly is attempting to escape. By contrast internal spaces throughout the film are often associated with the mob: the Tres Cruces bank that is robbed is a mob drop; bank president Maynard Boyle (John Vernon) who is in league with the Mafia, has an executive office in a high-rise building; the Mustang Ranch brothel is another mob-owned business; and two locations that Varrick visits in order to obtain a fake passport, Honest John's gun shop and photographer Jewell Everett's (Sheree North) apartment, are mob connected. Early in the film Varrick states that he left crop dusting because it had been taken over by the Combines, in much the same way the Mafia, as a corporate enterprise, has taken over the business of crime. This dichotomy between the independent contractor and big business is visualized by Siegel's use of external and internal space.

Film scholars have struggled with the issue of whether to regard Don Siegel as an "auteur" director or a "Hollywood professional." Barry Keith Grant addressing this issue notes that, "the jury on Siegel has yet to reach a convincing verdict."[7] As the epigram that opened this essay suggests, Siegel himself did not take his work seriously. Yet, through skillful editing and manipulation of his central protagonist, the antisocial outcast within narrative space, a characteristic Siegel style emerges within his noir films. It is a style that depends on a naturalistic environment and characters that conflict or thrive within its oppositional spaces. It is a style that makes any Siegel film both recognizable and entertaining, which was Siegel's aim.

Notes

1. Don Siegel, *A Siegel Film*, London, Faber & Faber, 1993.

2. Raymond Borde and Etienne Chaumeton, *A Panorama of American Film Noir, 1941-1953*, translated by Paul Hammond, San Francisco: City Lights Books, 2002, p. 156.

3. Andrew Sarris, *The American Cinema: Directors and Directions, 1929-1968*, New York: Da Capo Press, 1996, p. 137

4. Alan Lovell, *Don Siegel–American Cinema*, London: BFI Publications, 1975, p 13.

5. Ibid, p. 14.

6. This use of narrative space should not be confused with Neo-formalist approaches as defined by David Bordwell in *Narration in the Fiction Film* (Madison: University of Wisconsin Press, 1985) or Stephen Heath's "Narrative Space," first published in *Screen* (Autumn 1976) 17: 19-75. I am less interested in the formal qualities of space, between viewer and subject, than I am with the psychological/emotional relationship the central character has with space itself.

7. Barry Keith Grant, *Invasion of the Body Snatchers*, London: BFI Palgrave Macmillan, 2010, p. 44.

Biography

Donald Siegel was born on October 26, 1912 in Chicago. Siegel worked briefly as a stage actor following training at the Royal Academy of Dramatic Art in Cambridge, England. Upon moving to Hollywood Siegel began working for Warner Bros. in 1933, initially as a film librarian, then as an assistant editor, and an assistant in the inserts department. Siegel became the editor and head of the newly formed montage department at Warner Bros. in 1938. There he directed and edited the time-transition sequences for such films as *Confessions of a Nazi Spy*, *Yankee Doodle Dandy*, *Action in the North Atlantic*, and *Casablanca*. Siegel was also the second unit director for such films as *Passage to Marseilles*, *Sergeant York*, and *Northern Pursuit*. In 1945 he directed two Academy Award-winning short subjects at Warner Bros., *Star in the Night* and *Hitler Lives*. This allowed him the opportunity to move into feature film direction with *The Verdict* (1946) also at Warner Bros. After a brief stint at RKO and Columbia Siegel became associated with independent producers such as Walter Wanger and Filmmakers, Inc. and distribution companies such as Allied Artists. The 1960s saw his return to a newly structured corporate studio system where he served as a contract director for Universal-MCA. Siegel also began directing for television during the 1960s and directed two episodes of *The Twilight Zone* as well as the first and third made-for-television movies: *The Killers* (1964) (although it was released theatrically when it was deemed too violent for television) and *The Hanged Man* (1964), a remake of Robert Montgomery's noir film, *Ride the Pink Horse*. It was during the last part of that decade that he forged an actor-director relationship with Clint Eastwood on five films: *Coogan's Bluff* (1968), *Two Mules for Sister Sarah* (1969), *The Beguiled* (1971), *Dirty Harry* (1971), and *Escape from Alcatraz* (1980). The commercial success of *Dirty Harry* allowed Siegel to work with larger budgets. In 1976 Siegel directed John Wayne's final film, the elegiac western *The Shootist*. Don Siegel died on April 26, 1991 following a long bout with cancer.

Noir Films

The Verdict (1946)
The Big Steal (1949)
Riot in Cell Block 11 (1954)
Private Hell 36 (1954)
Invasion of the Body Snatchers (1956)
Crime in the Streets (1956)
Baby Face Nelson (1957)
The Lineup (1958)
The Killers (1964)
The Hanged Man (1964)
Madigan (1968)
Dirty Harry (1971)
Charley Varrick (1973)

Siegel with Sydney Greenstreet and Peter Lorre on the set of *The Verdict*.

Above, Robert Siodmak on a lunch break in the Universal Studios commissary.

Robert Siodmak

Todd Erickson

Between 1944 and 1950 Robert Siodmak made eight noir films and two others that would qualify as well were it not for their period settings.[1] His volume of noir is unmatched by any other director during this seven-year span. It was during this time frame that the bulk of the film noir movement's most important titles were produced and although Billy Wilder's *Double Indemnity* (1944) and *Sunset Boulevard* (1950) are the two films cited most frequently as the brackets for this prolific phase of film noir, Siodmak's series of dark dreamscapes are just as compelling and perhaps even more significant.

From *Phantom Lady* (1944) where "Kansas" Richman's relentless stalking of Mac the bartender in the dead of night nearly gets her shoved off the el train platform to *The File on Thelma Jordon* (1950) with Cleve and Thelma's frantic scramble to cover up murder clues inside her dead aunt's home before the caretaker arrives, Siodmak's brand of film noir is known not only for his breathtaking expressionist visual flourishes and suggestively rich mise-en-scène, but also for his ability to create a heightened sense of tension and a visceral connection with the viewer.[2]

Siodmak's noir films performed well at the box office but critical praise for his work wasn't as effusive as one might imagine. However, in 1946 he reached the pinnacle of recognition and success in the motion picture industry with three of his films nominated for Academy Awards. *The Killers* earned four of those nominations with Siodmak getting a nod for best directing:[3] Anthony Veiller for his screenplay, Miklos Rozsa for his score, and Arthur Hilton for editing. *The Dark Mirror* received recognition with Vladimir Pozner's nomination in the original story category and Ethel Barrymore represented *The Spiral Staircase* with a nomination for best supporting actress.

Journey to Noirvana

The seeds of noir began taking root in Robert Siodmak's worldview years before reaching fruition in his American pictures. He had a ringside seat to his parents' unhappy marriage, left home at an early age, and saw firsthand the widespread ravages of World War I on his homeland. His filmmaking skills were developed during the peak of the German Expressionist movement and he was part of the sizeable fraternity of creative talent from Germany's Universum Film AG studio (UFA) that eventually made their way to Hollywood. Some, like him, stayed in France until Hitler's advancing forces made it too dangerous to remain in Europe. It was during his residence in Paris that he became familiar with and assimilated some of the ideas and stylistic traditions of Surrealism and Poetic Realism into his cinematic palette.

Siodmak's exodus from Germany to America is marked with several signpost productions that clearly prefigure the noir films that would define him in Hollywood. *Der Mann, der seiner Mörder sucht* (*Looking for His Murderer*, 1931), co-scripted by Billy Wilder and Siodmak's brother Curt, and later remade by Rudolph Maté as *D.O.A.* (1950), is the story of a man crushed

Phantom Lady

by debt who arranges for his own murder. In the meantime he falls in love and has to race to locate the man he hired to kill him off only to find out that the contract on his life has been sold twice over. In *Stürme der Leidenschaft* (*Storm of Passion*, 1932), Siodmak posited Emil Jannings as a likable gangster who is betrayed by his girlfriend while doing time in prison. After his release he murders her lover, forcing him to hide out from the police. Meanwhile, she betrays him again at the first opportunity. His spirit broken, he concludes that it's better to surrender and return to prison. Siodmak capped off his exile in France with a stylish and moody crime drama titled *Pièges* (1939). Also known as *Personal Column* in English-speaking territories, the story is about the roommate of a serial killer's victim who is hired by police to go undercover and explore strange newspaper ads in search of the madman. She ends up meeting and falling in love with a cabaret singer who is looking for a maid only to see him arrested as the killer.

Leaving France wasn't any easier than leaving Germany was for Siodmak. One can scarcely imagine the utter weariness and isolation he and other Jewish refugees experienced trying to stay a step ahead of the Nazi advance through Europe. Years removed from the danger, Curt Siodmak said the after-affects still lingered: "We refugees suffer from the past, the Hitler persecution, which we will never be able to absorb completely. We were often so close to death that we are branded for life. No success could wipe out the past which we went through."[4]

Perhaps more than any other single influence, it is this chilling perspective coupled with the Expressionist style that German refugee filmmakers like Robert Siodmak brought with them that led to the emergence of the film noir movement in the American cinema in the 1940s.[5] Siodmak arrived in Hollywood attuned to subject matter dealing with obsession, alienation, existentialism, fatalism, and haunted pasts. All he needed was the right material: hard-boiled narratives that explored the dark edges of human experience and the criminal underworld. But first, he had to pay his proverbial dues to the old boys network in Hollywood. In an undated letter to his brother Werner, Siodmak wrote:

> I worked in Germany and France—and I worked there successfully--but I must say, nowhere else in the world is the way to success as hard as here in Hollywood. There are no personal sentimentalities and considerations—it is very tough--if you don't elbow your way through you are left behind."[6]

Siodmak's first six assignments in Hollywood between 1941 and early 1944 were B-movies. Borde and Chaumeton observed that Hollywood producers, "with their customary contempt for European directors...bestowed on Siodmak subjects that were unworthy of him."[7] Nevertheless, he quickly assimilated into the assembly line nature of the studio system's low budget productions, finding a bit of comfort amidst his frustration in the familiar faces of fellow expats who served on his casts or crews including art director Hans Dreier, cinematographer Theodore Sparkuhl, writer Hans Kraly and actors Martin Kosleck and Albert Basserman.

Fly-By-Night

Two of the six pictures from this B-film period demonstrate that Siodmak's noir sensibilities were beginning to ripen. *Fly-By-Night* (Paramount, 1942) featured a wrong-man-on-the-run storyline reminiscent of Hitchcock. The first 15 minutes of the picture are pure noir. The story begins on a stormy night where a man imprisoned in a sanitar-

Above, Dracula (Lon Chaney, Jr.) lands in "the swamplands of the Deep South" in *Son of Dracula*.

ium escapes and commandeers a ride with a young doctor whose car had temporarily broken down while passing through the area. The man claims to have secret information about a substance known as "G-32" which the Nazis are trying to get from him, but when he ends up mysteriously stabbed to death, the doctor has to go on the run and find a way to prove he's innocent of the murder. Although the story meanders from that point and loses its noir bearings, working with cinematographer John Seitz was a brief but valuable artistic exchange for Siodmak; it was the only time the two men would ever collaborate. Seitz's next film was *This Gun for Hire* (1942) at Paramount and he would end up shooting eight more noir films in his career including *Double Indemnity* and *Sunset Boulevard*.

Siodmak directed three more B-pictures during the next year and he co-wrote an original story with Alfred Neumann titled "The Pentacle" which they sold to Warner Bros. for Curtis Bernhardt to direct. Shot in August 1943, Warner Bros. didn't release the film (titled *Conflict*) until June 1945 because of a disagreement with Humphrey Bogart. In the film, Bogart plays

Richard Mason who murders his wife to be with her sister. Sydney Greenstreet plays his psychiatrist friend Dr. Mark Hamilton who solves the crime.

Thanks to his brother Curt's influence following a string of recently successful horror pictures he'd written, Robert landed a single picture deal with Universal to direct *Son of Dracula* (1943) which was based on his brother's story. The simple plot had Count Alucard of Budapest (Lon Chaney, Jr.) visiting the swamplands of the Deep South in search of his eternal love at the Dark Oaks plantation. It was the first time a Dracula movie made by Universal had been given a setting in America and Siodmak made the most of the love-death imagery, serving up a visual feast that was infused with a rich Gothic horror atmosphere and special bat transition effects, topped off with a fiery finale that William K. Everson referred to as "one of the bleakest endings to any horror film."[8] Universal's in-house producer Ford Beebe was so pleased with Siodmak's work just days after filming had commenced that the studio offered him a seven-year contract. This led to his first A-picture, the campy Technicolor production of *Cobra Woman* (1944) starring Maria Montez. Two months after wrapping production on *Cobra Woman*, Siodmak met with Joan Harrison, Universal's first female executive and a former screenwriter for Alfred Hitchcock (*Foreign Correspondent*, *Suspicion*, *Saboteur*) and came away with the assignment to direct *Phantom Lady* based on the Cornell Woolrich novel.

Reading Siodmak in Black and White

In Woolrich's novel, Siodmak finally had his hands on rich source material, plentiful in detailed character descriptions and heavy in atmosphere that defined the milieu of midtown Manhattan. And Harrison proved to be the perfect complement as his producer. Having worked closely with Hitchcock, she took a levelheaded approach toward nurturing talent and respected a director's vision and claim to screen authorship. The story is about civil engineer Scott Henderson (Alan Curtis) who is convicted of murdering his wife and the quest by "Kansas" Richman, his executive assistant, to prove his innocence. Henderson's only alibi is the titular "phantom lady" whom he shared his tickets with to a musical revue after meeting her in a bar one night following an argument with his wife. The one detail Henderson remembers about his anonymous date (Fay Helm) was that she was wearing an ornate hat identical to the one worn by the musical's headliner, Estela Monteiro (Aurora Miranda).

The production took place in September and October of 1943 and marked the beginning of a successful relationship Siodmak would enjoy with cinematographer Woody Bredell on two other noir films, *Christmas Holiday* (1944) and *The Killers* (1946). Their collaboration on *Phantom Lady* established a visual standard that many contemporaries would soon try to duplicate with its unambiguous portrayal of a haunting, gloomy cityscape drenched in paranoia, self-absorption, and the eerie haze of a sweltering heat wave in the air. Two sequences from the film, each focusing on Kansas and her quest to vindicate Henderson, are prime examples of the expressionist approach Siodmak brought to fruition in the American cinema. In both sequences, he combines the complete range of aesthetic elements in his palette to seamlessly create a pitch-perfect mixture of tension, suspense, and psychological intrigue. By depicting Kansas as a type of doppelgänger, Siodmak imbues her with a mysterious affect that tinges her relentless determination to exact confessions from Mac the bartender (Andrew Tombes) and Cliff the trap drummer (Elisha Cook, Jr.). The result is an eerily haunting vibe that presages the deaths of Mac, Cliff and Henderson's "best friend," the deranged sculptor Jack Marlow (Franchot Tone).

After learning that Henderson's legal options have been exhausted, Kansas commences tracking down witnesses she suspects were bribed. This is the precise moment in the picture where Siodmak begins to amplify the viewer's identification with her through expressive detail. The first shot we see of Kansas in her quest is a reflection in the mirror of Anselmo's Bar

and Grille as the camera tracks down the counter to find her taking a seat. At first glance, Kansas bears a strong resemblance to the "phantom lady" with her dark hair pulled back close to her head, her delicate facial features and piercing eyes, sans the flashy hat. Mac takes her order and then Siodmak confirms our initial instinct that the two women look similar by emphasizing Mac, his pate glistening with beads of sweat, double-take a troubled look at Kansas as he mixes her drink. Siodmak ensures that we read Mac's concern correctly by emphasizing another troubled expression that he makes as he walks to the other end of the counter.[9]

The following night Kansas takes the same seat at the bar, her intense gaze cutting through the hubbub of a noisy, packed house. Again, we see her reflection in the mirror behind the counter—one of Siodmak's pet trademarks to connote the inner struggle or dual nature of a character's personality. Mac nervously drops a glass and a bottle of liquor he is pouring. The third night it's closing time and the bar is empty except for Kansas seated in the same place, Anselmo and a buddy who are leaving, and a visibly shaken Mac who says, "Boss, she's been staring at me all night, like last night and the night before." And then to Kansas, "We're closing up, Miss." She doesn't move or say a word. Mac ducks behind a jut in the wall and grabs his hat and coat. He pauses behind the wall, hoping she'll leave, and repeats himself: "We're closing up, Miss." He listens for a response. Nothing. He gathers his courage and steps out from behind the wall, but Kansas is gone, leaving a powerful sense of tension and suspense lingering on the screen.

After locking up for the night, Mac cautiously makes his way down the wet sidewalk. Siodmak uses extreme camera angles and sound effects to increase anxiety in the viewer, such as their shoes on the pavement and the whir of passing el trains as Kansas follows him up to the train platform. The El platform is lit in pools of light that Mac passes in and out of as he walks to the far end, signifying the battle raging in his soul. A reverse shot shows Kansas standing alone at the other end. Mac walks back and stands directly behind her. We hear a train clattering closer and closer to the platform and we read in Mac's body language and facial expressions that he is contemplating pushing Kansas to her death. He moves a step closer. Kansas hears the creak of his body weight shifting and strains to see out of the corner of her eye. The train can be heard racing closer and then just as Mac steps forward to shove Kansas onto the tracks we hear the click of a turnstile token, -and startled, -he halts his murderous thrust, turning quickly to see a nicely dressed middle-aged woman enter the platform.

After the train unloads at 23rd Street, Kansas resumes shadowing Mac down several empty streets until he turns around and confronts her. Two male onlookers jump to her defense but she tells them to back off. Mac lunges for Kansas when she demands to know who bribed him but the men leap forward to protect her. He wriggles free and bolts into the street only to be hit by a passing vehicle.

Kansas' stalking turns to seduction and she poses as an easy target for Cliff with a front row seat at the musical revue. Dressed like a hooker with heavy makeup and fishnet stockings, she calls herself "Jeanie" and claims she's a "hep kitten." After the show, they descend from street level down a crooked concrete stairway and into a jazz den where Cliff's musician friends are in the throes of a jam session. He weaves Kansas through the band to a chair by his drum

Counter-clockwise from top left opposite, *Phantom Lady*: "Kansas" Richman (Ella Raines) flees down the stairway of Cliff's apartment building after he tries to assault her.

Mac the bartender (Andrew Tombes) struggles to remember where he's seen his new patron before; "Kansas" stalks Mac the bartender after he leaves work. Mac contemplates shoving "Kansas" off the platform at the Elevated train station

Crazed murderer Jack Marlow (Franchot Tone) fights off a seizure in his art studio/ apartment. The distorted sculpture he created signifies the turmoil raging inside his mind.

kit; the overtly sexual nature of the music is manifested by the trombonist and the clarinetist thrusting their instruments toward her in rhythmic displays of phallic energy. Kansas pours him a drink and he kisses her aggressively. Trying to mask her revulsion, she quickly wipes her mouth and reapplies her lipstick using a mirror on the wall. Her disgust is evident in her reflection but she's determined to get the information she needs and the scene concludes with unconventional frantic intercutting between high angle shots of Cliff banging away on a drum between his legs and low angle clips of Kansas' taunting body language that excites him to a metaphorical climax. He tosses his drumsticks aside and whisks her out of the jam session to his apartment. Ultimately, the noir-laden irony of Kansas' successful quest to find the phantom lady and free her boss from death row is the body count of three dead men left in the wake of her nightmarish journey through the malignant New York cityscape.

Siodmak's next picture, *Christmas Holiday* (1944), came to him through executive producer Felix Jackson, a fellow German émigré who was previously a composer, playwright and drama critic in Berlin. He also happened to be married at the time to leading lady Deanna Durbin. Based on a brilliant screenplay that Herman J. Mankiewicz adapted from the W. Somerset Maugham novel, both Gene Kelly and Durbin were cast against type—two dysfunctional young lovers who end up as convicted murderer and prostitute, respectively. The essence of the story is told in fragmented flashbacks by Jackie Lamont (Durbin)—as a confession of sorts--to newly commissioned Army Lt. Charles Mason (Dean Harens) who is waylaid in New Orleans by a storm while trying to get home to California on his Christmas holiday break. Lamont, who changed her name from Abigail Manette after her husband Robert Manette (Kelly) went to prison for murdering a bookie, has banished herself to an upscale brothel in an act of self-persecution, rather than live with her creepy mother-in-law. On the second day of Lt. Mason's holdover, Manette breaks out of prison and hunts Jackie down at the brothel, but he is shot by a police officer before he can kill her.

Christmas Holiday is drenched in atmosphere and heavily stylized with Siodmak's Germanic sensibility. He masterfully contrasts the vibe of a war-weary nation through the character of Lt. Mason and his reality against the cloistered life of the Manette home revealed

Christmas Holiday

through Jackie's flashbacks. Siodmak's expert eye for depth staging and character choreography packs each frame with verisimilitude, and his use of music is nothing short of masterful.[10] Durbin (as Jackie) doesn't appear until eleven-and-a-half minutes into the movie, after we've learned that Mason has been commissioned an officer, jilted by his fiancée, forced to land in New Orleans, and steered to the Maison Lafitte by a slimy press agent named Simon Fenimore (Richard Whorf). It's Christmas Eve, but there's no semblance of holiday cheer in this depressing alternate reality. Accompanied by a jazz sextet, Jackie sings a bluesy version of "Spring Will Be a Little Late This Year" while Siodmak's staging and Woody Bredell's deep focus divulge the flow of activity around her; couples dancing and client tables being waited on in the foreground with other customers ascending a staircase in the background.

Shortly after being introduced to Lt. Mason, Jackie persuades him to take her to the St. Louis Cathedral's midnight Mass. The scene is memorable for the authentic depiction of the religious service, Jackie's remorseful weeping as the boys' choir sings "Adeste Fidelis," and Mason's self-consciousness as curious onlookers stare when she crumples to the floor. It's the turning point at the end of the first act and a perfect transition to her confessional that unfolds in flashback at the diner where they go to grab a bite to eat.

Jackie's story, which comprises the entire second act, is packed with material Siodmak thrived on in his noir films: a fractured family setting, triangulated relationships, obsession, and criminal psychology. In one scene the morning after Robert has murdered his bookie, she finds stains on his trousers and Mrs. Manette (Gale Sondergaard) snatches them from her and discovers a wad of cash in the pocket. Robert demands the

Jackie (Deanna Durbin) is overcome with grief and weeps uncontrollably at the feet of Lieutenant Charles Mason in New Orleans' St. Louis Cathedral on Christmas Eve.

Robert Manette (Gene Kelly) struggles with his mother (Gale Sondergaard) over a wad of cash she found in his pants.

money and there's an uncomfortable but rather obvious Oedipal moment where he angrily embraces his mother in an intimate manner. Siodmak cuts to a reaction shot of a startled Abigail (Jackie's real name), and then back to Robert who is embarrassed with the awkwardness of the revelation. If that isn't subtle enough, Jackie's voiceover later reveals that "when it was all over, a psychoanalyst said that Robert's relations with his mother were pathological ... he wasn't just her son, he was her everything."

Through the flashbacks we learn that Mrs. Manette proposed to Jackie, not Robert, and that he was a compulsive liar and gambler, easy to anger, and violent. Immediately after his mother's marriage proposal, he takes Abigail to a seedy bar that he frequented, promising it was the last time he'd ever go there. Here we see his relationship to Simon Fenimore and Teddy Jordan, the bookie, and he says, "Well, now you've seen the worst. This is the den of iniquity I used to spend so much time in." And yet, after he breaks out of prison and traces Abigail/Jackie to her own chosen den of iniquity—the Maison Lafitte—Robert informs Fenimore that he's got a gun and he's going to "straighten out" his family life.

Siodmak uses music to punctuate the conclusion of the most poetic of his noir films. Having established in flashback that the song "Always" was special to Abigail and Robert, he shows Jackie singing a mournful rendition of the tune before Fenimore signals to her. Waiting

Jackie/Abigail (Deanna Durbin) tries to convince her husband, Robert Manette (Gene Kelly) that she's only worked at the Maisson Lafitte as a matter of self-persecution since his imprisonment.

in Bredell's carefully crafted shadows in one of the brothel's side rooms, Robert confronts Abigail about her infidelity with the intent to be her executioner. Instead, he takes a bullet from the gun of an alert policeman patrolling outside the window and dies in her arms. Lt. Mason, who has become Jackie's de facto confessor, tells her, "You can let go now, *Abigail*." "Liebestod" from Richard Wagner's *Tristan and Isolde* cues in—the same fateful track that played in her flashback when they first met at the symphony—and she sets Robert's head down and rises as if summoned by an otherworldly power. Abigail walks to the window and gazes at the clouds parting in the starlit night sky, and suddenly, there's a glimmer of hope that the storm raging in her own soul can be quelled.

Siodmak reunited with producer Joan Harrison in the summer of 1945 to make *The Strange Affair of Uncle Harry* starring George Sanders, Geraldine Fitzgerald, and Ella Raines. It was his third consecutive picture with Raines and second with cinematographer Paul Ivano and editor Arthur Hilton following *The Suspect* (1944), and it was his third noir film made with H.J. Salter helming the music. Eugène Lourié, an old friend from Siodmak's stint in France, served as co-art director. Based on the play "Uncle Harry" by Thomas Job, the story is pregnant with irony, and dark family secrets that are subtly exposed scene by scene. It's an impressive film that lingers with you long after viewing it, but one can only imagine how much more powerful this film might have been if the original story structure Siodmak mapped out with screenwriter Stephen Longstreet had been approved by the Production Code Administration

Clockwise from above: Harry Quincy (George Sanders) contemplates murdering his sister Lettie with the poison she used to kill the family dog. Lettie Quincy (Geraldine Fitzgerald) is stunned to learn that Harry is going to frame her for the murder of their older sister, Hester. Lettie walks down the prison corridor to her execution after rejecting Harry's attempt to free her. Siodmak's close-up of Lettie confronting Harry in the prison warden's office before her execution is reminiscent of close-ups of Brigitte Helm in German Expressionist films like Fritz Lang's *Metropolis*.

(PCA).[11]

The film's opening title music is suitably melodramatic, playing over a compelling art deco title design, and leaving little doubt about the tone of the story about to unfold. However, in direct contrast, the opening shots are bright, daylight views with a travelog-like voiceover narration: "This is the Warren Mill. Most of the town works here. Now, don't let it frighten you, even if it does look like a prison. Harry Quincy works here from nine to five. Day in – day out." Harry Melville Quincy is introduced to us in his work setting and as mundane as it appears we soon learn it's preferable to the virtual prison he calls home. Deborah (Ella Raines), the company's New York fashion expert, is also introduced in this scene while on a tour of the mill with John Warren and she shares an immediate attraction with Harry. He arrives home from work that afternoon to his sister Hester's (Moyna MacGill) greeting, "You're late, Harry." Quoting Robert Frost, he responds, "As the poet said, 'Home is where you go and they have to let you in.'" This type of banter is par for the course in the Quincy home, but it's much more venomous and discordant between middle-aged Hester and Harry's attractive younger sister Lettie (Fitzgerald), who remarks at the dinner table, "It's like turning off a radio when Hester stops talking." Ratcheting the chatter factor even higher in the household is the Irish housemaid Nona (Sara Allgood) who's been around the family long enough to chime in with her two cents whenever she pleases.

Most of the film takes place in the Quincy home which has the ambience of an old funeral home with its stodgy Victorian era furniture, veiled stained glass windows, patterned wallpapers, and Siodmak's requisite touch of mirrors, stairways, ornate banisters, and assorted middle class furnishings. There are two stairways that dominate the home's floor plan. One leads to the second floor and Lettie's bedroom and the other is a wide five-step approach leading to what Hester describes as a "green, dark den" where her "spoiled, selfish" sister "sits among those horrible plants and reads poetry."

Siodmak establishes the triangular conundrum that will lead to Harry's murderous impulse through first-rate performances, costume design and skillful editing. He reveals Harry as a likable and diplomatic fellow attracted to Deborah but encumbered with his possessive and conniving younger sister. Having already established Lettie's jealousy for Deborah, a woman she's heard about but never met, Siodmak escalates the enmity in their first scene together when Deborah, attired in a chic modern-tailored suit and her hair in a casual, side-

Uncle Harry

parted contemporary look, visits the Quincy home. Alone in the spacious family room together after manipulating both Harry and Hester to fetch items for their guest, Lettie, wearing a strict looking yesteryear outfit with her hair in a dated, uptight style, asks Deborah to leave her hands off Harry's old dog, Weary. Deborah rejects the request and scratches the dog's head. Lettie then lectures Deborah about what's best for Harry and the family name in the community, asking her to reject Harry's visits to her hotel. Deborah stands her ground and replies "If Harry wishes to stop by my hotel at any time, I'll always be glad to see him." Siodmak juxtaposes Lettie's icy stare at the close of that scene with Harry burying Weary in the backyard.

Later, Harry stumbles across the poison Lettie used to kill Weary and retires to his art studio to contemplate murder. Dissolving into Harry's dream, Siodmak takes us along for a ride that ends up with Hester mistakenly killed by the tainted hot cocoa Harry intended for Lettie, and Lettie convicted of her sister's murder. Wracked with grief for the wrong he's unleashed on his sisters, he tries to persuade the prison warden that Lettie is innocent, but she rejects his attempt to rescue her from the gallows, declaring, "I died months ago." Then, in a sharp focus, close-up shot that's reminiscent of the aloof gaze Brigitte Helm displays as "Maria" in Fritz Lang's 1925 expressionistic masterpiece, *Metropolis*, Lettie foretells Harry's condemnation, "You'll not be good company for yourself all the long years that stretch ahead, when you can't think, or sleep, or eat, or read. Poor Harry." The most chilling noir shot in the film comes just moments later as we see Lettie, dwarfed by a much larger prison matron following her, walking away from the camera down a long, dreary concrete columned hall with barred window pattern shadows angled across the walls and the floor. The shot stirs a feeling of horror at the prospect of Lettie being hanged for a crime she didn't commit and there is a sense of relief when it dissolves to Harry awakening from the nightmare. In a fitting off-screen finale to an otherwise laudable film, producer Joan Harrison joined Siodmak and Geraldine Fitzgerald in their refusal to shoot the ending dictated by the PCA that undercut the original script's piercing psychological and emotional payoff.

The Killers is Siodmak's tour de force and one of the most quintessential

Hit men Max (William Conrad) and Al (Charles McGraw) approach and intimidate George (Harry Hayden) in Henry's Diner as they await the arrival of their target.

noir films in the original cycle. From the very first strains of Miklos Rozsa's emphatic overture, Siodmak stakes his claim on the definitive and proceeds to cover a wide range of noir themes including fatalism, obsession, alienation, nihilism, existentialism, futility, and greed. Faithful to the source material that independent producer Mark Hellinger bought and set up at Universal, the first 13 minutes of screen time depicts Ernest Hemingway's same-titled short story in heart-pounding fashion. Two hit men (William Conrad and Charles McGraw) visit a small New Jersey town at night, terrorize a local diner for information, and execute a former boxer turned criminal known as Swede (Burt Lancaster) in his boarding room. From there, the screenplay by Anthony Veiller (with significant contribution from John Huston who couldn't take the credit while under contract to Warner Bros.) follows an obsessed insurance investigator named Reardon (Edmond O'Brien) who finds out there's more to the mysterious killing than the victim's $2,500 life insurance policy benefiting a hotel maid in Atlantic City. He discovers that Swede was part of a gang that robbed a hat factory insured by his firm, and that he was the stooge in a double-double-cross pulled off by Kitty (Ava Gardner), the moll of gang leader Big Jim Colfax (Albert Dekker).

Reardon's investigation unfolds through a fragmented yet riveting narrative structure that emphasizes the past, relying on eleven flashbacks voiced by eight different characters. The trail he follows—in person or via the flashbacks—leads us through a laundry list of archetypal noir locations including a morgue, a boxing arena, seedy hotels, tenement housing, a pool hall, a prison cell, night clubs, the prison ward of a hospital, and of course, lonely, threatening city streets at night. The film is drenched in cynicism and irony. Swede is a fighter but he gives up. A gang member named "Dum-Dum" kills Colfax, the "brains" of the gang. The safest location it seems is the prison cell that Swede and a past-his-prime con named Charleston share. Life insurance man Reardon brings about the deaths of five men during the course of his investigation with the net result of reducing his company's policy rates by one-tenth of one percent. Even the Brentwood sheriff claims that Swede's murder is of "no concern to him at all," that his only concern is protecting the lives and property of Brentwood's citizens, despite the fact Swede lived and worked in the town.

Brutal violence punctuates *The Killers* from start to finish. The two hit men fling open the door to Swede's room in the boarding house and blast away at him mercilessly with their .38 caliber handguns. Later, Plufner, the coroner, describes his findings to Reardon in the morgue, "Got eight slugs in 'em. Near tore 'em in half." When Reardon's boss, Kenyon, reads the news article about the "sensational robbery" of the Prentiss Hat Company, Siodmak reveals the entire heist from an omniscient point of view in a continuous two-minute crane shot. The scene culminates in a gun battle outside the plant's front gate where one of the security guards doubles over and falls to the ground "with a bullet in his groin." As Reardon advances deeper into the investigation he starts packing a gun and risking his own life. He sets a trap for Dum-Dum in the room where Swede was murdered only to fall for the old "mind if I have a cigarette" trick and gets the side of his skull kicked in before the police backups arrive. After Reardon finally makes a connection with Kitty, they head to the Green Cat to talk. Max and Al, the two hit men, tail Kitty to the nightclub to knock off Reardon, but Lubinsky of the Philadelphia police department is there in wait and guns them down. The film climaxes inside Colfax and Kitty's opulent mansion where Dum-Dum tumbles down the grand staircase after being shot by Big Jim, who lies dying on the upper stairway landing surrounded by Reardon, Lubinsky and Kitty. She pleads with him to absolve her, "Jim! Tell them I didn't know those gunmen were coming. Say, 'Kitty is innocent.' Say, 'I swear Kitty is innocent!'" To which Lubinsky reacts, "Don't ask a dyin' man to lie his soul into hell."

Siodmak makes the most of Ava Gardner's brief time on screen as a figurative Medusa.[12] Her first appearance is in flashback from the viewpoint of the understandably jealous Lily when she was Swede's old flame. At a party hosted by Jake "The Rake" in Colfax's Philadelphia penthouse, Swede is captivated by Kitty from the instant he sees her. It's a hyper-realized moment where the punch-drunk fool can't take his eyes off her. The conversation turns to Swede's boxing and Lily proudly states that she's seen all of his fights. "How wonderful of you," Kitty coos condescendingly. "I could never bear to see a man I really cared for being hurt." The fact that we already know her hands are stained with Swede's blood is the essence of film noir. It's a dark, dreamlike vortex we willingly get sucked into because we have to know the "why?"

The Killers was the last motion picture Siodmak made with Woody Bredell but the collection of cinematic images they left behind from their trio of collaborations will forever define the noir look. Three scenes in particular typify the ominous yet alluring nature of the final story they told together: The silhouettes of two figures (under the opening credits) walking slowly down a lonely small town street at night. They look in the window of a small gas station office that is closed, and then turn so we briefly see the pudgy, mustachioed face of William Conrad (Max) and the chiseled jawline of Charles McGraw (Al) before they become silhouettes again, walking toward Henry's Diner. Following Swede's last fight, the camera tracks with him and Sam Lubinsky walking down a Philadelphia city street past the closed shops and one-way alley entrances. They talk about his future and Sam extols the police department's

Opposite, top and center, the stylized and brutal sequence of the Swede's murder. Bottom, Ava Gardner's figurative Medusa captivates Burt Lancaster's Swede.

pension benefits of "twenty-two hundred a year to start." Swede stops sharply and retorts, "You know somethin'? Some months I made that much in one month." He turns away and walks down an alleyway where the overhead construction scaffolding makes it look like he's walking into a small tunnel. The end of the alleyway is bathed in light creating a silhouette effect on Swede and casting his shadow against the alley wall. It's the final shot of Swede as an honest man, foreshadowing the fatal choices he'll soon make. The third example captures Reardon staking out the boarding room where Swede was murdered. He knows Dum-Dum is coming to look for the gang's stolen loot. The room is patterned with early evening shadows. A tapestry blanket hangs on the wall above Swede's bed (where a shelf with a radio had previously been in the murder scene) to cover the bullet holes in the wall. Reardon hears the landlady talking to Dum-Dum downstairs and he moves into the adjacent room. The suspense builds as we hear the gangster tearing the room apart just before Reardon decides to make his move. The room is markedly darker, the shadows more prominent. The cat and mouse game of extracting information from each other ends with Dum-Dum turning the tables on Reardon, leaving him unconscious and bleeding on the floor.

If it wasn't already apparent to movie critics and filmgoers that Robert Siodmak was drawn to exploring the human psyche in his pictures, *The Dark Mirror* (1946)[13] made it perfectly clear. Based on a story by Vladimir Pozner and screenplay by producer Nunnally Johnson,

Center, Jim Riordan (Edmond O'Brien) shakes down "Dum-Dum" Clarke (Jack Lambert) in the boarding house bedroom where the Swede was murdered.

Bottom, Lt. Lubinsky (Sam Levene) and Riordan flank Kitty Collins as she tries to extract a false confession from her dying husband "Big Jim" Colfax (Albert Dekker).

the film is a psychological study of identical twin sisters Terry and Ruth Collins (both played by Olivia de Havilland) who confound and frustrate Detective Stevenson (Thomas Mitchell) from solving a murder he's convinced one of them committed. The story sets up nicely with Terry and Ruth covering for each other (we learn they share a job under Terry's name so they can take turns having time off) and casual acquaintances that find out they didn't know there was two of them. Dr. Scott Elliott (Lew Ayres) happens to be one of those acquaintances that thought he knew "Terry" from his frequent lemon drop purchases at the medical plaza magazine stand where "she" worked, and he's astonished to find out that Terry has an identical twin when he's summoned to an inquiry at the district attorney's office. When Stevenson learns that Dr. Elliott is a specialist in behavioral genetics and the study of twins, he enlists his help to figure out which of the twins is guilty.

Siodmak's direction and de Havilland's performance are quite impressive, considering both Collins characters had to be filmed separately for the scenes where they would appear on the screen together. Complicating the production even further, Siodmak and de Havilland were at odds from the start regarding how the story should be told. He saw it as a psychological thriller and she saw it as a character study of paranoid-schizophrenia.[14] Fortunately, Siodmak prevailed. His fascination with the good sister/bad sister scenario was already evident in *Cobra Woman* (1944) and *The Strange Affair of Uncle Harry* (1945), and a story featuring identical twins provided the perfect opportunity to further explore the doppelgänger motif that he'd been intrigued with since Fritz Lang's *Metropolis* (1927). Working with cinematographer Milton Krasner (who shot Lang's *Woman in the Window* and *Scarlet Street*), Siodmak also hired Eugen Schüfftan, an old colleague from UFA, to assist with the visual effects.[15] There are more

Clockwise from below left, *The Dark Mirror*: Ruth Collins (Olivia de Havilland) reacts to another cruel provocation by her scheming sister. Terry, shown in mirror reflection in bed, questions her sister Ruth. Lieutenant Stevenson (Thomas Mitchell) conducts a line-up with Terry and Ruth. Terry Collins, standing in the shadow, tries to provoke her sister Ruth, seated on the bed.

than three-dozen shots in the film where mirrors are present; some are for ambience, but most are used to convey the discord between the inner states of the twins while emphasizing their physical likeness.

The two most prominent mirrors seen in the film serve as visual bookends for the story. In the opening scene, Siodmak uses a long, probing camera maneuver through two rooms of an apartment to establish that it's 10:48 p.m. at night in a city where a struggle has taken place and a man has been stabbed in the back with a pair of scissors. We also note that a large mirror over the fireplace has sustained a sizable spider web-shaped crack during the struggle. This image foreshadows the complete shattering of a mirror by Terry at the climax of the movie when, tricked by Stevenson into believing that her sister has committed suicide, she is finally caught in her web of lies. She becomes emboldened in her claim that she's actually Ruth and tells the detective how "Terry" really hated her because men always found it easiest to like her (Ruth). This is a reverse on the typical transference pattern of a doppelgänger (where evil is transferred to the good person, rather than the evil person claiming a transference of good attributes from their double). Dr. Elliott's comment in the end supports this phenomenon when he tells Ruth, "That's what twins are you know, reflections of each other, everything in reverse."

At first, one questions why the good sister Ruth is willing to play along and cover for Terry, especially when she is the victim of Terry's cruel mind games that nearly push her to the brink of insanity. Gradually, though, it becomes apparent that the more she sees of Terry's dark side, the more she might be reluctant to inform on her, fearful that what she sees in

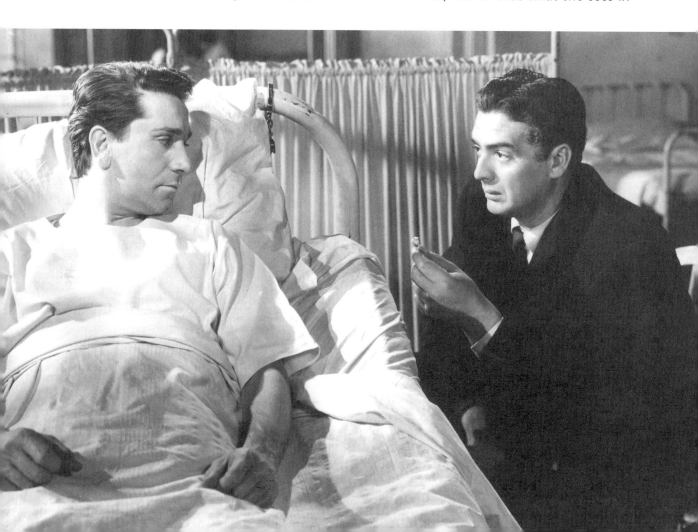

Terry – the potential to do evil, even murder – may very well dwell inside her, too. There's also the notion that Terry is like a mother to her (as the evil twin reminds her several times) and how could she ever betray her mother? Siodmak's chiaroscuro is conspicuously restrained in this picture and aside from the opening scene, the only moments where he nuances the light and shadow is in the twins' bedroom. This, of course, is symbolic of the battleground Terry has created with Ruth and the perceived rivalry over the men in their lives. In the denouement, Stevenson tells Dr. Elliott that he decided to trick Terry because he was fearful for Ruth's safety. "Even a nut can figure out that it's simpler to get rid of a rival than to go on knocking off her boyfriends all the rest of her life."

Cry of the City (1948) reunited Siodmak with producer Sol Siegel with whom he made three Paramount B-films shortly after settling down in Hollywood in the early 1940s, and it was also the first Siodmak film noir to shoot extensively on location. Based on the novel *The Chair for Martin Rome* by Henry Edward Helspeth, the plot borrows from a familiar story device of its time, pitting two men that grew up in the same neighborhood as kids against each other in their adulthood. We saw this in *The Killers* with Sam Lubinsky, who became a cop, and Swede, who turned to crime, although that relationship wasn't the dramatic driver in the story and it played out rather passively because it was revealed in flashback rather than in linear narrative.[16]

Working from Richard Murphy's screenplay,[17] Siodmak introduces in the first three minutes the three main characters that form a triangulated relationship and propel the story toward its conclusion. He opens the movie with a priest administering last rites at the hospital bedside of smalltime crook Martin Rome (Richard Conte) who was wounded in a restaurant robbery shootout with a police officer that he claims to have killed in self-defense. His nemesis Lt. Candella (Victor Mature) and sidekick (Fred Collins) cause a bit of a stir at the entrance to the room as they try to pump a nurse for information. After Candella's family and the two detectives exit the room, Rome's young girlfriend Teena (Debra Paget) quietly slips in from a back entrance, accompanied by Alfred Newman's sympathetic theme for

Cry of the City: opposite, longtime friend of the Rome family, Lieutenant Candella (Victor Mature), visits Martin Rome (Richard Conte) in the hospital. Below, Candella (foreground) shoots Rome in the back on the street outside the local cathedral, Bottom, in the family apartment with Mama Rome (Mimi Aguglia) looking on, Rome holds Candela at gunpoint.

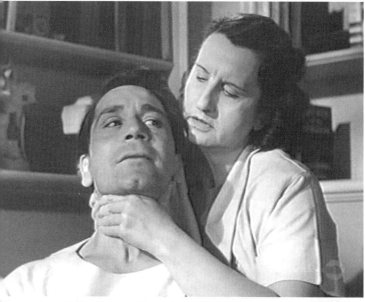

Top, the masseuse by day/murderous thief by night Rose Given (Hope Emerson) puts a choke hold on Martin Rome demanding the jewels from the de Grazia case. After his daring escape from jail, Rome shakes down criminal attorney W.A. Niles (Barry Kroeger).

her character. She serves as a Madonna figure and stimulates his conscience ("Oh Marty, why did you have to shoot? Why did you kill?"). When a nurse casually mentions to Candella that she saw Rome's "wife" in his room, the detective is hell bent on finding her because a sleazy lawyer named Niles (Barry Kroeger) is trying to pin a jewelry theft/murder (called "the de Grazia case") on Rome and a key piece of evidence points to a woman being involved in that crime.

Siodmak builds the tension from that point, revealing the foul characters that inhabit the dark side of Rome's life and the violence required to survive among them. Niles pays a visit to Rome at the hospital, and circling his bed like a ravenous hyena, offers ten grand to take the blame for the de Grazia Crime ("Be practical, my friend, you're going to the chair anyway.") Rome repels the offer, but Niles probes harder and mentions his girlfriend. Siodmak's camera gradually closes in tighter, and cutting between the two men, he emphasizes Niles' superior perspective with high angle shots of Rome, including one from Niles' perspective standing behind Rome's hospital bed looking down at him ("She must be beautiful, Marty...but if we worked on her for a couple of days...maybe she wouldn't look the same. Maybe even you wouldn't recognize her.") The scene ends with Rome trying to choke Niles from his bed. After escaping the city jail hospital ward, Rome heads straight for Niles' office. Wielding a switchblade, this time he's the aggressor and Siodmak shoots Rome's perspective of Niles seated at his desk with high angle shots. Rome finds the de Grazia jewels in his safe and squeezes Niles for the name of the woman involved in the crime–Rose Given. The scene climaxes with Niles making a play for his gun and Rome knifing him through the back of his chair. Rome stuffs the jewels in his coat pocket and Siodmak crafts a macabre ending to the scene with the sound of Niles plopping on the floor followed by an odd repetitious sound. The camera pans and tilts to show Niles' desk chair spinning around, with Niles sprawled on the floor behind it, and then we notice the puncture mark of Rome's knife that tore through the back of the chair.

With Niles out of the way, Rome has to dodge the police dragnet, get unlicensed medical treatment and find Rose Given (Hope Emerson). The night scene of Rome on the doorstep of her massage parlor is a masterpiece of Siodmak's staging and cinematographer Lloyd Ahern's deep focus and lighting. Shooting over Rome's shoulder through the glass window of Given's front door, we see Given open the door of a back room, and then advance toward the camera, turning on the light in each of the three rooms she passes through, growing increasingly larger until she opens the door and fills half the frame. Once inside, Rome cuts a deal with her for the de Grazia jewels: a car, $5,000 and safe passage to South America. Siodmak's direction reveals Given to be yet another of the city's deadliest creatures. She massages his back and shoulders and talks about her clientele of "fat, old women who have too much money and too many jewels." Her hands gradually move up his shoulders and around his neck like the coils of a python until she has him in a choke hold and demands the jewels for his life. It's the most frightening moment in the film because Candella's earlier description to Rome of how the elderly de Grazia woman was tortured to find the whereabouts of her jewels becomes clear. That Rome manages to evade these predators and Candella is a testament to his streetwise resourcefulness. Siodmak brings the story full circle with Rome seeking refuge at his neighborhood cathedral in a rendezvous with his mythical Madonna. But following a tip, Candella finally catches up with his quarry, just in time to warn and counsel Teena, ("If he really loved you, would he ask you to share the kind of life he's got to live?") She understands her future with Rome is a dead end, crosses herself, and slips away. He must now pay for his transgressions, and the obsessive Candella does the honors, commanding, "In the name of the law, Rome, stop!" before pulling his trigger. Rome's end is fittingly noir. Before taking Candella's bullet in the back, Siodmak shows him trudging down the wet city pavement, streetlights and neon signs glaring, backlit fog framing his dark silhouette; a veritable dead man walking.

Mark Hellinger planned to make *Criss Cross* (1949) a year earlier with Siodmak, but he died unexpectedly and his widow sold the rights to Universal. The studio hired Michel Kraike (*Desperate*, 1947) to produce and Daniel Fuchs was contracted to revamp Anthony Veiller's half-finished screenplay that had changed the armored car robbery from Don Tracy's 1934 pulp novel of the same title to a racetrack heist. Siodmak also brought in William Bowers (*Pitfall*, 1948, uncredited) to kick up the dialog. Shot almost entirely on location in Los Angeles, the picture opens under Miklos Rozsa's doom-laden score (reminiscent of his *Double Indemnity*

composition) and the opening credits with a nighttime aerial shot that slowly hovers along what appears to be the downtown of the city. Then, as Siodmak's directorial credit fades, the camera swoops down like an angel of death toward a parking lot where Steve (Burt Lancaster) and Anna (Yvonne De Carlo) are illuminated in their embrace between parked vehicles by an arriving car's headlights. The visual of the startled couple and Anna's impassioned dialog presage their fate ("After it's all over... it'll be just you and me...the way it should've been all along from the start."). It's the perfect hyper-realized set up for the grand finale.

Siodmak next introduces the other third of the triangle, Slim Dundee (Dan Duryea). Decked out in a white tuxedo with boutonniere and shot from a low angle—juxtaposed against the high angle shots of Anna and Steve in the previous parking lot scene—Slim is immediately posited as the confident man of his domain in contrast to Steve, the noir chump.[18] He rips on the maitre d' for not keeping tabs on Anna, and then she appears, still decked out in fur and jewelry from the previous scene, but here she's in full peacock display descending the stairway from the upper level of the club. In these first two scenes, Siodmak establishes the sexual sparks between Steve and Anna, her contempt for Slim and the power he wields over her, and the distrust Slim holds for both of them. This triangle is similar to *The Killers* in that both Swede and Steve fall for gangster's girls and end up embroiled in high stakes crimes where they get double-crossed and pay for their stupid choices with their lives. Steve's motivation is much deeper, though, because he was previously married to Anna. This element of their past disguises Anna's real intent. Is she as simpleminded as the Anna we see straddling her barstool at the drug store counter like a teenager enjoying a dish of ice cream waiting for Steve, or does she really possess the cunning of a genuine femme fatale? "This fundamental complexity of Siodmak's human beings," wrote Borde and Chaumeton, "demonstrates ... that even within the framework of film noir we're in the presence of one of the finest psychologists of the screen."[19]

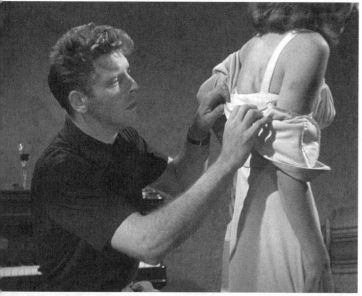

Criss Cross possesses an oneiric quality unlike any other Siodmak noir film, primarily because of the 48-minute flashback Steve narrates while driving the armored truck to the Bliss Plant where the heist will occur. The flashback is cued by Anna's opening scene line echoing in Steve's mind ("After it's all over ... it'll be just you and me ... the way it should've been all along from the start.") with Steve repeating the words "from the start" at the beginning of his narration. His voice-over is packed with unmistakable noir fatalism and counters the bright daytime setting used throughout much of the film. Getting off the trolley and climbing the steep steps to his Bunker Hill family home, Steve recalls, "From the start, it all went one way. It was in the cards, or it was fate, or a jinx, or whatever you want to call it, but right from the start." The heavy emphasis the dialogue and Steve's narration place on "the start" of his and Anna's doomed relationship punctuates the tragic ending that they are powerless to avert. Inside the early moments of the flashback, there's a pensive cue in Rozsa's score that intensifies just as Steve enters The Round-Up nightclub. The daylight casts him in silhouette in the doorway, and the light pouring in illuminates a narrow passage of the floor along the bar. The narration is equally wistful and dreamlike ("And then somehow, there I was--in The Round-Up, the old place, the old hangout, there I was alright, looking for her."). As Steve proceeds inside the bar entrance, his shadow stretches across the sunlit floor until the door closes behind him. The dreamlike feel of the scene is enhanced by the reluctance of the bartender and resident lush to acknowledge him as a real customer and by the emptiness of the nightclub in the daytime ("It was a little strange to see the place in the daytime – empty, quiet, dim.").

Siodmak's successful evolution from studio sets to location production is evident in *Cry of the City* but it's fully realized in *Criss Cross*. Working with cinematographer Franz Planer (*The Chase*, 1946), he achieves a realistic noir atmosphere throughout the film, deftly juxtaposing exterior location shots with studio and location interiors thanks to his distinctive mise-en-scène and Planer's collaged lighting and crisp deep focus. In the Union Station sequence, amidst the continuous bustle of arrivals and departures, and countless other visual distractions that contribute to verisimilitude within Siodmak's frame, Steve sees Anna – for a moment – and then she's gone. Well, sort of. As fate dictates, they bump into each other at a crosswalk outside the station and the sequence ends with a brilliant deep focus shot of Steve in the foreground looking at Anna as she stands next to a "STOP" traffic sign on the street. Vincent, one of Slim's gang members, is in a car at the intersection parallel to Anna, waiting for a green light, and in the background, over Anna's shoulder is a Chinese restaurant with its name ("Dragon's Den") painted in large white letters on the brick

Opposite top, Steve (Burt Lancaster) examines the wounds inflicted on Anna's (Yvonne De Carlo) back courtesy of her gangster husband, Slim Dundee. Bottom. Steve watches Anna outside Union Station. Note the three symbolic visual warnings Siodmak has placed in the frame: Slim's driver in the car to the left, the STOP sign, and the "Dragon's Den" restaurant sign in the extreme background.

Top, Extreme low angle shot of Steve and Anna from the perspective of one of Slim's gang members at the base of the stairway after the couple have been caught meeting in his home. Above, Slim Dundee (Dan Duryea) makes himself at home in Steve's living room as Anna (Yvonne De Carlo) tries to help explain why they were meeting.

wall. The next scene juxtaposes Steve in the proverbial dragon's den (one of Slim's pads) and Anna is on the piano plunking out the notes to Siodmak's oft-used harmonic harbinger of bad news, "I'll Remember April." You get the point. Another vivid example of the Siodmak/Planer visual collaboration (the signature noir sequence of the movie) begins with two of Slim's gang members climbing the steps up the street in the Bunker Hill district of Los Angeles. The camera pulls back as they turn the corner and scale another set of steps to the entrance of a seedy building and we see just enough of the city skyline and the traffic in the street below to establish a sense of veracity. Siodmak cuts inside and follows the gang members through the building's serpentine hallways and multiple inner stairwells to the bookshelf-cramped apartment of Finchley (Alan Napier), their alcoholic mastermind for the heist. With Finchley onboard, the intricate planning of the armored truck robbery unfolds in another cramped apartment and the pecking order within Slim's gang becomes apparent.

As the story emerges from the flashback, Siodmak's depiction of the plant robbery is surrealistic. The score intensifies, mirroring the tension of the impending violence. A low angle shot of the armored truck entering the plant's security gate emphasizes the massive concrete and steel structures in the back-

Top, Steve Thompson driving the armored truck at the point where his flashback begins.

Center, extreme high angle shot of the armored truck making its way down an alley inside the Bliss Plant where Slim Dundee's gang waits to pull off their heist.

Bottom, Anna and Steve dead at the Palos Verdes boathouse after being gunned down by Dundee.

Opposite, framed by his broken arm, Steve is helpless in the hospital.

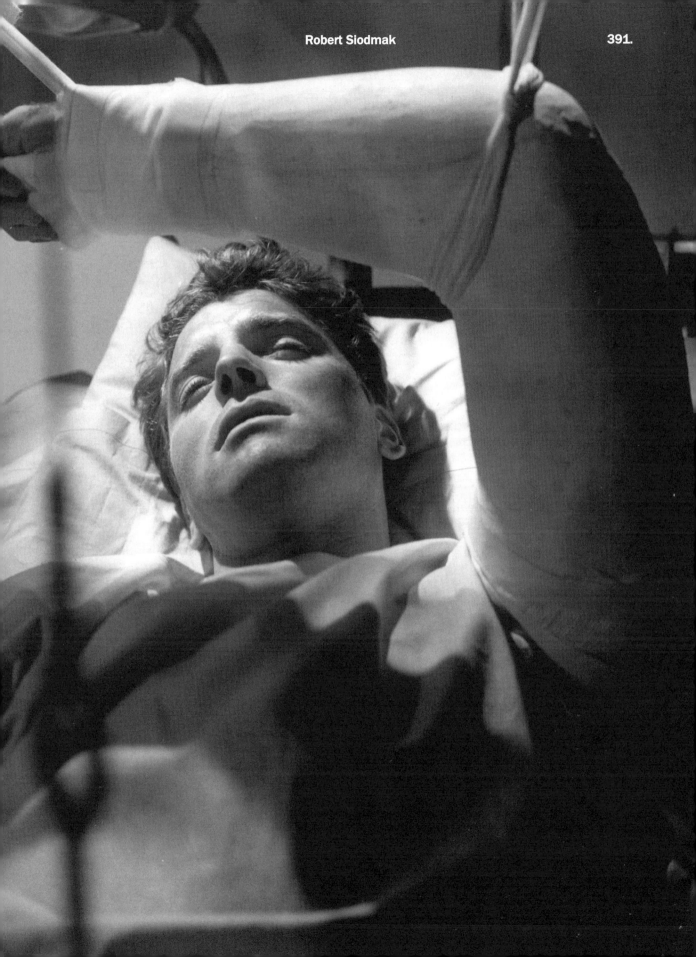

ground, and then he cuts to an eerie and disorienting extreme high angle shot from the top of one of the buildings to follow the truck's maze-like path toward its destination. Back at ground level, Slim's gang members are in disguise and situated for the armored truck's arrival. As canisters of tear gas explode around Steve and Pop, the sudden appearance of gas-masked killers from within the thick blanket of smoke is nightmarish. Siodmak extends the nightmare to the next scene, dissolving out of focus from the robbery and into focus in Steve's hospital room where he's in traction and delirious with a severe gunshot wound to his shoulder. He drifts in and out of consciousness, interrupted by visits from his immediate family and their doctor, and then detective Pete Ramirez (Stephen McNally), Steve's conscience throughout the story, now there to deliver his epitaph. Siodmak's fully developed sensibility extracts all the noir that his anti-hero can handle in his final celluloid moments. There's the feverish entrapment in his hospital bed, battling paranoia, disorientation and delusion. The ten grand bribe to get Slim's driver to detour to the Palos Verdes boathouse. Then, Anna's final betrayal as she readies to leave with the loot and he whimpers, "You love me," but she rips his heart out, retorting, "Love, love – you have to watch out for yourself." The fact that Steve is so willing to flush his life down the toilet for Anna makes it all the more fitting that she dies draped across his corpse, fulfilling her vow from the first scene, "After it's all over ... it'll be just you and me."

The File on Thelma Jordon (1950) was the last film noir that Robert Siodmak made. It's only fitting that he would close out his contribution to the original noir cycle with the oppor-

Clockwise from below, *The File on Thelma Jordon*: Thelma (Barbara Stanwyck) appears at the office of Miles Scott to report an alleged burglary attempt on her aunt's estate. Thelma informs Cleve Marshall (Wendell Corey) outside her aunt's estate of a murder. Thelma and Cleve race down the stairs to cover up any evidence that would incriminate Thelma. Miles Scott (Paul Kelly) informs Cleve that Thelma has confessed everything about her crime, except the identity of "Mr. X." Defense attorney Kingsley Willis (Stanley Ridges) and Thelma stride confidently toward the courthouse to find out the jury's verdict. Pam Marshall (Joan Tetzel) confronts her husband Cleve about the other woman in his life.

tunity to direct Barbara Stanwyck, she the versatile actress who helped popularize the noir femme fatale as Phyllis Dietrichson in *Double Indemnity*. As Thelma Jordon, Stanwyck schemes her way into the life of unhappily married assistant district attorney Cleve Marshall (Wendell Corey) and turns it upside down by implicating him in the murder case of her wealthy aunt.[20] Thelma's mysterious appearance in Cleve's life is actually a mistake, but it spells doom for him from the outset. She appears in the doorway of chief investigator Miles Scott, his close colleague in whose office he sits drinking himself foolish one night. She wants to report a burglary attempt to Miles whom we later learn was her intended fall guy. But Cleve's immediate availability and wandering heart make him the easier mark.

Working with a script by Ketti Frings (*The Accused*, *Dark City*) for producer Hal B. Wallis and Paramount, Siodmak's sure touch is evident throughout the picture, from his clever unveiling of the triangle with Thelma's accomplice to the suspenseful handling of Aunt Vera's murder, the ensuing trial, and colorful supporting characters like defense attorney Kingsley Willis. There are also the brief but telling juxtapositions where Siodmak reveals the nature of his protagonist through bit characters. In the scene where Cleve comes home the morning after his drunken night out with Thelma, he finds his wife Pam (Joan Tetzel) packing for the summer beach house and misreads it, assuming she's leaving him. ("You've always threatened to do it, but I never thought you would.") They share a romantic kiss and he makes a case for dropping the summer beach routine. Pam laughs. ("You sound as if there's some blonde after you and you're frightened.") Well, she's right about the other woman but Cleve's not scared, it's the 120-mile round trips to the beach house that will be an inconvenience for him to carry on the affair he's contemplating. A mirror shot reflects the two in a loving embrace but the scene ends with a sour expression on his face. In the next scene Cleve's kicked back in his office chair, smoking a cigarette, and the exchange he has with his secretary Dolly (Laura Elliot) informs us that she's been more than office help to him in the past.

The murder sequence of Thelma's aunt is fourteen screen minutes of Siodmak at his finest. Shadows of tree limbs whip across the interior walls through the windows, a door slams open and shut downstairs in the parlor, and a baroque staircase lit in chiaroscuro provides the death descent for Aunt Vera. Victor Young's score nuances and tantalizes the action. Sidney the caretaker (Harry Antrim) overhears an incriminating call between some man (Cleve) and Thelma. Arriving at the estate in a panic, his plans to get away with Thelma for the weekend dashed, Cleve dismisses every warning sign indicating he's a patsy in the crime. Thelma meets him outside and the revelation of the murder takes place behind the property's vertical-barred iron fence. The symbolism is obvious yet aptly motivated. Driven by a combination of his lust and survival instinct, Cleve retraces Thelma's account of what happened step by step throughout the mansion, instructing her where to leave evidence that might strengthen her defense. With Sidney making his way to the mansion by flashlight from the caretaker house, Siodmak ratchets up the tension even more, thanks to a lost note from Thelma to her aunt and Cleve's steel pencil that must be found. The sequence ends with Cleve narrowly escaping through a window. Siodmak then cuts to an appealing summer beach house shot with two quiet little children playing in the sand and Pam lounging nearby to underscore the comfortable middle-class world Cleve has chosen to swap for a living hell.

Like all of Siodmak's noir films, irony plays a significant role in exploring and exposing relationships for what they are, none more so than Cleve serving as prosecutor for Thelma's case. Kingsley Willis' description of himself to Thelma in their first meeting ("To me the world is full of innocent lambs, and I'm their lawyer.") as he leans back into a shadow that covers his face is a delicious noir moment, as is his amusement playing a bit of cat-and-mouse with Thelma over who her protector might be, the mysterious Mr. X. ("He must be a lawyer with his

SIODMAK

inside knowledge about the court system.") Thelma's confident march from the jail to the courthouse for her verdict is a spectacular sequence; it grows into a procession as she's joined by Willis, a mob of news reporters, and spectators. Siodmak intercuts shots of Miles and Cleve as they cross the walkway bridge from the D.A's offices to the courthouse and notice the spectacle. The energy of the moment crescendos as Thelma and Willis and the throng of followers ascend the massive public staircase leading to the courtroom.

Following her acquittal, Cleve confronts Thelma and Tony at her aunt's estate and she confesses ("I'd like to say I didn't intend to kill her, but when you have a gun, you always intend if you have to.") Cleve claims he can bring Tony to trial as an accomplice, but Tony counters, "Where would that put you, Mr. X? That's the convenient part about a fall guy. Once you've got him hooked you've always got him hooked." Siodmak punctuates the final minutes of the picture with graphic violence. Tony pummels Cleve unconscious with the butt of his gun, and later Thelma plunges a red-hot cigarette lighter into Tony's face causing their car to plunge off a cliff. Thelma's deathbed confession at the hospital is the only moment that doesn't ring true in the film. Her face is untouched following the horrific accident. Siodmak was galled that he had to compromise verisimilitude in order to keep his leading lady happy, but it's illustrative of the power shift that was taking place in the rapidly changing American studio system. It's also one of the reasons why, less than two years later, he chose to return to Europe – the incubator for many of the classic period's finest noir filmmakers.

Endnotes

1. Alain Silver and Elizabeth Ward, eds., *Film Noir: An Encyclopedic Reference to the American Style*, 3rd ed. (Woodstock, NY: Overlook, 1992). 330-331. The two films not addressed are *The Suspect* (1944, Universal Pictures) and *The Spiral Staircase* (1945, MGM). Both of these productions come as close as any period pictures in succeeding as noir, but "the requirements and expectations associated with genre prevent an audience from relating to them as it would *film noir*. In that sense and varying with individual productions in the genre, the period film may be said to participate at once marginally and substantially in the noir cycle."

Raymond Borde and Ettiene Chaumeton. *A Panorama of American Film Noir*. San Francisco: City Lights Books. 2002. *(Translated from Panorama du film noir Américain 1941-1953*. Paris: Les Editions de Minuit. 1955. Borde and Chaumeton referred to these films as a "noirified period style."

Jack Shadoian. *Dreams and Dead Ends: The American Gangster/Crime Film*. Cambridge: MIT Press, 1977. Outlines that gangster/crime films must have characters that are a "product of an advanced, urban civilization."

2. The French referred to this viewer co-experience as *effet de réel*, which is typically translated as "reality effect."

3. Siodmak was in good company for best directing in 1946 going up against Frank Capra, David Lean, and William Wyler. The most glaring omission by the Academy was the failure to nominate Woody Bredell in the category of best black and white cinematography for *The Killers*.

4. Pat McGilligan. *Backstory 2*. Berkeley: University of California Press, 1991.

5. Mark T. Conrad, ed. *The Philosophy of Film Noir*. Lexington: University of Kentucky Press, 2006. "If one views the director as central to the creation of a movie, suddenly film noir begins to look about as American as apple strudel … however American the subject matter of film noir may seem to be, it was often presented through European eyes behind the camera, and the formal characteristics of the genre owe more to European than American directors, above all, to the masters of the German expressionist cinema."

Opposite, Siodmak with Barbara Stanwyck on the set of *The File on Thelma Jordon*. Right, a secretary (Lois Regan) stands by while Siodmak confers with Burt Lancaster and Mark Hellinger (white tie) on the set of *The Killers*.

Robert Gerald Porfirio. *The Dark Age of American Film: A Study of the American Film Noir 1940-1960.* Doctoral dissertation, Yale University, 1979. Porfirio points out that "the most visible evidence of Expressionism in Hollywood can be traced back to the growth of the studio art departments which took on a definite Germanic tone in the Twenties...when Hans Dreier began his association with Paramount, Anton Grot with Warner Bros., and Herman Rosse with Universal." This was the first wave of émigrés that inadvertently laid the groundwork for the likes of Siodmak, Wilder, Lang, Bernhardt, et al.

6. Barbara Steinbauer-Grötsch. *Die lange Nacht der Schatten: Film noir und Filmexil.* Berlin: Bertz + Fischer GbR. 2005.

7. Borde and Chaumeton, 50.

8. William K. Everson. *More Classics of the Horror Film.* New York: Citadel Press. 1986.

9. Siodmak pays off the correlation between Kansas and the phantom lady in the final act of the film when Kansas finally locates Ann Terry who is under doctor's care at her family's estate in Long Island. They both wear their dark hair down on their shoulders and the similarity is there again, at first glance. Terry talks of her dead fiancé and it's a verbal mirror being held up to Kansas' feelings about Henderson on death row—echoing the physical mirror Terry sits in front of as she holds the mystery copy of Monteiro's hat that can set him free.

10. Porfirio, 227, discusses the manner in which "a commercial tune can serve as a hermeneutic guide to the film text.... The American preoccupation with commercial music was given a new and 'Germanic' twist by the film noir, which often exaggerated the cloying sentimentality of an established tune, or played upon the ironic connotations of its banal lyrics." In *Christmas Holiday*, Siodmak used the popular tunes "Spring Will Be a Little Late This Year," "I'll Remember April," "Always," and "Liebestod" from Richard Wagner's *Tristan und Isolde* to communicate aurally the character's inner feelings.

11. Joseph Greco. *The File on Robert Siodmak in Hollywood: 1941-1951.* USA: Dissertation.com. 1999. The original screenplay Siodmak agreed to direct began with a prologue where Harry, a psychological and emotional wreck from the death of Hester and execution of Lettie, is at the train station with his doctor headed for an insane asylum. Deborah, now a widow, shows up and wants to marry him. Harry explains it can't happen and the story goes into flashback. In the epilogue, Harry's doctor prevents Deborah from following him on the train as it rolls out of the station.

12. Mark Hellinger Collection. Department of Special Collections, Doheny Library, University of Southern California. Producer Mark Hellinger's first choice to play Kitty was Dorothy Comingore, who played Susan Alexander Kane in *Citizen Kane* (1941).

13. Production on the film actually wrapped before *The Killers* began filming, but Universal-International couldn't release it until later because of the time-consuming post work involved in the composite shots with Olivia de Havilland.

14. Greco, 18-19. Greco notes that Siodmak shut down production for three days and questions if it was because of the disagreement with de Havilland over how the twins should be portrayed.

15. Schüfftan created visual effects for Lang's *Metropolis* and he was Siodmak's cinematographer on his first picture, *Menschen Am Sonntag* (1929), as well as *Abschied* (1930) for UFA, and *La Crise est Finie* (1934) for Nero Film in Paris.

16. This literary device is also present in *Criss Cross*, the third consecutive noir film by Siodmak to implement it in some fashion. Although it's rather passive because of the flashback structure, Steve's boyhood friend Pete Ramirez is a police detective who serves as his metaphorical conscience, warning him to steer clear of Anna and Slim.

17. The script has significant fingerprints left by first drafters Ben Hecht and Charles Lederer, and

three more drafts from John Monks, Jr. (*The House on 92nd Street*, 1945, *13 Rue Madeleine*, 1947, *Knock on Any Door*, 1949).

18. Later in the film, when the gang is planning the armored car robbery in the Bunker Hill hideout, Steve temporarily holds all the cards and demands a 50-50 split of the loot, Siodmak shoots Slim from a high angle. In the final scene where Slim shoots Anna and Steve, he is shot from a low angle again.

19. Borde and Chaumeton, 80.

20. It is interesting to note that Stanwyck also played a ruthless, domineering wife of an alcoholic district attorney in *The Strange Love of Martha Ivers* (1946), one of three noir films she made with producer Hal B. Wallis.

Biography

Robert Siodmak was born on August 8, 1900 in Dresden, Saxony, Germany–contrary to the myth that he was born in Memphis, Tennessee–a deception necessary to get an entry visa to France in 1933. Siodmak studied at the University of Marburg and flirted with acting before succumbing to pressure from his father to work in the family banking business. He then had a brief stint in magazine editing that led to writing German subtitles for American silent films. In 1927, he parlayed his nascent film industry connections and secured an opportunity at UFA in Berlin where he worked as a script assistant, editor, and assistant director. Siodmak independently co-produced his directorial debut, *Menschen am Sonntag (People on Sunday*, 1929), a simple yet compelling film with an uncommonly modern visual flair for its time, which also launched the careers of co-director Edgar G. Ulmer, brother Curt Siodmak and Billy Wilder, who both assisted with the script, and assistant cameraman Fred Zinnemann. He then helmed five feature length films under producer Erich Pommer for UFA Studios and one for Deutsche Universal Film before fleeing the Nazi regime for France. There he joined several German film industry émigrés and directed seven more films. On the day before Hitler's army invaded Poland in 1939, Siodmak was on a ship bound for the United States. At the recommendation of Preston Sturges, Paramount hired him and he made three B-films, as well as one each for 20th Century-Fox and Republic Pictures. Dejected with the material he was assigned, his brother Curt (by then a successful horror genre screenwriter) came to the rescue and helped him land a directing job at Universal on *Son of Dracula* (1943). That was the beginning of a successful seven-year stint at the studio, interspersed with solo pictures made for RKO, 20th Century-Fox, MGM and Paramount. Although Siodmak directed 53 feature films over a span of nearly five decades, he is best remembered for the noir films he made within the American studio system between 1944 and 1950. Siodmak died on March 10, 1973 in Locarno, Ticino, Switzerland.

Noir Films

Right, Siodmak poses with Olivia de Havilland and Lew Aryes during *The Dark Mirror*.

Phantom Lady (1944)

Christmas Holiday (1944)

Uncle Harry (1945)

Conflict (1945) co-story credit with Curtis Bernhardt

The Killers (1946)

The Dark Mirror (1946)

Cry of the City (1948)

Criss Cross (1949)

The File on Thelma Jordon (1950)

Jacques Tourneur at the time of *Nightfall*.

Jacques Tourneur

Corey Creekmur

Although generally well regarded, Jacques Tourneur has rarely been acclaimed one of Hollywood's greatest auteurs, and only a few of his thirty-three feature films may be comfortably identified as film noir. However, Tourneur enjoys the distinction of having directed one of film noir's acknowledged masterpieces, *Out of the Past* (1947). Indeed, for many fans and critics, *Out of the Past* is paradigmatic, a virtual catalog of many of the key thematic, narrative and stylistic elements that distinguish film noir from more conventional thrillers and detective films. Early on, in *A Panorama of American Film Noir, 1941-1953* (1955), Borde and Chaumeton asserted that "*Out of the Past* raises the extravagance of *film noir* to its highest pitch," and later commentary on the film typically deems it "quintessential" or "seminal." Yet the acknowledged excellence of this film from a director not otherwise regularly associated with film noir might argue for the power of the genre's conventions themselves, or for the "genius of the system" when the components and collaborations constituting a Hollywood studio product effectively align. Indeed, in *More Than Night* James Naremore analyzes the film's lighting and cinematography not because they are unique but "because this particular film represents such an impressive use of what had become standard Hollywood procedures." In such cases a director might only be required to supply competence: otherwise the genre's mythic elements and the well-oiled factory produce the quality product on display. Yet Chris Fujiwara, Tourneur's greatest critical champion, has suggested (in *Jacques Tourneur: The Cinema of Nightfall*) that what is best about *Out of the Past* stems from the vision of its director: "If *Out of the Past* seems in some ways like a typical film noir, this is only because Tourneur's constant preoccupations – the unreliability of appearances, the helplessness of people to resist their obsessions and avoid becoming the victims of an apparently impersonal fate – are also those of the genre."

If, as Fujiwara suggests, Tourneur's work across various genres nonetheless maintains concerns close to film noir, the fact that the director made so few explicitly noir films seems curious and regrettable. However, Tourneur's affinities with film noir do appear to extend beyond the few films

Below, *The Cat People* features "a supernatural version of the noir *femme fatale*."

in his oeuvre that clearly fit the category. His background directing low-budget but unusually artful horror films, including at least two masterpieces of the genre, as well as his European roots (though he actually arrived in Hollywood as a child, following his famous father Maurice Tourneur) associate him with some of the commonly cited precursors of film noir, and noir themes if not style can be located in his distinctive Westerns and costume adventures, which often maintain an air of mystery and ambiguity atypical of such genres.

However, like Edgar G. Ulmer, who preceded the larger wave of European directors who would help turn Hollywood noir, Tourneur's work in the horror genre seems to have most directly anticipated his later achievements in film noir. The three B-films he directed at RKO for producer Val Lewton are commonly described as "atmospheric," the term signaling not only an effective evocation of mood, but a triumph of technique over small budgets and tight shooting schedules. Before their more explicit conclusions, both *Cat People* (1942) and *The Leopard Man* (1943) derive their best effects from suggestions and shadows rather than explicit scenes of horror. *Cat People* especially locates the risk its European heroine presents to its "normal," American characters in sexual desire that cannot be contained: Irena is a supernatural version of the noir femme fatale, more dangerous and therefore more exciting than her all-American counterpart (anticipating the pair of women who dramatize the hero's conflicted desire in *Out of the Past*). Tourneur's remarkable *I Walked with a Zombie* (1943), despite its lurid title, is a genuinely poetic, dreamlike film, indebted to Charlotte Bronte's *Jane Eyre* and, for a Hollywood movie, a respectful treatment of Afro-Caribbean culture.

Experiment Perilous

Although Borde and Chaumeton, in their groundbreaking book on film noir, briefly mention Tourneur's *Experiment Perilous* (1944) as a "crime film in period costume" its actual relation to noir seems slim even as it confirms the director's affinity with psychological crime stories as well as supernatural horror. In the Hollywood Gothic tradition of *Gaslight* (released the same year), its most relevant link to film noir derives from the film's lengthy flashbacks and often ambiguous voiceover narration, as well as an inventive use of multiple camera positions to depict single events. Set (unlike its source novel) in 1903, and taking place for the most part in an ornate Victorian house, whatever noir elements Borde and Chaumeton detected in the film seem muted by its period detail. For his next film, the excellent color Western *Canyon Passage* (1946), Tourneur retreated further into the historical past for a story set in Oregon in 1856. The subsequent *Out of the Past* is therefore not only a shift in genre that fully embraces film noir, but a remarkable focus on the style, language, and mood of post-World War II America, a vision of the present after two successful forays into the past.

Again, once the critical identification of film noir was underway, and otherwise defined Hollywood crime films were repositioned under the new rubric, *Out of the Past* was often cited as a flawless example of the elusive form. It simply has it all: the very embodiment of the world-weary, doomed detective hero in Jeff Bailey, played by Robert Mitchum in a gen-

Below, a wary Jeff Bailey (Robert Mitchum) peers out from behind pneumatic equipment in his small-town garage in *Out of the Past.*

Out of the Past: above Jane Greer as the prototypical femme fatale with gun in hand. Opposite, the consequence of consorting with her is a dead partner.

uinely iconic performance; Kathy Moffat, perhaps the greatest femme fatale in American cinema, played by Jane Greer in an unforgettable performance (for many viewers, the minor star Greer is known for this film alone); a simultaneously charming and terrifying villain, Whit Sterling, played by a pitch-perfect Kirk Douglas, as well as memorable character actors in minor but vivid roles, including Virginia Huston in the role of the good small town girl who we know we should prefer over Kathy, but who simply cannot compete for our attention or the hero's desire. The film's skillful cinematographer, Italian-born Nicholas Musuraca, had already worked with Tourneur on *Cat People*, and other key film noir titles (including the prototypical *Stranger on the Third Floor* [1940], about which Naremore notes that, while it does not indulge in the more ostentatious techniques often associated with film noir, it nevertheless provides a textbook example of the crucial role of lighting in a style devoted to darkness). The intricate screenplay, by Daniel Mainwaring (using the pseudonym Geoffrey Holmes), was adapted from his novel *Build My Gallows High* (a line that remains in the film, and the film's original British release title), with uncredited contributions from Frank Fenton and James M. Cain. It's also a tight, witty model of hard-boiled dialog that includes a half dozen memorable lines ("A dame with a rod is like a guy with a knitting needle") in a genre known for memorable lines, and formally the film offers many of the devices with which *film noir* is associated, including elaborate flashbacks, existential voiceover narration, and cinematography designed to capture the cigarette smoke that pervades the film. (The film also contains one of the most casually respectful treatments of African Americans in any Hollywood film of the period, a nightclub sequence that implies Black leisure and popular culture apart from White folks.) At the same time, the film's celebrated opening and conclusion in nature and a small town provide an effective, symbolic contrast to the urban settings of most of the film and the genre overall. The equally famous sequence in Mexico, including a self-reflexive location across the street

Out of the Past

from a movie theatre, also gives the film the exoticism and eroticism that film noir often associates with risky border crossings. Aside from the perpetual enjoyment the film provides, it has been a source of endless interpretation by critics, and thus crucial to the development of film noir as an academic as well as popular category.

Tourneur's following film was *Berlin Express* (1948), based on a story by Curt Siodmak. Although another film emphatically set in the present, it is perhaps more of a traditional spy thriller than an example of film noir, and most remarkable overall for its documentary-like location shooting (by cinematographer Lucien Ballard) in the rubble of Berlin and Frankfurt immediately after World War II. Whereas the war and its aftershocks are commonly cited for their usually off-screen and often unstated impact on film noir, Tourneur's film makes the vivid depiction of that devastated world one of its central concerns, creating a curious hybrid of a Hollywood thriller and a documentary suggestive of the emerging works of Italian Neo-realism. The sense of a destroyed world that underlies a good deal of film noir is in this case on vivid display, even if the film finally projects a somewhat hopeful future through characters that bluntly represent the national powers that will determine the future of a reconstructed Germany. Although the film relies on a slangy voiceover narration (by Paul Stewart), it does not admit the weary resignation of the typical noir hero, functioning instead to

Berlin Express: top, the assembled agents identified in the elaborate tracking shot outside the train. Bottom, at work in the field.

advance the film's unambiguous ideological message. And while the film's ostensible star, Robert Ryan, is as significant as Robert Mitchum in the pantheon of noir actors, his role in *Berlin Express* as agricultural agent Robert Lindley is designed to display the confidence of the American victors rather than the angst of the recovering Europeans in the rebuilding of postwar Germany.

Robert Ryan and Merle
Oberon in *Berlin Express*.

Along with *Out of the Past*, Tourneur's other work easily defined as film noir is *Nightfall* (1957), which carries the pedigree of a 1947 source novel by David Goodis, one of the definitive creators of the *roman noir*. Critics have frequently noted that *Nightfall* seems like a reworking of elements of *Out of the Past*, with ultimately less grim and therefore perhaps less effective results. As Fujiwara notes, both films map "the dualism of past and present onto that of country and city" and both dramatize "the hero's flight from destiny by relocating and changing his name." Otherwise, *Nightfall* seems designed to rescue its characters from the fate of their precursors: the hero, commercial artist Jim Vanning (Aldo Ray), vanquishes the criminals following him and proves his innocence in the murder of a father figure. Moreover, Marie (Anne Bancroft), the model and apparently deceptive femme fatale he meets at the beginning of the film, turns out to be as innocent as he is, and a helpful companion in his quest rather than agent of his doom: along with Jim, we are also initially deceived by her.

Like *Out of the Past*, *Nightfall* also relies on flashbacks to structure a portion of the film rather than the whole; however, the first portion of *Nightfall* relies upon a slightly comic pattern of clever cuts joining scenes, although the technique is oddly dropped along the way. Playing an innocent man on the run, Aldo Ray provides a compelling if often awkward performance. Jim and Marie seem to bond because they are both bruised rather than jaded individuals, but the actors (and their characters) simply lack the sexual chemistry that sizzles between Mitchum and Greer in Tourneur's earlier film. The film's villains, on the other hand, seem distinctive to film noir: like Kirk Douglas' Whit, Brian Keith's John is a chatty, often charm-

Below, *Nightfall*: Vanning (Aldo Ray) and the false femme fatale Marie (Anne Bancroft).

Above and below, Vanning is under the guns of John and Red in *Nightfall*.

ing criminal, while Rudy Bond's Red is a psychopath, giggling throughout the film even when being restrained by John from the killing he obviously enjoys. In an otherwise finally upbeat film, Red's sadism is one of the few elements that links *Nightfall* to the more hysterical elements often found in late the phase of the original cycle of film noir, although the use of a snowplow as a weapon has undeniable novelty. As Alain Silver writes in *Film Noir, the Encyclopedia*: "When Vanning is first seen skulking in the shadows of a back street, the visual inscription could easily be that of a culpable figure trying to avoid detection. This contrasts markedly with the introduction of Bailey in *Out of the Past*, who is out by a lake fishing. As such it does not recruit but extends the ironies of that earlier film. Vanning is basically innocent of any wrongdoing and Bailey clearly was not, so the trap into which Vanning has fallen can and must be interpreted as impersonal or deterministic not retributive. Vanning has a socially motivated paranoia. Physically and temporally removed from the violent events that threatened him before, Bailey seems to expect that his new life will not be disrupted by something out of his past. When Vanning is misjudged and incriminated in the doctor's death, he is unable to restore equilibrium to his life, as Bailey did for a considerable amount of time. Vanning's initial belief that Marie, whose ultimate influence on him is as beneficent as Kathie Moffat's was malign for Bailey, has betrayed him to John and Red is symptomatic of how Vanning's trauma has distorted his outlook. Since Vanning is not haunted by a particularly dark or distant past but driven by an unsettled and immediate one, perhaps the subtlest ironies that Tourneur attaches to this situation are visual rather than narrative. Contrary to common noir usage, for Vanning the black streets promise some measure of safety while the bright snow-covered landscape recalls pain and near death. Low angles and side-light around the oil derrick turn the mechanism into a huge, nightmarish mantis waiting to devour Vanning. In the climactic sequence, the snowplow lumbering after him like a gigantic beast becomes the final metaphor for the larger-than-life terrors that have plagued him."

Like most Hollywood directors, Tourneur's films were not confined to one or even two genres, but compared to his contemporaries like Fritz Lang or Otto Preminger his contributions to the canon of film noir are few, a limitation perhaps offset by the high quality of *Out of the Past*, a standout in his career and in the history of film noir. *Nightfall* is a solid but ultimately secondary contribution, and works like *Experiment Perilous* and *Berlin Express* seem most reasonably located along the borders of film noir.

Biography

Jacques Tourneur was born In Paris in 1904, but came to the United States in 1914 when his father, the legendary director Maurice Tourneur (originally Thomas), came to Hollywood. Jacques became an American citizen in 1919 and appeared as an actor in bit parts before returning to Europe to join his father in 1928. After working his way into the film industry as his father's assistant director and editor (and marrying Marguerite Christiane Gebb in 1930), as a contract director for Pathé-Natan he directed *Tout ça ne vaut pas l'amour* (1931), followed by three more French films. In 1934 he returned to Hollywood, where he directed shorts (often under the name Jack Turner) and second unit work at MGM, until directing his first feature film, *They All Come Out* in 1939. Dropped by MGM, his artistic (if not commercial) break came when he directed producer Val Lewton's inaugural film at RKO, the first in a series of low budget horror films. Tourneur directed three films for Lewton, *Cat People* (1942), *I Walked with a Zombie* (1943), and *The Leopard Man* (1943), the first two considered masterpieces of the horror genre. Bigger budgets for four A-features at RKO followed, and as a freelance director for various studios and independent producers, Tourneur demonstrated his ability to work effectively in a range of genres, including Westerns and costume adventures, as well as in film noir. His last feature film was *War Gods of the Deep* (1965). For the last two decades of his career (between 1954 and 1966) Tourneur was an active director of television series. He died in 1977 in his native France.

Noir Films

Experiment Perilous (1944)
Out of the Past (1947)
Berlin Express (1948)
Nightfall (1957)

Tourneur on the set of *Berlin Express.*

Edgar G. Ulmer

Edgar G. Ulmer

Julian Stringer

Edgar G. Ulmer's career as director of American film noir ostensibly starts and ends in the realm of the Hollywood B-movie. It was while working in the 1940s and 1950s in Los Angeles for Poverty Row studio Producers Releasing Corporation (PRC) that he helmed the handful of dark crime thrillers that have secured his reputation as Hollywood outcast and cult auteur. Indeed, Ulmer is perhaps the ultimate "King of the Bs," a filmmaker able to "take a rat and make Thanksgiving dinner out of it."[1] Yet this seemingly inauspicious industry location was neither where Ulmer started from nor where he ultimately ended up. Since his death in 1972, Ulmer's posthumous reputation has travelled along new career routes, subject to close critical analyses that seek to place his life and work in historical context and to re-evaluate his achievements.[2]

Although Ulmer never had the opportunity to direct prestigious A-film noirs for a Hollywood major, his low-budget genre pieces have attracted increased attention for two main reasons—namely, his independent spirit and his talent. During the heyday of classic period film noir, Ulmer forged a unique position for himself. According to James Naremore, "he was dubbed 'the Capra of PRC,' which meant that he had his own crew and relative freedom at a sub-minor-league studio."[3] It was this singular arrangement that enabled Ulmer to transcend limitations of time and budget by directing a

Left, a whip-wielding Hedy Lamarr in a publicity pose for *The Strange Woman*. Even when Ulmer got some name actors and slightly higher budgets, the movies he made still had to be sold based on their most sensational aspects.

group of titles that deepen the film noir corpus with their thematic strangeness and formal intensity.

Ulmer's early career gives a clear sense of his artistic qualities and motivations. He belongs to the group of distinguished European émigré filmmakers who traveled abroad in the wake of political repression under Hitler and created influential film noirs in the U.S. in the post-war period (cf. Fritz Lang, Otto Preminger, Robert Siodmak, Billy Wilder). Similar to other members of this loose-knit group, Ulmer had a background in both high art and popular culture (for example, he had worked at famed German film studio UFA). Unlike them, however, he wound up toiling away on Poverty Row rather than for a leading Hollywood studio. This situation injected ambivalent energies and emotions into Ulmer's work. Freedom meant lack of constraint, but possibilities for innovation and ideas came at the price of a lack of success.[4]

In making the transition to Southern California, Ulmer's specific artistic temperament and ambivalent industry position added an extra dimension to the European migrant sensibility imported into the U.S. crime thriller. Interviewed for the documentary *Edgar G. Ulmer: The Man Off-Screen* (dir. Michael Palm, 2004), German director Wim Wenders describes the intriguing sense of "dissonance" found in Ulmer's American films. His work abounds with displaced figures lost in the wasteland, expressing not just a doubled-tiered émigré consciousness but also the mixture of complex feelings that characterize what Naremore terms a "true aesthete of the lower depths."[5] To this already heady cocktail of cultural factors should be added the no less important fact, discussed at length by film historians Noah Isenberg and Vincent Brooke, that Ulmer's is also a resolutely Jewish sensibility.[6]

Ulmer's emergence as an important creator of films noirs occurred after a lengthy apprenticeship producing other kinds of American B-movies. Across the course of his career he worked in a veritable throng of diverse genres, including documentaries, instructional films and "ethnic" movies. However, a dark strain of mystery and suspense nevertheless infiltrates much of his output. It has been argued, for example, that titles such as the horror film *Bluebeard* (1944), the melodrama *Club Havana* (1945), the science fiction *The Man From Planet X* (1951) and the Western *Naked Dawn* (1955) all contain noir-like elements.

Arguments rage into the night about which of Ulmer's films to include in the corpus of film noir. While acknowledging the perennial slipperiness of any such definition, therefore, five titles may be identified. These have played a key role in the establishment of Ulmer's cult reputation as well as his ongoing canonization as major film artist. Certainly, legendary—albeit frequently variable—accounts circulate concerning Ulmer's fast pace of production (six days and nights for one feature), paucity of available film stock (15,000 feet per picture), high rate of camera setups (as many

Below, *Strange Illusion* Regis Toomey (left) and Jimmy Lydon were typical of the actors PRC could afford. Opposite, star and executive producer Hedy Lamarr as period femme fatale Jenny Hager in the arms of George Sanders. Lamarr packaged the project for United Artists and delivered to Ulmer actors such as Sanders and Louis Hayward.

Above, *Murder Is my Beat*: the noir tragedienne (in life and in film) Barbara Payton as Eden Lane, with Paul Langton (left) as Det. Ray Patrick, who clears her, and Robert Shayne as Captain Bert Rawley.

Opposite, a somewhat frumpy and less-than-svelte Payton made for an atypical *chanteuse* and potential femme fatale vis-a-vis the sympathetic Det. Patrick who lights her cigarette .

asleighty a day) and low shooting rations (two-to-one). How many other significant American film noirs have been produced under such pared-down circumstances?

     For anyone wishing to program a late night Edgar G. Ulmer film noir double bill, *Strange Illusion* (1945) and *Murder Is My Beat* (1955) would form an appropriately unusual duo. The former is a disturbing tale of murder and male intuition involving Paul Cartwright (James Lydon), a young man whose violent dream starts to become a reality. Enmeshed in a psycho-

sexual web of tangled family relations and sinister forebodings, the film unravels through exploration of the danger posed by a mysterious stranger, Brett Curtis (Warren William), to Paul's father, mother and sister. Conversely, the latter title is another mystery of human perception in which a young nightclub singer, Barbara Payton (Eden Lane), is suspected of a violent killing. However, the convoluted plot soon brings her to the point where she thinks she has set eyes on the very man she is supposed to have murdered.

Another suitably odd Edgar G. Ulmer crime-themed double bill is the pairing of *The Strange Woman* (1946) and *Ruthless* (1948). The earlier film is a period piece about an ambitious femme fatale, Jenny Hager (Hedy Lamarr), in 19th century Maine who rides roughshod over the men who love her in a mad dash for wealth and power. Her achievements include coaxing a young man, Ephraim Poster (Louis Hayward), into murdering his father Isaiah (Gene Lockhart)—an act which earns him nothing but her cold-hearted contempt. On the other hand, the later film, which in its complex use of multiple flashbacks is often compared to *Citizen Kane* is a dissection of brutal male ego. It revolves around Horace Vendig (Zachary Scott), an immoral investment tycoon who takes his revenge on a bad childhood by ruthlessly pursuing wealth at the expense of human relations.

Ruthless is difficult to class in terms of film noir despite the obvious parallels to *Citizen Kane*, which itself is a significant noir prototype in terms of narrative organization that integrates flashbacks and vignettes with a distinctive visual style. *Ruthless* was Ulmer's second (and last) opportunity for Ulmer to make a modestly budgeted picture anchored by minor studio stars. Zachary Scott, best known for the arrogant Monte Beragon opposite Joan

Above, Lamarr with Gene Lockhart and Louis Hayward (center). Below, Zachary Scott as Ulmer's "Charles Foster Kane," Horace Woodruff Vendig.

Crawford in *Mildred Pierce*, was also very effective in other Warners noir as the suspicious stranger in *Danger Signal* and as the betrayed husband in *The Unfaithful*. With Scott as an anchor, Eagle Lion also got Sydney Greenstreet from Warners and contract players from other studios such as Diana Lynn and Lucille Bremer. As it happens two blacklisted writers worked on the script of *Ruthless*. Alvah Bessie–one of Hollywood Ten—has had his credit restored years later. Gordon Kahn would not be blacklisted until after this movie's release. Again like *Citizen Kane* and other surveys of a fictional and notorious life, *Ruthless* relies on its narrative structure for control of point of view. Because events are filtered through Vendig beginning with key moments in his childhood, the viewer has to maintain an identification with him no matter how "ruthless" he may be. The sort of ongoing commentary by Louis Hayward's character Vic Lambdin may refine the perception of Vendig but it cannot refocus the film away from him. The audience reaction to his exploitation of other characters may be negative but in terms of both storyline and principal character there are no alternates.

While high for Ulmer, the B-budget production values were no impediment to the interest and achievement of films such as *The Strange Woman* and *Ruthless*. Instead, they are a key part of their fascination. Here, necessity is made a virtue. Paul Kerr writes of the B-film noir's "[a]rtistic ingenuity in the face of economic intransigence," and states that "a number of

Opposite, Scott and Diana Lynn in the dual role of Martha Burnside/Mallory Flagg, Below, Scott's Vendig with Louis Hayward as Vic Lambdin.

noir characteristics can at least be associated with—if not directly attributed to—economic and therefore technological constraints. The paucity of 'production values' (sets, stars and so forth) may even have encouraged low budget production units to compensate with complicated plots and convoluted atmosphere."[7] This is certainly true in the case of Ulmer. As the various testimonies in *Edgar G. Ulmer: The Man Off-Screen* demonstrate, this is a director renowned for his camera choices. Roger Corman remarks that Ulmer tried to tell his stories in interesting ways and to make his films look bigger than they actually were, while John Landis adds that he "used the lack of material to help the bleakness of the tale."

These qualities are best observed in *Detour* (1945), Ulmer's masterpiece and a standout title that could be programmed in double bills alongside cognate classics produced by any major Hollywood studio. Andrew Britton describes *Detour* as "not only one of the greatest film noirs but also one of the most demanding and audacious narratives ever produced in Hollywood," and proceeds to explicate the film's systematic use of an unreliable narrator, subversive gender play, and coruscating assessment of key American values linked to the advent of capitalism.[8] The film chronicles a bizarre death trip undertaken by a self-deluding piano player, Al Roberts (Tom Neal), whose girlfriend leaves him in New York to pursue the Hollywood dream. Taking to the road to follow her, Al encounters two characters destined to change his life forever—Haskell (Edmund MacDonald) and the unforgettable Vera (Ann Savage), a spider woman of astonishing spunk and vitality.

Ulmer's reputation in the area of film noir was established largely on the basis of *Detour*. In no other film did he make such vivid use of minimal cast and sets or explore such wilfully perverse subject matter. In *Edgar G. Ulmer: The Man Off-Screen*, Joe Dante calls *Detour*

a "dark, nasty, twisted little movie" and celebrates the fact that "even today it has its own grimy, 'wanna-take-a-shower after you watch it' quality." Yet it is now the only B-picture ever to be included in the National Film Registry of the Library of Congress, and, such is the power it casts on audiences, that it continues to overshadow all of Ulmer's other endeavours.

Detour, then, has allowed Ulmer to transcend the historical confines of Poverty Row. Today he is routinely identified as the "most celebrated director of this sort of 'supporting' cinema...who, had he not existed, would probably need to be invented."[9] As Peter Bogdanovich states in his landmark 1970s interview with the director, "[n]obody ever made good films faster or for less money than Edgar Ulmer."[10] He is known for injecting a personal sense of style and high class European value into cheaply made Hollywood B- productions. He developed a name for his ability to adapt to anything and everything, with *Detour* as the proof.

The cult that has subsequently grown up around the life and work of Edgar G. Ulmer, and around *Detour* in particular, demonstrates that the cultural status of

Opposite, *Detour*: the hapless Al Roberts (Tom Neal) and the hitch-hiking, blackmailing, femme fatale Vera (Ann Savage), Below, the mirror reflects Roberts' reaction to a situation that has managed to go from very bad to even worse.

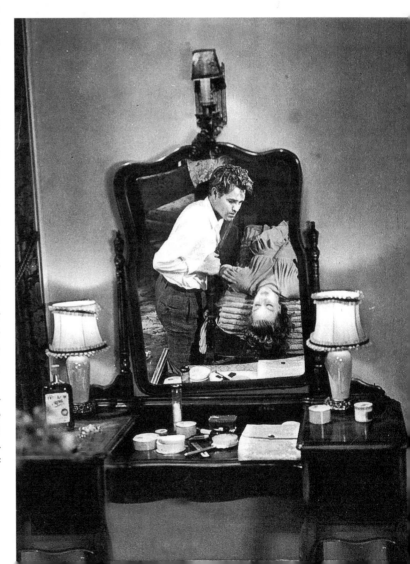

Detour

film noir is never fixed. The distinction between A- and B-crime thrillers is not hard or fast. (Over time A-pictures could fail at the box-office or sink into obscurity, just as B-pictures could achieve ongoing success and attain enhanced respectability.) Aside from being interesting and significant in his own right, therefore, Ulmer is representative of the changing status of film noir in general. The twists and turns of the making of his cult and auteur reputations have seen him progress from trash to classic, from genre hack to expressive artist.

Indeed, so dramatic has been the transformation of Ulmer's reputation that these days the trajectory of his life story is often written up as if it were itself a film noir. In this reading, the protagonist constructs complex and possibly unreliable flashback narratives concerning his own life and career; he embellishes facts at every opportunity; and, like a thief, he steals bits of cultural pedigree whenever and wherever he gets the chance. As his numerous biographers point out, Ulmer's own films even uncannily chronicle the wayward and at times "murderous" ups and downs of his artistic life.

Aside from achieving canonization through the accumulated weight of interviews, movie revivals, documentaries, critical revaluations, book publishing and other forms of status verification, a final reason why Ulmer's work extends across time is his influence over fellow filmmakers. A host of directors from other countries and film movements—including the French New Wave of the 1950s/1960s, the New German Cinema of the 1960s/1970s, and the New Hollywood of the 1970s/80s—have testified to his impact on their own artistic practice. Wim Wenders sums it up best: like any good film noir, Ulmer's story involves ambition and frustration—he exists "between desire and capability." Clearly, Ulmer never achieved all he wanted to in Hollywood. Yet only a production system as adept at giving European émigré directors a shot at helming dark thrillers could have produced a filmmaker as compelling as Edgar G. Ulmer, or a movie as powerful as *Detour*.

Notes

1. Publicity material for Kino DVD release of Austria/US documentary *Edgar G. Ulmer: The Man Off-Screen* (dir. Michael Palm, 2004).

2. Numerous books have been published on Ulmer since the release of *Edgar G. Ulmer: The Man Off-Screen*. These include, *inter alia*, Gary D. Rhodes (ed.), *Edgar G. Ulmer: Detour on Poverty Row* (Lanhan, MD: Lexington Books, 2008), Noah Isenberg, *Detour* (London: British Film Institute, 2008), and Bernd Herzogenrath (ed.), *Edgar G. Ulmer: Essays on the King of the B's* (Jefferson, N.C.: McFarland, 2009).

3. James Naremore, *More Than Night: Film Noir in Its Contexts* (Berkeley: University of California Press, 1998), p. 144.

4. Symptomatically, after Wilder directed the A-title *Double Indemnity* (1944) for Paramount,

Ulmer's response was to plan production of his (uncompleted) B-film *Single Indemnity*.

5. Naremore, p. 144.

6. See Isenberg, op. cit.; Vincent Brooke, *Driven to Darkness: Jewish Émigré Directors and the Rise of Film Noir* (New Brunswick: Rutgers University Press, 2009), especially pp. 145-66.

7. Paul Kerr, "Out of What Past?: Notes on the B *Film Noir*," in Alain Silver and James Ursini (eds.), *Film Noir Reader* (New York: Limelight Editions, 1996), p. 116. Originally published in *Screen Education* nos. 32/33 (1979-80).

8. Andrew Britton, "*Detour*," in Ian Cameron (ed.), *The Movie Book of Film Noir* (New York: Continuum, 1993), pp. 144-83.

9. Naremore, op. cit., 144.

10. Peter Bogdanovich, "Edgar G. Ulmer," in Todd McCarthy and Charles Flynn (eds.), *Kings of the Bs: Working Within the Hollywood System* (New York: E. P. Dutton, 1975), p. 377.

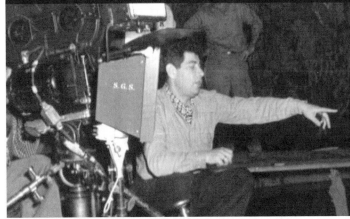

Biography

Edgar G. Ulmer was born in Olomouc in 1904 and lived as a young man in Vienna. The exact facts of his early life and career are often uncertain, but it is known that he started out in the German stage and screen, working with distinguished collaborators Max Reinhardt, F. W. Murnau, Billy Wilder, and Fred Zinnemann, among others, and that he travelled extensively between Europe and the U.S. In 1926, Ulmer worked in Hollywood on Murnau's *Sunrise*. His first notable success as director in the U.S. came with a German Expressionist-influenced horror movie, *The Black Cat* (1934), for Universal. However, his career in the upper echelons of Hollywood soon ended when he was "blacklisted" from the major studios after his affair with a studio executive's daughter-in-law. He then made a series of career moves on the fringes of the U.S. movie industry, directing ethnic minority films like *Cossacks in Exile* (1939), *Green Fields* (1937), *Moon Over Harlem* (1939), and *The Light Ahead* (1939), as well as documentaries and instructional films. Ulmer joined Producers Releasing Corporation in 1942 and helmed many of the titles for which he is now highly regarded, including *Bluebeard* (1944), *Strange Illusion* (1945), *Club Havana* (1945), and *Detour* (1946). Over the next two decades, Ulmer directed films in Mexico, Italy, Spain, and elsewhere, but his career fizzled out amid a lack of wider recognition. However, his work has recently been revived and re-evaluated, and his legacy is now preserved by the Edgar G. Ulmer Preservation Corporation.

Noir Films

Detour (1945)

Strange Illusion (1945)

The Strange Woman (1946)

Ruthless (1948)

Murder Is My Beat (1955)

Top, Ulmer directs *Ruthless* with his eyes closed. Above, eyes wide open, not imagining that "fate, or some mysterious force, can put the finger on you or me for no good reason at all."

High Sierra: Humphrey Bogart and Raoul Walsh.

Raoul Walsh

Constantine Verevis

In 1939, with two boxoffice flops directed in Europe and mediocre reviews for recent films made for Paramount in Hollywood, Raoul Walsh moved to revitalize a career in pictures–already a quarter-century long–signing with Warner Bros. to enter a prodigious period of filmmaking that lasted almost two decades. Of the thirty-plus features Walsh went on to direct at Warner Bros., several have been labeled noir, or regarded as containing noir themes and sequences, but together these films also stress the trans-generic classification of the category and the fact that Walsh (like other directors of his generation) moved freely between genres. Walsh pictures notable for their presentation of noir elements include: the gangster films, *High Sierra* (1941) and *White Heat* (1949); the westerns, *Pursued* (1947) and *Colorado Territory* (1949); the woman's picture, *The Man I Love* (1947); and the police procedural or social problem film, *The Enforcer* (1951).

Walsh began his career at Warner Bros. with *The Roaring Twenties* (1939), a film based on an original story by Mark Hellinger, the former newspaper columnist and (later) producer of such films as *The Killers* (1946) and *The Naked City* (1948). On its completion Walsh immediately exercised his option to work outside the studio directing John Wayne in a Republic Picture, *Dark Command* (1940), based on a work by novelist and screenwriter W. R. Burnett. Walsh retuned to Warner Bros. to direct George Raft and Ida Lupino in the trucker film *They Drive By Night* (1940), and during the production the studio negotiated with Burnett–whose first novel, *Little Caesar*, had been turned into the 1931 gangster film at Warner Bros.–for the purchase of his latest work, *High Sierra*.

Loosely based on the life of John Dillinger, Burnett's book tells the story of veteran gangster Roy Earle, newly released from prison, who joins an unseasoned crew to rob a casino in a Californian mountain resort. The job goes disastrously wrong and Earle flees with a

Below, *They Drive By Night*

High Sierra (clockwise from top left):

Bogart in a Dillinger-like pose

With Ida Lupino as Marie

The robbery at the lodge.

woman, Marie Garson, whom he meets through the crew, to the Sierras where he is cornered and shot down by police. Hellinger came aboard the project as associate producer and Walsh was assigned to direct the story, adapted for the screen by relative newcomer John Huston along with Burnett himself. George Raft was offered the lead but when he refused to take a role that required the character pay with his life for crimes committed, the part went to Humphrey Bogart. The latter drew upon his performance as Duke Mantee in *The Petrified Forest* (1936) to fashion the Earle character, "a mixture of old-fashioned decency and sharp rebellion against the average man's role in society" (*New Republic*, 8 Apr. 1940), into a sympathetic, country style outlaw.

Walsh's biographer, Marilyn Ann Moss, writes that *High Sierra* provides opportunity for the expression of one of the fundamental motivations in a Walsh picture: namely, "the hope that a man and a woman would come together–or at least die trying" (*Raoul Walsh: The True Adventures of Hollywood's Legendary Director*, 2011). More particularly, a key noir element of *High Sierra* is the sense of alienation–of loneliness, loss and desperation–that defines its central characters, Earle and Marie (Ida Lupino). From the moment Earle is released from prison and finds brief respite from the concrete city in a local park where he can finally breathe clean air and feel the grass beneath his feet, it is clear that the fate of the anachronistic gangster, a Western style bandit, literally out of time, has been predetermined. Earle initially attempts to find a way through the new society he has entered, but the ex-convict is soon frustrated in turns, first by the opportunistic Velma for whom he develops a romantic interest and (emotional and financial) investment only to be spurned, and next by his quarreling and inept gang members who not only challenge the aging gangster but ultimately make a mess of the robbery and give up Earle to the police. Only the fallen girl, Marie, can understand the gangster's frustration and desire to find true freedom in his expressed longing "to crash out." But Earle does not recognize her love until it is too late, shot dead by a police marksman as he emerges from his mountain refuge to protect Pard, the dog whose devotion he has similarly ignored. Asked years later if he wished Earle had escaped, Walsh admitted "Yes. Him and the girl and the little dog. I would have liked to see them ride away into the desert somewhere with the sun setting" (Patrick McGilligan, *Film Crazy: Interviews with Hollywood Legends*, 2000), but Walsh also understood that the culmination of the drama, Earle's longing for freedom, inevitably meant an appointment with death. In a key inversion of the rise and fall trajectory of the gangster story, Earle's literal fall from his lofty hideout to his metaphorical rise to freedom helps mark out *High Sierra* as an important transition piece in the movement from gangster picture to film noir.

Walsh followed *High Sierra* with a film he claimed was his favorite of the sound era, the old-time musical *The Strawberry Blonde* (1941), and then directed a string of pictures with lifelong friend Errol Flynn, including: *They Died with Their Boots On* (1941), *Gentleman Jim* (1942) and *Objective, Burma!* (1945). In 1947 Walsh returned (obliquely) to noir themes with *The Man I Love*, a film more obviously categorized as a family melodrama or woman's picture. The story follows world-weary nightclub singer Petey Brown (Ida Lupino, again) who, at the beginning of the film, moves from New York to Long Beach to be near her three siblings. Upon arrival in California, Petey takes a job at a club run by sleazy entrepreneur Nicky Toresca (Robert Alda), and develops a relationship with a former jazz pianist, the melancholy San Thomas (Bruce Bennett), but most of Petey's time is devoted to helping resolve family problems, including the difficult relationship that exists between Petey's sister Sally and her emotionally damaged husband Roy, who is recuperating from a breakdown in a hospital for WWII veterans. In this respect *The Man I Love* takes a noir interest in psychological effects and the period of post-war adjustment for traumatized returning servicemen, but the film's representation of "damaged"

Ida Lupino as Petey and Bruce Bennett as San in *The Man I Love*.

men extends beyond this specific relationship to the film's larger concern with post-war changes in the societal role of women. Each one of the women in the film—Petey's two sisters, Sally and Ginny, and their neighbor, Gloria—deals with the redefinition of gender roles, but none more so than Petey herself who, abandoned (by San) at the end of the film, still finds the courage (much like Marie at the end of *High Sierra*) to lift her head and move forward. A film about intimate relationships, *The Man I Love* expresses its noir sensibility through the pathos and vulnerability of its key characterizations.

Walsh's next picture, *Pursued* (1947), more obviously featured visual and thematic elements of film noir, but like *The Man I Love* could also be

Above, a noir visual style applied to the Western by Walsh and cinematographer James Wong Howe in *Pursued*.

discussed as a family melodrama or—given its historical setting and iconography—as a Gothic Western. *Pursued* was written by Niven Busch who had recently co-scripted the MGM adaptation of James M. Cain's *The Postman Always Rings Twice* (1946) and, from his own novel, the blockbuster Western melodrama *Duel in the Sun* (1946) for producer David O. Selznick. The inspiration for *Pursued* came from an old newspaper article about a bloody feud between two families that left a boy from one side orphaned, and subsequently raised by the family that had murdered his parents. Walsh's psychological Western—most of which unfolds in flashback years later from the burnt-out homestead of the killings—tells the story of Jeb Rand (Robert Mitchum), a lone and alienated character who has witnessed the slaughter of his family but repressed the scene that returns to him only as a nightmare image of a pair of boots with flashing silver spurs. Jeb is taken into the home of Ma Callum (Judith Anderson) and raised alongside her two children, Thor (Teresa Wright) and Adam (John Rodney). When Jeb and Thor become adults they develop feelings for each other but Jeb must deal not only with Adam's resentment but also Ma's brother, Grant Callum (Dean Jagger), who is determined to eliminate Jeb, the sole survivor of the Rand family. A series of conflicts ensues but all is resolved when Ma—who was actually Jeb's father's lover—kills her brother Grant, freeing Jeb from his nightmare and enabling him to marry Thor. The complex material, which Busch described as a Greek tragedy set in a western terrain (Julian Fox, "Hollow Victories," *Films and Filming*, Aug. 1973)—made for a psychological mystery replete with Freudian themes of childhood trauma, repressed memories and forbidden sexuality.

The depiction of Jeb's disturbed mental state (and associated Freudian themes: incestuous longings and murderous impulses) all contribute to the fatalistic mood of *Pursued*, as do

Pursued.: Robert Mitchum has Western garb even as his character has a noir persona.

the film's dark interiors, shadowy night sequences, and haunting black-and-white landscapes. In shooting the film, Walsh worked with cinematographer James Wong Howe with whom he had already collaborated on such films as *The Strawberry Blonde* and *Objective, Burma!* In the case of *Pursued*, Walsh and Howe devised a visual style appropriate to the alienated psychological state of Jeb Rand, notably isolating him, a lone rider dwarfed and vulnerable, against the backdrop of massive mountain defiles. Walsh would subsequently reprise this type of shot (with another favored cinematographer, Sid Hickox) in *Colorado Territory* (1949), an uncredited (for Burnett) remake of *High Sierra*, which retained the original film's narrative units but

Above, Virignia Mayo (with Henry Hull and Joel McCrea) as a frontier woman in *Colorado Territory*. Below, Mayo as a more typical and treacherous femme fatale, the cheating wife, with James Cagney as her sociopath husband, Cody Jarrett in *White Heat*.

reworked the material as a Western with Joel McCrea and Virginia Mayo in the (transformed) leading roles of outlaw Wes McQueen and his companion, Colorado. Biographer Moss signals a further connection between these three Walsh films, noting that the loss and grief felt by the homeless soul, Jeb, a character who sets out to recover a part of himself that has been lost, is not unlike the experience of the displaced couples Roy and Marie, and their remake pair Wes and Colorado, who yearn for some idealized past. In the latter instance, Walsh emphasizes the childlike innocence of the outlaw couple, altering the ending so that Wes and Colorado die together to underline the kind of psychological darkness and defeatism associated with contemporaneous noirs.

Soon after *Colorado Territory*, Walsh began work on *White Heat*, a film derived from an original treatment by former *Los Angeles Times* correspondent Virginia Kellogg that was substantially transformed by screenwriters Ivan Goff and Ben Roberts into a gritty mobster story about deranged urban outlaw Arthur "Cody" Jarrett. James Cagney returned to Warner Bros. to take the lead—his first gangster role since *The Roaring Twenties*—and together with Walsh worked to further twist the character of Jarrett into a psychopath, "a mean grin with an Oedipus complex and migraine headaches" (Fox, "Hollow Victories"). Following the daring train robbery (that opens the film), Cody pleads guilty to a minor felony to avoid the electric chair for lives claimed, entering instead a penitentiary from where he can continue to run his crew. The authorities realize his strategy and plant an undercover man, Hank Fallon/Vic Pardo (Edmond O'Brien), in the prison to befriend Cody and expose his actions. The famous mess hall sequence, in which Cody goes berserk, swimming down the length of dining tables before

Left, *White Heat*: Cody Jarrett is visited by the real object of his obsessive love: mother.

At right, Bogart's last project with Walsh: *The Enforcer*.

being restrained by guards, occurs when news reaches Cody that Ma Jarrett (Margaret Wycherly) has died after challenging gang member Big Ed (Steve Cochran) who has taken up with Cody's disloyal wife Verna (Virginia Mayo). Cody breaks out of prison to take revenge on Big Ed and Verna, and subsequently plans a big payroll heist at a petroleum refinery. In the equally well-remembered finale, the authorities–tipped off by Fallon who has won Cody's trust–trap the wounded gangster atop one of the refinery tanks where Cody repeats his Ma's words—"top of the world!"—just before firing bullets into the tank to explode into a (symbolically apocalyptic) gigantic ball of flame.

Like *High Sierra*, *White Heat* challenges generic conventions to fall somewhere between gangster picture and film noir, but the vicious paranoiac Cody Jarrett is far removed from the ineffably sad and sympathetic character of Roy Earle. Building on his explosive tough guy roles, in particular Tom Powers from Warner Bros.' *The Public Enemy* (1931), Cagney and Walsh fashioned Cody as a "terrifying, unruly force of psychological chaos," and symptom of postwar American angst (Moss, *Raoul Walsh*). In this way Walsh extends his depiction of emotionally damaged war veterans (from *The Man I Love*) through the character of Cody, who becomes a representative figure of post-war anxieties around compromised masculinity and the kind of disturbances that could erupt. The failure of masculine socialization is amplified through Cody's mother fixation and excessive brutality, and by contrasting his abnormal behavior to the properly rational actions of (comparatively bland) organization man, Hank Fallon. Cody's psychological instability—his depravity and frailty—is further linked to (and twisted by) the alienating urban landscape, and also dangerous technological forces, such as the steam generated by the railroad engine that scalds a crew member in the opening heist and the dehumanized petroleum refinery complex which Cody's gang invades in the film's spectacular final sequence. Fallon's final assessment, "He finally got to the top of the world. And it blew right up in his face," indicates the annulment of the criminal threat but, as filtered through Cagney's magnetic performance, there lingers still a film noir challenge to conformist, bureaucratic postwar culture.

In the early 1950s Walsh returned from directing *Captain Horatio Hornblower R.N.* (1951) for Warner Bros. in England to complete a picture, *The Enforcer* (1951), begun by contract director Bretaigne Windust but whose work did not meet with the approval of producer Milton Sperling. Although Walsh received no screen credit for the film he later stated that he "directed more than half of it, and retook some scenes," such as the climatic shoot-out in which a mortally wounded gunman is caught in a revolving door (McGilligan, *Film Crazy*). *The Enforcer* (known in the UK as *Murder, Inc.*) is one of several films, such as *The Big Heat* (1953), *The Big Combo* (1955) and *Underworld U.S.A.* (1960)–inspired by Senate Crime Investigating Committee hearings into the extent of modern-day syndicated crime in the U.S. After the death of a key witness, Rico (Ted de Corsia), the film follows District Attorney Martin Ferguson

One of Cagney's most quoted moments: "Top of the World, Ma!"

(Humphrey Bogart) as he spends the night before a big trial trying to find some piece of evidence that will enable him to convict underworld crime boss Albert Mendoza (Everett Sloane). As Ferguson works through the files, the story unfolds as an elaborate series of flashbacks (and flashbacks within flashbacks) in the form of the testimonies of criminals and their informers previously interrogated by Ferguson. Gradually Ferguson assembles the pieces of a gangland puzzle of organized crime, a new corporate-style gangsterism of "fingers," "hits" and "contracts," that culminates in a race against time to save a final witness, Angela Vetto, for whom Mendoza has issued a contract (via his lawyer) from the confines of his cell. Whereas *White Heat* had presented the gangster as a psychopathic individual, *The Enforcer* worked with the idea of the criminal as a company man, just another anonymous employee in a large organization with different branches across the country. Perhaps more significantly, the convoluted structure of *The Enforcer* (most likely inherited from Windust) seems unusual for Walsh—a director who said his films were characterized by "continuous action"—but the origins of the film link it to a tradition of "semi-documentary" police procedurals (notably *The Naked City*) and further mark out Walsh's contribution to film noir.

Biography

Raoul Walsh is known as a cinematic storyteller, a physical filmmaker of great action and adventure films, but also as a teller of stories, an enigmatic character who was an adventurer in his personal life as well as a filmmaker. Walsh (1887–1980) was born Albert Edward Walsh in New York City, and entered the film industry initially as an actor, notably playing the role of John Wilkes Booth in D. W. Griffith's *The Birth of a Nation* (1915), before going on to direct one- and two-reelers under Griffith's supervision. Walsh left Griffith's company to make *Regeneration* (1915) at the Fox Film Corporation where he stayed for more than twenty years, directing such films as the Sgt. Quirt and Capt. Flagg trilogy of war dramatic-comedies—*What Price Glory?* (1926), *The Cock-Eyed World* (1929) and *Women of All Nations* (1931)—and *The Thief of Bagdad* (1924) and *Sadie Thompson* (1928), both for United Artists. Throughout the 1930s Walsh worked variously at Fox, MGM, Paramount and RKO, and directed two films in the UK, before signing with Warner Bros. where he enjoyed a long and prodigious director-studio relationship from his initial feature *The Roaring Twenties* (1939), through several pictures with favored actor Errol Flynn, and on to his final film, *A Distant Trumpet* (1964). Walsh expressed a preference for adventure and melodrama, but like other filmmakers of his generation worked across several genres, as is evidenced by *Colorado Territory* (1949), a western remake of his own gangster film noir, *High Sierra* (1941). After making in 1964 the Western *A Distant Trumpet*, Walsh retired from movies. He died in 1980.

Noir Films

High Sierra (1941)

The Man I Love (1947)

Pursued (1947)

Colorado Territory (1949)

White Heat (1949)

The Enforcer (1951)

Walsh (smoking by the camera) on the set of *They Drive By Night*.

Orson Welles directs Charlton Heston on the set of *Touch of Evil.*

Orson Welles

Steven Sanders

It is only a slight exaggeration to say that the historical sequence of classic film noir is book-ended by the first and last Hollywood studio films directed by Orson Welles. *Citizen Kane* (1941) marks the beginning of the sequence and *Touch of Evil* (1958) signals its transition to stages variously known as "post-classic noir" and "neo-noir." *Citizen Kane* is a landmark in American cinema and a compendium of cinematographic and narrative techniques that subsequent noir filmmakers would mimic, borrow, and build on, a profusion of brilliant images and narrative innovations and a masterwork that filmmakers would go to school on for decades to come. Depth-of-field, chiaroscuro, flashback, off-kilter framings and composition are just a few of the techniques that Welles brought to full fruition in *Citizen Kane* and can be seen in noir films throughout the 1940s and 1950s. As Chuck Berg writes in his 2003 entry on *Citizen Kane* in *The Encyclopedia of Orson Welles*, "*Citizen Kane* is a virtual textbook of sophisticated techniques exemplifying the artistic best in mise-en-scène, cinematography, lighting, editing, music scoring, and sound design." Of course, no one would deny that Welles employed to the fullest the contributions of many talented participants including screenwriter Herman J. Mankiewicz, editor Robert Wise, composer Bernard Herrmann, and principally his gifted cinematographer, Gregg Toland, who famously told Welles he could teach him everything he needed to know about cinematography in a few weeks and then took the fledgling filmmaker in hand as the two worked their magic.

The central theme of *Citizen Kane*—as it is in so many of Welles' films, from *The Stranger* and *Mr. Arkadin* to *F for Fake* (1973)—is identity, its loss, fragmentation, concealment, or discovery. The film opens on Xanadu, the castle of the dying newspaper magnate, presidential candidate, and possessor of the world's sixth-largest private fortune, Charles Foster Kane (Welles). Kane utters the gnomic word "Rosebud" as he dies, dropping a snow globe that shatters into pieces indicating the disparate shards of his life. This scene transitions abruptly to a projection room where reporters watch a newsreel depicting Kane's career in all its color and controversy. The editor of *News on the March* (Philip Van Zandt—a bit player who would go on to appear in many noir films including John Farrow's *Where Danger Lives* (1950) and *His Kind of Woman* (1951)—has screened this newsreel for his reporters and now charges them to go out and get the real story: Who was Charles Foster Kane? What clue, if any, does "Rosebud" provide? The remainder of the film consists of their attempts to reconstruct his identity out of its biographical fragments, an enterprise that is

Previous page, Paul Stewart supervises the Xanadu inventory in *Citizen Kane*,

Left, passengers are treated to a magic show in *Journey into Fear*.

Opposite, Welles as the Nazi fugitive in *The Stranger*.

carried out from perspectives by Kane's mother (Agnes Moorehead), his trustee Thatcher (George Couloris), his newspaper associates Bernstein (Everett Sloane, Welles' nemesis in *The Lady from Shanghai*) and Leland (Joseph Cotten, who stars in Welles' *Journey into Fear* [1943] and Hitchcock's *Shadow of a Doubt* [1943]), his first and second wives (Ruth Warrick, Dorothy Comingore), and his butler at Xanadu (Paul Stewart, later to be seen as the mobster Carl Evello in Robert Aldrich's *Kiss Me Deadly* [1955]). In the end, Kane remains a cipher, as does the significance of "Rosebud," the name emblazoned on his boyhood sled.

Nevertheless, for all its originality, vitality, and influence, *Citizen Kane* is not ordinarily regarded as a film noir at all. Berg, in the entry previously cited, suggests that the film is "in many respects...a noirish mystery," and, as illustrated above, one of the subordinate enjoyments of viewing the film is to see how many members of its cast turn up in noir films throughout the 1940s and 1950s. Whatever verdict one may reach on *Citizen Kane*, it seems clear that if we are to assess Welles as a director of noir films we are left with the four films he directed within a mere twelve year period: *The Stranger* (1946), *The Lady from Shanghai* (1947), *Mr. Arkadin* (1955), and *Touch of Evil* (1958). Of course, Welles also acted in several noir films including *Journey into Fear* (directed by Norman Foster and uncredited Welles) and, most famously, *The Third Man* (Carol Reed, 1949).

The films for which Welles will be remembered as a noir director have in common what R. Barton Palmer describes, in another context, as a narrative which exposes a present crisis in the protagonist's life stemming from and focused on his or her "dark past." "Thus noir characters...cannot avoid the fatal entanglements they themselves have chosen because in the end these answer to their nature." (R. Barton Palmer) A hallmark of the predicament of the noir protagonist is an unresolved conflict from the past and Welles' noir films can be typically understood as meditations on protagonists who are trying to escape their pasts even if they must confront them in order to do so, as does Franz Kindler, a Nazi war criminal who has been living in a small New England hamlet and is about to marry the daughter of a U.S. Supreme Court justice. When Kindler learns he is the target of a Nazi hunter from the Allied War Crimes Commission, he knows he must kill him or be destroyed by the disclosure of his Nazi past.

The Stranger

The Stranger was regarded by Welles himself as his weakest film, and it underwhelmed critics. The film is reminiscent of the Eric Ambler/Graham Greene tradition of international intrigue with an element of political realism that would be developed in fuller form in such films as *The Spy Who Came in from the Cold* (Martin Ritt, 1965) and *The Quiller Memorandum* (Michael Anderson, 1966). *The Stranger* incorporates a fairly conventional narrative, although that does not prevent it from being "filled with perverse relationships and equally perverse characterizations" in which "the mockery of a marriage and the underlying thread of violence found in Kindler's pulpish characterization underscore the noir quality to *The Stranger*," as Carl Macek observes in his entry on *The Stranger* in *Film Noir: An Encyclopedic Reference to the American Style*.

    The Stranger exemplifies film noir not only in the way the narrative adverts to the dark past of its protagonist Kindler (Welles) but also in the way the film locates evil just beneath the surface of the small town of Harper, Connecticut, where Kindler has taken on the identity of Charles Rankin, a teacher at the Harper School for Boys. The small town setting features what Irving Singer in his *Three Philosophical Filmmakers* calls "quotidian verisimilitude," a feature often found in the non-urban noir and which has its paradigmatic instances in Hitchcock's *Shadow of a Doubt* (1943) and *The Birds* (1963): a calculated departure from normality in which unspeakable evil exists side-by-side with, or descends upon, the innocuous. In *The Stranger*, Welles modulates this feature to include the whimsical: the owner of the general store cheats at checkers.

    Kindler is being pursued by Inspector Wilson (Edward G. Robinson) under the auspices of the Allied War Crimes Commission. Wilson has arranged for one of Kindler's executive officers, Konrad Meinike (Konstantin Shayne), to escape from prison in Germany where he is awaiting execution. Meinike, while in prison, has found God, travels to America to find Kindler and convince him to confess and repent. When Kindler runs into Meinike on the street he knows this must be due to a plan to apprehend him. He meets with his former associate in the nearby woods on the same day he is to marry Mary Longstreet (Loretta Young). Rankin stran-

Welles and Rita Hayworth in *The Lady from Shanghai*.

gles Meinike and buries him in the woods.

Wilson, who has not yet identified Rankin as the notorious Kindler because he was knocked unconscious by Meinike before he had a chance to trace him to Rankin, encounters Rankin at a dinner party where the latter is expatiating on the history of Germany. He remarks that "the basic principles of equality and freedom never have [and] never will take root in Germany." Mary's brother, Noah (Richard Long), rebuts with the case of Karl Marx. When Rankin replies that "Marx wasn't a German. Marx was a Jew," Wilson knows he has found his man. After all, he reasons, "Who but a Nazi would deny that Karl Marx was a German because he was a Jew?" Once Wilson convinces Mary of her husband's Nazi past, and the atrocities he is responsible for, she is able to confront him in the town's clock tower, where he is hiding. She shoots and injures him and Kindler meets his death when he is impaled by a sword-wielding angel that runs along the outside track at the top of the tall clock tower and Kindler falls to his death. In images thus suggestive of vengeance and wrongs put right, Welles reaffirms his essentially moral vision of the human condition. But the film's final image of the tower clock's hands spinning wildly out of control suggests it is unlikely that things will return to normal in the once quiet town of Harper.

The Lady from Shanghai

As Robert Garis opines in *The Films of Orson Welles*, this "brilliant and overwrought" film is "the most overheated film Welles directed." *The Lady from Shanghai* may also be Welles' most ambiguous film. The story is told that when Harry Cohn, the head of Columbia Pictures, first screened the film, he offered anyone in the room one thousand dollars to explain the plot to him. It is not recorded whether Welles was in the room at the time but in any event no one took Cohn up on the offer.

Welles plays a sailor, Michael O'Hara, who provides a flashback voiceover narration. While strolling through Central Park, O'Hara sees an attractive woman (Rita Hayworth) in a horse-drawn cab and offers her a cigarette (which she folds in a handkerchief and tucks into her handbag). Later, he hears a cry for help and rescues her from three young thugs. He then takes her home and on the way they talk of many things, including allusions to the time she spent in Macao and Shanghai, which suggest that she is more hard-bitten than she appears. O'Hara asks why she never used the gun she had in the handbag that he retrieved when he first heard her screams in the park. She tells him she meant for him to find the bag and that she doesn't even know how to shoot. She is Elsa Bannister, the wife of Arthur Bannister (Everett Sloane), a famous, highly successful criminal defense attorney. She offers O'Hara a job on the Bannister yacht, which O'Hara declines. Bannister himself seeks out O'Hara in the seamen's hiring hall waiting for a ship. When Bannister passes out after too many drinks, he has to be taken back to the yacht by O'Hara where he encounters Elsa again. She implores him to take the job and he cannot resist. In the ensuing trip in the Caribbean, Elsa wastes no opportunity to stoke the fires of O'Hara's desire, and it is evident who has taken control in this protracted and elaborate seduction. The tropical landscapes, the sea's whorls and eddies, and the many shots of Elsa in shorts, bathing suits, and supine on the yacht's deck represent the tropics where Michael finds himself in both a geographical place and an inescapably erotic state of mind.

O'Hara is increasingly repulsed by the wealthy lawyer in all his arbitrariness and power and this is shown in two sequences. The first occurs on board Arthur's luxury yacht as the lawyer humiliates Elsa, Grisby, and his black maid Bessie (Evelyn Ellis) in turn by indicating how much each of them needs him because he is wealthy and they are not and depend on his benefice. The second sequence occurs at Arthur's nighttime beach picnic where O'Hara observes the way the three—Arthur, Elsa, and Grisby—resemble a group of sharks he once saw off the coast of Brazil, fighting and feeding on each other until they became so frenzied that they began to eat at themselves. O'Hara tells them, "I never saw anything worse until this little picnic tonight." The shark scene is very likely Welles' metaphor for the worst excesses of predatory capitalism, and it leads O'Hara to tell them, anticipating the film's ending, "And you know, there wasn't one of them sharks in the whole crazy pack that survived."

When the yacht docks at Acapulco, Grisby takes O'Hara aside and offers him $5,000 to kill him—or, more accurately, to confess to killing him. Grisby tells O'Hara that he wants to get far away from the site of an imminent nuclear apocalypse; that he wants to get away from his wife who will not give him a divorce; and that he wants to collect on an insurance policy. However, these reasons could not possibly support such a plan because Grisby is not married and obviously could not collect on a policy if he were dead, but O'Hara, having fallen hook, line, and sinker for Elsa and dreaming of taking her away with the $5,000, is oblivious to these flaws, a common condition among film noir fall guys. When he shows Elsa the phony confession that Grisby wants him to sign, she warns O'Hara that it is a trap set by Arthur. In fact, the trap is one that she and Grisby have set for Arthur and O'Hara, the former to be killed and the latter to take the fall. When Grisby is found dead in Arthur's office, O'Hara is arrested for the murder forthwith and hires Arthur to defend him.

The famous trial sequence in *The Lady from Shanghai* has Arthur Bannister doing what he can to see to it that O'Hara is found guilty, but Elsa helps him engineer an escape to a Chinese theater. He discovers that Elsa has the gun that killed Grisby but passes out before he is able to take action. He awakens in a deserted amusement park, sufficiently lucid to realize that all along Elsa and Grisby were planning to murder Arthur. In a striking, proto-psychedelic visual, O'Hara zigzags down a chute to the hall of mirrors where Elsa and Arthur, guns drawn, have confronted each other, and as Arthur laments that "Killing you is killing myself. It's the same thing. But I'm pretty tired of both of us," Elsa starts to shoot and Arthur shoots back, shattering the various images reflected in the mirrors, indicative of a Wellesian motif where distorted images and shattered glass are visual metaphors for the distortions of reality by poses and masquerades and the dispersal of identity into a multitude of shards and guesses. By the time the shooting has stopped, both have received fatal injuries, and Elsa lies dying, imploring O'Hara not to leave her. But O'Hara's narration has nearly come to an end as he now explains how the past continues to "exist" in his present and, indeed, in his future, as an unre-

Left. Everett Sloane and Rita Hayworth outside the stylized courtroom in *The Lady from Shanghai.*

Opposite, Welles as the title character in *Mr. Arkadin.*

solved and perhaps never-to-be resolved conflict, as he says, "Maybe I'll live so long that I'll forget her. Maybe I'll die trying."

Mr. Arkadin

The difficulty of analyzing and evaluating *Mr. Arkadin* comes from its elusive production history. Although Welles spent five months shooting the film and another eight months in post-production, there is no canonical text. At least five versions (including two Spanish language edits) exist. The differences among them have to do chiefly with variations in the flashback structure, the order of scenes, the transitions between episodes, the editing of the recorded score, and the redubbing of lines—all due in large part to the fact that after Welles failed to deliver the final edit on schedule, the footage was taken from him by producer Louis Dolivet, who assigned the editing to Renzo Lucidi. This led Welles to call the making of *Mr. Arkadin* "the real disaster of my life."

Gregory Arkadin (Welles), an eccentric billionaire, hires Guy Van Stratten (Robert Arden), a young American opportunist, to delve into his past prior to 1927, the year he claims he lost his memory, to find out who he is. ("The great secret of my life is that I do not know who I am.") In fact, Arkadin is using Van Stratten to ferret out people from his past so he can do away with them in order to conceal that past from his daughter. It is a past replete with criminal acts through which Arkadin has acquired his fortune. Of course, Van Stratten is using Arkadin

Mr. Arkadin.

as well, in the hopes of supplementing his fee with a payoff many times larger for agreeing to keep his silence about what he may discover. And what he does discover is a story of criminal activity, primarily White slavery, and, ultimately, that the people he finds from Arkadin's past turn up dead almost immediately after he has found and talked to them. Even Van Stratten's girlfriend Mily (Patricia Medina), who put him onto the trail of Arkadin in the first place, meets her death after partying with the magnate aboard his yacht. Arkadin himself comes across as a kind of Felliniesque ringmaster of the grotesque, damaged, and absurd, as illustrated in Welles' casting of Mischa Auer as the flea trainer, Akim Tamiroff as a onetime employee, now in hiding, Michael Redgrave as an effeminate antiques dealer, and Katina Paxinou as a former mistress living in Mexico. The masquerade party sequence at Arkadin's castle, where Arkadin entertains his guests with the story of the scorpion who cannot help but sting the frog who is carrying him across a pond on his back, illustrates Welles' sense of noir fate. ("It's my character," the scorpion tells the frog, to which Arkadin adds, "Let's drink to character!") In an attempt to speak to his daughter Raina (Paola Mori) before Van Stratten has a chance to turn her against him, Arkadin obtains a private plane and flies to meet her. But Van Stratten has persuaded her to tell her father that he has already revealed Arkadin's truth, and when she does, the communication between Arkadin and his daughter goes silent and, we must assume, he has jumped from the plane to his death.

 Mr. Arkadin is reminiscent of *Citizen Kane* in its recapitulation of the noir themes of the penetration of the past in the present and the inescapability of the constraints of character.

Even without *Kane*'s budget, formidable structure, or superb cast, *Mr. Arkadin* deserves attention as an exercise in Wellesian extravagance and a source of guilty pleasure for the viewer with its baroque sets, exotic visuals, over-the-top acting by Welles, moving and hilarious characterizations respectively by Katina Paxinou and Michael Redgrave (hairnet and all), and multiple voice dubs by Welles. Doubtless a second- or third-tier entry in Welles' body of work, it is worth reminding ourselves, as Chuck Berg points out in *The Encyclopedia of Orson Welles*, that *Mr. Arkadin* was once ranked as one of the dozen best films ever made by no less than the French film critics at *Cahiers du Cinema*.

Touch of Evil

In a 1982 interview with Leslie Megahy for the BBC, Welles described the Hollywood crowd of his acquaintance while he was filming *Touch of Evil*. It provides perspective on a career in which he had not made a film in Hollywood in ten years and, after this film, all his films as director would be made outside the Hollywood system. "I gave a dinner party not long after I started the picture, for my producer friends and big star friends, the old Hollywood brigade. My wife laid on a splendid meal and I was a little late so they were all there having their drinks before they were to sit down. I came in, in order to arrive in time, in my make-up and costume. (Welles wore an extra 80 lbs of padding and was made-up to look grotesque, bloated, and dissipated.) And they all said, 'How are you Orson, you're looking great.' (He laughs.) You know, I was an absolute monster."

Touch of Evil, a film Paul Schrader calls "film noir's epitaph," opens with a bravura three minute and twenty second tracking shot, one of cinema's most remarkable and memorable, admired by cineastes everywhere. (It is, Welles told Peter Bogdanovich in *This is Orson Welles*, "one of those shots that *shows* the director 'making a great shot'.") In close-up a hand sets a timer and a bomb is placed in an automobile. As the camera rises up and over Los Robles, on the Mexican/American border, we pick up a couple, Miguel "Mike" Vargas (Charlton Heston), a Mexican drug enforcement prosecutor, and his American wife Susan (Janet Leigh). When the bomb explodes and kills Rudi Linnekar and his companion, the investigation is put into the hands of an American police detective, Hank Quinlan (Welles), who suspects a Mexican, Manolo Sanchez (Victor Millian), and frames him with evidence that Vargas quickly establishes was planted. The antagonism between the two thus established, Vargas sets out to discredit Quinlan even as Quinlan attempts to discredit Vargas by sending racketeer Uncle Joe Grandi (Akim Tamiroff) and his minions to the motel where Susan Vargas is staying to intimidate and drug her. Once he learns of this scheme, Vargas pulls out all the stops to rescue his wife, and Quinlan realizes he must kill Grandi, which he does in the motel room in which Susan Vargas has been drugged. But Quinlan incriminates himself by leaving the cane he uses for his injured leg at the scene of Grandi's murder. Irving Singer in *Three Philosophical Filmmakers* says that Quinlan "leaves it by accident at the scene of Grandi's murder," but if there is a flaw in *Touch of Evil* it is that Quinlan, a seasoned detective who needs the use of his cane, would leave the scene of the murder and *forget* to take his cane, a vital piece of incriminating evidence—unless, of course, he *wanted* to be discovered as the murderer. But this is implausible once we understand that Quinlan's remorseless pursuit of the men he knows by what he calls his "intuition" to be guilty is done out of a sense of justice. We learn that Quinlan's wife was murdered by strangulation but the killer was never found, or at least never brought to trial, because strangulation leaves such weak evidence by which the killer might be convicted. But Quinlan's "intuition" has been remarkably effective in his crusade to find the guilty.

Vargas knows he needs to gather evidence to establish the corrupt cop's deeds. He succeeds in doing so by convincing Pete Menzies (Joseph Calleia), Quinlan's devoted sidekick, to engage Quinlan in conversation (which Vargas is taping) that will implicate him in framing indi-

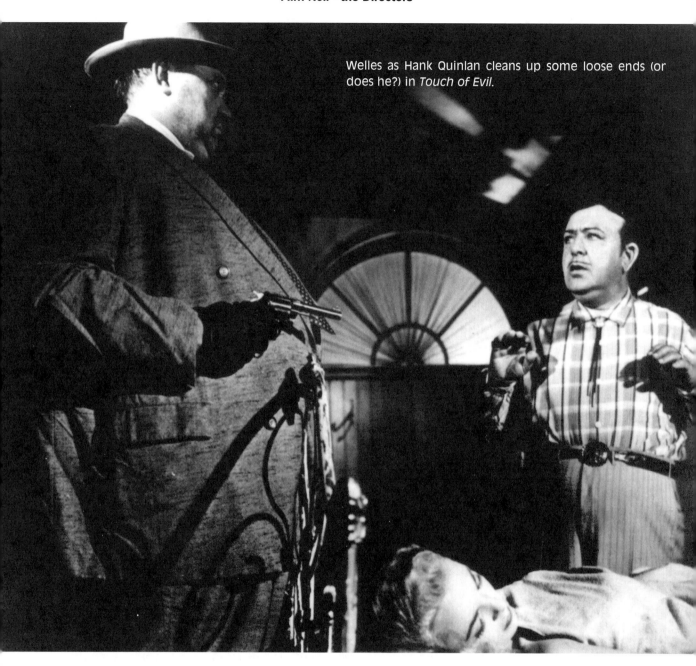

Welles as Hank Quinlan cleans up some loose ends (or does he?) in *Touch of Evil*.

viduals Quinlan "knew" were guilty without having the proper evidence to indict them. This Menzies does, and in a shootout, both men are killed. As Singer recognizes, *Touch of Evil* transcends the B-film noir it resembles so much even as it exemplifies it with its action sequences, overlapping dialogue, and Russell Metty's exquisite chiaroscuro lighting.

The master narrative of Orson Welles' career is often thought to be one of meteoric rise quickly followed by rapid decline. While this is an oversimplification, it comes close to describing the boom-and-bust aspect of Welles' Hollywood years. It is disheartening to contemplate what the director-screenwriter-actor underwent in Europe and how divided his time was between scriptwriting, performing, and fulfilling the contractual and financial obligations he had made in the course of paying the large debts he incurred as a result of his many projects (to say nothing of his efforts to fulfill the promise of his masterwork, *Citizen Kane*). This pattern of his financial career was to use, in the words of Robert Garis in *The Films of Orson Welles*, "whatever money he was earning in a current project to repay debts contracted in past projects, only to contract new debts in the new project." Welles' filmmaking career is often described as a trajectory of decline, and the oft-described "boy genius" who appeared regularly on TV talk shows and in wine commercials is dismissed by some, but in the precincts of serious film commentary and criticism his achievements as a creative artist are secure.

Biography

Orson Welles was born on May 6, 1915 in Kenosha, Wisconsin. He is perhaps best known to the general public for his Mercury Theater of the Air broadcast of the H.G. Wells' story of a Martian invasion, "The War of the Worlds," a radio drama whose documentary form and realistic effects panicked an entire nation.

Brought to Hollywood by RKO in 1939, Welles was given the unheard-of "final cut" on a project of his choosing. He co-wrote (with Herman J. Mankiewicz), directed, and starred in *Citizen Kane* (1941), a film widely regarded as one of the best ever made but a commercial disappointment. Welles followed *Kane* with a film version of Booth Tarkington's novel, *The Magnificent Ambersons*. This time around, he was not given final cut and the version released by the studio included edits by others that ran contrary to his intentions. It was another financial loss for RKO. While he was in South America to film a semi-documentary called *It's All True*, RKO severed its ties with Welles, refusing to produce the South American film. In Hollywood, Welles came to be regarded as unreliable, so in order to demonstrate his ability to work within the constraints of the studio system, he directed and starred in a conventional suspense thriller, *The Stranger* (1946). Impressed by his ability to complete a film on time and within budget, Columbia Pictures hired him to direct and co-star with one of its biggest stars, Rita Hayworth (Welles' former wife) in *The Lady from Shanghai* (1946). In terms of steadying his reputation with the Hollywood studios, the often incomprehensible film was an unmitigated disaster. Welles spent the next nine years in Europe, acting with distinction in *The Third Man* (Carol Reed, 1949), and completing two of his own pictures, *Othello* (1952) and *Mr. Arkadin* (1955). Back in Hollywood, Welles was offered the opportunity to co-star in *Touch of Evil*, a film he wound up scripting and directing and ultimately lamenting once the studio took it out of his hands, adding scenes shot by studio director Harry Keller and cutting others. The remainder of Welles' films were produced in Europe: *The Trial* (1962), *Chimes at Midnight* (1966), and *F for Fake* (1974). Other projects, such as *Don Quixote* and *The Other Side of the Wind* remained uncompleted or hostage to litigation at the time of Welles' death on October 10, 1985.

Noir Films

Journey into Fear (1943)
The Stranger (1946)
The Lady from Shanghai (1947)
Mr Arkadin (1955)
Touch of Evil (1958)

Left. Welles directs *The Lady from Shanghai.*

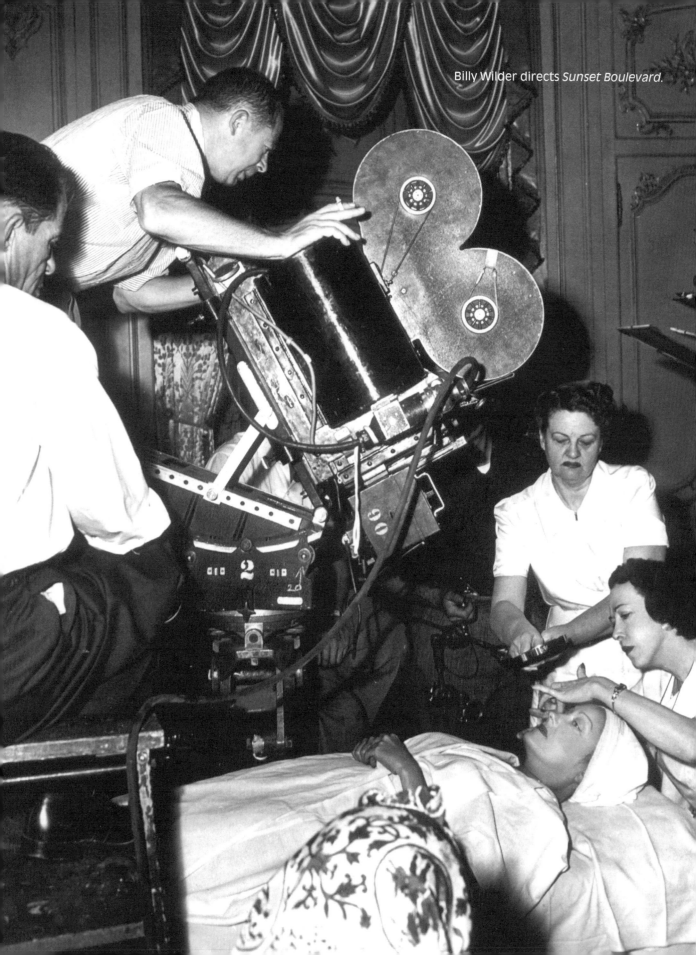

Billy Wilder directs *Sunset Boulevard*.

Billy Wilder

Sheri Chinen Biesen

Writer-director Billy Wilder made four noir pictures—*Double Indemnity* (1944), *The Lost Weekend* (1945), *Sunset Blvd.* (1950) and *Ace in the Hole* (1951)—influential films depicting a brooding visual and psychic landscape laced with cynical biting wit. Wilder's films show how noir style influences many different genres. None of Wilder's noir pictures are conventional detective films or criminal narratives. Instead, they concern self-destructive ordinary people led to commit sordid criminal acts where anti-heroes are caught in labyrinths of deceit.

Double Indemnity is a shadowy exemplar of noir style and a key film spurring the dark trend. Its significance was recognized in the U.S. during the war, before noir was coined in 1946 by French critics overseas. Wilder brilliantly establishes the quintessentially dark atmosphere of film noir immediately in *Double Indemnity* with beautifully chiaroscuro (low-key, high-contrast) shrouded visual style, bleak tone, ambient milieu and evocative voice-over narration. Visually Wilder's blackest noir, its embedded sense of paranoia highlights the subjective psychological point-of-view of an unlikely illicit lover-turned-criminal lured to his doom by a cold-blooded, gold-digging femme fatale.

Wilder creates an existential abyss that envelopes the viewer from the very opening of *Double Indemnity* as a silhouette moves forward to visually swallow the screen and a car races through a black night to the suspenseful strains of Miklós Rózsa's riveting music score. Cynical insurance salesman Walter Neff (Fred MacMurray) is shot tangling with a lethal married femme fatale, spider woman Phyllis Dietrichson (Barbara Stanwyck)—who he's just murdered (after having an affair and murdering her husband). As Neff dictates a late-night murder confession (the story's plot) into his Dictaphone machine to his investigator boss Barton Keyes (Edward G. Robinson) he bleeds to death smoking a cigarette in his pitch-black office. "I did it for money. And a woman. I didn't get the money. I didn't get the woman. Pretty isn't it."

Collaborating with hardboiled writer Raymond Chandler (*The Big Sleep, Farewell My Lovely, The Blue Dahlia*), Wilder's adaptation of James M. Cain's salacious *Double Indemnity* was a watershed: a vanguard film in how to adapt censorable Cain material successfully (after being banned for nearly a decade) providing a road map for getting noir past Hollywood censors. Wilder's *Double Indemnity* featured racy dialogue with dark visual style to suggest a shady sordid milieu. Wilder and Chandler reworked Cain's story to maximize sexual innuendo and verbal wit in cunning repartee invented for the film not found in Cain's novella, such as the classic conversation about accident insurance as Neff's eyes drop to Phyllis' anklet. Neff asks her name, saying he'd have to "drive it around the block a couple of times," and "was sorta getting over the idea" of talking to her husband. When she warns "There's a speed limit," Neff replies "Suppose you get down off your motorcycle and give me a ticket." Venetian blinds splinter Neff as he enters Phyllis' house conveying his doom. His inferior point-of-view looks up at her (shot with an extreme power-angle backlit so she's visually ablaze) in a towel at the top of the stairs looking down at him.

Moody voiceover narration accompanies Neff's drive home: "It was a hot afternoon, and I can still remember the smell of honeysuckle all along that street. How could I have known that murder can sometimes smell like honeysuckle?" It accentuated Neff's doomed, conflicted protagonist in Wilder's oppressive fatalistic milieu, structuring action with his guilt-ridden male point of view. Wilder's flashback narrative evokes a hardboiled detective story, but reveals the criminal up front—as self-destructive anti-hero—to emphasize futile immoral deeds. On a dark street near Neff's apartment he takes a walk after the murder; his narration conveys moral retribution: "That was all there was to it. Nothing had slipped, nothing had been overlooked, there was nothing to give us away." With growing paranoia, "Yet...as I was walking down the street...suddenly it came over me that everything would go wrong. It sounds crazy...I couldn't hear my own footsteps. It was the walk of a dead man."

Deep shadows cloak Neff's apartment and Phyllis' house where they shoot each other, night-for-night shots of railroad tracks where they drop her husband's body after they murder him as the sedan engine fails, and Neff's walk home after the murder. Wilder's film was suspenseful and unsettling from the moment it opened as Neff swerves his car, screeching through dark, wet city streets. To avoid showing censored violence and sex, Wilder uses off-screen sound and visuals to suggest taboo material. Wilder frames a tight close-up of Phyllis' face as the horn blows and Neff strangles her husband. Wilder seated the couple at opposite ends of a couch in Neff's apartment, fully dressed and smoking cigarettes, after fading from a passionate embrace to imply sex, splintered by venetian blind shadows to forebode their fatally doomed affair.

Wilder's chiaroscuro lighting and shadowy noir visual style was a savvy aesthetic response to censorship and Hollywood's wartime filmmaking climate with blackouts and rationing of lighting, electricity, film, set materials. His mise-en-scène reveals a corrupt American city, sordidness shrouded in shadow, fog and smoke, light splintered in oblique pat-

Double Indemnity: above, Keyes (Edward G. Robinson) finds a wounded Neff (Fred MacMurray) dictating his story. Opposite, Neff admires a "honey of an anklet" on the leg of Phyllis Dietrichson (Barbara Stanwyck).

terns or glistening reflections on rain slicked streets, pools of water, shattered windows and mirrored surfaces. Wilder explained, "We had to be very realistic...you had to believe the situation and the characters...*Double Indemnity* was based on the principal of *M*...I tried for a very realistic picture...that looked like a newsreel. You never realized it was staged. But like a newsreel, you look to grab the moment of truth, and exploit it." Cinematographer John Seitz shot in art director Hans Dreier's house. Wilder described Stanwyck's femme fatale as "not much of a housekeeper." He wanted to achieve a shrouded look: "Whenever I opened the door and the sun was coming in, there was always dust in the air. Because they never dusted it." His most expressionistic noir, Wilder insisted, "There was *some* dramatic lighting, yes, but it was newsreel lighting...sometimes even in a newsreel you get a masterpiece shot. That was the approach. No phony setups.... Everything was meant to support the realism of the story." The war played a key role in his bleak vision of authenticity. Wilder's family perished at Auschwitz as he shot *Double Indemnity*. The popularity of Wilder's stylish *Double Indemnity* launched a booming noir trend in Hollywood by the end of the war.[1] (See Biesen, *Blackout*.) Wilder cast comedic MacMurray, Stanwyck and former-gangster Robinson against type in fine performances creating ambiguity and suspense that were critically acclaimed. Hollywood critics, industry executives and director Alfred Hitchcock noted Wilder made film history with *Double Indemnity*. Nominated for seven Academy Awards, Wilder's *Double Indemnity* set the standard for film noir.

It also paved the way for *The Lost Weekend*. Wilder's *Double Indemnity* and *The Lost Weekend* were two of the original dark American pictures cited by the French as "film noir" in

The Lost Weekend: above, Ray Milland as Don Birnam suffers from delirium tremens. Opposite, lying to those trying to help him, brother Wick (Phillip Terry) and girlfriend Helen (Jane Wyman).

1946, highlighting the importance of Wilder's contribution to noir's development. Influenced by documentary newsreel style, *The Lost Weekend* was a social realist drama with extensive location shooting on the streets of New York, anticipating later social problem noir (and Neo-realist) pictures following the war. Based on Charles Jackson's lifelike novel on the perils of alcoholism, like Cain's *Double Indemnity*, censors deemed it sordid and objectionable in its unvarnished portrayal of excessive drinking, illicit sex/prostitution and suicide.

While not as visually dark or hardboiled as Wilder-Chandler's punchy repartee in *Double Indemnity*, *The Lost Weekend* (adapted by Wilder and Charles Brackett [who refused to adapt *Double Indemnity*]) was a brooding narrative of obsession with noir style (shot by Seitz) depicting the bleak vision of its unglamorous, self-destructive antihero writer Don Birnam (Ray Milland). Rather than a noir focusing on sex or murderous crime, *The Lost Weekend* instead centered on his addiction to drink and his downward spiral. Birnam ends up plummeting down a flight of stairs on an alcoholic binge culminating in a shrouded horrifying Caligari-like psychiatric ward with oppressive shadows and crisscrossing bars of entrapment (undulating to splinter Milland as doors swing shut) that consume its inhabitants suffering delirium tremens, a "disease of the night," and Birnam's horror-inspired hallucination (amplified by Miklós Rózsa's creepy score) of a bat eating a rat in a hole in the wall. (Though Wilder denied it, Milland's tormented *Lost Weekend* writer seemed to resemble *Double Indemnity* collaborator Chandler.)

In *The Lost Weekend* "that nice young man who drinks" is driven not by sex or money or violent sadistic thrill but by thirst for booze. He steals a woman's purse in a swanky bar to pay for his liquor, but is humiliated when he is caught and thrown out. (Wilder shows the chandelier where his liquor's hidden and his hand clasping her purse under the table.) He pawns his typewriter, his girlfriend's leopard coat, gets a gun and attempts suicide. Birnam describes his autobiographical novel as "morbid stuff…a horror story, confessions of a booze addict" simply titled *The Bottle* about his drinking obsession "merry-go-round, you got to ride it all the way" (resembling the lethal trolleycar in *Double Indemnity* where criminals ride "straight down the line" together to their doom).

While *Double Indemnity* dealt with an unscrupulous insurance salesman out to score some cash and sex in murderous fatal attraction, Wilder's later noir such as *The Lost Weekend* centered on flawed washed-up writers filled with cynical loathing hitting rock bottom. *The Lost Weekend* projected noir urban jungle: pawnshops, Bellevue Hospital psychiatric ward, 55th and 3rd Avenues, the Metropolitan Opera (Wilder's dark sense of humor torments Birnam with *La Traviata*'s "Drinking Song"). Unlike dangerous femme Phyllis, played with ice-cold perfection by Stanwyck, his girlfriend Helen (Jane Wyman) is a warm hearted maternal redeemer who tries for over three years to reform/cure his addiction (he eventually survives to write his story). Even the prostitute Gloria (Doris Dowling) is portrayed as humane, comical and sympathetic as he exploits her for money to buy another bottle, feeding his obsession. (Censors insisted Wilder clean up his depiction of unsavory prostitution, drinking, and suicide.)

Wilder's *The Lost Weekend* ends where it begins: with a bottle of booze stealthily hanging outside the apartment window as he tries to hide his drinking from his girlfriend and brother. "I stood in there packing my suitcase, only my mind wasn't on the suitcase, and it wasn't on the weekend, nor was it on the shirts I was putting in the suitcase either. My mind was hanging outside the window. It was suspended, just about eighteen inches below. And out there in that great big concrete jungle, I wonder how many others there are like poor bedeviled guys on fire with thirst, such colorful figures to the rest of the world as they stagger blind-

ly towards another binge, another bender, another spree." After Wilder's *Double Indemnity* was nominated the year before, *The Lost Weekend* won Best Picture Oscar, Best Director for Wilder, Best Actor (Milland), and Best Screenplay (Brackett [who produced] and Wilder).

Wilder worked with Brackett for the last time on *Sunset Blvd.* featuring an unlikely romantic pairing of washed-up misfits: a delusional eccentric past-her-prime silent-screen star Norma Desmond (Gloria Swanson [originally intended for Mae West]) and her younger kept man Joe Gillis (William Holden [replacing Montgomery Clift]), a frayed, unemployed B-movie screenwriter hiding out from a collection agency. *Sunset Blvd.* is another example of noir as a style rather than a genre: there are not many films about Hollywood writers moving in with old silent movie stars. Wilder's *Sunset Blvd.* includes iconic examples of noir visual style and a noir love triangle with a classic noir gender paradigm contrasting "good girl" redeemer (Betty, the fresh-faced young script reader [Nancy Olson]) vs. femme fatale (manipulative aging star Desmond) who embodies unstable noir psychosis.

Below, kept-man Joe Gillis (William Holden) consoles his mistress Norma Desmond (Gloria Swanson). Opposite, Gillis trying to find inspiration as a screenwriter.

Wilder takes shots at Hollywood; as in his other noir films, he includes social criticism in *Sunset Blvd*. Wilder comments that "psychopathy sells" in writing pictures, a self-reflexive commentary on film noir, exploring the difference between his noir films *Double Indemnity*, *The Lost Weekend* (a "message" picture) and *Sunset Blvd*. "Message kid" script girl Betty says: "I just think that pictures should say a little something…I think you should throw out all that psychological stuff—exploring a killer's sick mind." Joe replies, "Psychopaths sell like hotcakes." Betty insists people's "threadbare lives, their struggles…worry about getting enough money to resole their shoes… can be as exciting as any chase, any gunplay."

Wilder captures a dying era of old Hollywood in *Sunset Blvd*. casting famous silent stars such as Swanson, Buster Keaton, filmmakers Erich von Stroheim, Cecil B. DeMille, and gossip columnist Hedda Hopper shot in shadowy noir style (by Seitz) providing scathing critique and insider commentary on the motion picture industry with an ugly glimpse backstage behind-the-scenes of Tinseltown. Wilder invokes horror conventions: Norma's rundown mansion embodies a haunted house of surreal insanity (with a dead monkey as rats scurry in concrete remains of a pool) that becomes a prison entrapping Joe. He is entombed in a shrine to flamboyant fading star Norma's dead career. Images of Swanson as a young ingénue are everywhere. Spider Woman Desmond sinks her claws into Joe as they watch Swanson's real life silent films (*Queen Kelly* directed by Stroheim) backlit by the projector in the dark; Norma pantomimes Chaplin's Tramp. Desmond's obsessive web closes in, controlling and manipulating Joe's every move with compulsive mania. (Norma's mansion had been owned by oil tycoon J. Paul Getty.)

Wilder introduces a creepy atmosphere of eccentric ruin that's strange and destroys lives, yet hypnotically alluring and seductive from a lost indulgent age. The grandiose excess of Norma's ostentatious empty mansion personifies her overwhelming silent-era presence deglamorized and dissected in Wilder's noir as tragic, oppressive, a suffocating, bizarre relic of faded grotesque splendor. Joe admits, "The whole place seemed to have been stricken with a kind of creeping paralysis, out of beat with the rest of the world, crumbling apart in slow motion...I knew there was something wrong...It sure was a cozy set-up." As in *Double Indemnity,* they sprinkled dust before the camera to enhance a musty shrouded look. Wilder employs an ornate baroque visual style of worn opulence and decadent decay with cluttered claustrophobic mise-en-scène. *Sunset Blvd.* reveals a clash of styles and eras: Norma's melo-dramatic intensity, hyperbolic exaggerated gestures, makeup and silent performance style vs. caustic barbed wit and mocking deadpan humor of cynical hardboiled sound-era screenwriter Joe. "You're Norma Desmond. You used to be in silent pictures. You used to be big." She replies, "I am big. It's the pictures that got small," as Wilder recognizes Hollywood's rival: small screen television. Wilder visually articulates Joe being drawn into Norma's web with snarled dead branches as he climbs dark stairs to his room above the garage, smug in his "cozy setup" sug-gesting he has no idea of the dangerous mess he's getting into.

Sunset Blvd. features iconic noir elements: doomed antihero, entrapment, claustro-phobia, femme fatale, naïve redeemer. Wilder reveals a corrupt Hollywood with crooked agents, washed-up stars, writers trying to get a gig where life is an unhappy struggle. Joe never lands a job on a picture; he instead becomes Norma's gigolo selling out sex and services for some hard cash while moonlighting afterhours with another woman on the side and writ-ing for free. *Sunset Blvd.* evokes melodrama and police procedurals in its crime-oriented open-ing with Franz Waxman's exhilarating score, police cars blaring across asphalt at shadowy dawn with screaming sirens and newsreel cameras. "Yes, this is Sunset Blvd...the homicide squad—complete with detectives and newspaper men. A murder has been reported from one of those great big houses... You'll read all about it in the late editions...You'll get it over your radio, and see it on television because an old-time star is involved, one of the biggest. But before you hear it all distorted and blown out of proportion, before those Hollywood colum-nists get their hands on it, maybe you'd like to hear the facts, the whole truth...If so, you've come to the right party..."

Sunset Blvd. reimagines *Double Indemnity*'s sardonic hardboiled noir in a classic black

Sunset Blvd: Wilder mocks myths and reveals the unglamourous reality behind the camera: at right, the mad Norma Desmond gives her news conference about her "comeback."

Left, Gillis takes an apple break with co-writer Betty Schaefer (Nancy Olson) on Paramount's New York street back lot.

comedy/drama set in Los Angeles, especially Hollywood (with recognizable locations such as Schwab's Drug Store) and Paramount's backlot with the interiors of Norma's mansion filmed on sound stages. Wilder's dark melodrama with biting humor concerned an illicit crime-of-passion. While *Double Indemnity* conveys its story via a murder confession given by a dying man, Wilder tops himself in *Sunset Blvd* with voiceover narrated by a dead man floating facedown in a pool! (Wilder shot the sequence with a mirror to show the corpse's face through the water from below.) Wilder's love triangle is doomed from the start: his narrator is a guy already murdered. Joe ends up shot, but *Sunset Blvd.* is not really about crime in the usual sense of a detective-mystery story; like *Double Indemnity* it's revealed up front. (Originally opening in the morgue with Joe's corpse talking to cadavers, Wilder reshot after preview audiences laughed.)

Wilder mocks Hollywood myths; he ridicules romance, glamour, fame, stardom and starry-eyed couples. Norma brags: "I'm richer than all this new Hollywood trash! I've got a million dollars." Unimpressed, Joe replies, "Keep it." Undeterred, she boasts, "Own three blocks downtown, I've got oil in Bakersfield, pumping, pumping, pumping! What's it for but to buy us anything we want!" But she can't buy Joe's love, a career or public adulation. She is lonely, desperate, suicidal, egomaniacally yearning for her silent-era accolades. Betty stopped pursuing fame: "What's wrong with being on the other side of the cameras?" Norma's director/husband-turned-butler Max admits, "I could have continued my career, only I found everything unendurable after she had left me." (Swanson fired Stroheim from uncompleted *Queen Kelly*, ending his career.) Everything is a sham, a front, a façade like hollow Hollywood soundstage sets creating false illusions. (Betty prefers the phony backlot because she was raised by a "picture family": her parents and grandparents worked at the studio for generations, which is why she has a job.) Max sends fake fan letters to Norma. Joe thinks Betty's a fool not to sense "something phony" in his setup. Norma asks Betty: "Exactly how much do you know about him? Do you know where he lives?" Joe sells out for money, as Walter "did it for money and a woman" in *Double Indemnity*. "This is an enormous place...It's lonely here, so she got herself a companion. A very simple setup: An older woman who is well-to-do. A younger man who is not doing too well... Look, sweetie, be practical. I've got a good thing here. A long-term contract with no options. I like it that way. Maybe it's not very admirable." When Betty can't look at him anymore, he coldly replies, "How about looking for the exit." Norma is lost, "sleepwalking," reliving a lost career, literally playing to an empty house the audience left years ago.

When Joe tries to leave, Norma attempts suicide; then in manic delusion she breathes, "No one ever leaves a star. That's what makes one a star," and shoots him dead. Wilder ends his noir where it began with Joe's sardonic narration: "They got a couple of pruning hooks from the garden and fished me out...ever so gently. Funny, how gentle people get with you once you're dead. They beached me, like a harpooned baby whale, and started to check the damage...By this time the whole joint was jumping—cops, reporters, neighbors, passersby." Wilder skillfully handles Production Code censorship: Norma is arrested after gunning down Joe, but her famous departure becomes a memorable moment showing she is crazy. Joe dies for his actions and speculates she might get off. As newsreel cameras roll, "Life, which can be strangely merciful, had taken pity" on Norma, deluded by fame as the "dream she had clung to so desperately had enfolded her." Swanson delivers a mesmerizing performance. Self-absorbed, she exclaims to imaginary fans, "I'll never desert you again...this is my life!...I'm ready for my close-up."

While *Double Indemnity*'s success spurs the noir trend, executives later criticized Wilder and *Sunset Blvd.* for its unvarnished portrayal of Hollywood. It was a metaphoric wake-up call signaling the end of a creative, economic and political era in a changing Hollywood by 1950. Revealing the period's Cold War xenophobia, MGM's Louis B. Mayer called émigré Wilder a "foreigner" disparaging the industry at *Sunset Blvd.*'s premiere for studio executives. Darryl Zanuck said that "*Sunset Blvd.* was a masterpiece until it was released throughout the country and failed to do business. It is not so big a masterpiece today." (Biesen, *Blackout*.) It earned acclaim as one of Hollywood's finest films. Nominated for eleven Academy Awards, including best picture, director, cinematography, performances, editing, *Sunset Blvd.* won Oscars for writing (Wilder/Brackett [who produced]), art direction, music; and Best Picture, Director (Wilder), and performance (Swanson) at the Golden Globes.

Sunset Blvd.'s critical success enabled Wilder to produce-write-direct *Ace in the Hole*, his last and most cynical noir (based on a true story of the tragic death of Floyd Collins). Ruthless reporter Charles "Chuck" Tatum (Kirk Douglas) exploits a collapsed cave accident burying a man alive to further his career while having a toxic affair with the victim's unfaithful wife Lorraine (Jan Sterling); her trapped war-veteran husband Leo dies after Tatum delays his rescue a week to milk his sensational tabloid story while thousands cash in on the tragedy with a carnival and media circus that makes the hoopla in *Sunset Blvd.* look tame. *Ace in the Hole* amplifies Wilder's scathing cultural critique of media sensationalism with Cain-like illicit sex and misogyny.

Wilder's sunlit visual style set outdoors in stark rural New Mexico daylight shows a brighter noir look while his bleak worldview slams media, reporters, TV, radio, even the American public. Wilder constructed a huge set near ancient ruins with chiaroscuro tunnels where Tatum shines a flashlight for eerie demon lighting. His antihero reporter is a failed writer (in an extraordinary cold hearted performance by Kirk Douglas) who is caustic and unsympathetic, toying with a philandering married blonde femme. Lorraine tells sleazy Tatum: "I've met a lot of hard-boiled eggs in my time, but you're twenty minutes." Wilder refers to his earlier noir films opening with Tatum riding up in a convertible on a tow truck suggesting Joe's car being towed in *Sunset Blvd.*, paying homage to Cain (Lorraine's illicit affair with Tatum

Below, *Ace in the Hole*: the jibes of Leo Minosa's wife Lorraine (Jan Sterling) ultimately prompt a physical response from reporter Chuck Tatum (Kirk Douglas).

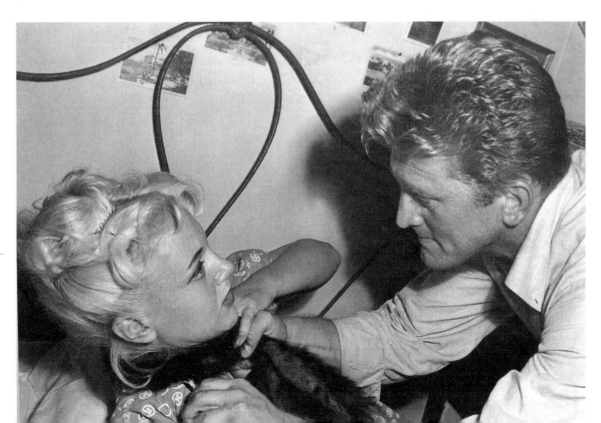

resembles that of *Postman*'s Cora and Frank) and *Double Indemnity* (referring to Neff's insurance company Pacific All Risk, casting *Double Indemnity*'s Medford Oregon witness "Jackson" Porter Hall as Tatum's disapproving editor).

In *Ace in the Hole* everyone is corrupt—Leo's "friend" Tatum, his wife, the crooked sheriff, the contractor hired to rescue him (and paid off to delay), the news media who should be helping him but exploit him, and the public feeding on the carnival frenzy. No one is innocent; even dying victim Leo was exploiting Indian burial sites. Nothing can save Leo, not his doctor, priest, heartbroken father or his mother's prayers. He is doomed.

Eventually, Wilder's antihero endeavors to

redeem himself. When Tatum realizes Joe will die, he tries to save him, but it's too-little, too-late: in his guilt Tatum nearly strangles Lorraine until she stabs him in the stomach with scissors. Instead of getting a doctor for his wound, Tatum gets a priest to honor Leo's dying wish to receive the last-rites. (Similarly, Neff had the perfect fall-guy but couldn't let him take the blame, driving to confess when he could still get away; Joe redeems himself driving away Betty for her own good though he plans to leave Norma.) It's a bleak vision. In the end, Tatum literally "takes the fall," dying in an incredible shot by Wilder (and DP Charles Lang) of Douglas visually crashing facedown before the camera on the floor, shifting from ironic extreme power-angle to extreme close-up of his dead face in the lens.

Wilder's harsh noir faced a hostile reception from the press and the public and was not successful at the box office. (Paramount retitled it *The Big Carnival,* a bungled release.) After its commercial failure, *Ace in the Hole* was Wilder's last noir; the noir cycle fades throughout the 1950s. Wilder explained there was no reason why he never made another noir, however, he had a shrewd commercial sensibility, turning to comedy. Wilder was a remarkable noir stylist, an inspired trendsetter. His cynical vision, biting wit and perceptive human insight was miles ahead of its time and continues to have contemporary resonance.

Notes

1. Sheri Chinen Biesen, *Blackout: World War II and the Origins of Film Noir* (Baltimore: Johns Hopkins University Press, 2005).

Biography

Billy Wilder (1906-2002) was born in Austria-Hungary. He was a journalist before becoming a screenwriter in Berlin, Germany, where he worked with Robert and Curt Siodmak, Edgar Ulmer, and Fred Zinnemann. After a brief stay in Paris, he moved to America following Hitler's rise to power, became an American citizen in 1934, and worked in Hollywood as a screenwriter. Given the chance to direct by Paramount, his comedy *The Major and the Minor* (1942) was a success, and he went on to become an important hyphenate filmmaker. Although he and his brother had escaped Germany, his mother and other family members were murdered at Auschwitz. His *Double Indemnity* (1944) was a key development in the rise of noir, and each of his four films in the noir style were not typical detective genre fare. After 1951, his films included *Stalag 17* (1953), followed mainly by classic comedies such as *Sabrina* (1954), *The Seven Year Itch* (1955), *Some Like It Hot* (1959), and *The Apartment* (1960). He won two Academy Awards for Best Director (*The Lost Weekend*, and *The Apartment*), and three for screenwriting (*The Lost Weekend, Sunset Blvd.,* and *The Apartment.*) His last film was *Buddy, Buddy* (1981).

Noir Films

Double Indemnity (1944)
The Lost Weekend (1945)
Sunset Blvd. (1950)
Ace in the Hole (1951, aka *The Big Carnival*)

Opposite, *Ace in the Hole*'s "Big Carnival" and Tatum "in the hole" screaming at Leo Minosa. Right, Wilder directs Stanwyck in *Double Indemnity.*

Robert Wise

Wheeler Winston Dixon

> I didn't want to become a director all along. I didn't really think about it that way. You know, I just took it one step at a time. Once I got to be an editor, I learned the game, learned about filmmaking and directing, and I wanted to move on and become a director.

Robert Wise, "My Three Ps"

Robert Wise's case as a noir director is a curious one. Wise seemingly freelanced throughout his career, and never really came down decisively in any one genre or movement, swinging all the way from horror films through noir to musical epics, with every possible stop in-between.

Criminal Court (1946) is arguably Wise's first full-on noir film. Steve Barnes (Tom Conway) is a criminal defense lawyer who has made a name with his showy courtroom tactics. He is now running for district attorney on a "clean government" platform. Barnes' nemesis is gangster Wright (Robert Armstrong), who threatens him if he reveal the incriminating evidence he has compiled about Wright's syndicate. During a fight Barnes kills Wright. Unfortunately it is Barnes' girlfriend, Georgia Gale (Martha O'Driscoll, better known for her light comedies and appearances in Universal horror movies), the featured singer at Vic's place, the Club Circle, who discovers the body, and is charged with Vic's murder. Barnes immediately goes to the police and confesses, but no one will believe him. Further, Barnes suggests that the reason he didn't report the murder immediately is because Vic deserved to die; true, perhaps, but unconvincing to the police. However, none of this is developed in any way, shape, or form; *Criminal Court* just sits there, with nothing much happening for its 60-minute running time after a solid first six minutes, dominated by Armstrong's brash and assured performance. When Vic dies, the film dies with him, and nothing can bring it back to life. As Barnes, Tom Conway mopes his way through the film with an air of resigned fatality, and really doesn't do anything to effect Georgia's eventual exoneration. Wise's seeming lack of interest in the project

Below, *Criminal Court*

is also evident in his lack of dollies, sharp editing, or even close-ups; most of the action is covered with a master shot whenever possible. Not even Steve Brodie's presence in the supporting cast can help *Criminal Court*, which was released on the bottom half of a double bill, and quickly vanished into oblivion. It is perhaps Wise's least interesting film.

But from this undistinguished effort, Wise rebounded with *Born to Kill*, one of the greatest noirs ever made, and the first definitive proof that Wise was a talent to watch behind the camera. His apprenticeship work as an editor and director with Val Lewton and Orson Welles at RKO is accomplished enough, but the stunning brutality of *Born to Kill* recalls the bleakly amoral appeal of Jacques Tourneur's (another Lewton alumnus) brilliant noir *Out of the Past*, made the same year, 1947, for the same studio, RKO. Based on James Gunn's novel *Deadlier Than the Male*, *Born to Kill* tracks the psychotic progress of the homicidal Sam Wild,

Below, Claire Trevor and Lawrence Tierney in *Born to Kill*.

played with brazen conviction by Lawrence Tierney. Sam is a time bomb waiting to go off at any moment, and as the film opens, he kills his girlfriend Laury Palmer (Isabel Jewell) in a momentary fit of jealousy, and is forced to leave town until the heat dies down. Sam's side-kick, Marty "Mart" Waterman, played by noir's perennial fall guy Elisha Cook, Jr., looks after Sam with an almost wifely concern, rushes Sam out of town on the next train, where he runs into the equally unbalanced Helen Trent (Claire Trevor), who is engaged to a rich man she doesn't really love, the colorless Fred Grover (Phillip Terry).

Helen doesn't have a penny of her own, but like Sam, she's "no turnip," as she put it, and the two recognize in each other the clear hallmarks of the opportunistic social climber who will stop at nothing to get what they want. Helen wants Fred's money, and the security that marriage to him will bring, but treats him like dirt, which, for the moment, Fred tolerates. But Sam Wild promises much more excitement for Helen, as his name clearly implies, and soon the two are involved in a passionate affair, even as Sam engineers a marriage to Helen's half-sister, the somewhat clueless but filthy rich newspaper heiress Georgia Staples (Audrey Long). But no sooner are Sam and Georgia married than Sam demands to immediately take over editorship of the newspaper she owns, without any prior experience in the business, while at the same time, smarmy smalltime detective Matthew Arnett (Walter Slezak) is on Sam's trail for the Laury Palmer murder, egged on by Laury's former landlady, Mrs. Kraft (Esther Howard), who has made solving Laury's murder a personal vendetta. Matters come to head when Sam, wrongly convinced that his pal Mart is making a play for Helen, knifes him to death on a deserted stretch of beach, even as Mart, ironically, is trying to murder Mrs. Kraft to put an end to her meddling in their affairs. Kraft survives, but is cowed into silence by Helen; yet the Palmer matter refuses to go away, and Arnett eventually brings the police in, resulting in a violent shootout in which both Sam and Helen are killed.

But what is most striking about the film is Wise's skill with the actors: Lawrence Tierney was well known for getting into scrapes of one kind or another off screen, and Claire Trevor was also equally volatile. Phillip Terry and Audrey Long, portraying the ostensibly "normal" people in the film, are absolutely without interest or sympathy, and in many ways are drawn entirely as one-dimensional characters; Wise's narrative sympathy is with Sam, Helen, and Mart, even as the world they inhabit alternately repels and fascinates the viewer. By this time, also, Wise had developed a utilitarian visual style that he would employ in all his work, adapting his camera work and editorial decisions to the material at hand, rather than employing one distinctive visual approach throughout his work, as in Hitchcock's precise storyboarding of his films, or Fritz Lang's meticulous pre-production and detail-oriented process. Wise responded to his material on the set, on a day-by-day basis, blocking out his camera movement as he went along. Of his early days at RKO, Wise remembered that "I'd get to the set very early in the morning, maybe at seven o'clock or something. They probably would have a nine o'clock call for people. I'd get there at seven, and I'd fool around with the set, with my finder, figuring different angles and that kind of thing. I had to get an idea of how I wanted to go, and eventually down the line I got to working with a sketch artist. We would try to sketch stuff out ahead of time so we'd have an idea, always leaving room to move away from the sketches, if what you thought just wouldn't work with the actors."

Born to Kill is a tour de force in every department, and its unrelieved pessimism, coupled with its memorably cynical dialogue—threatening Mrs. Kraft in an attempt to get her to stop pursuing the Laury Palmer murder, Helen Trent notes that "perhaps you don't realize. It's painful being killed. A piece of metal sliding into your body, finding its way into your heart. Or a bullet tearing through your skin, crashing into a bone. It takes a while to die, too. Sometimes a long while." *Born to Kill* is almost unique in its absolute vicious view of human existence.

Indeed, for many, Wise would never top the film in his work within the noir genre.

But after this triumph, for the next year Wise's career seemed to proceed in low gear; *Mystery in Mexico* (1948) is a routine crime thriller with little to recommend it, and at 66 minutes is clearly a B film, with William Lundigan toplined in a film of little ambition or audience interest, redeemed only by Wise's visual flair, and the economy of the film's running time. As insurance investigator Steve Hastings, Lundigan is sent to RKO's back lot Mexico in search of a missing colleague, seeking aid from the missing man's sister, Victoria Ames (Jacqueline White). Despite help from the dependable Ricardo Cortez in the supporting cast, the film unravels in a rather routine, offhand fashion, as if no one involved in the film really cares what happens.

But the same cannot be said of Wise's next film, the brutally violent boxing drama *The Set-Up* (1949), which stars noir icon Robert Ryan as Bill "Stoker" Thompson, a washed-up fighter who refuses to go down for the count. Teamed with the equally capable Audrey Totter as his wife Julie, who pleads with him to quit the fight game, Ryan and Wise propel the film through a taut 72 minutes, aided considerably by Art Cohn's tough script, and Milton Krasner's nightmarish cinematography.

Stoker is finished, but he doesn't know it; one more fight, just one more, he thinks, will put him back at the top of the game again. As he tells Julie, "I'm just one punch away" from the championship. To which Julie wearily replies, "I remember the first time you told me that. You were just one punch away from the title shot then. Don't you see, Bill, you'll always be just one punch away?" Stoker is unconvinced, and his unscrupulous manager, Tiny (George Tobias), sets up a match which will supposedly bring him back as a contender, but which Tiny is certain that he will lose, and in fact bets heavily on Stoker to do just that. When one of Stoker's handlers, Red (the always unscrupulous Percy Helton), tells Tiny that he should inform Stoker that the fight is fixed, and to simply take a dive, Tiny has a ready comeback: "How many times I gotta say it? There's no percentage in smartenin' up a chump."

Above, William Lundigan in *Mystery in Mexico*.

Opposite, Robert Ryan (dark trunks) in *The Set-up*.

Sent into the ring against up-and-comer Tiger Nelson (Hal Fieberling), Ryan is unaware that Tiny has cut a deal with gambler Little Boy (Alan Baxter), and fights with courage and conviction, finally gaining the upper hand in the contest. Desperate that he'll lose everything and get beaten up, or worse, by Little Boy's thugs, Tiny pleads with Stoker to throw the fight, but Stoker refuses, and in a brutal finish, pounds Tiger into the canvas.

But, as predicted, Little Boy doesn't take losing easily, and his henchmen converge on Stoker and beat him to a bloody pulp. Little Boy seems satisfied with his "revenge" on Stoker, but the boxer has one last ace up his sleeve; with a final burst of strength, he punches Little Boy in the face. Outraged, Little Boy grabs a brick and smashes one of Stoker's hands with it. The gangsters depart, and Stoker staggers to his feet,

and into the arms of Julie; Stoker's fighting days are definitively over, but he's managed, at least, to scrape out a moral victory of sorts in an utterly amoral universe.

The Set-Up is one of the classics of late 1940s noir, and Ryan's performance as Stoker is one that resonates in the memory; like so many foredoomed noir heroes, he simply refuses to accept defeat, and doesn't know when to quit. He can't trust anyone around him; everyone betrays him except for Julie, who sees the world Stoker inhabits for what it really is. The black-and-white, low-key cinematography employed throughout the film, coupled with the verisimilitude of the boxing sequences—arguably some of the most authentic in film history until the advent of Martin Scorsese's searing *Raging Bull*—makes the film an authentic representation of an unholy netherworld of dingy gyms, down-and-out "contenders," and two-bit hoods who control the destinies of the pathetic pawns of the fight game. Only in its ending, in which Julie realizes, as she says that they "both won tonight"— that she will have her husband back from the rackets, retiring as a winner—does *The Set-Up* back away from the hopeless essence of pure noir. But until that redemptive moment, the film is a headlong descent into deceit and betrayal, which Wise handles with efficiency and excruciatingly intense detail.

From here, Wise's next noir was *The House on Telegraph Hill* (1951), in which a young Valentina Cortese (here billed as Valentina Cortesa) plays Victoria (Vicky) Kowelska, a young

Robert Ryan as the beaten "winner" Stoker Ace being consoled by Audrey Totter as his wife Julie.

Polish woman who has somehow survived internment in a Nazi concentration camp during World War II, and flees to the United States with identity papers taken from a dead friend, assuming the friend's identity, and being accepted by her family as their long lost daughter in their crumbling but palatial home in San Francisco. This strains credulity a bit, but more is to come; Victoria finds that she is now an heiress, as well as the godmother of a young boy, Chris (Gordon Gebert), who stands in line to inherit a fortune. But trouble lurks in the person of Alan Spender (Richard Basehart), who plans to marry Victoria, and then kill both her and the young boy, thus inheriting the estate for himself. Spender is actually in love with Margaret (Fay Baker), the boy's nanny, who is equally bent on getting her hands on the estate. Alan and Margaret almost immediately set their homicidal plans in motion.

Soon a series of mysterious "accidents" occur in which the young boy narrowly escapes injury, and Victoria finally becomes suspicious. The film's rather melodramatic conclusion, in which Alan is killed by his own poisoned glass of fruit juice, which he had intended for Victoria, brings the film to a rather clumsy and formulaic ending; the film, made for 20th Century-Fox, is a distinctly minor effort, and although Wise handles the preposterous scenario with his customary professionalism, the film as a whole fails to come off.

Equally colorless is *The Captive City* (1952), a routine crime drama in which crusading newspaperman Jim Austin (John Forsythe) takes on the local mob in the small town where he lives. Though the film has the requisite number of beatings and betrayals, it never really catches fire, and plods through its running time like a police procedural, as if Wise were obliged to direct the film, rather than having any real interest in it. Despite the element of organized crime, one really can't call the film a noir. Unlike Fritz Lang's similarly-themed *The Big Heat* (1953), the cast simply can't sustain interest in the rather predictable narrative, which ends

Below, suave villain Alan Spender (Richard Basehart) meets the woman (Valentina Cortese, right) impersonating Victoria Kowelska, her "son" Christopher (Gordon Gebert), and governess Margaret (Fay Baker) in *The House on Telegraph Hill.*

Above, John Forsythe in *The Captive City*.

Bottom, Robert Ryan and Harry Belafonte as the race-conscious partners-in-crime in *Odds Against Tomorrow*.

with Austin successfully defying the mob through the justice system, actually invoking the real-life figure of Senator Estes Kefauver and his Special Senate Committee to Investigate Crime in Interstate Commerce, to which Austin turns in a last, desperate attempt to thwart the mob, and which, in turn, embraces his testimony, in a rather desultory happy ending. Shot for the most part on location in austere black-and-white, *The Captive City* has all the elements for a compelling crime drama, but never really takes off.

Odds Against Tomorrow (written by blacklistee Abraham Polonsky) is a much more promising enterprise on all counts, a crime thriller reminiscent of Stanley Kubrick's *The Killing* (1957) or John Huston's *The Asphalt Jungle* (1950) and features Harry Belafonte, Robert Ryan, Shelley Winters, Gloria Grahame and Ed Begley, Sr. in a surprisingly effective heist yarn with distinct racial overtones. Dave Burke (Begley) is an ex-cop who has gone "bad." After serving time in prison, Burke wants to set up a big bank robbery, and hires White, racist ex-con Earle Slater (Ryan) and African-American gambler Johnny Ingram (Belafonte) to assist him. At first, both men want nothing to do with the enterprise, partly because Slater is such an obvious racist, and hates Ingram on sight. But Ingram owes gambling debts, and Burke sees to it that the squeeze is put on him; Slater, too, needs cash to impress his girlfriend, Lorry (Winters).

So an uneasy alliance is formed, but the viewer is aware from the outset that the entire

plan is ready to unravel at any moment. After lengthy preparations, the robbery goes off more or less according to plan, except that the nearly psychotic Earle starts slugging the bank employees and using strong-arm tactics where none are needed, and refuses to let Johnny drive the gang's getaway car. Instead, he gives the keys to Burke, who is almost immediately shot and killed by the police exiting the bank as the burglar alarm goes off; this leads to a shoot-out between Johnny and Earle, which ends with both men fighting it out atop an oil refinery tank (an obvious nod to the justly famous climax of Raoul Walsh's *White Heat* [1949]), which blows up, killing them both. Wise keeps things moving at a rapid clip throughout the film, and Belafonte, Begley and Ryan all give excellent performances. If the film is perhaps a bit derivative and overwrought at times, it's still a solid piece of filmmaking, with a then-contemporary touch, coming at the end of the first cycle of classic noir.

One could probably make the case that the death row procedural *I Want To Live!* (1958), in which Susan Hayward's portrayal of accused murderess Barbara Graham won Hayward an Academy Award for Best Actress in 1959, as a noir of sorts; certainly, it is one of the most clinical and disturbing examinations of capital punishment to ever hit the screen, and was responsible for the elimination of the death penalty in a numbers of states after its release. As with all his films, Wise does his homework here, and actually attended an execution by lethal gas in preparation for the shooting of the film. The film itself is unrelieved by any ray of hope. Graham's final days and hours are depicted with mechanical brutality; the film pushes the reality of the death penalty into the collective laps of the audience with unapologetic defiance.

But after this film, Wise moved on to bigger budgeted projects with wider audience appeal, such as *West Side Story* (1961; co-directed with Jerome Robbins), the Lewtonesque but overwrought ghost story *The Haunting* (1963), and of course, *The Sound of Music* in 1965, which is about as far from being a noir as a film can possibly be.

Taken all in all, Wise's career *is* a curious one. In hopping from genre to genre, Wise reminds one of Howard Hawks, who could make superb noirs (*The Big Sleep*, 1946) and effortlessly switch to westerns (*Red River*, 1948) or musicals (*Gentlemen Prefer Blondes*, 1953) without missing a beat, but Hawks brought a distinctive world view to all of his films (honor, professionalism, the idea of the "Hawksian woman," who could take care of herself in a man's world). Wise subsumed himself to his material, and when he hit, as with his superb science fiction parable *The Day the Earth Stood Still* (1951), oddly made the same year in which Hawks "ghost-directed" the much more noirish sci-fi thriller *The Thing from Another World* (officially credited to Christian Nyby), the results could be spectacular. But Wise was always a front office man, too willing to go along with his bosses on scripts he sometimes didn't believe in, even after he hit complete "A" status, and when he picked his own projects, as with *Star!* and *The Sand Pebbles*, his box-office instincts were often wrong. Wise was a man who directed many remarkable films, but he remains an inconsistent stylist.

Biography

Robert Earl Wise was born on September 10, 1914 in Winchester, Indiana, the youngest of three brothers, and the son of a butcher and a stay-at-home mother. He attended high school in Connersville, Indiana, but spent most of his spare time at the local movie theatre. In 1933, with the Depression in full force, Wise moved to California looking for work. Through the aid of his older brother, David, who worked in the RKO Radio Pictures accounting department, he found a job as a gopher in the editorial department. From there, Wise swiftly began his rise to the top of the profession, starting as an apprentice editor in the music and sound effects department. Wise cut the music and effects tracks for such films as *Of Human Bondage* (1934), *The*

Above and opposite, two genre movies directed by Wise and photographed in the noir style: noir icon Robert Mitchum in the Western, *Blood on he Moon*, and Michael Rennie as the space-ship-flying alien on the run in *The Day the Earth Stood Still.*

Gay Divorcee (1934), *The Informer* (1935) and *Top Hat* (1935), before moving into the cutting room full time in 1939, most famously editing *Citizen Kane* for Orson Welles in 1941. He also presided over the editing and later, the recutting and reshooting of Welles' *The Magnificent Ambersons* (1942), which was substantially altered and truncated in the editing room, much to Welles' chagrin. But Wise's big break came with his association with producer Val Lewton, who was tasked with creating a series of B-horror films at RKO, and tapped Wise as the director for *The Curse of The Cat People* (1944), when the film's original director, Gunther von Fritsch, fell behind schedule; he also directed an adaptation of Robert Louis Stevenson's horror classic *The Body Snatcher* (1945) for Lewton's RKO unit. Once in the director's chair, Wise was unstoppable, hitting his stride with films like the noir *Born to Kill* (1947) as well as the noir Western *Blood on the Moon* (1948), science fiction classic *The Day the Earth Stood Still* (1951), the big business drama *Executive Suite* (1954), the prison drama *I Want To Live!* (1958), the socially aware noir *Odds Against Tomorrow* (1959), and the musical *West Side Story*, before scoring his biggest commercial success with *The Sound of Music* (1965). Wise served as president of the Academy

of Motion Picture Arts and Sciences (he won four awards, two each for directing and producing) and the Directors Guild of America and was active in helping preserve the history of the industry until his death in September, 2005.

Noir Films

Criminal Court (1946)

Born to Kill (1947)

Mystery in Mexico (1948)

Blood on the Moon (1948)

The Set-Up (1949)

The Day the Earth Stood Still (1951)

The House on Telegraph Hill (1951)

The Captive City (1952)

Odds Against Tomorrow (1959)

Robert Wise lines up a shot on the set of *Odds Against Tomorrow*.

Key Largo: John Huston posed between Humphrey Bogart and Edward G. Robinson, while Lauren Bacall and Lionel Barrymore watch in the foreground.

Contributors

Sheri Chinen Biesen (entry on Billy Wilder) is professor of Film History at Rowan University and author of *Blackout: World War II and the Origins of Film Noir*, Johns Hopkins University Press, 2005. She received her Ph.D. at University of Texas at Austin, M.A. and B.A. at University of Southern California School of Cinema-Television and has taught film at USC, University of California, University of Texas, and in England. She has contributed to *Film Noir Reader 4*; *Gangster Film Reader*; *Film Noir: The Encyclopedia*; *Film and History*; *Historical Journal of Film, Radio and Television*; *Quarterly Review of Film and Video*; *Literature/Film Quarterly*; *American Jewish History*; *The Historian*; *Television and Television History*; *Popular Culture Review*; and edited *The Velvet Light Trap*. Her next book on noir is due soon.

William B. Covey (entry on John Huston) is associate professor in the English department at Slippery Rock University of Pennsylvania where he coordinates the Film and Media Studies minor program. He has previously published articles on film history and theory in *CineAction*, *Film Noir The Encyclopedia*, *Film Noir Reader 2*, *Journal of Film and Video*, *Mfs: Modern Fiction Studies*, and *Quarterly Review of Film and Video*.

Corey Creekmur (entry on Jacques Tourneur) is an Associate Professor of English and Film Studies at the University of Iowa, where he also directs the Institute for Cinema and Culture; he has published on various aspects of both American and Hindi cinema, including "Bombay Bhai: The Gangster in and Behind Hindi Cinema."

Chris D (aka Chris Desjardins; entries on Joseph Losey and Otto Preminger) is author of the novel *No Evil Star* and the collection *Dragon Wheel Splendor and Other Love Stories of Violence and Dread*, both from New Texture Books. His anthology, *A Minute to Pray, A Second to Die*, a 500-page collection of selected short stories, excerpts from unpublished novels and scores of dream journal entries, as well as all of his poetry and song lyrics, was published in December 2009 from New Texture Books. His non-fiction *Outlaw Masters of Japanese Film* was published by IB Tauris (distributed by Palgrave Macmillan in the USA) in 2005. His first feature film as director, *I Pass for Human* was completed in 2004 (and released on DVD in 2006). He was a programmer at The American Cinematheque in Los Angeles, California from 1999-2009. Chris D. is also known as the singer/songwriter for the bands The Flesh Eaters and Divine Horsemen. He currently teaches film genre and film history courses part time, commuting to San Francisco from his residence in Los Angeles. Upcoming books include his long-in-the-works non-fiction *Gun and Sword: An Encyclopedia of Japanese Gangster Films 1955-1980*.

Wheeler Winston Dixon (entry on Robert Wise) is the Ryan Professor and Coordinator of the Film Studies Program at the University of Nebraska, Lincoln. As a filmmaker, the Museum of Modern Art presented a retrospective and acquired Dixon's work for its permanent collection. Since 1999, Dixon and Gwendolyn Audrey Foster have served as editors-in-chief of *The Quarterly Review of Film and Video*. Among his most recent books are *A History of Horror* (Rutgers University Press, 2010); *Film Noir and the Cinema of Paranoia* (Edinburgh University Press/Rutgers, 2009); *Film Talk* (Rutgers, 2007); *Visions of Paradise* (Rutgers UP, 2006); *American Cinema of the 1940s: Themes and Variations* (Rutgers, 2006); *Lost in The Fifties: Recovering*

Phantom Hollywood (Southern Illinois University Press, 2005); and *Film and Television After 9/11* (Southern Illinois, 2004). Dixon received his Ph.D. (in English) from Rutgers University.

Todd Erickson (entry on Robert Siodmak) is a veteran communications professional by day and a film noir aficionado by night. He coined the term "neo-noir" in the early 1980s while researching for his master's thesis, *Film Noir in the Contemporary American Cinema* (Brigham Young University, 1990) under the mentorship of film historian James V. D'Arc and film noir experts Alain Silver and Robert Porfirio. A condensed version of his thesis titled "Kill Me Again: Movement Becomes Genre" was published in *Film Noir Reader* (Limelight, 1996), and ten of his neo-noir title essays were published in *Film Noir The Encyclopedia* (Overlook, 2010).

Geoff Fordham (entries on Edward Dmytryk and Alfred Hitchcock) is a retired public policy adviser in the field of urban regeneration and neighborhood renewal. He was formerly visiting professor in the faculty of Community Development at Birkbeck College, University of London. His film interests focus on crime in the movies; his essay on *The Godfather* movies appeared in the *Gangster Film Reader,* and he was a contributor to *Film Noir: the Encyclopedia.* He now grows vegetables and is trying to learn to paint.

Jake Hinkson (entry on Felix Feist) has written extensively for the Film Noir Foundation, and his essays have appeared in *Bright Lights Film Journal* and *CriminalElement.com*. His novel *Hell on Church Street* is available from New Pulp Press. He teaches composition and literature at Monmouth University.

Richard T. Jameson (entry on Fritz Lang) was educated at Washington & Jefferson College in Washington, Pa. and made an abortive pass at a graduate degree in English at the University of Washington in Seattle. Since catching up with new foreign and classic movies in local theaters was more interesting, he went on to write voluminous program notes for university film series, help operate two art theaters, co-found the nonprofit Seattle Film Society, edit its journal *Movietone News* (1971-81), write reviews for sundry other local and national publications, and devise and teach film courses at the UW from 1969 to 1982. He became a member of the National Society of Film Critics in 1980 and edited its 1994 anthology *They Went Thataway: Redefining Film Genres*; served as film critic of *7 Days* magazine in Manhattan (1989-90) until it folded. He then edited *Film Comment* magazine for ten years beginning in 1990. Currently he maintains a movie website, *Straight Shooting*, at queenannenews.com and has been married to film critic Kathleen Murphy since 1973.

Geoff Mayer (entry on Joseph H. Lewis) is a Reader and Associate Professor at La Trobe University (Australia) where he is head of the School of Communications, Arts and Critical Enquiry. His previous books include *Encyclopedia of Film Noir* (Greenwood, 2007), *The Cinema of Australia and New Zealand* (Wallflower, 2007), *Roy Ward Baker* (Manchester University Press, 2004), *Guide to British Cinema* (Greenwood, 2004), *The Oxford Companion to Australian Film* (Oxford University Press, 1999) and *New Australian Cinema* (Cambridge University Press, 1992). His forthcoming book is *Historical Dictionary of Crime Films* (Scarecrow Press, 2012).

R. Barton Palmer (entries on Andre de Toth and Henry Hathaway) is Calhoun Lemon Professor of Literature and Director of Film Studies at Clemson University. Among his books on American filmmaking are *Hollywood's Dark Cinema: The American Film Noir*; *Perspectives on Film Noir* (editor); *Joel and Ethan Coen*; *A Little Solitaire: John Frankenheimer and American Film* (with Murray Pomerance); *The Philosophy Of Steven Soderbergh* (with Steven Sanders); and *Michael Mann and Philosophy* (with Steven Sanders and Aeon Skoble).

Homer B. Pettey (entry on Anthony Mann) is Associate Professor of English at the University of Arizona, where he teaches literature and film. Currently, he is working on a book on film noir.

Tom Ryall (entry on Jules Dassin) is Emeritus Professor of Film History at Sheffield Hallam University. He has written on various aspects of British and American cinema including the films of Alfred Hitchcock, genre theory, and the history of the British film. His books include *Alfred Hitchcock and the British Cinema* (1986), *Britain and the American Cinema* (2001), and *Anthony Asquith* (2005). He has contributed various articles on British and American cinema to collections such as *A Companion to Film Noir* (2012), *A Companion to Alfred Hitchcock* (2011), *The British Cinema Book* (2009), *The Cinema of Britain and Ireland* (2005), *The Oxford Guide to Film Studies* (1998); and to journals such as *Sight and Sound* and *The Journal of Popular British Cinema*.

Steven Sanders (entry on Orson Welles) is professor emeritus of philosophy at Bridgewater State University in Massachusetts. His work on film noir can be found in *The Philosophy of Film Noir* (UPKY, 2006), *The Philosophy of TV Noir* (UPKY, 2008), *The Philosophy of Science Fiction Film* (UPKY, 2008), *Film Noir: The Encyclopedia* (Overlook Duckworth, 2010), *The Blackwell Companion to Film Noir* (Blackwell, 2013), and *Miami Vice* (Wayne State University Press, 2010), his monograph on the film noir heritage of the 1980s television series. He is currently co-editing a volume of philosophical essays on the films of Michael Mann.

Jesse Schlotterbeck (entry on Nicholas Ray) is an Assistant Professor of Cinema Studies at Denison University. His work on film noir appears in *M/C–A Journal of Media and Culture* and the *Journal of Adaptation in Film and Performance*. He has also published in *Scope: An Online Journal of Film and Television Studies* and the *Journal of Popular Film and Television*.

Alain Silver (entries on John Farrow and Max Ophuls) wrote and edited the books listed on page 2. His articles have appeared in *Film Comment, Movie, Wide Angle,* anthologies on *The Philosophy of Film Noir*, *The Hummer*, and Akira Kurosawa as well as the online magazines *Images* and *Senses of Cinema*. His produced screenplays include *White Nights* (from Dostoyevsky), the Showtime movie *Time at the Top*, and *Nightcomer* (which he also directed). He has also produced a score of independent feature films (including *Palmer's Pick-up, Beat, Bel Air, Cyborg 2*, and *Crashing*) and forty soundtrack albums. His commentaries may be heard and seen on numerous DVDs discussing Raymond Chandler, the gangster film, and classic period movies from *Murder, My Sweet* to, most recently, *Kiss Me Deadly*. His Ph.D. in Theater Arts/Motion Pictures, Critical Studies is from the University of California, Los Angeles.

Julian Stringer (entry on Edgar G. Ulmer) is Associate Professor in Film and Television Studies at the University of Nottingham. He has published widely on U.S. and East Asian cinemas and is the editor of *Movie Blockbusters* (Routledge, 2003), co-editor (with Chi-Yun Shin) of *New Korean Cinema* (Edinburgh University Press, 2005) and co-editor (with Alastair Phillips) of *Japanese Cinema: Texts and Contexts* (Routledge, 2007). He has recently contributed a chapter (co-authored with Nikki J. Y. Lee) on the historical development of South Korean crime thrillers to *A Companion to Film Noir* (Wiley-Blackwell, forthcoming).

Grant Tracey (entry on Samuel Fuller) is a professor of English at the University of Northern Iowa where he teaches Film and Creative Writing. He has published three collections of fiction and articles on James Cagney and Samuel Fuller (in *Film Noir Reader 2*); contributed to *Film Noir The Encyclopedia* (2010); and been nominated for a Pushcart Prize. He also edits *North American Review*.

James Ursini (entries on John Brahm, John Farrow, Max Ophuls, and Gerd Oswald) wrote and edited the books listed on page 2 and provided text for the Taschen Icon series on Humphrey Bogart, Marlene Dietrich, Elizabeth Taylor, Mae West, and Rovert De Niro. His early study of Preston Sturges was reprinted in a bilingual edition by the San Sebastián Film Festival. Forthcoming in 2012 is *American Neo-Noir, the Movie Never Ends*. His film noir DVD commentaries (often with Alain Silver) include *Out of the Past, The Dark Corner, Nightmare Alley, Lady in the Lake, Kiss of Death, Brute Force, Crossfire, The Lodger, The Street with No Name, Where Danger Lives, Kiss Me Deadly* and other titles such as *Hobson's Choice* and the limited edition of *The Egyptian*. He has been a producer on features and documentaries, and lectured on film-making at UCLA and other colleges in the Los Angeles area where he works as an educator.

Constantine Verevis (entry on Raoul Walsh) is Senior Lecturer in Film and Television Studies at Monash University, Melbourne. He is author of *Film Remakes* (Edinburgh UP, 2006) and co-editor of *Second Takes: Critical Approaches to the Film Sequel* (SUNY P, 2010) and *After Taste: Cultural Value and the Moving Image* (Routledge, 2011). He is presently completing the co-edited volumes *Film Trilogies* (Palgrave-Macmillan) and *B for Bad Cinema* (Wayne State UP) and the co-authored book *Australian Film Theory and Criticism Vol 1: Critical Positions* (Intellect).

Jans B. Wager (entry on Ida Lupino) is a Professor of English and Literature, and chair of Cinema Studies and Interdisciplinary Studies at Utah Valley University. She is the author of *Dames in the Driver's Seat: Rereading Noir* (Texas UP, 2006) and *Dangerous Dames: Women and Representation in the Weimar Street Film and Film Noir* (Ohio UP, 1999). Her current book project is tentatively titled *Jazz and Cocktails: Censorship and Representation in Film Noir*

Susan White (entries on Anthony Mann and Max Ophuls) is Associate Professor of Film and Comparative Literature in the Department of English at the University of Arizona. She is the author of *The Cinema of Max Ophuls* and numerous essays on film, including recent work on Alfred Hitchcock and Nicholas Ray.

Tony Williams (entry on Robert Aldrich) is the co-author of *Italian Western: Opera of Violence*, co-editor of *Vietnam War Films* and *Jack London's The Sea Wolf: A Screenplay by Robert Rossen*. He is the author of *Jack London: the Movies*; *Hearths of Darkness: the Family in the American Horror Film*; *Larry Cohen: Radical Allegories of an American Filmmaker*; *Structures of Desire: British Cinema 1949-1955*; and *John Woo's Bullet in the Head*. His articles have appeared in *Cinema Journal, CineAction, Wide Angle, Jump Cut, Asian Cinema, Creative Filmmaking*, and several *Film Noir Reader*s. He is an Associate Professor and Area Head of Film Studies at Southern Illinois University, Carbondale.

Ronald Wilson (entry on Don Siegel) is an instructor with the Department of Film and Media Studies and the Graduate Writing Program at the University of Kansas. He has published essays in *Film Genre 2000* (SUNY Press) and *Mob Culture; Hidden Histories of the American Gangster Film* (Rutgers University Press). He is currently working on a book about the television series *The Untouchables* for Wayne State University Press.

Left, cinematographer Stanley Cortez stands behind director Fritz Lang on the set of *Secret Beyond the Door.*

Right, on the set of *Christmas Holiday* Deanna Durbin sits on the lap of director Robert "See-odd-mack."